LANDMARK
SUPREME COURT
CASES

A Reference Guide

DONALD E. LIVELY

GREENWOOD PRESS
Westport, Connecticut • London

Library of Congress Cataloging-in-Publication Data

Lively, Donald E., 1947–
    Landmark Supreme Court cases : a reference guide / Donald E.
Lively.
        p.   cm.
    Includes bibliographical references and index.
    ISBN 0–313–30602–8 (alk. paper)
    1. Constitutional law—United States—Cases. I. Title.
    KF4549.L58   1999
    342.73'00264—dc21   98–44220

British Library Cataloguing in Publication Data is available.

Library of Congress Catalog Card Number: 98–44220
ISBN: 0–313–30602–8

First published in 1999

Greenwood Press, 88 Post Road West, Westport, CT 06881
An imprint of Greenwood Publishing Group, Inc.
www.greenwood.com

Printed in the United States of America

The paper used in this book complies with the
Permanent Paper Standard issued by the National
Information Standards Organization (Z39.48–1984).

10 9 8 7 6 5 4 3 2 1

Contents

Preface

The purpose of this work is to provide readable discussions of important Supreme Court cases so that they can be easily understood by students and lay readers. The selection of cases was made with this readership in mind. A book on landmark cases in constitutional law has a rich and extensive list of candidates from which to select. Because review by the United States Supreme Court is discretionary, and justices select only a minute number of the cases annually presented for the Court's consideration, mere achievement of a hearing before the nation's highest tribunal is a veritable landmark. Technically, and in the sense used to identify cases for this work, landmark decisions are those that represent more than just the resolution of a major issue or a dispute that had a high profile in its time. To qualify as a potential landmark decision, a ruling must not only resolve a controversy but have a meaning that transcends the impact upon the immediate parties. Actual landmark status is reserved, however, for those decisions that have defined for society the moment and the future in a profound fashion.

Constitutional rulings by their nature determine the scope of governmental power or the breadth of fundamental rights and liberties. Resolution of conflicts between individual freedom and official authority define their respective meanings. Landmark rulings, therefore, consist of those decisions that both mark how governmental power is exercised and point the way toward economic, social, or political change. Because many of the nation's most intense controversies arise when government power collides with basic expectations of liberty and equality, it is not surprising that many of the most significant landmark decisions have emerged in these contexts.

This work is divided into four parts. The first part focuses upon rulings that have been critical in defining the framework of national government and the distribution of power among its various branches. The second part consists of cases that have been crucial in determining the relationship between the nation and its states, the concept of federalism, and regulation of the country's economy. The third part concerns decisions regarding equality principles and race following Reconstruction. The final and most expansive part of the book identifies landmark cases on personal rights and liberties. This part includes cases on key guarantees of the Bill of Rights, as well as rights and liberties that, although not specifically enumerated by the text of the Constitution, have been recognized as fundamental under the Fourteenth Amendment.

Each part begins with a discussion of the issues pertinent to the topic. The cases within each part are organized by topic, and generally in chronological order so that the reader can trace the progression of the Court's thinking on the issue. In those instances when cases are not ordered chronologically, the purpose is to achieve a more logical presentation. The discussion of each case consists of a fact box of pertinent information for quick reference, a summary of the case and its impact, and an annotated bibliography of sources for further reading. Citations in the fact boxes are to United States Reports, and are abbreviated as "__ U.S. __." Brackets are used in the text to indicate a change with respect to upper or lower case from the original or modification of a word or words used in the original. Such changes in terminology are for purposes of efficiency, and do not change the original meaning. Law review articles are often cited in the bibliographies that follow the cases. Typically, such works are intended for an academic or professional readership and have been accessible only in law libraries. Many of these journals increasingly are accessible on-line. Even so, their citation is intended for more serious students performing research or seeking to satisfy intellectual curiosity. References to other cases that are main entries in this work are cited in italics.

It is unlikely that constitutional scholars would debate or dispute the landmark nature of most, if not all, of the cases chosen for this book. Some might quibble with certain decisions that have been excluded. These disagreements are an inevitable byproduct of any effort to construct a list that by its nature must have a cutoff point. The most difficult editorial decisions are usually those requiring a choice between two or more highly influential rulings on the same subject. Constitutional law evolves from case to case, and the interrelationship of decisions makes it particularly challenging in some instances to prioritize one as more defining than another. The case of *Gideon v. Wainwright* (1963), for instance, was selected because it effectively defined the Sixth Amendment right to appointed counsel for indigent defendants. Its landmark status is illuminated not just by its significance but by the numerous books that have been written about it for both mainstream and academic audiences. A significant predecessor case,

Powell v. Alabama (1934), actually announced the Sixth Amendment principle. The Powell decision's significance is reflected in part by the fact that the case became the basis for not only books but also a movie. Even though the Powell decision represented the Supreme Court's initial step in recognizing a right to appointed counsel for indigent defendants, it was the *Gideon* decision that extended that guarantee from a principle of limited impact to one of broad applicability. As with other cases rooted in a previous decision, it is the author's responsibility to establish the historical linkage of the landmark to its past. Those who might be disappointed that Powell was excluded in favor of *Gideon*, or with similar editorial judgments, hopefully will be pleased with the attention that is devoted to the antecedents of and other historical influences upon the cases selected for inclusion.

The Supreme Court defines the Constitution through the interpretation of it. Appreciation of this process and of the context in which constitutional controversies arise provides an enriched understanding of how the law has shaped and reflects American history. This work makes an effort to identify and include those cases that represent defining statements not only of the law but of the society. The objective, in sum, is to present those decisions that are most relevant to American history as studied in high school, and that illuminate the constitutional issues raised in that curriculum.

Stewart A. Rea, a student at Florida Coastal School of Law, helped research several of the cases selected for this book. Lynn Wunderlich provided invaluable technical assistance in preparing the manuscript. I am grateful to my colleagues at Florida Coastal School of Law, who, despite the rigors and anxiety of developing a new institution, indulged the periodic spells of inattention that enabled me to write this book.

Separation and Distribution of Powers

The Constitution creates a structure of government that separates power among three branches. It also divides responsibilities between the federal and state governments. The doctrine of separation of powers is not established by any specific constitutional provision. Rather, it emerges from the framers' establishment of three branches of government with the understanding that each was to function as a check and balance upon the other. Consistent with this idea, the legislative, executive, and judicial branches are set forth, respectively, in Articles I, II, and III of the Constitution.

The framers' interest in separating the federal government's powers reflected a fear and distrust of centralized authority. With the colonial experience still fresh in their memories, but recognizing the need for an effective federal government, the founders viewed separation of powers as a means to achieve two important goals. By distributing the federal government's powers among three branches, they anticipated that liberty would be safeguarded from excessive concentrations of authority, and effective governance would be achieved through balance, coordination, and cooperation.

Supreme Court cases regarding separation of powers typically have resulted from conflicts between the branches of government over how far their respective authorities extend. Cases typically arise when one branch of government takes action that another department views as an encroachment onto its turf. For instance, the power of judicial review emerged from a dispute over whether the Supreme Court could bind the president by its interpretation of the Constitution. Both the judicial and legislative branches have challenged presidential authority over the course of history. Issues have concerned whether the president can claim privilege or immunity from the judicial process or under certain circumstances take action that otherwise is reserved for Congress. Questions of legislative power most frequently have concerned the scope and extent of lawmaking authority and Congress's ability to delegate its responsibility or reconstruct its processes for purposes of efficiency.

Part I examines the power of judicial review, which gives federal courts the final word in defining the Constitution's meaning. Although this authority is not set forth in the Constitution, it has become a well-settled principle of American government. It also has become the basis for constitutional decision making that sometimes challenges and even invalidates the work of representative government. The responsibilities assigned and the scope of power defined for the president and Congress also are focal points of this part. Decisions concerning the interaction of the executive, legislative, and judicial branches and setting limits on the exercise of their power reflect the continuing transformation of the doctrine of separation of powers into action.

1

The Power of Judicial Review

The judiciary's authority to interpret the Constitution so that its decisions are binding on other branches of government is not specifically set forth in the text of the Constitution. Because of the underdeveloped record left by the framers of the Constitution on this subject, it is impossible to identify meaningful support for the proposition that they even anticipated, much less agreed upon, the judiciary's role. The power of judicial review, which gives the Supreme Court the final word on the Constitution's meaning, derives not from the terms of the Constitution but from the Court's own definition of its function. The appropriate starting point for any discussion of judicial review is *Marbury v. Madison* (1803). Against the backdrop of sharp political conflict between the president and the Court, Chief Justice John Marshall established the judiciary's power "to say what the law is."

Although this role has become a settled constitutional reality, the way in which the judiciary interprets the Constitution is a source of controversy that actually predates the *Marbury* ruling. In *Calder v. Bull* (1798), the Court debated whether it could identify and establish rights and liberties that limit governmental power even though they are not enumerated by the Constitution. The *Calder* decision shaped a debate over whether judicial review should be an exercise in activism or restraint, a controversy that is no more resolved now than it was two centuries ago.

In the *Slaughter-House Cases* (1873), the Court considered whether the Bill of Rights, which originally was conceived as a check on federal power, also applied to the states. Although the Court rejected this proposition at the time, several decades later it decided differently in *Adamson v. California* (1947).

Marbury v. Madison

The power and influence of the judiciary are distinguishing characteristics of the American political system. Although the authority of courts to review legislative or executive action is a well-established norm, it would be unsafe to assume that the Constitution's framers intended it that way. Neither the text of the Constitution nor history provides many clues to what the Republic's founders contemplated about the judiciary's relationship with the political branches. As the learned constitutional historian Leonard W. Levy has observed, those "who say the framers intended [judicial primacy] are talking nonsense, and the people who say they did not intend it are talking nonsense."

Because of uncertainty about its role, the Supreme Court's origins were decidedly humble. Those who served on the Court during its early years earned little of the esteem and prestige that would be experienced by justices of future generations. Following a term as the nation's first chief justice that included extensive travel over poor roads to preside over circuit courts, John Jay refused reappointment on grounds that the position lacked stature and clout. Within a decade after Jay stepped down, however, the judiciary's future was defined in terms that established it as the branch of government with the final say on the Constitution's meaning.

Citation:	5 U.S. 137.
Issue:	Whether the Supreme Court may order the president to deliver a judicial commission that was signed but not delivered by his predecessor in office.
Year of Decision:	1803.
Outcome:	Although the Court determined that it could not order the president to deliver the commission, it asserted that it had ultimate authority to interpret the Constitution.
Author of Opinion:	Chief Justice John Marshall.
Vote:	6–0.

The emergence of the judiciary as a coequal branch of government in fact as well as in form is attributable to the vision and achievements of Chief Justice John Marshall. His appointment to the bench in 1801 and his decisions over the course of three decades reflected the intense turn-of-the-century political conflict between President John Adams's Federalist Party and Vice President Thomas Jefferson's Democratic-Republican Party. Profound ideological differences, apparent during the Constitution's framing and ratification processes, had continued to divide the citizenry between the Federalist view of a strong national government and Jeffersonian thinking, which favored decentralization. When Jeffersonians were poised to capture the executive and legislative branches after the election of 1800, President Adams sought to neutralize their influence by packing the federal courts with judges sympathetic toward the Federalist agenda. Chief Justice Marshall, who was appointed by Adams and served simultaneously as secretary of state during the Federalist administration's final days, presided over the rush to appoint these "midnight judges" before Jefferson's inauguration.

Several judges-designate appointed just before Adams's term ended, including William Marbury, did not receive their commissions before Jefferson took office. Not surprisingly, when Marbury demanded delivery of his commission, Jefferson's secretary of state, James Madison, refused to give it to him. Marbury then sued Madison in the Supreme Court of the United States, seeking a writ of mandamus—an order that would have required the Jefferson administration to deliver the commission. Chief Justice Marshall thus was presented with the opportunity to resolve the controversy that he had had a hand in creating. Despite the apparent conflict of interest, Marshall decided that the judiciary has the authority to decide whether legislative or executive action is constitutional or not. This decision became what Justice Felix Frankfurter described in a *Harvard Law Review* article as a ruling "deemed by great English-speaking Courts [as] an indispensable, implied characteristic of a written Constitution."

This lasting impression, however, was the result of some artful analysis and reasoning that essentially sacrificed Marbury's claim to establish the judiciary's constitutional role and relationship with the political branches of government. In passing the Judiciary Act of 1789, Congress had conferred original jurisdiction upon the Supreme Court for writs to officers of the United States. The act thus cast the Court in the rather rare role of a court of first resort rather than its usual function as a court of last resort. Operating under the premise that it was the judiciary's power to determine "what the law is," Marshall established the power of judicial review and proceeded to measure the Judiciary Act of 1789 against the Constitution. Article III of the Constitution confers upon the Supreme Court original jurisdiction "[i]n all Cases affecting Ambassadors, other public Ministers and Consuls, and those in which a State shall be Party, . . . [but] [i]n all the other Cases before mentioned, [gives it] appellate Jurisdiction." Put simply, Article III defines the Court as an appellate tribunal except in specific instances. Because the Judiciary Act did not fit into any of these limited categories, Marshall struck it down as unconstitutional. Marbury's request for a writ of mandamus, which would have required President Jefferson to comply with the Court's command, thus was denied for lack of jurisdiction. Marbury did not receive his commission.

The staying power of the *Marbury* decision is especially notable given Jefferson's belief that the judiciary was not supreme in interpreting the

Constitution and his resolve to ignore any court order requiring him to deliver the judicial commissions. The opinion's significance and survival are tributes not only to Chief Justice Marshall's reasoning but also to his political dexterity. By denying Marbury a remedy, the Court resolved the immediate political issue in Jefferson's favor and defused a conflict with the president that the Court could not have won. Because the Court depends upon the executive branch for enforcement of its orders, a decision against the president most likely would have been ignored and the judiciary would have been trivialized. The net result was a ruling that not only avoided the judiciary's marginalization but established it as the Constitution's primary guardian and interpreter.

Because Marshall was writing on a virtually blank slate in the Republic's formative years and cited no clear precedent for the Court's self-assertiveness, it may be argued that his reasoning was not airtight. Although Article III identifies specific instances in which the Supreme Court may exercise original jurisdiction, these settings need not be viewed as exhaustive or restrictive. A reasonable interpretation of the Judiciary Act might have been that Congress, without any constitutional prohibition, legitimately was expanding the Court's jurisdiction. The act also might have been regarded merely as the basis for mandamus as a remedy when the Court otherwise possessed jurisdiction. By declining to issue a ruling that the president inevitably would have ignored, however, Marshall prioritized the judiciary's vitality in a constitutional system based upon an effective balance of powers.

Poignantly illustrating the *Marbury* decision's enduring influence was the compliance of another president 171 years later with a Court order requiring him to produce tape recordings that he claimed were protected by executive privilege. By acceding to what Jefferson would have resisted, President Richard Nixon demonstrated how secure the judiciary's primacy had become in deciding the Constitution's meaning. Reflecting the vitality and security of Marshall's operating premise was the Court's reaffirmation in *United States v. Nixon* [1974] that "[i]t is emphatically the province and duty of the judicial department to say what the law is."

On its face, the *Marbury* decision may seem a departure from Federalist doctrine that typically urged policies that facilitated a strong national government. Trimming congressional sails at an early point in the Republic's development, which Marshall's ruling did, may seem inconsistent with a general theory in support of centralized legislative authority. The ruling proved instrumental, however, in creating a platform from which Chief Justice Marshall through the mid-1830s solidified and extended Federalist vision and principle. Having established the power of judicial review, Marshall authored a series of significant decisions that helped forward the evolution of a nation rather than a confederation. Rulings that prohibited states from interfering with contractual obligations (Dartmouth v. Woodward [1819]), denied them the power to tax and destroy the national bank (*McCulloch v. Maryland* [1819]), and defined commerce and Congress's power to regulate it in expansive terms (*Gibbons v. Ogden* [1824]) reflect a legacy of nation shaping consistent with Federalist doctrine. Until 1857, when the Court upheld slavery in *Dred Scott v. Sandford*, the *Marbury* decision represented the only instance in which it struck down a federal law.

Even if the Court's emergence as a powerful factor in defining the Constitution was rooted in partisanship, its role has been fortified rather than eroded by history. During the early years of desegregation, when judicial authority was being challenged by states bent on resistance and evasion, *Marbury* was cited in support of the proposition that the Court's rulings were "the supreme law of the land" (*Cooper v. Aaron* [1958]). The extent to which the judiciary may review the political branches' output was then and is now subject to debate. Although differences persist over whether the Court merely interprets or makes law, the debate would be much less significant in a society governed by Jefferson's rather than Marshall's vision of the judicial function.

Bibliography

Raoul Berger, *Congress v. the Supreme Court* (1969). A critical inquiry into the historical basis for judicial supremacy in interpreting the Constitution.

Felix Frankfurter, "John Marshall and the Judicial Function," 69 *Harvard Law Review* 217 (1955). A noted Supreme Court justice's assessment of the *Marbury* decision's significance.

Robert McCloskey, *The American Supreme Court* (1960). A comprehensive history of the United States Supreme Court's evolution and role through the midpoint of the Warren Court.

James Bradley Thayer, *John Marshall* (1901). The primary biography of Chief Justice John Marshall contains an argument that the *Marbury* decision did not confront the hard questions concerning judicial power and its nature.

William W. Van Alstyne, "A Critical Guide to Marbury v. Madison," 1969 *Duke Law Journal* 1 (1969). A detailed examination of the *Marbury* opinion.

Charles Warren, *The Supreme Court in United States History* (1932). A multivolume treatise on the United States Supreme Court, rich in description and analysis of the politics surrounding the *Marbury* decision.

Calder v. Bull

The Supreme Court's decision in *Marbury v. Madison* may have established the Court's supremacy in defining the Constitution, but it neither addressed nor resolved the extent to which the judiciary may exercise its power of review. Whether the judiciary may refer only to the rights and liberties enumerated by the Constitution in striking down a law or may identify rights not enumerated by the Constitution was the source of debate that preceded and followed the *Marbury* decision.

Whether courts can strike down laws because they violate unenumerated rights and liberties is a fundamental issue regarding the role of the judiciary in a democratic society. When a federal court strikes down a law, the will of the people as expressed through their political representatives is superseded by the decision of an unelected official. In determining that legislation is at odds with an enumerated right or liberty, a court relies upon a superior body of law (the Constitution) that has been ratified and directly consented to by the governed. Enumerated rights and liberties essentially are those set forth in the Bill of Rights. Unenumerated rights and liberties, which the Court typically characterizes as being "rooted in the Nation's traditions and conscience" or "implicit in the concept of ordered liberty," have the same force as textual guarantees when they are applied to legislative action. Critics of such "rights making" maintain that judicially identified freedoms,

Citation:	3 U.S. 386.
Issue:	The technical issue was whether a state law that set aside a probate decree violated the constitutional provision against ex post facto laws. The broader issue was whether the judiciary can recognize rights that are not enumerated by the Constitution.
Year of Decision:	1798.
Outcome:	The state enactment was not an ex post facto law. The larger question of the judiciary's power to recognize rights not enumerated by the Constitution was unresolved.
Author of Opinion:	Consistent with Supreme Court practice before 1801, each justice authored a separate opinion. No opinion represented the entire Court. The pertinent opinions, providing competing perspectives, are those of Justices James Iredell and Samuel Chase.
Vote:	6–0.

such as a woman's liberty to obtain an abortion, reflect antidemocratic tendencies because policy making is transferred from elected to unelected officials.

Arguments for and against these respective models of judicial restraint and judicial activism were sounded early in the Supreme Court's history in an otherwise unremarkable case. *Calder v. Bull* arose from a garden-variety probate dispute that initially was resolved by a state court decree. Caleb Bull and his wife had been denied rights under a will, and the time for appeal from the probate court judgment had expired. Connecticut legislature passed a law that set aside the decree. At issue before the Supreme Court was whether the state had passed an ex post facto law. Legislation that retroactively punishes or penalizes a person is barred by Article I, Section 10[1], of the Constitution, which provides that "[n]o State shall ... pass any ... ex post facto Law." Because the prohibition against ex post facto laws applies only to criminal enactments, as opposed to civil legislation, the Court found that the legislature's setting aside of the probate decree was not unconstitutional.

Despite its modest factual origins, the *Calder* case is memorable for its effective presentation of what has been an unending debate over the judiciary's role. The Court's finding that the state law was not unconstitutional thus was secondary for historical purposes to the competing perspectives on the judiciary offered by Justices James Iredell and Samuel Chase. Both voted to uphold the law, but for different reasons that are crucial for purposes of understanding the continuing debate over the judiciary's role.

In voting to uphold the Connecticut law, Justice Iredell expounded a philosophy of judicial restraint. As he saw it, the will of the people was represented through the political branches of government and was restricted only by the specific terms of the Constitution. From Iredell's perspective, therefore, legislation could not be struck down unless it conflicted with an explicit constitutional provision. He maintained that when the judiciary relied upon an unenumerated right or liberty to strike down a law, it subordinated the will of the people to subjective preferences and values of unelected judges. Such a function, in his view, was fundamentally antidemocratic.

Justice Chase agreed that the state law was constitutional, but he argued that the Court's role in interpreting the Constitution should not be restricted to the Constitution's express terms. From his perspective, governmental power is limited not only by the Constitution's specific restrictions but by natural rights and liberties—those freedoms that natural-law theorists view as implicit in human existence. The Constitution limits governmental powers not only by textually specified checks, but by natural rights and liberties. Iredell and Chase concurred that the will of the people, as expressed through their elected representatives, is subject to a higher law in the form of the Constitution. They disagreed, however, on whether the Constitution was the only source of higher law that could be used in reviewing legislation.

The language of judicial opinions since *Calder* largely reflects the concerns of Justice Iredell. Courts frequently stress that their role does not include second-guessing the wisdom of the legislature. Judicial rulings, however, often tend to be in line with Justice Chase's perspective. Over the course of the nation's history, the Court has identified several rights and liberties that, although they are not specified by the Constitution, have been recognized as fundamental. These rights have included the liberty to contract, which, during the first third of the twentieth century, was used to strike down social- and economic-reform legislation such as minimum-wage, maximum-hour, and child-labor laws. The right of privacy has emerged as a restriction on the political process during the final third of the century, not because it is mentioned in the Constitution, but because the judiciary has established it through the case law that interprets the document. This right has been found broad enough to include a woman's liberty to obtain an abortion, the right to marry, aspects of family freedom, and a right to refuse unwanted medical treatment.

These unenumerated rights and liberties have been recognized as fundamental and thus as a basis for curbing legislative power. However, Justice Iredell's concerns have continued to reverberate in jurisprudence. Justice Hugo Black, for instance, asserted in *Griswold v. Connecticut* (1965) that "I like my privacy as well as the next one, but I am nevertheless compelled to admit that government has a right to invade it unless prohibited by some specific constitutional provision." Stressing his concern with appointed judges substituting their wisdom for elected representatives, he further observed that "[f]or myself it would be most irksome to be ruled by a bevy of Platonic guardians, even if I knew how to choose them, which I assuredly do not." Such arguments and concerns reflect the philosophy underlying Justice Iredell's contention that a law cannot "be void, merely because it is, in [the Court's] judgment, contrary to the principles of natural justice."

The actual content of natural law is difficult to define and defies consensus. The Court's reference in Fletcher v. Peck (1831) to natural law as a body of "general principles which are common to free institutions" demonstrates the problem. In a diverse society, significant differences in opinion can be anticipated over these "general principles." For some, abortion is a choice that belongs to the mother. For others, the procedure invades the rights of another life. The same problem was showcased by the Court's pre–Civil War decision in *Dred Scott v. Sandford* (1857), which upheld slavery. Slaveowners and their critics, especially abolitionists, disagreed on whether slavery was a "natural" human condition. Although the Constitution enumerates neither the rights of slaves or slaveowners, the Court drew upon the slaveowners' version of natural law. It thus determined that the right to own slaves was protected by the Fifth Amendment guarantee against deprivations of property without due process. Four decades later, in *Plessy v. Ferguson* (1896), the Court made a similar decision regarding "natural" human conditions when it determined that official segregation was "in the nature of things."

The Iredell-Chase debate persists not only in modern jurisprudence but in political and academic circles. Presidential candidates such as Richard Nixon, Ronald Reagan, and George Bush have made the Iredell-like case for "strict constitutionists"—persons who will read and interpret the Constitution as it exists rather than alter it through the process of judicial review—primary campaign themes. Competing against this perspective have been Chase-like arguments that the Court develops and uses unenumerated rights and liberties rather sparingly and typically does not step far beyond the mainstream of what the people expect and will support. Opinion polls suggest that despite vigorous debate over the Supreme Court's ruling in *Roe v. Wade* (1973) determining that a woman has the freedom to obtain an abortion, the vast majority of the public favors the decision's bottom line. The controversy over the judiciary's function is no closer to resolution now than it was two centuries ago. The contrast between the strong political appeal of judicial restraint and popular acceptance of many decisions based upon unenumerated rights or liberties suggests an inconsistency that is fundamental and perhaps irreconcilable.

Bibliography

Alexander Bickel, *The Least Dangerous Branch* (1962). This work influenced the work of Robert Bork cited here.

Robert Bork, *The Tempting of America* (1990). Sets forth the argument for judicial restraint comprehensively, with detailed arguments against theories for recognizing rights not enumerated by the Constitution.

John Hart Ely, *Democracy and Distrust* (1980). Discusses a middle ground that suggests that the judiciary should only be activist when the political process is not open to all because of discriminatory or exclusionary practices.

Thomas C. Grey, "Do We Have an Unwritten Constitution?" 27 *Stanford Law Review* 703 (1975); Mark V. Tushnet, "Following the Rules Laid Down: A Critique of Interpretivism and Neutral Principles," 96 *Harvard Law Review* 781 (1983). Notable articles among the numerous works that support development of rights and liberties that are not specified by the Constitution.

Griswold v. Connecticut, 381 U.S. 479 (1965) (Black, J., dissenting). Forcefully reaffirms Justice Iredell's position in response to the Supreme Court's announcement of a fundamental right of privacy.

The Slaughter-House Cases

Following the Civil War, formation of a more perfect union was the primary purpose of Reconstruction. The defining constitutional achievements of that period, which stretched from 1865 to 1877, were the Thirteenth, Fourteenth, and Fifteenth Amendments. The Thirteenth Amendment, framed and ratified in 1865, prohibited slavery in the United States. The Fifteenth Amendment, drafted in 1869 and ratified in 1870, prohibited states from denying citizens the right to vote on the basis of race.

Significant though the Thirteenth and Fifteenth Amendments are, the linchpin of Reconstruction was the Fourteenth Amendment. Unlike the other Reconstruction Amendments, the Fourteenth Amendment speaks more broadly and ambiguously. The key passage for historical purposes is Section 1 which provides that

Citation:	83 U.S. 36.
Issue:	Whether the privileges and immunities of national citizenship include the Bill of Rights or other fundamental rights and thus limit the reach of a state's power.
Year of Decision:	1873.
Outcome:	The privileges and immunities of national citizenship are narrow and do not protect fundamental rights from state action.
Author of Opinion:	Justice Samuel Miller.
Vote:	5–4.

[a]ll persons born or naturalized in the United States, and subject to the jurisdiction thereof, are citizens of the United States and of the State wherein they reside. No State shall make or enforce any law which shall abridge the privileges or immunities of citizens of the United States; nor shall any State deprive any person of life, liberty, or property, without due process of law; nor deny to any person within its jurisdiction the equal protection of the laws.

The Fourteenth Amendment thus repudiated the Supreme Court's determination in *Dred Scott v. Sandford* (1857) that persons of African descent, even if they were born in the United States, could not be citizens. It also protected persons from actions by state government that would impair the privileges and immunities of national citizenship, deny citizens due process, or treat them unequally under the law.

Experience with slavery over the first several decades of the Republic's existence and the Civil War itself were sources for rethinking some of the nation's founding premises. The framing and ratification of the Constitution in the late eighteenth century reflected a dominant concern with the perils of centralized authority. The creation of a national government with limited powers and the adoption of a Bill of Rights were intended to minimize such risks. Slavery and civil war demonstrated that the states also could endanger civil rights and liberties. Southern resistance to Reconstruction, manifested by the adoption of Black Codes that severely curtailed the freedom of former slaves, reinforced the sense that state governments presented a threat to individual rights and liberties.

Against that backdrop, Congress enacted the Civil Rights Act of 1866 which guaranteed the freedom of all persons to contract, hold or transfer property, travel, sue and be sued, and have equal standing before the law. Concerned that an unrepentant post-Reconstruction South might have the votes to repeal the act, Congress proposed the Fourteenth Amendment to the Constitution. Unlike ordinary legislation that can be repealed by a simple majority, a constitutional amendment can be undone only by two-thirds of Congress and three-fourths of the states. In *Dred Scott v. Sandford* (1857), the Supreme Court had upheld slavery in part on grounds that national citizenship derived from state citizenship. The Fourteenth Amendment repudiated that understanding by establishing national citizenship as the basis for state citizenship and making the national government rather than the states the primary source and guardian of civil rights. As framed and ratified in 1868, the Fourteenth Amendment presented itself as a major restructuring of American government.

Five years after the amendment's adoption, the Supreme Court seized an opportunity to pass its own judgment on the extent to which state power and interests had been federalized. The first case decided under the Fourteenth Amendment seemed rather disconnected from the racial concerns and issues that dominated Reconstruction. The *Slaughter-House Cases*, however, represented a defining statement upon the Fourteenth Amendment that profoundly narrowed and redirected its operation. At issue in the *Slaughter-House Cases* was a Louisiana law that prohibited all but one slaughterhouse from operating within the New Orleans city limits. Butchers who were excluded by the monopoly challenged the state law as an interference with "the right to exercise their trade" that violated the Fourteenth Amendment. The Court rejected the argument on grounds that the alleged right was not a privilege or immunity of national citizenship.

Justice Joseph P. Bradley, who dissented from the Supreme Court's opinion, initially heard the case as a circuit judge. In his lower-court opinion, he found that the Fourteenth Amendment's privileges and immunities clause was broad enough to include the freedom to pursue a "lawful industrial pursuit." This expansive reading of the privileges and immunities of federal citizenship was rejected by the majority, which determined that the scope of federal protections was quite narrow and relatively inconsequential. As Justice Samuel F. Miller defined them, federal privileges and immunities included the right to assert claims or transact business with the government, have access to seaports, receive federal protection when a citizen was in a foreign country, peaceably assemble and petition for redress of grievances, file writs of habeas corpus, use navigable waters, and exercise those rights secured by the Reconstruction Amendments.

Conspicuously missing from the Court's definition of federal privileges and immunities were the Bill of Rights and any guarantees traditionally understood as being provided for by natural law. As a consequence, states retained much of the responsibility that they traditionally had exercised for the distribution and protection of fundamental rights and liberties. Under the majority's reasoning, for instance, a state law that abridged freedom of speech or of the press presented no more of a constitutional issue after the Fourteenth Amendment was adopted than before it existed. The enhanced significance of national citizenship and the consequent restrictions on state power were diminished by an interpretation that federal privileges and immunities were relatively narrow and mundane guarantees. Despite arguments that the Fourteenth Amendment had effected a major redistribution of power from the states to the national government, the *Slaughter-House Cases* decision reflected the Court's reluctance to "transfer the security and protection of all the civil rights we have mentioned, from the States to the Federal Government."

In his dissent, Justice Bradley reiterated that the privileges and immunities of national citizenship included the Bill of Rights and those fundamental guarantees enjoyed by "citizens of any free government." He further asserted that these rights and protections were extensive enough to include "the right to follow such profession or employment as ... one may choose." Justice Stephen J. Field dissented in similar terms, arguing that the Fourteenth Amendment's primary aim was to transfer responsibility for protecting basic rights and liberties to the national government. As he put it, "The fundamental rights, privileges and immunities which belong ... to a free man and a free citizen are attributes of federal rather than state citizenship." Field thus regarded the Fourteenth Amendment as the means for protecting "the citizens of the United States against any deprivation of their common rights by State legislation."

The *Slaughter-House* majority's interpretation of the privileges and immunities clause continues to be the defining understanding of that provision. Justice Bradley's and Justice Field's understandings of the Fourteenth Amendment, however, also have had lasting significance. Twentieth-century jurisprudence, which has incorporated most of the Bill of Rights through the Fourteenth Amendment's due process clause so that these guarantees apply to the states (see *Adamson v. California*), largely has achieved what Bradley had advocated through the privileges and immunities clause. Justice Field's contention that fundamental rights should be protected from state interference gained increasing currency toward the latter part of the nineteenth century. With rapid growth and developments in manufacturing, transportation, and communications, many states responded with regulation designed to control the economic and social impact of such change. The due process clause, rather than the privileges and immunities clause, soon became a source for economic rights and liberties that curbed states' ability to interfere with private enterprise. During the first third of the twentieth century, the Court regularly struck down labor and social-welfare legislation on grounds that it interfered with economic freedom. Although the *Slaughter-House* Court's narrow reading of the privileges and immunities clause did not permanently disable the Fourteenth Amendment, it nonetheless deferred much of the provision's impact until well into the twentieth century.

Bibliography

Raoul Berger, *Government by Judiciary: The Transformation of the Fourteenth Amendment* (1977); Harold Hyman, *A More Perfect Union* (1973); and Kenneth Karst, *Belonging to America* (1989). These works provide competing perspectives on the origins and aims of the Fourteenth Amendment.

Charles Fairman, *History of the Supreme Court of the United States*, vol. 7, *Reconstruction and Reunion, 1864–88* (1971) (1987). Provides a particularly detailed review of the Fourteenth Amendment's history and context.

Robert Kaczorowski, *The Politics of Judicial Interpretation: The Federal Courts, Department of Justice, and Civil Rights, 1866–1876* (1985). Discusses early judicial response to the Fourteenth Amendment.

James Kettner, *The Development of American Citizenship, 1608–1870* (1978). Examines the concept of national citizenship from a historical perspective.

Adamson v. California

As originally conceived, the Bill of Rights operated as a restraint on the power that the federal government could exercise over the people. For instance, the First Amendment states that "*Congress* shall make no law . . . abridging the freedom of speech, or of the press" (emphasis added). Modern understanding of the Bill of Rights is different, as most of its guarantees operate not only against the federal government but against state governments. This change is not directly attributable to any revision in the Constitution's text but to the power of judicial review and the Supreme Court's interpretation of the Fourteenth Amendment.

Early in the nation's history and prior to the Fourteenth Amendment's ratification, the Court considered and rejected the argument that the Bill of Rights limited the power of state government. In Barron v. Mayor and City Council of Baltimore (1833), it concluded that the question was "not of much difficulty" because "[t]he constitution was ordained and established by the people of the United States for themselves, for their own government, and not for the government of the individual

Citation:	332 U.S. 46.
Issue:	Whether all provisions of the Bill of Rights, including the Fifth Amendment right against self-incrimination, are incorporated through the Fourteenth Amendment and thus made applicable to the states.
Year of Decision:	1947.
Outcome:	Some but not all provisions of the Bill of Rights are incorporated through the Fourteenth Amendment, and the right against self-incrimination is not one of them.
Author of Opinion:	Justice Stanley Reed.
Vote:	5–4.

states." The original understanding thus was that each state, under its own constitution, provided "limitations and restrictions on the powers of its particular government, as its judgment dictated."

When the Fourteenth Amendment was adopted, it became a basis for revisiting the argument that the Bill of Rights applied to the states. In the *Slaughter-House Cases* (1873), the Court rejected the argument that the privileges and immunities of national citizenship included the Bill of Rights. Consequently, it refused to incorporate into the Fourteenth Amendment the same rights and liberties that check federal power. Despite having foreclosed what many scholars consider to be the most logical pathway toward incorporation, the Court by the late nineteenth century began curbing state powers that it believed interfered unreasonably with individual rights and liberties. The Court based its decision to limit state authority not on the Bill of Rights but on the Fourteenth Amendment's due process clause, which prohibits states from "depriv[ing] any person of life, liberty, or property, without due process of law." Through the mid-1930s, the Court identified a broad range of freedoms and rights that governmental power at any level was required to respect. These guarantees, which the Court incorporated into the Fourteenth Amendment, paralleled and in some instances exceeded those enumerated by the Bill of Rights. When the Court struck down a state law that prohibited "malicious, scandalous and defamatory newspapers" in *Near v. Minnesota* (1931), it thus cited the Fourteenth Amendment's due process clause rather than the First Amendment's guarantee of freedom of speech and of the press.

By the late 1930s, the makeup and philosophy of the Supreme Court had changed dramatically. Among the most dramatic changes resulting from this turnover in personnel and ideology was the Court's use of the Fourteenth Amendment as a source of fundamental rights and liberties. The Court's identification and development of rights and liberties not specifically enumerated by the Constitution, as noted in the discussion of *Calder v. Bull* (1798), has been a persistent source of controversy. Critics maintain that these methods of review enable unelected judges to override the will of the people as expressed through their elected representatives. Although the Court largely abandoned use of the due process clause as a basis for identifying and developing specific rights and liberties, it did not restore state immunity from the Bill of Rights. Instead of viewing the Fourteenth Amendment due process clause as a basis for rights and liberties that checked state authority, the Court began to view it as a conduit through which the Bill of Rights could be made applicable to the states.

The fundamental question confronting the Court as it shifted gears was whether the Fourteenth Amendment incorporated some or all of the guarantees in the Bill of Rights. In Palko v. Connecticut (1938), the Court determined that the Fifth Amendment guarantee against double jeopardy did not apply to the states. Although the Palko Court refused to incorporate the provision, it introduced an analytical formula that largely would govern the future of incorporation. What the Court asked in Palko, and in most future incorporation cases, was whether the enumerated right or liberty was so fundamental as to be "implicit in the concept of ordered liberty" or "so rooted in the traditions and conscience of our people as to be fundamental." In Palko, the Court found that the guarantee against double jeopardy was neither so implicit nor so rooted. Three decades later, in Benton v. Maryland (1969), the Court changed that result and decided that the double jeopardy provision was "fundamental to the American scheme of justice." This result was achieved through the process of "selective incorporation," a method that determines on a case-by-case basis whether a particular provision of the Bill of Rights applies to the states.

Competing against the selective incorporation model, which inquired on a case-by-case basis whether the provisions of the Bill of Rights applied to the states, was the concept of "total incorporation." A particularly crucial moment for the future of incorporation theory occurred when the Court held in *Adamson v. California* (1947) that the Fifth Amendment privilege against self-incrimination was not incorporated into the Fourteenth Amendment. Therefore, the Court determined that although the privilege operated in the federal context, it did not apply to the states. The case concerned the conviction of Admiral Dewey Adamson for first-degree murder. He argued that the conviction was obtained in violation of his privilege against self-incrimination. Writing for the Court, Justice Stanley Reed found no support for the proposition that the Fourteenth Amendment's framers or ratifiers intended the "due process clause to draw within its scope the earlier amendments to the Constitution." Demonstrating the Court's commitment to selective incorporation, he noted that the Fourteenth Amendment incorporated only those provisions that the judiciary found "implicit in the concept of ordered liberty."

For purposes of historical significance and impact, the Court's refusal to incorporate the privilege against self-incrimination proved less significant than the debate among the selective incorporationists (represented by Justice Reed), total incorporationists (represented by Justice Hugo Black) and nonincorporationists (represented by Justice Felix Frankfurter). This controversy reached its peak in the *Adamson* case. Stating the case for total incorporation of the Bill of Rights, Justice Black referred to statements by the Fourteenth Amendment's framers. These sponsors and supporters "proclaimed its purpose to be to overturn the constitutional rule" of Barron and "to make the Bill of Rights applicable to the states." Black argued that unless the court incorporated the entire Bill of Rights, it would give "much less effect to the Fourteenth Amendment that some of the public men active in framing it had intended it to have." He added that "the people of no nation can lose their liberty so long as a Bill of Rights like ours survives and its basic purposes are conscientiously interpreted, enforced and respected so as to afford continuous protection against old, as well as new, devices and practices which might thwart those purposes."

In concurring with the majority opinion, Justice Frankfurter rejected both total and selective incorporation theory. Responding to Justice Black's detailed inquiry into the Fourteenth Amendment's history, Justice Frankfurter dismissed the relevance of any framer's or supporter's statements on grounds that "[w]hat was submitted [for ratification] was [a] proposal, not [a] speech." Frankfurter argued that if the framers really had intended to incorporate the Bill of Rights into the Fourteenth Amendment, they would have done so in less ambiguous terms. Noting the rather broad and indeterminate terminology of the due process clause, he observed that "[i]t would be extraordinarily strange for a Constitution to convey such specific commands [as the Bill of Rights] in such a round-about and inexplicit way." Because many states that ratified the Fourteenth Amendment afforded protections to their citizens that were less rigorous than those provided by the Bill of Rights, Justice Frankfurter doubted whether they intended to uproot and replace their "established methods."

Frankfurter's argument is best remembered as a rebuttal to Justice Black's total incorporation theory, but he was equally unimpressed with the selective incorporation premise. His concern was that correlating the concept of due process with the Bill of Rights would distort the meaning of both and would "tear up by the roots much of the fabric of law in the several States." Particularly worrisome to him was the prospect of judges making subjective determinations of which amendments were "indispensable to the dignity and happiness of free men"—an exercise in selection that Justice Black would have avoided through total incorporation.

Although the theoretical dispute was resolved in favor of selective incorporation, actual results over the course of time have realized most of the aims of total incorporationists. Through the case-by-case process of selective incorporation, the only provisions of the Bill of Rights that have not been found applicable to the states are the Fifth Amendment right to grand-jury indictment, the Seventh Amendment right to trial by jury in civil actions, and the Eighth Amendment freedom from excessive bail. In Malloy v. Hogan (1964), the Court revisited the right against self-incrimination and concluded that it should be incorporated through the Fourteenth Amendment. Some have argued that despite almost full incorporation of the Bill of Rights, the guarantees do not necessarily apply to the states with the same force that they do to the federal government. The Court, however, has refused to dilute the impact of incorporated rights and liberties upon the states. Rather, case law has forwarded and largely finalized the judicially driven application of the Bill of Rights to all forms of American government.

Bibliography

Hugo Black, "Unfinished Business of the Warren Court," 46 *Washington Law Review* 3 (1970). Further amplifies Justice Black's thinking on incorporation.
Charles Fairman, *History of the Supreme Court of the United States*, vol. 7, *Reconstruction and Reunion, 1864–88* (1971) (1987). Fairman's analysis of

the Fourteenth Amendment was a particularly significant influence upon Justice Frankfurter's thinking.

Jerold H. Israel, "Selective Incorporation Revisited," 71 *Georgetown Law Journal* 253 (1982). Offers postincorporation insights.

Jacobus ten Broek, *Equal under Law* (1965). Sets forth the argument for total incorporation, and that the privileges and immunities clause was the logical provision for incorporation.

2

The Power of the President

Under a system of separation of powers, conflict between branches of government is inevitable. Because the Constitution speaks in broad and general terms, boundaries of authority are not always clear or precise. Disputes also may arise over the interests, needs, and circumstances of different branches. In *Youngstown Sheet and Tube Co. v. Sawyer* (1952), President Harry S. Truman and Congress clashed over the chief executive's seizure of the nation's steel mills during the Korean War. At issue was whether the president was making or executing the law. Two decades later, in *United States v. Nixon* (1974), President Richard Nixon's interest in maintaining the confidentiality of executive communications collided with the criminal justice system's need for evidence. Typically, the judiciary is highly deferential toward executive power when national security interests are at stake. If such a concern is not present, however, the Supreme Court is not shy about asserting its own interests over those of another branch.

Youngstown Sheet and Tube Co. v. Sawyer

The Constitution initially was conceived and ratified for purposes of establishing and distributing power among three primary departments of government—the legislative, executive, and judicial branches. Because the Constitution generally speaks in broad terms rather than detailed specifics, the precise contours of each branch's scope are often difficult to pinpoint. Article II, Section 1, vests "[t]he executive Power . . . in a President of the United States of America." Among the constitutional responsibilities of the president are functioning as "Commander-in-Chief" and ensuring "that the Laws be faithfully executed." These provisions were the focal points of the Supreme Court's ruling in *Youngstown Sheet and Tube Co. v. Sawyer* (1952).

Whether the president's power to execute the law enables him or her to make the law under certain circumstances is a question that has significant implications. In 1952, during the Korean War, President Harry S. Truman seized the nation's steel mills. His reason for nationalizing the steel industry was to avoid a strike that would have shut down the mills and, from Truman's perspective, undermined the war effort and threatened national security interests. Although Congress had the power to authorize such presidential action, it specifically had rejected the idea in enacting federal labor legislation. Truman notified Congress of the seizure, which was executed formally by Secretary of Commerce Charles Sawyer. Although Congress raised no objection, affected steel companies challenged the seizure on grounds that it exceeded the scope of the executive branch's power.

The president's primary arguments were that the seizure was justifiable as (1) a legitimate exercise of his power as "Commander-in-Chief" of the armed forces under Article II, Section 2[1], and (2) an exercise in "tak[ing] Care that the Laws be faithfully executed" under Article II, Section 3. Typically when military affairs or national security interests are at issue, the Court shies away from challenging or second-guessing the president. Writ-

Citation:	343 U.S. 579.
Issue:	Whether the president has power under the Constitution to make domestic law.
Year of Decision:	1952.
Outcome:	The president has no power to make the nation's laws.
Author of Opinion:	Justice Hugo Black.
Vote:	6–3.

ing for the majority in this instance, however, Justice Hugo Black found that the president's seizure of the steel mills exceeded the scope of his authority and thus was unconstitutional. As the Court saw it, the Constitution neither explicitly authorized the chief executive to take such action nor implied that he could. The Court concluded that the power "to take possession of private property in order to keep labor disputes from stopping production . . . is a job for the Nation's law-makers, not for its military authorities."

The Court also determined that the seizure could not be justified under the president's duty to ensure "faithful execut[ion]" of the law. The duty to execute the law thus was limited to carrying out rather than making the law. The Court further observed that the power to make law is vested exclusively with Congress, which is authorized, under Article I, Section 8[18] of the Constitution, "[t]o make all Laws which shall be necessary and proper for carrying into Execution [its legislative] Powers." Although Truman notified Congress of the seizure, and Congress took no contrary action, the Court found no ratification or acceptance of the president's action. Because Congress specifically had prohibited such presidential conduct, the Court concluded that the chief executive was making rather than faithfully executing the law.

Although Justice Black spoke for a majority of the Court, the concurring opinions of Justices Felix Frankfurter and Robert Jackson are notable. Justice Frankfurter suggested that the seizure might have been upheld if it had not been inconsistent with federal law prohibiting such action by the president. He also was willing to expand executive authority to the extent that it represented "a systematic, unbroken, executive practice, long pursued to the knowledge of the Congress and never before questioned." The influence of Frankfurter's reasoning manifested itself three decades later when, in Dames & Moore v. Regan (1981), the Court upheld executive orders and regulations nullifying attachments and liens on Iranian assets in the United States. This action freed these assets so that they could be transferred to Iran as a basis for resolving a hostage crisis generated by seizure of the American embassy in Teheran. As the Court put it, "Crucial to our decision today is the conclusion that Congress [over the years] has implicitly approved the practice of claim settlement by executive agreement."

Justice Jackson presented a more complex profile of presidential power. From his perspective, executive authority varied in relationship to congressional action or lack thereof. Presidential power was at its apex when it was exercised in concert with specific congressional authorization. Without congressional authorization, the president must stand on his or her own power. What Jackson referred to as "a zone of twilight" exists when the distribution of authority is uncertain or shared. Under such circumstances, an absence of congressional action may allow for presidential action. Executive power was at its low point when it was exercised contrary to legislative will. Under Jackson's formula, the president's seizure of the steel mills might have been supportable had Congress not prohibited such action. Congress's specific rejection of such action thus relegated Truman's power to its "lowest ebb." The impact of Justice Jackson's thinking also was evident in the Dames & Moore decision. Writing for the Court in that decision, Justice William Rehnquist cited Jackson's concurring opinion in *Youngstown Sheet and Tube Co.* and noted that because presidential action in this instance "was taken pursuant to specific authorization, it is supported by the strongest of presumptions and the widest latitude of judicial interpretation, and the burden of persuasion would rest heavily upon any who might attack it."

In a dissenting opinion in *Youngstown Sheet and Tube Co.*, Chief Justice Fred Vinson expressed concern that the Court did not take the national security interest seriously enough. The seizure occurred within the context of an "existing emergency," and, as the chief justice noted, "a work stoppage would immediately jeopardize and imperil our national defense." Despite the Court's insistence upon a clear line between the law's makers and its executors, it is not impossible to imagine scenarios in which the majority might have been forced to rethink its position. If the battle was being waged on American soil, rather than in a distant country, a greater sense of urgency might offset the Court's interest in a strict division of responsibility. At some point, even if it was when foreign soldiers were marching on the Capitol, it would seem that formality would have to give way to the greater imperative—unless the principle's survival was viewed as more important than the nation's.

Bibliography

Edward Corwin, *The President: Office and Powers, 1787–1957* (1957). Examines historical perspectives dating back to those of the founders.

E. Donald Elliot, "Why Our Separation of Powers Jurisprudence Is So Abysmal," 57 *George Washington Law Review* 506 (1989). Sets forth the argument that a formalistic separation of powers doctrine of powers disserves the concept of separation of powers.

Louis Henkin, *Foreign Affairs and the Constitution* (1972). Discusses constitutional roles and responsibilities in the field of foreign affairs.

Harold H. Koh, *The National Security Constitution: Sharing Power after the Iran-Contra Affair* (1990). Addresses the relationship of national security to separation of powers concerns.

Philip Kurland, ed. *Felix Frankfurter on the Supreme Court* (1970). Examines the case for elasticity and fluidity in separation of powers doctrine.

United States v. Nixon

The judicial branch's defining moment in constitutional history occurred when Chief Justice John Marshall announced in *Marbury v. Madison* (1803) that "it is emphatically the province and duty of the judicial department to say what the law is." The power of judicial review was established in *Marbury*, despite President Thomas Jefferson's belief that the judicial branch had no power to define the Constitution's meaning for the executive branch. More than a century and a half later, the Court confronted another president who viewed executive authority in terms not unlike Jefferson's. Although Chief Justice Marshall avoided a showdown with Jefferson by ruling for the president, the Supreme Court in *United States v. Nixon* demanded that the chief executive comply with an order contrary to his constitutional views. In so doing, the Court again asserted its authority in another test of its constitutional authority.

This constitutional controversy arose in the aftermath of the Watergate affair, a burglary of Democratic Party national headquarters during the 1972 presidential election campaign. Two years later, in the course of a special prosecutor's investigation, a grand jury indicted several of President Richard Nixon's executive aides and advisers and named Nixon as an unindicted coconspirator. The district court, at the special prosecutor's request, subpoenaed documents and tapes relating to conversations between the president and his aides and advisers. Although Nixon provided edited transcripts of these conversations, he moved to quash the subpoena on grounds that the tapes and other materials were protected by executive privilege. After the district court rejected the president's arguments, the controversy was presented to the Supreme Court.

Although the Constitution makes no reference to executive privilege, President Nixon argued that it was implicit in the concept of separation of powers. The president maintained, and the Supreme Court agreed, that without such a privilege, candid discussions and frank exchanges among

Citation:	418 U.S. 683.
Issue:	Whether the president must disclose information, sought in criminal proceeding, that he or she claims to be confidential and privileged.
Year of Decision:	1974.
Outcome:	The president's claim of executive privilege must be reviewed by the judiciary to determine whether it is justified and outweighs the interest of the criminal justice process.
Author of Opinion:	Chief Justice Warren Burger.
Vote:	8–0.

policy makers would be inhibited. The Court thus subscribed to the basic proposition that "government . . . needs open but protected channels for the kind of plain talk that is essential to the quality of its functioning." If communications could not take place on a confidential basis, without the risk of public disclosure, officials would be more guarded in their comments and less inclined to take intellectual risks in discussing policy. But although the Court agreed with the president on the value of executive privilege and its grounding in separation of powers doctrine, it rejected arguments that a presidential claim of privilege was immune from judicial review and that executive privilege was absolute. The Court thus ruled against the president, and he was forced to turn over the tapes.

Responding to the contention that the president's privilege claim was unreviewable, the Court reiterated the central meaning of *Marbury v. Madison*—that the judiciary has the ultimate power to decide "what the law is." As the Court viewed it, separation of powers doctrine cut against rather than in favor of the president's position. The Court noted that an absolute, unqualified executive privilege would impede the primary constitutional duty of the judicial branch to do justice in criminal prosecutions. It thus concluded that foreclosure of judicial review "would plainly conflict with the function of the courts" under the Constitution. Although the Court acknowledged that a presidential claim of confidentiality is presumed to be privileged, it refused to cede authority to review whether such a claim was justified. The Court then proceeded to balance the need for confidentiality under the circumstances. From its perspective, the privilege as asserted rested upon a "broad, undifferentiated claim of public interest in the confidentiality of such conversations." Although a different result might have followed if military, diplomatic, or sensitive national security secrets were at stake, the Court determined that the criminal justice system's specific need for evidence admissible at trial outweighed the president's right to confidentiality. Further diminishing the chief executive's privilege claim was the right of the judiciary to review the materials on an *in camera* basis— that is, within the privacy of chambers—so that only tapes and documents relevant to the criminal proceeding would be disclosed. The president's interest in confidentiality thereby was subordinated to "the legitimate needs of the judicial process." Justice could not be done, the Court observed, without the ability to obtain "evidence needed either by the prosecution or defense."

The decision thus turned in significant part upon "the ancient proposition of law . . . 'that the public . . . has a right to every man's evidence.' " Although the Court determined that the president was not above the law under the particular circumstances, the recognition that the "confidentiality of Presidential communications has . . . constitutional underpinnings" suggests that the president may be untouchable in other instances. As noted previously, a need to protect military, diplomatic, and national security secrets might heighten the need for confidentiality. The needs of the judicial process also might carry less weight in noncriminal proceedings because public interest is less of a factor, particularly if the evidence is relatively insignificant and is available from other sources. If the government is suing a private party, however, it would seem fundamentally unfair to allow the government to pursue its interests by denying the defendant access to relevant information.

The decision in *United States v. Nixon* is notable because it reaffirms the power of judicial review. Like *Marbury*, the *Nixon* case represented a constitutional showdown between the executive and judicial branches of government. Unlike President Jefferson, who threatened to resist any judicial demand for delivery of the contested judicial commissions at issue in *Marbury*, President Nixon immediately complied with the Court's order to turn over documents and tapes. An argument similar to Nixon's, that the "character of the office" justified deferral of a civil lawsuit against President William Clinton until his term in office expired, was rejected in Clinton v. Jones (1997). Citing its decision in *Nixon* and rejecting President Clinton's claim that litigation would impose an unacceptable burden upon him and impair his performance in office, the Court reiterated "that the President is subject to judicial process in appropriate circumstances." In President Nixon's case, the disclosure of material he sought to protect confirmed his participation in covering up the Watergate burglary and led to his resignation soon thereafter. At the cost of losing not just his argument but his office, Nixon reaffirmed the judiciary's primacy in "say[ing] what the law is."

Bibliography

Raoul Berger, *Executive Privilege: A Constitutional Myth* (1974). Examines the need for executive privilege for the president to govern effectively.

Archibald Cox, "Executive Privilege," 122 *University of Pennsylvania Law Review* 1383 (1974). The first special prosecutor in the Watergate controversy sets forth his insights into the scope of executive privilege.

Patricia A. Krause, ed., *Anatomy of an Undeclared War: Congressional Conference on the Pentagon Papers* (1972). A critical perspective upon the motives and reliability of executive privilege claims.

Charles Warren, *The Making of the Constitution* (1937). Contains a discussion of why the Constitution's framers considered secret meetings essential to their work and productivity.

3

The Power of Congress

The mistrust and suspicion of centralized authority that characterized the nation's founding persisted long after the ratification of the Constitution. Early in the Republic's history, debate turned to the scope of Congress's authority. Specifically at issue in *McCulloch v. Maryland* (1819) was whether legislative power should be limited strictly to what the Constitution specified or whether the Constitution allowed for action that enabled Congress to exercise its authority more effectively. Separation of powers controversies typically arise from disputes over which branch of government should exercise authority in a particular context. Constitutional turf wars between branches of government, however, are not the sole source of intragovernmental controversy. As federal powers have expanded over the course of the twentieth century, Congress has initiated efforts to increase the efficiency of governmental operations. Its ability to delegate legislative authority to administrative agencies that are charged with the responsibility to manage increasingly complex social and economic problems and needs within Congress's scope of responsibility was the subject of *Yakus v. United States* (1944). Some controversies concerning a branch's exercise of power reflect less a conflict with another branch than a question over the existence of authority altogether. Congressional power to legislate in excess of the Constitution's own provision for civil rights is addressed in *Katzenbach v. Morgan* (1966).

McCulloch v. Maryland

A primary strength of the Constitution is its brevity and simplicity. Because it is written in broad and magisterial terms, its meaning is capable of adapting to changes in and the evolution of the society that it governs. Because the judiciary's role is "to say what the law is," it typically is the source of interpretation and understanding that gives the Constitution meaning under those circumstances when it does not speak clearly for itself.

A fundamental constitutional premise is that the federal government is an institution of enumerated powers. The federal government thus only exercises those powers that the Constitution specifically assigns to it. This understanding was evidenced in the framing of the Constitution and in debate that has continued since its ratification. From the Constitutional Convention emerged a blueprint for government that contained inherent tensions. The federal government was to exercise only those powers that the Constitution assigned to it.

Citation:	17 U.S. 316.
Issue:	Whether Congress's powers are limited to those that are specifically enumerated by the Constitution.
Year of Decision:	1819.
Outcome:	Congress possesses not only those powers that are specified by the Constitution but those that are reasonably necessary to exercise its enumerated powers.
Author of Opinion:	Chief Justice John Marshall.
Vote:	7–0.

The states, whose existence preceded formation of the national government under the Constitution, retained those powers that were not granted specifically to the federal government. The resulting system of dual sovereigns that functioned under a Constitution that presented itself in broad rather than detailed terms created a condition in which jealousy and conflict over the exercise of power in "gray areas" was inevitable. During the process of framing and ratification of the Constitution, Federalists argued for a strong central government that effectively could reckon with national problems. Anti-Federalists resisted an expanded federal role on grounds that it encroached upon interests and powers reserved to the states. The Bill of Rights reflected an early compromise between these rival ideologies. It imposed formal curbs upon federal power and was a compromise that was essential to achieve ratification of the Constitution. Competition to define the relative scope of federal and state powers did not vanish with the Constitution's framing and ratification. On the contrary, as noted earlier, the document's broad and sometimes indefinite terminology extended an invitation to both sides to continue the debate.

A particularly significant moment in the definition of federal and state power occurred when the Supreme Court reviewed the state of Maryland's attempt to collect taxes from the Bank of the United States. Central to the state's case in *McCulloch v. Maryland* was the argument that the Constitution does not empower Congress to create a bank or corporation. The bank, which had been chartered in response to economic turmoil following the War of 1812, soon became a target of critics who believed that it caused a worsening of the nation's economic condition. In response to these concerns, many states enacted laws designed to neutralize its role and influence. Maryland imposed a tax on the federal bank. When James McCulloch, the cashier of the Baltimore branch of the national bank, refused to pay it, the state sued. Although the Maryland Court of Appeals upheld the tax, the Supreme Court found it unconstitutional.

The state's argument was premised upon the theory that the federal government's powers were limited to those that the Constitution specifically enumerated. From its perspective, the national government derived its authority from the states, whose powers predated the Constitution. In support of its argument, the state noted that delegates to the Constitutional Convention had been elected by state legislators, and the states had ratified the Constitution. Competing against these contentions were arguments that the federal government possessed powers necessary to implement its enumerated powers, and its authority derived from the people rather than the states. Resolution of the controversy proved consistent with the strong pro-Federalist sentiments characterizing Chief Justice John Marshall's tenure on the Supreme Court. Marshall had been chosen by President John Adams in the waning days of the last Federalist administration to slow the rising tide of Jeffersonianism that favored broadened state autonomy and interests. Marshall's opinion confirmed his abiding commitment to establish the power of the national government.

In resolving the controversy over the source of federal authority, the Court found that the national government "is, emphatically and truly, a government of the people." Because the "government of the Union . . . emanates from them, . . . [i]ts powers are granted by them, and are to be exercised directly on them, and for their benefit." Having identified the source of federal authority, the Court further concluded that its power, "though limited . . . , is supreme within its sphere." If Congress legislated within the scope of its authority, federal law must necessarily bind the nation's component parts. Put simply, when federal legislation addresses a legitimate federal concern, the states cannot stand in the way of the national interest.

The most pivotal aspect of the case was the Court's interpretation of Article I, Section 8 [18], of the Constitution, which provides that Congress has the power "[t]o make all Laws which shall be necessary and proper for carrying into Execution the foregoing Powers, and all other Powers vested by this Constitution in the Government of the United States, or in any Department or Officer thereof." From the state's perspective, the necessary and proper clause limited Congress's power to enact laws to those that "are indispensable, and without which [an enumerated] power would be nugatory." If this interpretation had been accepted, it would have limited Congress's choice of legislative means to those that are "absolutely necessary." For Marshall, such a narrow view of federal power was unacceptable because it would deny Congress the right to select appropriate means and would lead to absurd results. Noting that Congress had the enumerated power "to Establish Post-Offices and Post-Roads" under Article I, Section 8[7], he reasoned that the power and duty of carrying the mail existed only because they were inferred. Neither was indispensable to the power to create postal offices and routes, but a system of mail delivery was "essential to the beneficial exercise of the [enumerated] power." The Court thus understood "necessary" as permitting "any means calculated to produce the end, and not as being confined to those single means, without which the end would be entirely unattainable."

Although the Court acknowledged that the federal government is an institution of enumerated powers, it concluded that implied and incidental powers are not precluded. This understanding reflected the sense that Congress should not be impaired from exercising its best judgment in choosing the methods for executing its constitutional powers. Consistent with that understanding, the Court determined that the necessary and proper clause permits Congress in pursuing a "legitimate end" to use "all means which are appropriate, which are plainly adapted to that end, which are not prohibited, but consistent with the letter and spirit of the Constitution." The national bank thus was found to be a reasonable means of exercising its "powers, to lay and collect taxes; to borrow money; to regulate commerce; to declare and conduct a war; and to raise and support armies and navies."

A final reason for striking down the state law was that it conflicted with federal law. Under Article VI, Section 2, the United States Constitution and federal law are "the supreme Law of the Land." When federal and state laws conflict, the national interest prevails unless Congress has exceeded the scope of its authority. Allowing the state to tax the bank would have been inconsistent with this supremacy principle. As Marshall noted, "the power to tax involves the power to destroy."

The Court's decision represented a landmark in defining the relative scopes of federal and state powers. Conflict and debate over each sovereign's range of interest, nonetheless, have been a persistent feature of the nation's constitutional history. Four decades later, continuing debate over the respective powers of federal and state governments caused the union's rupture and civil war. The Court's order to desegregate public schools during the latter half of the twentieth century has been surrounded by arguments over federal power and states' rights. Writing on a relatively blank slate in the early nineteenth century, Chief Justice Marshall not only drew an initial line between federal and state powers but helped define the nature of the Constitution. Distinguishing it from laws that are enacted by a legislature, he observed that its nature "requires that only its great outlines should be marked, its important objects designated, and the minor ingredients which comprise those objects be deduced from the nature of the objects themselves." Noting further that "we must never forget that it is a *constitution* we are expounding," Marshall strengthened both the federal government's power and the judiciary's hand in "say[ing] what the law is." The net result is what one constitutional historian describes as "the greatest decision John Marshall ever handed down—the one most important to the future of America, most influential in the Court's doctrinal history, and most revealing of Marshall's unique talent for stately argument."[1]

Note

1. Robert McCloskey, *The American Supreme Court* 66 (1960).

Bibliography

Daniel Farber and Suzanna Sherry, *A History of the American Constitution* (1990). Describes debate over federal and state powers among the Constitution's framers.

Gerald Gunther, ed., *John Marshall's Defense of McCulloch v. Maryland* (1969). Provides further insight into Chief Justice Marshall's views on the issues raised in *McCulloch v. Maryland.*

Robert G. McCloskey, *The American Supreme Court* (1960). Contends that *McCulloch v. Maryland* represents Chief Justice Marshall's "greatest decision."

Charles Warren, *The Supreme Court in United States History* (1932). Discusses the circumstances and impact of the national bank.

Yakus v. United States

The Supreme Court's decision in *McCulloch v. Maryland* (1819) addressed the need for a strong central government that could deal with problems and concerns that were national in nature. Although this decision laid the foundation for a governmental structure that could reckon with the national interest and not be held hostage to the jealousies of the several states, it is unlikely that the *McCulloch* Court could have foreseen the dramatic social and economic changes that would take place over the course of the next century. During this time, American society was transformed from an agrarian to an industrial society. New transportation and communications methodologies facilitated a growing sense of national identity even as the number of states and the country's boundaries expanded rapidly.

Citation:	321 U.S. 414.
Issue:	Whether Congress could delegate legislative power to an administrative agency that enables it to adopt regulations implementing legislative policy.
Year of Decision:	1944.
Outcome:	Congress may delegate its legislative power to the extent that it establishes sufficient standards to guide the rulemaking process.
Author of Opinion:	Chief Justice Harlan Fiske Stone.
Vote:	6–3.

As the nation's borders enlarged population grew, and problems became increasingly complex, the federal government confronted new challenges to the effective and efficient exercise of its power. Against that backdrop, the utility of a constitution that, in Chief Justice John Marshall's view, only marked the "great outlines" of power was apparent. With the onset of the Great Depression, the need for constitutional adaptability was crucial to the survival of the many federal programs that were designed to cope with the national emergency. The centerpiece of President Franklin D. Roosevelt's first term in office during the early 1930s was a series of social- and economic-reform initiatives popularly known as the New Deal. During President Roosevelt's first few months in office, Congress passed the National Industrial Recovery Act of 1933 (NIRA). The purpose of this legislation was to stabilize wages and prices and restore confidence in the nation's economy. Under the NIRA, industrial and labor associations were authorized to develop codes of fair competition for the protection of consumers, competitors, employees, and the public interest. These codes were subject to presidential approval. Because they also had the force of law, the codes were challenged on grounds that Congress un-constitutionally had transferred its power to legislate.

In Schecter Poultry Corp. v. United States (1935), the Supreme Court concluded that "Congress is not permitted to abdicate or to transfer to others the essential legislative function with which it is . . . vested." From the Court's perspective, the delegation of authority provided no guidance to the private groups and the president and thus was too sweeping. The Court expressed concern that such an unfettered delegation of authority enabled private groups and the president to frame national policy on the basis of their own whims, priorities, and theories. Such a prospect suggested lawmaking that was not necessarily consistent with or reflective of the will of the people.

During the latter part of the 1930s, the Supreme Court experienced a wholesale turnover of its personnel. By 1941, the core group of justices in the Schecter majority had been replaced by appointees who were more favorably disposed toward New Deal aims and methods. That sympathy was evidenced when, in *Yakus v. United States* (1944), the Court again confronted the nondelegation doctrine. At issue was the Emergency Price Control Act, which delegated power to control prices during World War II. By vesting authority in a price administrator to control prices, the law aimed to stabilize prices, prevent speculation, and enhance the efficiency of the war effort. Albert Yakus was one of several defendants convicted for violating the Act. The only guideline provided by the law was that when prices rose or threatened to rise in a manner inconsistent with the act, the price administrator must set prices that were "fair and equitable." Argua-bly, this principle was no more intelligible than the "fair competition" stan-dard rejected as inadequate in Schecter. The Court, however, determined that the price administrator's scope of responsibility was sufficiently fixed by the statute. The key to this conclusion was the Court's sense that the "fair competition" standard enabled it to identify a basis for any finding by the price administrator. The delegation of legislative power was per-missible because, as the Court saw it, Congress had stated its legislative objective and had set adequate standards to guide administrative decision making regarding the need for price controls. Unlike the codes of compe-tition in Schecter, the guidelines for the price administrator provided stan-dards to which regulations must conform. Although this point may be debatable, as noted previously, another key point of distinction was that the delegation of power did not leave the formulation of policy to private individuals who are unaccountable to Congress.

By upholding the transfer of legislative power to the price administrator, the Court validated an increasingly significant dimension of modern gov-ernment. The magnitude, complexity, and extent of problems confronting Congress make it impossible for that body to identify and manage the many problems and needs for which it is responsible. The emergence of administrative agencies, which multiplied especially under the New Deal and its aftermath, has represented a primary structural response to that challenge. Administrative officials, however, are appointed rather than elected. Concern exists, therefore, about the possibility of conflict between administrative action and democratic principles. The Court's ruling in *Yakus* responded to this concern. Although the Court noted that Congress is not required to find for itself every fact upon which legislative action or policy is based, it identified a legislative responsibility to specify the basic conditions of fact upon which an administrative agency may act. Congress thus must provide intelligible principles that guide an agency's development of rules and regulations or, as the *Yakus* Court put it, "sufficiently mark [ ] the field within which the Administrator is to act so that it will be known whether he has kept within it in compliance with the legislative will."

The requirement of meaningful standards as a condition for delegation of legislative power has not been a daunting criterion for the past half century. Not since Schecter has the Court actually invalidated a law under the nondelegation doctrine. The Court itself has acknowledged the extreme to which this doctrine has swung. Half a century after Schecter, it observed that "restrictions on the scope of the power that could be delegated [have] diminished and all but disappeared." This record is not without its detractors, some of whom currently sit on the Supreme Court. Both Chief Justice William Rehnquist and Justice Antonin Scalia have expressed concern that loose delegation standards enable legislators to avoid responsibility for informed policy making and choices among policy options. These arguments arise at a time when uneasiness that too much power is being exercised by "faceless bureaucrats" in Washington has become widespread. This uneasiness is not surprising given the sense, expressed by one court, that "administrative agencies may well have a more far-reaching effect on the daily lives of all citizens than do the combined actions of the executive, legislative and judicial branches." Congress itself has expressed concern about the influence of administrative agencies in the political system. To reassert control over the administrative process, it established a legislative veto that enabled either the Senate or the House of Representatives, rather than both, to review and negate any action under a delegated power. In Immigration and Naturalization Service v. Chadha (1983), the Court struck down the legislative veto, basing its argument on separation of powers theory. What Justice Robert Jackson referred to as "a veritable fourth branch of the Government" thus persists as a pervasive phenomenon reflecting what its architects and supporters view as a logical response to societal evolution and a changed society and what its critics regard as a threat to representative governance.

Bibliography

Sotirios A. Barber, *The Constitution and the Delegation of Congressional Power* (1975), Examines delegation issues.

Stephen Carter, "From Sick Chicken to Synar: The Evolution and Subsequent De-Evolution of the Separation of Powers," 1987 *Brigham Young University Law Review* 719 (1987). Explores the Supreme Court's theories of review in developing delegation principles.

Kenneth Davis, *Administrative Law Treatise* (1982). A comprehensive description and analysis of administrative government, including attention to the non-delegation doctrine.

Robert H. Jackson, *The Struggle for Judicial Supremacy* (1941). Discusses the significant changes in the federal government's structure, operations, and responsibilities and the judiciary's role in the transformation.

Geoffrey Miller, "Independent Agencies," 1986 *Supreme Court Review* 41 (1986). Discusses the argument for formal division of responsibilities among the branches of the federal government, and its implication for administrative agencies.

Katzenbach v. Morgan

The Fourteenth Amendment was one of three constitutional amendments conceived, adopted, and implemented during Reconstruction in response primarily to the nation's experience with slavery. The Fourteenth Amendment's key guarantees are the derivation of state citizenship from national citizenship, the protection of privileges and immunities of citizenship, safeguards against deprivation of life, liberty, and property without due process of law, and the guarantee of equal protection of the law.

These provisions, set forth in Section 1 of the Fourteenth Amendment, represent substantive constitutional guarantees that limit state power. As explained by the amendment's architects, these provisions were intended to transfer responsibility for protection of civil rights from the states to the federal government. Historically, states had been the primary source for creating and protecting civil rights. The Fourteenth Amendment, based mainly upon the slavery experience, achieved a redistribution of accountability for these interests. Recourse for violations of guarantees secured by

Citation:	384 U.S. 641.
Issue:	Whether a state law restricting the right to vote should be struck down because it conflicted with federal law enacted pursuant to the Fourteenth Amendment.
Year of Decision:	1966.
Outcome:	The state law conflicted with properly enacted federal legislation and thus should be invalidated.
Author of Opinion:	Justice William Brennan.
Vote:	7–2.

Section 1 was provided for through the judicial system. Included in the amendment, however, was another significant method for securing those interests identified in Section 1. Under Section 5 of the Fourteenth Amendment, Congress was empowered to enforce "by appropriate legislation" the substantive terms of the amendment.

The extent to which congressional enactments under Section 5 might exceed the terms of Section 1 became a question for the Supreme Court when Congress enacted civil rights and voting rights legislation during the 1960s. Several years after the end of Reconstruction, the Court in the *Civil Rights Cases* (1883) determined that Congress could reach no further than what courts prohibited under Section 1. Because the equal protection clause only barred official action, the Civil Rights Act of 1875 was invalidated because it outlawed private discrimination. Enactment of the Civil Rights Act of 1964, which prohibits racial discrimination in numerous private contexts, avoided the impact of the *Civil Rights Cases* ruling by basing itself upon Congress's power to regulate commerce among the several states. The question of whether Congress might regulate activities not squarely within the ambit of Section 1 presented itself when a New York law that conditioned the right to vote on the ability to read and speak English was challenged under the Voting Rights Act of 1965.

The Voting Rights Act, which was designed to eliminate barriers that had denied the right to vote on the basis of race, included a provision that prohibited literacy tests for persons who had attained at least a sixth-grade education in Puerto Rico. Affected by a conflict between New York and federal laws were large numbers of Puerto Ricans living in New York. Those Puerto Rican immigrants who had been educated in Spanish and were unable to read and write English were disqualified by the New York law from voting. Because the Voting Rights Act prohibited enforcement of the state law, a group of registered voters challenged its constitutionality in *Katzenbach v. Morgan*. Nicholas Katzenbach was Attorney General of the United States. John P. Morgan and other voters sued him, the Attorney General of New York, and the New York City Board of Elections when the city indicated it would comply with the Voting Rights Act. Their basic argument, consistent with the *Civil Rights Cases* decision, was that federal law enacted pursuant to Section 5 took precedence only if the state law violated Section 1 of the Fourteenth Amendment.

Writing for the majority, Justice William Brennan upheld the federal law without determining whether the state law violated the equal protection clause. In so doing, Brennan maintained that the congressional power granted by Section 5 would be redundant and meaningless if legislation was restricted to the terms and reach of Section 1. Because the state law could be challenged in court as a violation of Section 1, the ability of Congress to proscribe only the same activity added nothing. From the Court's perspective, Section 5 needed to be measured not only in its relationship to the Fourteenth Amendment but on the basis of whether it was an appropriate means for enforcing the equal protection guarantee. Rather than viewing Section 5 as a parallel measure, the Court determined that it vested Congress with the same powers afforded by the necessary and proper clause set forth in Article I, Section 8 [18] of the Constitution. As noted in *McCulloch v. Maryland* (1819), this provision enables Congress to make "all Laws which shall be necessary and proper for carrying into Execution the foregoing Powers, and all other Powers vested by this Constitution in the Government of the United States, or in any Department or Officer thereof." In *McCulloch*, the Court determined that legislative ends that are legitimate and within the scope of the Constitution allow for "all means which are appropriate, which are plainly adapted to that end, which are not prohibited, but consistent with the letter and spirit of the Constitution."

The focus of the Court's inquiry thus was upon whether the federal law was "plainly adapted" to the ends of the equal protection clause and whether it was consistent with, rather than barred by, the Constitution's "letter and spirit." The Court found that the Puerto Rican community's interest in voting justified congressional action that superseded state interests, and therefore the "plainly adapted" standard was satisfied. The Court noted that the literacy requirement had originated as a device to encourage non-English-speaking immigrants to learn English and to ensure informed voting. Because the literacy test provision contained several exemptions, and some evidence suggested that prejudice played a prominent role in the enactment of the requirement, the Court determined that Congress might well have had reason to question the state's purpose. Noting the "specially informed legislative competence" of Congress regarding the subject, the Court deferred to Congress's judgment.

Turning to whether the Voting Rights Act provision was consistent with and not prohibited by the Constitution's letter and spirit, the Court rejected arguments that the law discriminated against persons who were educated through at least the sixth grade in Spanish-speaking schools. Its reasoning was that Congress had neither denied nor diluted the right to vote but merely extended the opportunity to a group previously unable to exercise it. Unless there was any burdening of a fundamental right or invidious discrimination, the Court concluded that Congress could address denials of the right to vote on a selective rather than wholesale basis.

In a dissenting opinion joined by Justice Potter Stewart, Justice John Harlan, Jr., maintained that the Court had violated separation of powers principles by enabling the legislature to perform a judicial function. As Harlan framed it, the question was not whether the federal law constituted "appropriate remedial legislation to cure an established command of the Constitution" but whether that constitutional provision had been violated. Stressing that the question was for judicial review rather than legislative determination, he warned that Congress otherwise "would be able to qualify this Court's constitutional decisions . . . by resorting to the Necessary and Proper Clause." Particularly risky, if Congress could define the substantive reach of Section 1, was the possibility that Congress also could "dilute equal protection and due process decisions of this Court."

Allowing Congress to define constitutional violations and respond to them by expanding rights arguably transfers a judicial function to the legislative branch. Justice Brennan suggested that the risk of diluting rights could be avoided by allowing Congress only to expand but not diminish them. This so-called ratchet theory of congressional enforcement power has never been presented as a formal holding. It has been supported over the years, however, by numerous justices and commentators and has generated case law that extends voting and civil rights beyond the specific terms of the Constitution. Although the result is not constitutional law in the form of a protected right or liberty, and legislation always is subject to repeal, congressional action, when it is upheld, effectively extends the Constitution's reach.

Bibliography

Archibald Cox, "The Role of Congress in Constitutional Adjudication," 40 *University of Cincinnati Law Review* 199 (1970). Advocates and amplifies the so-called ratchet theory of the Fourteenth Amendment.

Donald E. Lively, *Foreshadows of the Law* (1992). Explores the long-term impact of the *Civil Rights Cases* as they relate to congressional power to enforce the Fourteenth Amendment.

Stephen Ross, "Legislative Enforcement of Equal Protection," 72 *Minnesota Law Review* 311 (1987). Examines the debate over whether Congress should be allowed to enact laws that reach beyond the Fourteenth Amendment itself.

II

Power to Regulate or Affect
the National Economy

The structure of American government in the period immediately after the Revolution was influenced strongly by experience with the abuses of power that generated the struggle for independence. The Articles of Confederation evidenced lingering uneasiness with centralized authority. They attempted to minimize the risk of peril to individual freedom by assigning the primary powers of government to the states. Experience under the Articles of Confederation soon demonstrated their inadequacy and the necessity to balance the dangers of tyranny against the need for a viable political and economic union.

Particularly disastrous to the imperative of nation building was the power of each state to define its own economic policies. The country's initial postcolonial political order provided the federal government with no power to regulate commerce among the states or with foreign nations. Because each state reserved to itself the power to regulate commerce, economic policy was competitive, divisive, and even destructive. Restrictive tariffs and trade wars became the norm as states sought to protect or advance their economic interests, typically at the expense of their neighbors. The result was a system that choked commercial intercourse, facilitated economic stagnation, undermined cooperation and harmony, and ultimately generated a consensus for change.

Delegates to the Constitutional Convention did not abandon concern with the risks of centralized power. Authority was divided and distributed among three branches of government that would check and balance each other. The blueprint for a political union, moreover, reflected an understanding that the federal government would be a government of limited power. Consistent with that expectation, the Bill of Rights established specific limits on the reach of federal authority. The Tenth Amendment in particular preserved the role and status of the states and people by providing that "[t]he powers not delegated to the United States by the Constitution, nor prohibited by it to the States, are reserved to the States respectively, or to the people."

The framers of the Constitution, however, also sought to create a more viable, efficient, and productive union. Drawing upon experience under the Articles of Confederation, they vested the national government with power "[t]o regulate Commerce with foreign Nations, and among the several States." By transferring this authority from the states to the federal government, the Constitution established the basis for an integrated national economy that represented movement beyond the intramural squabbles and self-destructive policies of states under the Articles of Confederation. Granting Congress the power to regulate interstate commerce, however, posed the risk that the federal government's role would expand beyond the limited range of interests originally contemplated for it. Particularly as the nation became increasingly industrialized, the federal government's interest in economic regulation pushed beyond just the interstate transit of goods. Economic crisis during the 1930s in the form of the Great Depression resulted in decisions that greatly enlarged the national government's ability to regulate activities that affected or were connected with commerce. The legacy of this expanded federal role has included an outpouring of federal regulation, including civil rights, criminal, and environmental legislation, that has been upheld by modern interpretations of Congress's power to regulate interstate commerce. These developments have not been without critical outcry over the diminished role and influence of the states under a system of dual sovereigns. Part II explores those Supreme Court decisions that have been critical in extending the federal government from a limited to a pervasive presence and balancing the competing interests of national and state authorities.

4

Federal Power to Regulate Interstate Commerce

The essential requirement for a viable economic union was power, vested in the federal government, to regulate interstate commerce. Failure to assign this authority to the national government was the fatal flaw of postrevolutionary government under the Articles of Confederation. By giving Congress the exclusive power to regulate commerce among the several states, the nation's founders responded to state practices and policies that had been ruinous to national growth and prosperity. Two centuries after the Constitution's framing and ratification, federal power far exceeds what the nation's founders contemplated. The basis for this expanded federal role can be found in the Supreme Court's initial expoundment of the commerce power in *Gibbons v. Ogden* (1824). By the early twentieth century, the Supreme Court defined this congressional authority in increasingly narrow terms. As a consequence, national policy initiatives aimed at addressing social and economic problems became hostage to constitutional interpretation. Conflict between the national political process and the judiciary peaked during the Great Depression, when the Court struck down numerous New Deal programs designed to alleviate the nation's economic crisis. Extensive turnover on the Court by the late 1930s, however, resulted in a doctrinal turnabout. In *Wickard v. Filburn* (1942), the Court set a constitutional tone that enabled Congress to use its commerce power as a basis for playing a vastly expanded role in the scheme of American governance.

Gibbons v. Ogden

Following the American Revolution, the thirteen former colonies grouped together under the Articles of Confederation. This initial effort at nation building quickly proved inadequate. Particularly fatal to the postcolonial system of governance were sectional and interstate rivalries that undermined economic growth and prosperity. Each state sought a competitive advantage over the others by means of high tariffs and taxes on interstate business transactions, and the confederation as a whole suffered from economic stagnation and selfdestructiveness.

The primary lesson of the Articles of Confederation was that a successful economic union required a national policy driven by common interests rather than petty jealousies. This understanding was shared by delegates from the several states who assembled in Philadelphia in 1787 to draft what became the United States Con-

Citation:	22 U.S. 1.
Issue:	Whether a state may regulate commerce with another state.
Year of Decision:	1824.
Outcome:	Congress has exclusive authority to regulate interstate commerce.
Author of Opinion:	Chief Justice John Marshall.
Vote:	7–0.

stitution. The Constitution thus was drafted with a collective sense that unless the states could overcome their economic rivalries and jealousies and function interdependently, they perpetually would flounder. To avoid the failures of the Articles of Confederation, authority over the national economy was centralized rather than fragmented. This change was effected by Article I, Section 8[3], of the Constitution, which vests Congress with power "[t]o regulate Commerce . . . among the several States."

Authority to regulate interstate commerce conferred a significant mantle of authority upon Congress. For a national government conceived with the understanding that it would have limited powers, the commerce clause established a power base that over time has competed with state interests and has expanded federal authority. That result was achieved not by the specific words of the Constitution but by its interpretation. Like many landmark disputes in the nation's early history, controversy over Congress's commerce power reflected a continuing debate over the roles of federal and state governments. As was the case in *Marbury v. Madison* (1803) and *McCulloch v. Maryland* (1819), Chief Justice John Marshall played a pivotal role in defining the nation's constitutional future.

The first test of Congress's power to regulate commerce among the several states arose in the context of a dispute between rival steamship companies. In 1798, New York granted an exclusive right to operate steamboats within its jurisdiction to John Fitch and Robert Livingston. Five years after Fitch and Livingston were granted their steamboat monopoly, the privilege was extended to Robert Fulton, whom history credits as builder of the first commercially viable steamboat. Under a licensing agreement with Fulton and Livingston, Aaron Ogden commenced steamboat service between New York and New Jersey. Despite the monopoly established by New York, Thomas Gibbons provided steamboat service on the same route under a license by Congress that enabled him to operate in coastal areas. Ogden sued Gibbons under a provision of the New York law that enabled him to obtain an injunction against anyone who violated his exclusive boating rights. Ogden's primary argument was that the exclusive right granted to him by New York related only to intrastate commerce, which Congress had no power to regulate. In response, Gibbons maintained that he was trading in interstate commerce, which Congress had exclusive power to regulate. Ogden initially was successful in obtaining an injunction from a New York court that protected his monopoly interest. Gibbons's appeal to the United States Supreme Court, however, reached an audience that was more receptive to his argument.

Writing for the Court, Chief Justice Marshall struck down the injunction on grounds that the state court had not interpreted the commerce clause properly. As the Court saw it, that provision gave Congress all power to regulate commerce among the several states. Ogden's view that the Tenth Amendment reserved to the states some power to regulate commerce thus collided with the Court's determination that congressional authority was exclusive. If Congress had enacted a law regulating commerce between or among states, conflicting state legislation was invalid and had to give way. This determination reflects not only the dominance of federal interest under the commerce clause but the principle of supremacy under Article VI, Section 2. Under the supremacy clause, congressional laws reflecting a dominant federal interest preempt state laws on the same subject.

No less important than this restatement of federal dominance, and of lasting significance for the scope of Congress's interest, was the Court's definition of commerce and the reach of the national interest. Marshall described commerce as commercial intercourse and viewed Congress's power as extending to wherever commerce existed. Given that broad characterization of the subject matter and the federal regulatory interest, it followed that navigation fell within the concept of commerce. As the Court put it, "The mind can scarcely conceive a system for regulating commerce between nations, which shall be silent on the admission of the vessels of the one nation [or state] into the ports of the other, and be confined to prescribing rules for the conduct of individuals, in the actual employment of buying and selling, or of barter." Particularly significant in establishing a broad federal interest over the long term was Marshall's refusal to use state boundaries as the dividing line between interstate and intrastate commerce. He observed that "[c]ommerce among the states cannot stop at the external boundary line of each State, but may be introduced into the interior." The basis thus was established for a federal interest that could reach within the state if some connection could be established to interstate commercial intercourse. Litigation under the commerce clause, as indicated over the years by Hammer v. Dagenhart (1918), Carter v. Carter Coal Co. (1936), and United States v. Lopez (1995), has focused upon the adequacy of that connection in either narrowing or expanding the scope of federal interest.

Although the Court's opinion established a dominant federal power over interstate commerce, it did not entirely preclude the ability of states to regulate activity of a commercial nature. The Marshall Court defined the federal interest in broad terms, but it left open the possibility that states could regulate in ways that affected commerce. A state's ability to do so, however, is dependent upon the identification of a legitimate interest unrelated to commerce. The police power that enables states to regulate health and safety, for instance, makes it possible for states to enact laws that impact commerce indirectly. The Marshall Court, in Willson v. Black-Bird Creek Marsh Co. (1829), thus upheld a state law regulating pollution of a navigable waterway as a legitimate health and safety measure.

Over the course of the nineteenth century, federal legislation under the commerce power was relatively rare. Even so, early decisions such as *Gibbons v. Ogden* established a federal interest that was not dependent upon an actual congressional enactment. Chief Justice Marshall's determination that Congress possessed all power to regulate interstate commerce established an authority that precluded states from directly regulating commerce even if it was not exercised. Modern case law refers to this barrier against state legislation as the "dormant commerce clause." Although the scope of federal interest has been debated and has varied over the years, depending upon how the line is drawn between interstate and intrastate commerce and how broadly commerce is defined, the Marshall Court's understanding of the federal interest represents the *Gibbons* decision's most significant legacy. Despite varying perceptions of how far congressional power extends under the commerce clause, it remains a basic constitutional premise that the federal interest is exclusive within its realm.

Bibliography

Charles Beard, *An Economic Interpretation of the Constitution of the United States* (1960). Provides insight into the various economic perspectives that influenced the Constitution's framing.

Claude Heathcock, *The United States Constitution in Perspective* (1972). Provides a long-term perspective upon the commerce power.

Carl B. Swisher, *American Constitutional Development*, 2d ed. (1954). Discusses the origins of the commerce power.

Charles Warren, *The Supreme Court in United States History*, vol. 2, pp. 75–76 (1932). Examines the impact of the *Gibbons* decision in facilitating interstate commerce.

Wickard v. Filburn

The Constitution was framed and ratified at a time when the United States was essentially an agrarian society. Protectionist economic policies adopted by the states in the years immediately following the American Revolution led to a restructuring and redistribution of governmental power. To avoid the destructiveness of interstate trade wars, the Constitution's framers established Congress's power "[t]o regulate Commerce with Foreign Nations, and among the several states."

Until the late nineteenth century, federal regulation under the commerce clause largely was restricted to governing trade among the several states and with foreign nations. American participation in the international slave trade, for instance, was prohibited in 1808. The national bank, discussed in the examination of *McCulloch v. Maryland* (1819), is another example of early federal law enacted in part under the commerce power.

Citation:	317 U.S. 111.
Issue:	Whether the production of wheat for home and local consumption was within Congress's power to regulate interstate commerce.
Year of Decision:	1942.
Outcome:	A local activity substantially affecting interstate commerce is within the scope of Congress's authority to regulate commerce among the several states.
Author of Opinion:	Justice Robert Jackson.
Vote:	9–0.

As the Industrial Revolution, urbanization, and advances in transportation and communication reshaped society in the late nineteenth century, federal regulatory interests began to expand. Concern with concentrated economic power and business abuses led to federal laws such as the Sherman Antitrust Act and the Interstate Commerce Act that responded to the profound social and economic changes caused by rapid industrialization. The Sherman Act, for instance, prohibits restraint of trade. The Interstate Commerce Act enabled Congress, among other things, to regulate rates charged by common carriers for interstate shipments. Both of these laws were challenged on grounds that Congress had exceeded its authority under the commerce clause in enacting them. The Supreme Court, however, found them within Congress's power and thus constitutional. These initial decisions upholding federal law did not reflect the restrictive understanding of the commerce clause and the political fallout that would characterize the debate over its meaning during the early twentieth century.

Typifying the Supreme Court's decisions during this period was the ruling in Hammer v. Dagenhart (1918) that struck down a law prohibiting the use of child labor for production of goods sold in interstate commerce. From the Court's perspective, the manufacture of goods was distinct from their production. Although Congress could regulate the interstate movement of goods, the manufacturing process itself did not constitute commerce. In defining the scope of the commerce power, the Court thus distinguished between regulation that directly affected interstate commerce and regulation that indirectly affected it.

The Court's restrictive view of congressional authority persisted even as the nation plunged into economic crisis. Responding to the onset of the Great Depression, President Franklin D. Roosevelt proposed and Congress enacted numerous laws regulating the national economy. These laws, collectively referred to as the New Deal, affected not only transportation and trade but manufacturing, mining, and agriculture. Despite the nation's grave economic condition, the Supreme Court maintained that the Constitution's meaning did not vary with circumstance and invalidated the multitude of economic reforms. The Court's reaction triggered a major political crisis when President Roosevelt presented a plan to increase the Supreme Court's size so that he could appoint justices more friendly to his position. Although Congress did not enact the Court-packing plan, significant turnover resulting from the death or retirement of several judges enabled Roosevelt to shape a Court more responsive to his political aims. In National Labor Relations Board v. Jones & Laughlin Steel Corp. (1937), the Court upheld a federal labor law that prohibited unfair labor practices by companies with operations in several states. Holding that Congress may regulate any "activities affecting commerce," the Court abandoned the distinction between direct and indirect affects. The ruling of Hammer v. Dagenhart itself was overruled in United States v. Darby (1941) when the Court determined that the commerce power enabled Congress to regulate the hours and wages of employees who produce goods shipped in interstate commerce. Finding that Congress has power to exclude goods and materials harmful to the public welfare, the Court accepted the argument that the movement of articles manufactured under substandard labor conditions had a negative impact upon commerce.

The Jones & Laughlin and Darby decisions represented significant turnabouts from commerce power decisions of the preceding decades. They opened the door for a much more active and pervasive federal role in governing conditions previously within the province of the states. The extent of that federal interest and the consequences for the balance of the twentieth century were previewed when the Court considered a federal law that restricted the production of wheat. Under the Agricultural Adjustment Act of 1938, the secretary of agriculture was authorized to set quotas for the growing of wheat. The act was designed to control the volume of wheat moving in interstate commerce and thus avoid surpluses and shortages that destabilized prices. Ignoring an order that allotted him 11.1 acres of wheat, Roscoe Filburn, an Ohio farmer, doubled his production quota. When he was ordered to pay a penalty for exceeding his allotment, he resisted on grounds that the excess crops were intended for his own consumption and thus were beyond the reach of Congress's power. Challenging the government's power to set quotas upon what he claimed to be a purely local activity, he sued Claude W. Wickard, the Secretary of Agriculture, to have the act declared unconstitutional.

Although the Court acknowledged that the farmer's "contribution to the demand for wheat by itself may be trivial," it refused to exempt him from the law's operation. It focused not upon his activity in isolation but upon the possibility that "his contribution, [if] taken together with that of many others similarly situated, [would be] far from trivial." The Court noted that Congress had a significant interest in production for home consumption because of its potential, if it was unregulated, to undermine the purposes of the act. Although one home-consumption producer might not affect market prices, the aggregate effect of many such producers might have a substantial influence upon them. The Court thus rejected the farmer's invitation to focus upon the local nature of his activity and concentrated upon the net result of cumulative effects, real or possible.

The essence of the Court's ruling was that even if an activity is local in nature, it is within the commerce power's reach if it has a substantial effect on interstate commerce. From this principle emerged the basis for a dramatically expanded federal regulatory presence over the course of the twentieth century. In the 1960s, federal civil rights laws that prohibited racial discrimination by hotels, motels, and restaurants were upheld on grounds that such practices burdened interstate commerce. The rule of *Wickard v. Filburn* was particularly instrumental in the Court's finding that an Alabama restaurant located several miles from an interstate highway and serving an essentially local clientele was subject to the Civil Rights Act of 1964. Although the restaurant was small and had a minimal effect on interstate commerce, its activities combined with those of others constituted a substantial effect. A significant connection to interstate commerce was established, moreover, by the fact that nearly half of the meat the restaurant served was purchased from a local supplier who obtained it from an outside source.

For nearly half a century, the Court consistently used the *Wickard* formula to reject constitutional challenges to federal regulation adopted under the commerce power. From 1937 through the early 1990s, federal interest and power extended pervasively into areas previously governed primarily by the states. This phenomenon of an expanding federal presence was facilitated by repeated reference to the reasoning of *Wickard v. Filburn*. The commerce power became a basis not only for federal civil rights legislation but for environmental legislation, criminal laws, and pervasive economic regulation. The regulatory latitude provided Congress under the commerce power expanded its authority to the point that critics, including some Supreme Court justices, questioned whether the commerce power had become the basis for a national police power at the expense of the states' Tenth Amendment interests. These concerns eventually became an influence upon case law during the 1990s. In New York v. United States (1992), the Court found that Congress could not require a state to enact a specific law. A few years later in United States v. Lopez (1995), it determined that the commerce clause does not confer a police power upon Congress. Striking down a federal law that made it a crime for students to carry firearms into a school, the Lopez Court determined that an activity must have a substantial effect upon interstate commerce to be a subject of federal regulation. Guns in schools, as the Court saw it, constituted a purely local activity. Noting that the commerce power must have some restrictions if the notion of the federal government as one of limited and enumerated powers is to have any meaning, the Court struck down a law that, if found, lacked any substantial effect on interstate commerce. The consequence of its determination, however, would appear to be an outer marking of rather than a narrowing of the *Wickard* formula or a retreat from the basic constitutional principles that greatly have expanded the federal role in social and economic regulation.

Bibliography

Raoul Berger, *Federalism: The Founders' Design* (1987). Argues against the expansive understanding of the commerce power.

Jesse H. Choper, "The Scope of National Power vis-à-vis the States: The Dispensability of Judicial Review," 86 *Yale Law Journal* 1552 (1977). Examines practical realities that limit the encroachment of federal power upon state interests.

Peter Irons, *The New Deal Lawyers* (1982). Discusses the Supreme Court's early resistance to the political initiatives of the New Deal.

5

State Police Power and the Dormant Commerce Clause

Congress's power to regulate interstate commerce is comprehensive and exclusive. Despite this authority, states retain their police power, which enables them to regulate health, safety, morals, and the public welfare. In exercising this authority, for example, when emission controls are established for motor vehicles, states incidentally may burden interstate commerce in the course of pursuing a legitimate interest. Such regulation is permissible provided it does not interfere with federal interests in efficient commercial intercourse and the needs of a viable economic union. A Pennsylvania law that required ships to use local pilots for navigation into and out of the port of Philadelphia was challenged in *Cooley v. Board of Wardens* (1851) on grounds that it exceeded the state's power. In *Southern Pacific Co. v. Arizona* (1945), the Court assessed whether a state safety regulation restricting the length of trains excessively impaired interstate commerce. In *Dean Milk Co. v. City of Madison* (1951), a city ordinance that prescribed methods for inspecting milk confronted Congress's power to regulate interstate commerce. These cases are examples of "dormant commerce clause" analysis, which assesses the constitutionality of state regulation that impacts the federal interest in interstate commerce. A constitutional violation is not contingent upon a state law being found in conflict with a federal law. The focal point instead is whether the state regulation compromises the national interest.

Cooley v. Board of Wardens

By vesting Congress with power to regulate commerce among the several states, the Constitution's framers and ratifiers provided for a system that would avoid the problems experienced under the Articles of Confederation, which created a weak national government. Because each state was able to set its own trade policies, economic warfare became the norm. Protective and retaliatory tariffs on the shipment of goods across state lines undermined the possibility of a prosperous economic union. The Supreme Court's decision in *Gibbons v. Ogden* (1824) to the effect that the Constitution gave Congress exclusive power over interstate commerce emphasized the primacy of national interest in the field.

Citation:	53 U.S. 299.
Issue:	Whether states may regulate aspects of interstate commerce that do not require national control.
Year of Decision:	1851.
Outcome:	States may regulate matters of local concern notwithstanding their effect on interstate commerce.
Author of Opinion:	Justice Benjamin Curtis.
Vote:	7–2.

Despite the strong and pervasive federal responsibility over commerce, many regulatory needs are of an essentially local nature. The placement of stop signs and the setting of speed limits on a community's roads, for instance, are actions that affect and may even burden interstate commerce. Nonetheless, such decisions logically are made by local governments, which are closer to and presumably have a better understanding of the nature and extent of needed regulation. The sensibility of an arrangement that enabled federal and state power to be exercised concurrently was not a foregone conclusion. Not until the mid-nineteenth century was it clear that Congress's power to regulate interstate commerce did not extinguish state authority to pass health, safety, and other laws that incidentally affected commerce among the states.

The question presented itself to the Supreme Court in the form of a challenge to a Pennsylvania law that required all ships to use a local pilot when they were navigating the Delaware River. Aaron B. Cooley was a merchant who argued that the local pilotage law imposed a tax on tonnage. He brought suit against the Board of Wardens for the Port of Philadelphia, which the state had authorized to receive fines from violators in the amount of half the cost of the pilotage fee. The basis for the constitutional claim was that the local regulation burdened interstate commerce. Responding to that contention, the state cited a federal law that provided that pilotage of the nation's rivers, harbors, and ports should remain within the state's regulatory domain. This argument set forth the basic concept of the "dormant commerce clause." Even though Congress may not have enacted a law, the commerce power nonetheless gives it an exclusive regulatory authority. The commerce power by itself, in its "dormant condition, is sufficient to bar any state law that directly regulates commerce." Put simply, the mere existence of federal power over commerce among the several states may be sufficient to disable them from regulating in the field. The question for the Court thus was not one of choosing between a national and a state law but determining whether a state law can coexist with the federal interest represented by the commerce power.

Writing for a majority of the Court, Justice Benjamin R. Curtis observed that Congress's power to regulate interstate commerce "does not contain any terms which expressly exclude the states from exercising an authority over its subject-matter." Noting that the "local necessities of navigation" may vary from place to place, the Court refused to frame the issue in terms of whether it should "affirm or deny that the nature of the commerce power requires exclusive legislation by Congress." Rather, the focus should be upon whether the activities subject to regulation under the commerce power "are in their nature national, or admit only of one uniform system, or plan of regulation." Only if the need for uniformity was established should a concern "be of such a nature as to require exclusive legislation by Congress." If a problem or condition was local in nature, such as a health or safety interest, it was appropriate for states to address that unique need.

The question of whether federal power was exclusive or states might regulate concurrently thus required a determination of whether a particular activity required a uniform national rule or was amenable to concurrent state regulation. Finding that pilotage was a local activity, and specialized navigational skills are required from one port to another, the Court determined that state regulation was appropriate. The finding of a concurrent state power, however, did not preclude Congress from asserting its power under the commerce clause on an exclusive basis. If Congress enacted a law that assumed responsibility for regulating usage of pilots in the nation's navigable waterways, the state interest and role then would be preempted. With respect to regulating pilotage, however, the Court found that Congress clearly and authoritatively had left the subject to the states unless and until it decided to "exert its power." Especially because the federal law itself provided for regulation of pilotage "by such laws as the states may ... enact," the Court determined "that the nature of this subject is not such as to require its exclusive legislation."

Although the Court upheld the Pennsylvania law and resolved the pilotage controversy in favor of the state, it provided little guidance for determining when an interest was primarily local or in need of a uniform national standard. The failure to provide such direction may not have been particularly crucial, given Congress's ability to assert its exclusive interest over commerce among the several states when it wishes to do so by legislation. The supremacy clause of the Constitution, set forth in Article VI, Section 2, provides that validly enacted federal legislation preempts conflicting state legislation. Because Congress has the authority to regulate exclusively in the field of commerce merely by exercising its power to do so, the line between local concerns and national needs is determined largely by how far Congress wants to push the national interest.

The majority decision reflected an accommodation of federal and state powers that was not entirely satisfactory to Justice Peter V. Daniel. In a concurring opinion, he argued that the power to regulate pilots was an attribute of inherent state power. From Daniel's perspective, the power to regulate pilotage inherently belonged to the states. A dissenting view was provided by Justice John McLean, who maintained that Congress had exclusive power under the commerce clause to regulate pilots. Responding to the point that federal law permitted states to regulate pilotage on the local level, he asserted that Congress could not delegate its power to regulate in the field. McLean thus agreed with the claimants that the challenged law was invalid.

The Court's ruling provided a needed bridge between the premise of *Gibbons v. Ogden* (1824), which emphasized the breadth and depth of congressional power under the commerce power, and modern case law that attempts to accommodate both federal and state concerns. In South Carolina State Highway Department v. Barnwell Bros. (1938), the Court determined that a state law that restricted the width and length of trucks using South Carolina highways was permissible. Although the law was a traffic safety measure, it burdened the movement of interstate commerce. Trucks that were too wide either had to stop and transfer their contents into other vehicles or detour around South Carolina. Application of Justice McLean's premise that congressional power in the field was absolute might have compromised a pressing safety interest. At the time, two decades prior to the interstate highway system, South Carolina roads were narrow and underdeveloped. Even on major highways used for interstate travel, trucks standing side by side were wider than the roads themselves. If the state had possessed no ability to regulate, a major safety hazard would have been unaddressed. The understanding that states possess power to regulate local circumstances on a concurrent basis, provided this does not conflict with the need for national uniformity or a federal law, reflected an interest in avoiding unnecessary tension or conflict between two sovereigns. It also established a model of dormant commerce clause analysis that still retains its vitality.

Twentieth-century case law under the dormant commerce clause acknowledges the validity of a state's interest in regulating health, safety, and the public welfare. This police power predated the Constitution's framing and ratification and carried forward into the new union. The Tenth Amendment acknowledges such state authority in stating that "[t]he powers not delegated to the United States by the Constitution, nor prohibited by it to the States, are reserved to the States respectively, or to the people." Modern standards of review have evolved beyond the criteria announced in *Cooley*. Provided that state regulations are not discriminatory or unduly burdensome to commerce, the Court upholds them as a concurrent exercise of power. Such case law is mindful of the national interest in avoiding the jealousies and frictions that undermined the Articles of Confederation. At the same time, it is attentive to the need for breathing room that enables the states to address their legitimate needs and interests.

Bibliography

Carl Swisher, *Roger B. Taney* (1935). Discusses Chief Justice Roger B. Taney's contribution to defining and understanding the relation and interaction between federal and state governments.

Laurence H. Tribe, *American Constitutional Law*, 2d ed. (1988). Examines the development of principles that accommodate the exercise of federal and state powers on a concurrent basis.

Southern Pacific Co. v. Arizona

The commerce clause, as noted in *Gibbons v. Ogden* [1824] and *Wickard v. Filburn* [1942], has become the basis for an expanded role and presence of the federal government, particularly over the past several decades. The commerce power's core purpose was to facilitate the nation's economic development and efficiency by ensuring that producers, traders, and service providers would have free access to markets in every state. Even when Congress has not used its authority by enacting legislation, state laws affecting interstate commerce must be reviewed against the commerce power. Although states are empowered to protect health, safety, and public welfare under their police powers, such legislation may impose a burden on interstate commerce. Legislation that restricts the length and width of trucks on state roads, for instance, may be enacted on grounds that it promotes public safety. Because it also may burden interstate commerce, and even if no conflicting federal law exists, the enactment must be measured against the "dormant" commerce clause.

Citation:	325 U.S. 761.
Issue:	Whether an Arizona law that limited the lengths of trains, adopted under its police power, imposes an unreasonable burden on interstate commerce.
Year of Decision:	1945.
Outcome:	State restriction on train length, even if enacted for purposes of promoting public safety, imposed an impermissible burden on interstate commerce.
Author of Opinion:	Chief Justice Harlan Fiske Stone.
Vote:	7–2.

When state law clashes with the commerce power, a constitutional conflict arises that requires judicial resolution. Such was the case when Arizona passed a law limiting trains traveling within or across the state to seventy freight cars. This restriction was justified on grounds that longer trains presented a heightened threat to public safety.

The limitation imposed burdens on trains operating through rather than within Arizona. Trains operating on interstate routes were required either to operate with fewer cars, even though longer trains were more economically efficient and were permitted in other states, or to decouple when they entered Arizona and recouple upon leaving the state. Either way, the law diminished the efficiency of commercial transportation.

Although the Arizona Supreme Court acknowledged the law's burden on interstate commerce, it upheld it on grounds that the regulation had a reasonable relationship to public safety. The state court's ruling drew upon an earlier United States Supreme Court decision, South Carolina State Highway Department v. Barnwell Bros. (1938), which upheld a state restriction on truck widths because it was reasonably related to safety concerns. In reviewing the Arizona high court's ruling, the United States Supreme Court reaffirmed the principle that states have significant leeway to address local health and safety needs. However, the Court stressed that when a state promotes such an interest, regulation must not significantly impede the free flow of interstate commerce or undermine any need for national uniformity. Both the policy of the commerce clause and the state's enactment reflected legitimate interests, at least in theory.

To sort out whether the federal constitutional interest or the state regulatory interest should prevail, the Court balanced the competing concerns. Specifically, it asked whether the benefits of the legislation exceeded the burdens imposed on interstate commerce. Noting that other states permitted longer trains than Arizona allowed, the Court found that the law undermined the interests of national uniformity that are "practically indispensable to the operation of an efficient and economic national railway system." The finding of a significant burden on interstate commerce weighed in favor of the dormant commerce clause but did not resolve the controversy. The ultimate outcome depended upon the strength of the state's interest. In examining the state's justification for the law, the Court found that the regulation had no reasonable relationship to safety. On the contrary, the Court noted that shorter trains in Arizona were not involved in fewer accidents than longer trains in other states. Because the law resulted in no real safety benefits, and the burden on interstate commerce was substantial, the Court found that the national interests of economic efficiency outweighed the regulatory concerns of the state.

Although the Court's decision established the basic method of dormant commerce clause review, the model is a source of continuing controversy. In a dissenting opinion, Justice Hugo Black set forth the primary objections to the Court's thinking. As he saw it, invalidation of the Arizona law transformed the Court into a "superlegislature" that merely second-guessed the wisdom of the state's policy. From Black's perspective, the regulation was struck down because the Court disagreed with the legislature's assessment of the safety risk, not because a reasonable relationship between regulatory means and ends was missing. Black, who believed that the decision reflected judicial usurpation of the legislative function, insisted that the Court must allow the states to make their own choices regarding methods for protecting public safety. In support of his position, it might be argued that Congress would have responded with legislation setting a uniform national standard if the Arizona law's burden on interstate commerce was truly significant.

Despite the force of Black's argument, which has been reiterated by other critics, including members of the Court, the majority opinion in *Southern*

Pacific Co. defines contemporary review of state safety regulations that impact interstate commerce. In Bibb v. Navajo Freight Lines (1959), a state law that required special mud guards on trucks was invalidated. The Court determined that this regulation did not meaningfully advance safety interests and was out of step with the law of virtually all other states. Because of the costs associated with compliance, moreover, the Court found that the requirement unreasonably burdened interstate commerce. Similarly, in Kassel v. Consolidated Freightways Corp. (1981), the Court struck down a law limiting the length of trucks on state highways. The Kassel Court observed that legitimate safety regulations have a strong presumption of constitutional validity, but noted that they still must be weighed against the needs of efficiency in interstate commerce. It also stressed that when a burden falls more upon out-of-state than in-state interests, the Court will examine the legislative design more closely. Such attention to possible discrimination or protectionism reflects a continuing appreciation of the historical realities that created and still define the commerce clause.

Bibliography

Donald H. Regan, "The Supreme Court and State Protectionism: Making Sense of the Dormant Commerce Clause," 84 *Michigan Law Review* 1091 (1986). Examines the Supreme Court's response to state protectionism.

Mark Tushnet, "Rethinking the Dormant Commerce Clause," 1979 *Wisconsin Law Review* 125 (1979). A comprehensive discussion of the dormant commerce clause and its purpose.

Dean Milk Co. v. City of Madison

The commerce clause, as discussed in *Gibbons v. Ogden* [1824] and *Wickard v. Filburn* [1942], was included in the Constitution to ensure that the states refrained from the jealous and economically ruinous trade policies that impeded the nation's economic development under the Articles of Confederation. Decisions in the early twentieth century that limited the commerce clause's force to processes closely related to transportation eventually gave way to rulings that any economic activity substantially affecting interstate commerce was within the provision's scope. Because the federal government's exclusive power to regulate interstate commerce barred states from implementing unduly burdensome transportation regulations, it followed that a state regulation of any economic activity sufficiently related to interstate commerce would be subject to constitutional review. Given the commerce clause's core concern with precluding protectionist state regulation, courts have been especially attentive to the possibility that health and safety measures actually may be a cover for policies that discriminate against out-of-state economic interests.

Citation:	340 U.S. 349.
Issue:	Whether a city ordinance that required out-of-state milk distributors to pasteurize their product locally discriminated against out-of-state commerce.
Year of Decision:	1951.
Outcome:	The ordinance discriminated against out-of-state commerce and thus conflicted with the commerce clause.
Author of Opinion:	Justice Tom Clark.
Vote:	6–3.

These questions of undue burdens upon interstate commerce and protectionist policy were at the heart of the Supreme Court's review of a Madison, Wisconsin, ordinance that regulated the terms of milk distribution within the city. The law prohibited distribution of milk labeled as pasteurized unless it was processed and bottled at a facility within a five-mile radius of the city. The plaintiff, Dean Milk Co., was headquartered in Illinois. None of its pasteurization plants was within the five-mile limit. Because it was denied the opportunity to distribute its milk in Madison, it sued on grounds that the ordinance unreasonably burdened interstate commerce.

Writing for the majority, Justice Tom Clark found that the regulation addressed health and safety interests that were within the scope of the state's police power. The Court nonetheless found that the measure constituted an economic impediment to out-of-state businesses that worked to the advantage of local milk distributors. It thus viewed the ordinance as a protectionist law that shielded local interests from the rigors of market competition and discriminated against interstate commerce. From the Court's perspective, reasonable alternatives existed for achieving the city's health and safety interests without denying out-of-state companies access to the city's milk consumers. Among those less burdensome possibilities were having city inspectors travel to distant plants and prohibiting the import of milk from communities that had lesser quality standards than Madison's. The bottom line, as the Court saw it, was that the city could achieve its health and safety goals by means that did not place out-of-state interests at a competitive disadvantage.

The Court's invalidation of the city ordinance on grounds that health and safety concerns could be met by alternative means generated a sharp dissent by Justice Hugo Black. Consistent with his criticism of the decision in *Southern Pacific Co. v. Arizona* (1945), Black maintained that the Court again was functioning as a superlegislature. He viewed the regulation as a bona fide attempt to protect public health and safety. Because the regulation was a good-faith effort to respond to a valid city concern, he believed that the Court should not second-guess the method that the city employed. For the Court to demand better ways to achieve a public health and safety goal, Black believed that it must have a knowledge base on the subject at least equivalent to that of the lawmakers. He particularly doubted whether the Court was qualified to pass judgment on what regulatory alternative best served the public's health interest. Because legislatures are not bound by rules of evidence, have greater expertise and resources for policy making, and are vested with the responsibility of legislating, Black concluded that the Court exceeded its authority and unwisely assumed the function of a health review board.

The majority's concern with discrimination against out-of-state milk distributors reflects a basic focal point of modern dormant commerce clause analysis. Its analysis of the ordinance's impact, however, may have been somewhat overstated. Because the regulation required all distributors to have milk processed and bottled within five miles of the city, it affected businesses both within and outside the state. Wisconsin distributors beyond the five-mile limit were subject to the same regulatory burden as out-of-state competitors. The commerce clause by its terms relates to commerce among the states rather than trade among communities within the same state. Because the ordinance disadvantaged any distributor that did not pasteurize its milk within the five-mile limit, the case might be understood better as one concerning an undue burden on interstate commerce rather than differential treatment of in-state and out-of-state interests.

Even if protectionism was a dubious basis for invalidating the Madison ordinance, it is a key factor in dormant commerce clause analysis. A law that prohibited the disposal of solid waste from other states was struck down in Philadelphia v. New Jersey (1978) on grounds that it discriminated on the basis of where the refuse originated. As the Court indicated in *Dean Milk Co.*, states may regulate aspects of commerce when they seek to protect public health or safety, at least to the extent that no conflicting federal regulation exists. Such uses of the police power are prohibited, however, if the resulting regulation discriminates on the basis of commercial origin or is unduly burdensome. A classic and patent example of such discrimination presented itself to the Court in Hunt v. Washington State Apple Advertising Commission (1977). In Hunt, the Court struck down a North Carolina law that prohibited the sale of apples in boxes labeled with the state of origin. This regulation was seen as a transparent attempt to neutralize the market advantage that Washington apple producers had obtained from the nationally recognized quality of their produce. Even when the state itself is a market participant as a producer, distributor, or purchaser, it is subject to dormant commerce clause principles. As the Court noted in South-Central Timber Development v. Wunnicke (1984), regulation that imposes burdens beyond the state's own market unduly interferes with interstate commerce and is unconstitutional. Cases of this nature evidence the Court's persistent vigilance and readiness to intercede if it senses that a state is reverting to the self-interested economic ways that preceded and necessitated the Constitution.

Bibliography

Richard B. Collins, "Economic Union as a Constitutional Value," 63 *New York University Law Review* 43 (1988). Explores the imperatives of a national economic union.

Daniel A. Farber, "State Regulation and the Dormant Commerce Clause," 3 *Constitutional Commentary* 395 (1986). Examines the tension between state regulatory interests and the dormant commerce clause.

Paul J. Hartman, *State Taxation of Interstate Commerce* (1953). A general review of issues concerning state tariffs and taxes on interstate commerce.

John E. Nowak and Ronald D. Rotunda, *Constitutional Law*, 5th ed. (1995). Includes an overview of the dormant commerce clause.

Martin H. Redish, *The Constitution as Political Structure* (1995). Discusses the role of the dormant commerce clause in the nation's scheme of governance.

6

Federal Preemption of State Law

Although Federal law emanates from a government of limited powers, it is supreme in its field of authority. Conflicts between federal and state laws thus are resolved in favor of the national government when Congress acts within the scope of its authority. This ordering of federal and state powers is dictated by the supremacy clause, which provides that laws made "under the Authority of the United States, shall be the supreme Law of the Land." Because federal law often does not indicate expressly whether it intends to preempt state regulation, the Supreme Court has developed standards for discerning and resolving any conflict. In *Pacific Gas & Electric Co. v. State Energy Resources Conservation and Development Commission* (1983), the Court considered whether federal regulation of the nuclear power industry was so pervasive that it allowed no room for state governance of it.

Pacific Gas and Electric Co. v. State Energy Resources Conservation and Development Commission

The commerce clause of the Constitution prohibits states from regulating in ways that unduly burden or discriminate against interstate commerce. This restriction applies, as noted in preceding discussions of dormant commerce clause cases, even if Congress has not exercised its commerce power by passing a law. When a state regulates in a field where Congress has passed a law, whether under the commerce clause or under some other enumerated federal power, a different set of principles determines whether the laws can coexist or whether one must give way. Such cases implicate the supremacy clause of the Constitution. This provision, set forth in Article VI, Section 2, establishes federal law as "the supreme Law of the Land" and necessitates the invalidation of conflicting state regulation. The key to what commonly is referred to as "preemption doctrine" is identifying whether in fact a conflict exists between federal and state laws. Because Congress does not always indicate explicitly an intent to preempt, the judiciary has developed criteria for determining when such a purpose may be inferred.

Citation:	461 U.S. 190.
Issue:	Whether a state moratorium on nuclear power plant certification was preempted by federal regulation of atomic energy.
Year of Decision:	1983.
Outcome:	Federal law did not deprive states of their traditional interest in regulating the economics of nuclear power.
Author of Opinion:	Justice Byron White.
Vote:	9–0.

Even though federal and state laws may regulate the same subject, they may complement rather than conflict with each other. Consistent with a preference for accommodation rather than preemption, judicial review of supremacy questions begins with a presumption in favor of a state law's validity. This desire to harmonize federal and state interests was reflected in the review of a California law that established a moratorium on the certification of nuclear power plants. The regulation reflected the state's concern that technology for disposal of radioactive waste was inadequate. Pending a demonstrably effective method for such disposal, the state wanted to safeguard against future risks. Specifically, it was concerned that inadequate disposal methods might require the shutdown of nuclear power plants. If that happened, consumers would be confronted with high costs of accessing alternative sources or bringing them on-line. The state's rationale thus reflected primarily an economic rather than a safety concern, a distinction that proved critical in the Court's resolution of the controversy.

The argument for preemption referred primarily to Congress's passage of the Atomic Energy Act of 1954. By that law, Congress vested the Atomic Energy Commission (now the Nuclear Regulatory Commission) with power over radiological safety matters relating to the construction and operation of nuclear power plants. Under the federal legislative scheme, the Nuclear Regulatory Commission had responsibility for licensing nuclear generating stations and for radioactive waste disposal. As the Court saw it, the state moratorium did not conflict with federal authority. Writing for the majority, Justice Byron White distinguished between federal concern with the safety of nuclear power plants and the state's interest in their economic viability. Noting that the Atomic Energy Act did not strip from states their power to regulate electric utilities with respect to need, cost, and reliability, the Court reasoned that the federal government could not compel approval or development of a nuclear power plant if the state thought it economically unwise to do so. Because federal and state law did not impose competing demands, the Court found no conflict and thus no basis for preemption. Had the state law been based upon safety concerns, it would have been at odds with federal regulation and subject to preemption.

In a concurring opinion, Justice Harry Blackmun maintained that the moratorium should have been upheld even if it was driven by safety concerns. He believed that the Atomic Energy Act was aimed at promoting nuclear power and diversifying resources for generating electricity. No reason existed, from this perspective, to deny states a concurrent interest in regulating the safety of nuclear power plants. Blackmun's argument that the state's motive should be irrelevant is not without significant logic. Inquiry into legislative motive often can be a futile exercise. In the realm of lawmaking, brokering and compromise are at the core of the process. Typically, laws are passed not just for one reason but for a variety of reasons ranging from ideology to payment of a political debt, a combination of motives, and even indifference. Federal law establishing the Food Stamp program is a classic example of legislation driven by multiple motives rather than one purpose. Its supporters included legislators from farm states, where agricultural interests benefit, and other representatives concerned primarily with indigency. The majority opinion in *Pacific Gas and Electric Co.* makes clear that a state law will survive preemption analysis if it states a purpose separate and apart from the federal interest. Lawmakers in other states who might oppose nuclear power development for safety reasons, therefore, could be assured that a moratorium would be upheld provided they articulated an economic rationale in support of it. The Court's analysis thus might be criticized for encouraging lawmakers to achieve their aims by disguising or being less than candid about their true motives.

The majority opinion nonetheless illustrates the primary principles governing preemption review. As noted previously, analysis begins with a presumption in favor of a state law's validity. If there is no specific language in federal law stating an intent to preempt state law, a court then looks for indications from which it may infer such a purpose. Three basic standards then come into play. If any one of them is satisfied, preemption follows. The first possibility is that preemptive intent may be discerned because a "scheme of federal regulation [is] so pervasive as to make reasonable the inference that Congress left no room to supplement it." The state moratorium on nuclear power plants did not satisfy this standard because, as both the majority and Justice Blackmun observed, responsibility over electric power generation was divided between federal and state governments. Preemption also is appropriate when "the federal interest is so dominant that the federal system will be assumed to preclude enforcement of state laws on the same subject." Again because the states maintain significant authority over and interest in the generation of electricity, the federal interest in the field is not preclusive. A final basis for preemption arises when a state law imposes regulatory demands that conflict with federal law. Because the Atomic Energy Act did not mandate nuclear power usage but focused upon safety concerns, state regulation that was concerned with economics of the industry did not create any demands that competed against the federal interest.

Critics may contend, as Justice Blackmun did, that the decision creates a barrier to state regulation that is more artificial than real. This argument reflects concern, as previously discussed, that a focus upon legislative motive may be futile because a singular purpose typically does not exist or lawmakers may cover their tracks in pursuing a particular agenda or aim. The decision, however, also may be viewed as friendly to the imperatives of federalism, which favor accommodating the differing policies and priorities of the several states. Particularly because the federal government was conceived as a government of limited power, analysis that avoids rather than identifies conflict would appear to be faithful to some of the union's most basic founding premises.

Bibliography

S. Candice Hoke, "Preemption Pathologies and Civic Republican Virtues," 71 *Boston University Law Review* 685 (1991). Explores the nature and complexity of preemption doctrine.

John E. Nowak and Ronald D. Rotunda, *Constitutional Law*, 5th ed. (1995). Provides a general overview of preemption.

Ronald D. Rotunda, "The Doctrine of the Inner Political Check, the Dormant Commerce Clause, and Federal Preemption," 53 *Transportation Practitioners Journal* 263 (1986). Examines the relationship between federal preemption doctrine and the dormant commerce clause.

7

Privileges and Immunities

Like the commerce power, the privileges and immunities clause of Article IV, Section 2, of the Constitution emerged in response to protectionist state practices that diminished the viability of an economic and political union. Resources and opportunities are distributed unevenly throughout the union. Minerals, fisheries, and public-sector employment, for instance, vary in availability from place to place. History has demonstrated the difficulty states have had resisting the temptation to give their own citizens favored treatment in resource use and opportunity exploitation. The privileges and immunities clause, as indicated in *Baldwin v. Fish and Game Commission of Montana* (1978), is a barrier against such self-interested policy that undermines the imperatives of a national union.

Baldwin v. Fish and Game Commission of Montana

Dormant commerce clause principles and preemption doctrine as discussed in preceding cases respond to common federal-state conflicts that require constitutional resolution. For instances in which states enact laws that affect interstate commerce, the Supreme Court has developed rules and standards to determine whether federal or state interests should prevail. Not all restrictions upon the exercise of state power involve the interaction of federal and state authority. Just as the federal branches of government are subject to constitutional restrictions on their power in relationship to each other, states also are limited in their ability to affect the interests of other states.

The commerce power in the Constitution ensures that states do not pursue self-interested economic policies at the expense of national economic interests. A state's policies, however, also may negatively impact other states' interests. When this happens, the privileges and immunities clause, set forth in Article IV, Section 2 [1], of the Constitution, may be implicated. This clause provides that "[t]he Citizens of each State shall be entitled to all Privileges and Immunities of Citizens in the several States." Put simply, the privileges and immunities clause establishes a rule that states generally must not discriminate against citizens of other states merely because of their citizenship. Like other constitutional guarantees, this clause is not absolute. Consequently, states can treat nonresidents differently under certain circumstances. Interpretation of the privileges and immunities clause thus has presented two primary challenges. The first is identifying interests that are protected under the clause. The second is determining the extent to which states may discriminate among persons on the basis of state citizenship.

The Constitution actually contains two privileges and immunities clauses. The Fourteenth Amendment secures the privileges and immunities of fed-

Citation:	436 U.S. 371.
Issue:	Whether a state law that established different licensing fees for in-state and out-of-state hunters violated the privileges and immunities clause.
Year of Decision:	1978.
Outcome:	Fees that distinguished between hunters on the basis of residency did not violate the privileges and immunities clause.
Author of Opinion:	Justice Harry Blackmun.
Vote:	6–3.

eral citizenship against state interference. These interests, delineated in the
Slaughter-House Cases (1873), include

> the right of the citizen . . . to come to the seat of government to assert
> any claim he may have upon that government, to transact any busi-
> ness he may have with it, to seek its protection, to share its offices,
> to engage in administering its functions, . . . [to] free access to [the
> nation's] seaports, . . . to the subtreasuries, land offices, and courts of
> justices of the several States, . . . to demand the care and protection
> of the Federal government over his life, liberty, and property when
> on the high seas or within the jurisdiction of a foreign government,
> . . . [t]he right to peaceably assemble and petition for redress of griev-
> ances, the privilege of the writ of *habeas corpus*, . . . [t]he right to use
> the navigable waters of the United States, . . . [and] all rights secured
> to our citizens by treaties with foreign nations.

Unlike its Fourteenth Amendment counterpart, the original privileges and
immunities clause focused upon interstate relations, particularly disparities
in state policy affecting citizens of a state and those of other states. An
early characterization of the privileges and immunities clause was provided
by Justice Bushrod Washington in Corfield v. Coryell (1823). Although
Washington's opinion was authored for a circuit court, it has been described by the Supreme Court as "the first, and long the leading, explication
of the Clause." In contrast with the rather narrow and pedestrian privileges
and immunities of federal citizenship set forth by the *Slaughter-House*
Court, Justice Washington described the privileges and immunities of state
citizenship in sweeping terms. As he put it, they included

> those privileges and immunities which are *fundamental*; which belong
> of right to the citizens of all free governments, and which have at all
> times been enjoyed by the citizens of the several States which compose
> this Union. . . . What these fundamental principles are, it would be
> more tedious than difficult to enumerate. They may all, however, be
> comprehended under the following general heads: protection by the
> government, with the right to acquire and possess property of every
> kind, and to pursue and obtain happiness and safety, . . . the right of
> a citizen to pass through, or to reside in any other state, for purposes
> of trade, agriculture, professional pursuits, or otherwise; to claim the
> benefit of the writ of habeas corpus; to institute and maintain actions
> of any kind in the courts of the state; to take, hold and dispose of
> property, either real or personal; and an exemption from higher taxes
> than are paid by other citizens of the state; [and] the elective franchise,
> as regulated and established by the law or constitution of the state in
> which it is to be exercised.

The privileges and immunities clause was the basis in the *Baldwin* case for challenging a Montana hunting-license system that imposed higher fees upon out-of-state residents. Lester Baldwin was a Montana resident who organized elk hunting trips for out-of-state customers. He challenged the fee structure, which enabled Montana residents to hunt elk for $9 a year but required out-of-state hunters to pay $225 for the same privilege. Because elk management is expensive, and demand for licenses by nonresidents was increasing dramatically, the state justified the differential as a means for distributing fairly the cost of effective game management.

In rejecting the claims of out-of-state hunters that the fee disparity violated the privileges and immunities clause, the Court, in an opinion authored by Justice Harry Blackmun, reaffirmed its understanding that the provision does not preclude all burdens or distinctions on the basis of state citizenship or residency. A ready example of a privilege that may be provided to state citizens only is the right to vote. As the Court noted, "No one would suggest that the Privileges and Immunities Clause requires a state to open its polls to a 'nonresident.' " Permissible distinctions between residents and non-residents "reflect the fact that this is a Nation composed of individual states." From the Court's perspective, the privileges and immunities clause concerned itself only with those "distinctions" that "hinder the formation, the purpose or the development of a single Union of [all] States." In assessing the Montana licensing scheme, the Court operated on the premise that "[o]nly with respect to those 'privileges' and 'immunities' bearing upon the vitality of the Nation as a single entity must the State treat all citizens, resident and non-resident, equally."

As the Court saw its analytical task, the critical factor in support of the state's regulatory scheme was whether it burdened a basic right. Because elk hunting was a recreational pursuit, engaged in by a wealthy few, the interest did "not fall within the purview of the Privileges and Immunities Clause." The Court noted that a different result might have followed if the fee differential deprived a nonresident of the means for a livelihood. Because out-of-state elk hunters were in pursuit of pleasure rather than plying a trade, the interest did not rise to a sufficient level of importance. Rather, the Court found that the pastime was "not basic to the maintenance of the well-being of the Union."

In a dissenting opinion joined by Justices Byron White and Thurgood Marshall, Justice William Brennan objected to the Court's inquiry into whether the interest in elk hunting was "fundamental." Brennan maintained that the magnitude of the interest was irrelevant to an inquiry that should focus merely upon the state's rationale for its discrimination. Distinctions on the basis of citizenship, he contended, should be permissible when a particular problem is attributable to nonresidents and the state's regulatory response "bears a substantial relation to the problems they present." Because out-of-state hunters constituted only 12 percent of Montana's hunting population, Brennan argued that their presence created no special danger to wildlife or the state's management program. Because the fee disparities exceeded the problems generated by out-of-state hunters, Brennan also contended that no "substantial relationship" existed between the problem and the discrimination.

The privileges and immunities clause limits distinctions that a state may make between its citizens and those of other states. It does not, as the *Baldwin* case demonstrates, prohibit them altogether. Students who attend a public university or college are familiar with different tuition rates for in-state and out-of-state students. Such a differential was challenged in Vlandis v. Kline (1973). The Court upheld the state's interest in a preferred tuition rate for in-state students. It viewed a residence requirement as a permissible means of ensuring that persons coming solely for an education could not take advantage of the lower rate. Such conditioning of benefits upon residence in a state for a certain length of time have been upheld when they are reasonable with respect to duration. When such requirements are found excessive or otherwise unreasonable, as in the case of *Shapiro v. Thompson* (1969), they have been held to violate the right to travel and migrate freely across state lines.

Bibliography

John E. Nowak and Ronald D. Rotunda, *Constitutional Law*, 5th ed. (1995); Laurence H. Tribe, *American Constitutional Law* (1988). These works include general discussions of the history and operation of the privileges and immunities clause.

William M. Wiecek, *The Sources of Antislavery Constitutionalism in America, 1760–1848* (1977). Discusses attempts to use the privileges and immunities clause to challenge slavery prior to the Civil War.

III

Equality Concepts

The American Revolution was inspired by a set of beliefs, set forth in the Declaration of Independence, that included the conviction that "all men are created equal." The United States Constitution as originally framed and ratified, however, made no reference to equality. On the contrary, the Republic's founders included provisions in the Constitution that reduced an entire race to slave status in many states. Even though some of the Constitution's framers objected to slavery, it was viewed as a necessary cost of forming a viable political union. Even slavery's most vocal detractors believed that without concessions to the Georgia and South Carolina delegates on this issue, the Constitutional Convention would be unsuccessful. Slavery's critics consoled themselves with the belief that, over the course of time, the institution either would wither away or that the political process eventually would resolve the controversy.

By the middle of the nineteenth century, however, positions for and against slavery had hardened to the point that compromise and resolution were beyond the political system's reach. Slavery ultimately was undone by the Civil War and the Thirteenth Amendment, which provides that "[n]either slavery nor involuntary servitude . . . shall exist within the United States." Reconstruction of the nation following the Civil War focused primarily upon the legacy of slavery. Central to the aim of forming a more perfect union was the Fourteenth Amendment, which, among other things, provided that no state could "deny to any person in its jurisdiction the equal protection of the laws."

Provision for equality under the law was a significant constitutional way station, but it did not preclude the emergence or perpetuation of official systems of discrimination. From the late nineteenth century through the middle of the twentieth century, the "separate but equal" doctrine compounded racial disadvantage. The separate but equal doctrine was the basis for a racial caste system that segregated persons on the basis of race and reinforced the ideology of white supremacy. Over the course of its operation, the separate but equal doctrine was the basis for laws that pervasively segregated persons by race and disadvantaged nonwhites. Racial segregation ultimately gave way to the understanding that separate was "inherently unequal." Not until nearly a century had elapsed since the Fourteenth Amendment's ratification in 1868, however, did the equal protection guarantee emerge.

Part III examines the evolution of constitutional equality principles, principally those concerning the issue of racial discrimination. Racial inequality is viewed through the prism of cases concerning slavery, Reconstruction, the separate but equal doctrine, desegregation, and affirmative action. The extension of equal protection on the basis of gender is also documented.

8

Economic Regulation

The government discriminates when in response to a problem or need it distributes burdens or benefits to some but not other individuals. The legality of such distinctions depends upon the meaning of "equal protection of the laws." As originally interpreted, the equal protection clause applied only to discrimination on the basis of race. For nearly a century, the equal protection guarantee offered no serious resistance to official racial segregation and oppression. Eventually, it was defined in terms that regarded racial classifications as "suspect" or presumptively invalid. When racial classifications are not at issue, or discrimination is not on the basis of some similarly objectionable basis relating to group status, the equal protection guarantee generally is inapplicable. Without the ability to differentiate among certain classes of persons, the government would be unable to set different tax rates for the wealthy and poor or distribute benefits to the needy. The equal protection guarantee's virtual irrelevance to the multitude of governmental programs and policies that affect some persons but not others is demonstrated in *Railway Express Agency v. People of State of New York* (1949).

Railway Express Agency v. People of State of New York

When government regulates, it frequently creates classifications of people that result in relatively favored or disadvantaged treatment of them. Income-tax codes and welfare-benefits programs, for instance, are examples of laws that affect different persons in different ways. Like many other regulations that classify on some basis, these laws have not been jeopardized by the equal protection clause. *Railway Express Agency v. New York*

dealt with a New York City law that prohibited the display of advertisements on vehicles using city streets unless they were "engaged in the usual business or regular work of the owner and not used merely or mainly for advertising." In other words, this law prohibited advertising on another person's or business's vehicle. The discrimination against advertising for hire was challenged by the Railway Express Agency, which operated a large fleet of trucks and sold space on the sides of its vehicles for advertising. The city maintained that vehicular advertising distracted other motorists and pedestrians and was a safety hazard. The New

Citation:	336 U.S. 106.
Issue:	Whether a municipal law that prohibited advertisements on motor vehicles except for those used in the owner's business violates the equal protection clause.
Year of Decision:	1949.
Outcome:	Government may differentiate between advertising on an owned or hired vehicle without violating the equal protection clause.
Author of Opinion:	Justice William O. Douglas.
Vote:	9–0.

York trial court agreed and found that the company had violated the ordinance. The New York Court of Appeals affirmed the judgment.

Although the Supreme Court noted "[t]he question of equal protection of the law is pressed most strenuously on us," it found no constitutional violation. The essence of the company's argument was that the discrimination was "not justified by the aim and purpose of the regulation." As the company noted, advertisements on motor vehicles might be a safety hazard, but the risk was unaffected by whose trucks carried them. "[T]he advertisement of a commercial house would not cause any greater distraction of pedestrians and vehicle drivers than if the commercial house carried the same advertisement on its own truck." Because the ordinance allowed one motor-vehicle owner to do what the other could not, the company maintained that the safety problem was not effectively addressed, and that it was the victim of unconstitutional discrimination.

The Court regarded the company's argument as "a superficial way of analyzing the problem." It also questioned its own ability to determine whether a particular type of advertiser presented an increased risk to traffic safety. As Justice William O. Douglas put it for the majority, the Court lacked the omniscience to determine "that those who advertised their own wares on their trucks do not present the same traffic problem" as those who offer space to others. The Court thus was unable to conclude that the classification was impermissible. Although a wholesale ban on advertisements on vehicles might address safety concerns more effectively, the Court considered the city free to remedy the problem in a piecemeal fashion. It thus concluded that "[i]t is no requirement of equal protection that all evils of the same genus be eradicated or none at all." The majority decision illustrates the point that not all discrimination violates the equal protection clause. Distinctions among persons for purpose of benefits or burdens are a common aspect of tax, welfare, and other regulatory schemes. The fact that wealthy individuals are subject to a higher tax rate than poor persons represents discrimination, but this is not unconstitutional. The equal protection clause does not prohibit all discrimination. If it did, many legitimate laws would not survive. The guarantee's prohibition thus extends to laws that classify persons in some objectionable way, most typically on the basis of race, gender, alienage, or illegitimacy.

Although Justice Robert Jackson concurred in the judgment, he urged a stricter standard of judicial review. Jackson emphasized that "equality is not merely abstract justice." Rather, the Fourteenth Amendment's framers understood "that there is no more effective practical guarantee against arbitrary and unreasonable government than to require that the principles of law which officials would impose upon a minority must be imposed generally." From his perspective, the distinction between carrying on a business for hire and for oneself would support regulation to the extent these "classes present different problems." Because the city discriminated between "two classes presenting identical dangers," Jackson believed that the regulation did not serve its purpose. Although he disagreed with the Court's reasoning, he thus was willing to support its judgment on grounds that cities must have broad discretion to protect citizens in their use of highways and public places.

The *Railway Express Agency* ruling demonstrates that the equal protection clause in most instances does not threaten legislation even when it classifies or discriminates. Case law over the past half century has established that stricter scrutiny is appropriate when official classifications are made on the basis of race or gender and, in some instances, on the basis of alienage or illegitimacy. Equal protection review also may be more rig-

orous when a group is singled out and denied a fundame
restriction on truck advertising had been raised a quarter c
it likely would have been struck down on grounds that it s
freedom of speech to some persons and companies. In *Virg*
of Pharmacy v. Virginia Citizens Consumer Council, Inc. (1
ruled that advertising was protected under the First Amenc
eral economic regulation, as the Court reaffirmed in *Wil*
Optical of Oklahoma (1955), "reform may take one step
dressing itself to the phases of the problem which seem mo:
legislative mind." Under this understanding, the equal protect
functions as a limited rather than a general charter of equal
law.

Bibliography

Michael Klarman, "An Interpretive History of Modern Equal Protection,"
igan Law Review 213 (1991). Raises questions regarding the Supreme
Court's deference toward legislative judgment when economic classifications
are made, as in the *Railway Express Agency* case.

Robert F. Nagel, *Constitutional Cultures* (1989). Argues the case for judicial deference toward legislative judgment, so that democratic processes are not impeded by equal protection principles.

Joseph Tussman and Jacobus tenBroek, "The Equal Protection of the Laws," 37
California Law Review 341 (1949). A classic inquiry into and exposition of
the nature of the equal protection guarantee.

9

Racial Issues

Race generally and slavery in particular were the Constitutional Convention's most divisive issues. The effort to resolve the conflict between North and South by allowing each state to decide the slavery question for itself set in motion forces that have struggled since to reckon with the framers' "unfinished business." Following decades of compromise that led eventually to political paralysis on the issue, slavery was upheld in *Dred Scott v. Sandford* (1857). Reconstruction after the Civil War eliminated slavery, established the citizenship of African Americans, and secured basic civil rights and the equality of all persons under the law. The Constitution's newfound intolerance of laws that implied racial inferiority was stressed in *Strauder v. West Virginia* (1880). Four years later in the *Civil Rights Cases* (1883), Congress's power to pass civil rights legislation was greatly eroded. Government's power to segregate on the basis of race was established in *Plessy v. Ferguson* (1896). The separate but equal era persisted for more than half a century. In *Korematsu v. United States* (1944), the Supreme Court enunciated equal protection standards that would be crucial to its determination in *Brown v. Board of Education* (1954) that racial segregation was "inherently unequal."

The demand that racially separate schools desegregate generated widespread resistance, evasion, and delay. In *Cooper v. Aaron* (1958), the Court responded to this intransigence by reaffirming its power "to say what the law is." A decade later, tired of foot dragging and delay, the Court in *Green v. County School Board of New Kent County, Virginia,* insisted on desegregation programs that promised to work "now." The power of federal courts to use a broad range of remedies to achieve desegregation, including busing, was delineated in *Swann v. Charlotte-Mecklenburg Board of Ed-*

ucation (1971). Desegregation peaked during the early 197
Court began to establish limits on its reach. If racially identi
resulted from causes other than legal requirements, the condit
tified as de facto segregation. This distinction was announce
School District No. 1, Denver, Colorado (1973). A year late
determined in *Milliken v. Bradley* (1974) that interdistrict bus
permissible unless segregation in one district was intentionall
the actions of another district. This ruling meant that many pre
black cities effectively would desegregate without achieving int

The *Brown* era accomplished the elimination of formal segr
only in schools but in a wide variety of public settings. Its le
general impermissibility of any law imposing burdens or distin
the basis of race. This achievement is evidenced effectively by
determination in *Loving v. Virginia* (1967) that prohibition of
marriage is unconstitutional. Because modern discrimination t
subtle rather than overt, constitutional standards have made it
minorities to prevail on equal protection claims. This reality is attributable
to the Court's decision in *Washington v. Davis* (1976) that an equal protection violation may be established only upon proof of intent to discriminate. Proof of discriminatory purpose is readily established when a law
provides favored treatment to a particular racial group. Such preferential
methods were the subject of *Regents of the University of California v.
Bakke* (1978) and *Richmond v. J. A. Croson Co.* (1989).

Dred Scott v. Sandford

The Constitution as originally framed and ratified included several provisions that accommodated slavery. Without concessions to proslavery delegates from Georgia and South Carolina, in particular, the union as conceived in 1787 might have been stillborn. Sectional friction over slavery dwarfed even the debate between large and small states over formulas for political representation. As James Madison observed, the primary schism at the Constitutional Convention arose "principally from the effects ... of having or not having slaves. These two causes concur in forming the great division of interests in the U. States. It did not lie between the large [and] small states; it lay, between the Northern [and] Southern."[1]

The Republic's founding was achieved by compromise on the slavery issue. The Constitution prohibited Congress from abolishing trade in the international slave market until 1808, contained a fugitive-slave clause, and counted a slave as three-fifths of a person for taxation and representation purposes. Compromise was facilitated by the misplaced sense of some northern delegates that slavery was a dying institution and that slavery issues that survived the Constitutional Convention could be dealt with through the political process.

Citation:	60 U.S. 393.
Issue:	Whether a slave could be a citizen of the United States and whether Congress had the power to prohibit slavery in federal territories.
Year of Decision:	1857.
Outcome:	No person of African descent could be a citizen, and Congress was denied the power to regulate slavery in federal territories.
Author of Opinion:	Chief Justice Roger Taney.
Vote:	7–2.

Contrary to these initial expectations, the problem of slavery became more vexing with the passage of time. As the nation's territory rapidly expanded westward, and slavery proved to be a flourishing rather than a dying institution, the political process confronted an increasingly daunting challenge in accommodating proslavery and antislavery systems. The Missouri Compromise in 1820 represented an effort to resolve the slavery controversy by allowing each new territory and state to decide the question for itself. Sectional differences, however, intensified rather than diminished. The abolitionist movement gained steam during the 1830s. Federal law that enabled slaveowners to recapture runaway slaves in the North without a hearing or proof of ownership heightened awareness that slavery was a national issue. With each new territory and state left to decide the issue for itself, political competition to shape the future intensified.

The Compromise of 1850 strengthened the fugitive-slave laws, admitted California to the union as a free state, and allowed slavery in the Utah and New Mexico territories. Although this compromise was touted as the long-awaited solution to the slavery controversy, subsequent developments indicated that the slavery issue had spiraled beyond the reach of the political process. Political turmoil in Kansas and Nebraska escalated into violence between proslavery and antislavery factions. Northern sentiment hardened against the westward expansion of slavery, political parties defined themselves by their positions for or against slavery's territorial extension, and political arguments evolved into competing constitutional theories. With these forces in motion, the slavery issue increasingly strained the capacity of the elected branches of government to deal with it effectively.

Because the political process had been unable to achieve an effective resolution of the slavery issue after seven decades of trying, the Supreme Court in 1857 attempted to complete the Constitutional Convention's "unfinished business." The Court's decision in *Dred Scott v. Sandford* was the culmination of litigation that had commenced in a Missouri state court in 1846. Having served as a slave to a military doctor in Illinois and the Minnesota territory, Dred Scott claimed that his travels to free soil had emancipated him from slavery. Scott alleged that his owner, John F. A. Sandford, had assaulted him, his wife, and his children by having them as slaves. Following numerous procedural twists and turns, the Supreme Court rendered a decision that President James Buchanan claimed would "finally settle" the slavery controversy. Specifically, the Court determined that no person of African descent could be a citizen of the United States. Technically, this determination meant that even "free" blacks could not be American citizens. The Court also concluded that Congress had no power to prohibit slavery in federal territory.

The Court might have resolved the case on the simple grounds that a slave was not a citizen and thus could not sue in federal court. Chief Justice Roger B. Taney, who authored the primary opinion of the Court, however, seized the opportunity to declare that the Constitution supported and protected slavery. Finding that persons of African descent had been excluded from citizenship and rights and regarded as "beings of an inferior order" when the Republic was founded, Taney reasoned that "they had no rights which the white man was bound to respect; and that the Negro might justly and lawfully be reduced to slavery for his own benefit." The conclusion that no person of African descent could be a citizen distorted history. Race was irrelevant to citizenship in several states at the time the Constitution was framed.

At the time of the *Dred Scott* decision, the key issue was the extent to which Congress had power to regulate slavery in federal territories. The

Republican Party, which burst onto the political scene in the 1850s, in large part was fueled by "free soil" sentiments that supported federal power to prohibit slavery in the territories. Taney acknowledged Congress's general power to "make all needful rules and regulations respecting the territory . . . belonging to the United States." However, he defined this authority narrowly. From his perspective, the Constitution conferred upon Congress general housekeeping power that did not enable it to regulate slavery in federal territory. Because the Missouri Compromise had prohibited slavery in the state and territory where he had resided, Dred Scott staked his claim to freedom on that law's validity. Having determined that Congress could only regulate territorial lands rather than conditions, Taney declared the Missouri Compromise unconstitutional.

Although this determination by itself was fatal to Dred Scott's case, Taney further fortified the constitutional security of slavery. He cited several provisions that, when the Constitution was framed, had achieved compromise on the slavery issue. From these terms, he constructed "a right to purchase and hold [slaves that] is directly sanctioned and authorized by the people who framed the Constitution." From Taney's perspective, a constitutional duty existed "to maintain and uphold the right of the master . . . , so long as the Government shall endure." He thus concluded that "the right of property in a slave is distinctly and expressly affirmed in the Constitution" and falls within the protection of the Fifth Amendment due process clause. By reconfiguring principles of compromise into fundamental rights, Taney twisted constitutional text beyond recognition and redefined a constitution that owed its existence to bypassing the question of slavery.

The decision, which was offered and anticipated as a final resolution of the slavery issue, proved to be a source of further division and tension between North and South. Because perceptions of African Americans as inferior were national rather than regional, northern criticism and outrage focused upon the curtailment of congressional power rather than the constitutional marginalization of an entire race. The immediate consequence of the ruling was that Dred Scott remained a slave, although he soon was emancipated by his owner. The broader impact of the decision soon was neutralized by the election of President Abraham Lincoln, who governed on the premise that he was not bound to accept or enforce the Court's ruling. Lincoln's announcement of the Emancipation Proclamation in 1863, which freed the slaves, typified his conviction that the nation was not bound by the decision.

The *Dred Scott* ruling has been described by constitutional scholar Derrick Bell, Jr., as "the most frequently overturned decision in history."[2] Eight years after the ruling, slavery was eliminated by the Thirteenth Amendment. The decision was further repudiated by the Fourteenth Amendment, which based state citizenship upon national citizenship and formally restored or conferred citizenship on persons of African descent. The legacy of *Dred*

Scott was further addressed a century later when, in *Brown v. Board of Education* (1954), the Court found the postslavery condition of official segregation "inherently unequal" and unconstitutional. Viewed from a historical perspective, the *Dred Scott* decision has been characterized by constitutional scholar Philip Kurland as a "derelict of constitutional law."[3] Despite its frequent repudiation, the ruling was a source of ideological inspiration for principles that maintained constitutional inequality long after it was overturned.

Notes

1. Max Farrand, *The Records of the Federal Convention of 1787* 486 (1937).
2. Derrick Bell, *Race, Racism, and American Law* 21 (1973).
3. Philip B. Kurland, *Politics, the Constitution, and the Warren Court* 186 (1970).

Bibliography

Derrick Bell, Jr., *And We Are Not Saved* (1987). A thought-provoking inquiry into the choices confronting the framers of the Constitution with respect to the slavery issue.

Don E. Fehrenbacher, *The Dred Scott Case* (1978). A comprehensive review of the *Dred Scott* case and assessment of its background and aftermath.

A. Leon Higginbotham, Jr., *In the Matter of Color* (1978). One of the most complete reviews of race and the law before and after the nation's founding.

Carl Swisher, *Roger B. Taney* (1935). The primary biography of Chief Justice Taney.

William M. Wiecek, *The Sources of Antislavery Constitutionalism in America, 1760–1848* (1977). A comprehensive examination of antislavery sentiment and influence prior to the Civil War.

Strauder v. West Virginia

The Supreme Court, in its first interpretation of the Fourteenth Amendment, doubted whether it ever would apply to any form of discrimination not based on race. In its own words, the Court found it unlikely that "any action of a State not directed by way of discrimination against the Negroes as a class, or on account of their race, will ever be held to come within the purview of this provision." This prediction, made in the *Slaughter-House Cases* (1873), has been disproved by twentieth-century decisions that have expanded the equal protection clause's scope to include discrimination on the basis of gender, alienage, and illegitimacy. Despite the *Slaughter-House* Court's prediction and the understanding that a particular racial group was the Fourteenth Amendment's primary beneficiary, early decisions generally blunted the clause's significance even for persons of African descent.

Judicial review that essentially marginalized the Fourteenth Amendment's impact was evident in the Court's early attitude toward civil rights claims. In Cruikshank v. United States (1876), the Court struck down a federal law that made interference with another person's civil rights a criminal offense. The Cruikshank case arose from the Colfax Massacre in 1873, a particularly violent outburst of racial conflict in Louisiana that resulted in large numbers of blacks being shot or burned to death. Despite this incident and the state of Louisiana's failure to control the hostilities, the Court characterized the matter as a state rather than a federal concern. Viewing the Fourteenth Amendment as rather inconsequential, the Court observed that it "adds nothing to the rights of one citizen as against another . . . [but] simply furnishes an additional guaranty against any encroachment by the States upon the fundamental rights which belong to every citizen as a member of society." This perspective was reaffirmed in United States v. Harris (1883), the Court struck down the Civil Rights Act of 1871. This law provided for federal prosecution of state law-enforcement officials charged with beating any person to death while in custody and thus conspiring to deny him or her equal protection of the

Citation:	100 U.S. 303.
Issue:	Whether a state law excluding persons of African descent from juries violated the Fourteenth Amendment.
Year of Decision:	1880.
Outcome:	The Fourteenth Amendment prohibits official exclusion of persons from juries on the basis of race.
Author of Opinion:	Justice William Strong.
Vote:	7–2.

laws. Consistent with its observations in Cruikshank, the Court observed that "[t]he duty of protecting all citizens in the enjoyment of an equality of rights was originally assumed by the States, and it remains there." These early understandings helped establish a foundation for forthcoming decades of racial segregation and terrorism that defined racial reality into the twentieth century. The rulings also refused to acknowledge Reconstruction's shift of responsibility for the protection of civil rights and equality interests from state to federal authorities.

Against this pattern of minimalist Fourteenth Amendment interpretation, the Court's ruling in *Strauder v. West Virginia* at least indicated the potential for more significant constitutional achievement. At issue was whether a West Virginia law excluding blacks from juries violated the Fourteenth Amendment. In assessing the racially exclusionary provision, the Court observed that the Fourteenth Amendment "cannot be understood without keeping in view the history of the times when [it] was adopted, and the general objects they plainly sought to establish." The amendment's primary purpose, from the Court's perspective, was to protect an exploited and disadvantaged race from further oppression. Elaborating on the background and need for the Fourteenth Amendment, the Court noted that those persons who had emerged from slavery confronted

> continuing jealousy and positive dislike, and . . . state laws [were] enacted or enforced to perpetuate the distinctions that had before existed. . . . The colored race . . . was abject and ignorant. . . . Their training had left them mere children, and as such they needed the protection which a wise government extends to those who are unable to protect themselves. They especially needed protection against unfriendly action in the States where they were resident. It was in view of these considerations that the Fourteenth Amendment was framed and adopted.

This passage reflected the most forthright characterization of the Fourteenth Amendment's meaning in the provision's early years and, as it turned out, for several decades. In accordance with understanding of the equal protection guarantee, the Court found that the racially exclusionary measure violated the principle "that all persons, whether colored or white, shall stand equal before the laws of the States."

The Court's ruling represented the first time that a racially exclusionary law was struck down on constitutional grounds. It also defined the Fourteenth Amendment in terms that were profoundly broader than those the Court had been willing to articulate previously. The equal protection guarantee emerged as a "right to exemption from unfriendly legislation" on the basis of racial status and as an "exemption from legal discriminations, implying inferiority in civil society, lessening the security of . . . enjoyment of the rights which others enjoy, and discriminations which are steps towards reducing them to the condition of a subject race."

In a related case, Ex parte Virginia (1880), the Court determined that the equal protection guarantee operated not only against laws excluding blacks from juries but against court rulings that achieved the same result. Taken together, the decisions demonstrated that the Fourteenth Amendment's teeth had been sharpened as potential cutting edges against official racial discrimination. Despite their rhetoric, the significance of these rulings remained dormant for several decades. Case law from the late nineteenth century through the mid-twentieth century upheld and facilitated systems of official segregation. These methods of racial management, driven by ideologies of racial superiority, emerged against the backdrop of the *Strauder* decision. Such developments, aimed at securing racial advantages, were unaffected by the *Strauder* Court's sense that racially exclusionary laws constituted "a brand upon [blacks], affixed by the law, an assertion of their inferiority, and a stimulant to that race prejudice which is an impediment to securing to individuals of the race that equal justice which the law aims to secure to all others." Not until 1954, when the Court in *Brown v. Board of Education* determined that official segregation was "inherently unequal," would a constitutional reawakening on this front take place. Despite the rhetorical promise associated with the determination that racially based exclusion of jurors was unconstitutional, many decades passed before the Court again became a source of encouraging words or deeds under the Fourteenth Amendment.

Bibliography

Charles Fairman, *History of the Supreme Court of the United States*, vol. 7, *Reconstruction and Reunion, 1864–88* (1971). Discusses early decisions under the Fourteenth Amendment.

Paul Finkelman, *An Imperfect Union* (1981). Studies reconstruction of the union.

Harold M. Hyman and William M. Wiecek, *Equal Justice under Law* (1982). Explores reconstructionist thinking as it related to civil equality.

Donald E. Lively, *The Constitution and Race* (1992). Examines the *Strauder* decision and rulings on related cases.

The Civil Rights Cases

The Thirteenth, Fourteenth, and Fifteenth Amendments commonly known as the Reconstruction Amendments, established new constitutional guarantees that responded to the nation's experience with slavery and civil war. They also curtailed state power over and responsibility for civil and political rights. The Thirteenth Amendment prohibited "slavery [and] involuntary servitude, except as a punishment for crime . . . within the United States." The Fourteenth Amendment, in addition to establishing the bases for national citizenship and the privileges and immunities incidental thereto, provided that no state shall "deprive any person of life, liberty, or property, without due process of law; nor deny to any person within its jurisdiction the equal protection of the laws." The Fifteenth Amendment ensures that "[t]he right of citizens of the United States to vote shall not be denied or abridged by the United States or by any State on account of race, color, or previous condition of servitude."

Citation:	109 U.S. 3.
Issue:	Whether Congress's power to enforce the Fourteenth Amendment reaches private as well as state action.
Year of Decision:	1883.
Outcome:	Congress in enforcing the Fourteenth Amendment only may prohibit state action.
Author of Opinion:	Justice Joseph Bradley.
Vote:	8–1.

Each of the Reconstruction Amendments establishes guarantees that provide grounds for constitutional challenge if they are violated by the states. Constitutional claims, however, are not the only means that these amendments provide against impermissible state action. The final section of each amendment confers upon Congress the "power to enforce" the respective guarantee. This enabling provision effectively transferred responsibility for the protection of civil rights from the state to the federal government. In part, this assignment of power to Congress may have reflected persisting doubt about the reliability of the judiciary in protecting those interests enumerated by the Reconstruction Amendments. A decade after the decision in *Dred Scott v. Sandford* (1857), the Supreme Court continued to be viewed disparagingly as "the citadel of Slaveocracy."[1] The enforcement provisions of the Reconstruction Amendments vested in "Congress the responsibility of seeing to it, for the future, that all the sections of the amendment are carried out in good faith, and that no State infringes the rights of person and property."[2]

Legislative activity under the Reconstruction Amendments was significant. Examples of congressional initiative included the Civil Rights Act of 1866, which identified and secured basic civil rights; the Enforcement Act of 1870, which criminalized private or public interference with the right to vote; and the Ku Klux Klan Act of 1871, which prohibited interference with civil rights under the color of state law or by private action. Passage of the Civil Rights Act of 1875, which prohibited racial discrimination in public accommodations, represented the legislative high point of Reconstruction. Under review were five cases concerning claims based upon exclusion from various public accommodations on grounds of race. Several years after the law's enactment, the Court considered a challenge to its constitutionality. Although the act was premised upon Congress's enforcement power under the Thirteenth and Fourteenth Amendments, it was contested on grounds that it overreached the scope of those provisions by prohibiting private as well as state action. At issue in the *Civil Rights Cases*, therefore, was the nature and extent of Congress's power to enforce these amendments that had redefined the union.

In reviewing Congress's authority to enforce the Thirteenth Amendment, the Court determined that the power to enforce the constitutional prohibition against slavery did not enable the federal government to pass civil rights laws. Although the Court acknowledged Congress's power to eradicate badges and incidents of slavery, it found that federal authority did not reach to racial discrimination in public accommodations. Accordingly, it observed that "[i]t would be running the slavery argument into the ground, to make it apply to every act of discrimination which a person may see fit to make."

With respect to the Fourteenth Amendment, the Court concluded that congressional enforcement power extended no further than action by the state. Because the Civil Rights Act of 1875 prohibited discriminatory private action, the Court determined that Congress had overstepped its bounds. As the Court put it, Congress's enforcement power did not confer authority "to create a code of municipal law for the regulation of private rights; but . . . provided modes of redress against the operation of state laws." It further emphasized that "[t]he wrongful act of an individual . . . is simply a private wrong . . . [that] cannot destroy or injure the right." The Court conceded that if "unjust discrimination" was the product of state action, Congress might have a basis for prohibiting it. The Court rejected any notion of state responsibility when a venue such as a theater, train, restaurant, or hotel was open to the public but privately owned. The Court also seemed convinced that the type of discrimination forbidden by the Civil Rights Act of 1875 was too inconsequential for serious constitutional attention. Because "thousands of free colored people" prior to Reconstruction were afforded civil rights conditioned by exclusion from public accommodations and other settings, the Court viewed the congressionally prohibited practices as "mere discriminations." Reflecting perhaps too a sense that Reconstruction goals had outlived their utility, the Court noted that

> [w]hen a man has emerged from slavery, and by the aid of beneficent legislation has shaken off the inseparable concomitants of that state, there must be some stage in the progress of his elevation when he takes the rank of a mere citizen, and ceases to be the special favorite of the laws, and when his rights, as a citizen or a man, are to be protected in the ordinary modes by which other men's rights are protected.

The tone of these observations indicated a mounting disinterest in using the Reconstruction Amendments as a barrier to state-imposed distinctions on the basis of race.

The Court's minimalization of the Thirteenth and Fourteenth Amendments and Congress's power to enforce them provoked a lengthy and sharp dissent by Justice John Harlan, Sr. From his perspective, slavery was rooted in principles of racial inferiority. It thus was appropriate for Congress to use its enforcement power under the Thirteenth Amendment to protect newly acquired civil rights or liberties from racially inspired deprivation. He also believed that the distinction between state and private action was inapt if the accommodations covered by the act were intended for public purposes. Harlan maintained that insofar as rights were impaired by racial discrimination, regardless of the source of the violation, the action "lay at the very foundation of the institution of slavery."

With particular respect to the Fourteenth Amendment's enforcement provision, Harlan identified a power "to enforce '*the provisions of this article*' of the Amendment—*all* of the provisions—affirmative and prohibitive." This charge, as Harlan saw it, conferred a broad enforcement mandate on Congress that extended beyond just the actions of state government. His core understanding of the Fourteenth Amendment was that it "necessarily imports at least equality of civil rights among citizens of every race in the same State. It is fundamental in American citizenship that, in respect of such rights, there shall be no discrimination by the State or its officers, or by individuals or corporations exercising public functions or authority, against any citizen because of his race or previous condition of servitude."

Several decades elapsed before the Court responded to Harlan's admonition that "there cannot be, in this republic, any class of human beings in practical subjection to another class, with power in the latter to dole out to the former just such privileges as they may choose to grant." The majority opinion disclosed an abiding commitment to antebellum principles and understandings that preceded framing and ratification of the Thirteenth and Fourteenth Amendments. It also previewed an emerging era of constitutional review that accommodated comprehensive schemes of racial management and discrimination. Evolution toward a societal structure based upon official segregation was facilitated by the Court's minimalist view of the Fourteenth Amendment. Such attitudes, which defined the amendment's meaning well into the twentieth century, provided an unfortunate response to the question Harlan posed in his dissent. The question he asked was whether the Reconstruction Amendments would prove to "be splendid baubles, thrown out to delude those who deserved fair and generous treatment at the hands of the Nation." As systems of official segregation soon became pervasive features of the societal landscape, it became clear that Harlan's question was more than merely rhetorical.

Notes

1. A. T. Mason, *The Supreme Court from Taft to Warren* 16 (1968).
2. *Congressional Globe*, 39th Congress, 1st session, 2766, 2768 (1866).

Bibliography

Robert Cover, *Justice Accused* (1975). A critical assessment of early interpretations of the Fourteenth Amendment.
Harold M. Hyman, *A More Perfect Union* (1973). Discusses the politics and impact of Reconstruction.
Robert J. Kaczorowski, *The Politics of Judicial Interpretation: The Federal Courts, Department of Justice, and Civil Rights, 1866–1876* (1985). Discusses the intended scope of the Thirteenth and Fourteenth Amendment.
Donald E. Lively, *Foreshadows of the Law* (1992). Examines the long-term significance of Justice Harlan's dissenting opinion in the *Civil Rights Cases*.

Plessy v. Ferguson

Official segregation on the basis of race was a defining feature of the South from the late nineteenth century through the middle of the twentieth century. During this period, Jim Crow laws separated persons on the basis of race and maintained white advantage in all quarters of society. To avoid conflict with the South, the federal government adopted segregation in the military and other settings. The actual role model for segregation derived from the laws of northern states that, before the Civil War, separated persons on the basis of race in education and other settings. Official segregation in the South commenced in 1887 when Florida passed a law that required racially separate transportation. Within a few years of its introduction, official segregation had spread throughout the South. Despite its northern roots, formal separation was well suited to the needs of those who still lamented the passage of slavery and were committed to maintaining their cultural advantage.

Citation:	163 U.S. 537.
Issue:	Whether a state law that required racially segregated seating on trains violated the Fourteenth Amendment.
Year of Decision:	1896.
Outcome:	Separate but equal seating accommodations did not violate the Fourteenth Amendment.
Author of Opinion:	Justice Henry Brown.
Vote:	8–1.

The rapid proliferation of laws that established comprehensive systems of racial segregation eventually triggered challenges to their constitutionality. The defining moment on this front occurred when a Louisiana law that required separate rail cars for whites and blacks was challenged on grounds that it violated the Thirteenth and Fourteenth Amendments. The law provided that railway companies "shall provide equal but separate accommodations for the white and colored races, by providing two or more passenger coaches for each passenger train, or by dividing the passenger coaches by a partition so as to secure separate accommodations." This law was challenged by Homer Plessy, who was described as a person of "seven eighths Caucasian and one eighth African blood, . . . [whose] mixture of colored blood was not discernible." In an effort to restrain the state from enforcing its law requiring racial segregation, Plessy sued Judge John H. Ferguson, who was assigned to preside at his criminal trial. Plessy's plea in this regard was denied, and he appealed to the United States Supreme Court.

In rejecting Plessy's challenge to the law's constitutionality, the Supreme Court demonstrated how minimally relevant the Thirteenth Amendment had become. The Court limited the amendment's role to prohibiting states of actual "bondage; the ownership of mankind as a chattel, or at least the control of the labor and services of one man for the benefit of another." The Thirteenth Amendment, as interpreted by the *Plessy* Court, thus extended only to slavery and its most immediate aftereffects.

Although the Court's discussion of the Fourteenth Amendment was more extensive, it was no less hostile to Plessy's constitutional claim. Acknowledging that the provision's purpose was "to enforce the absolute equality of the two races before the law," the Court nonetheless determined that the amendment did not "intend to abolish distinctions based upon color, or to enforce social, as distinguished from political equality, or a commingling of the two races upon terms unsatisfactory to either." In *Strauder v. West Virginia* (1880), the Court had determined that racial classifications that implied inferiority violated the Fourteenth Amendment. Official segregation, from the Court's perspective, however, did not imply inferiority. Rather, it reflected the reasonable exercise of a state's police power to promote the public good. In reply to those who might view segregation as stamping "the colored race with a badge of inferiority," the Court maintained that such a perception was not the fault of the law but of the interpretation that "the colored race chooses to put . . . on it." It thus concluded that segregation was a reasonable means of maintaining "the established usages, customs, and traditions of the people, . . . [for] the promotion of their comfort, and the preservation of the public peace and good order."

Having determined that official segregation did not violate the Constitution, the Court further observed that legislative policy or judicial review that favored racial commingling would be unwise and futile. It accordingly noted that "legislation is powerless to eradicate social instincts or to abolish distinctions based upon physical differences." Attempts to do so, as the Court saw it, would be counterproductive. Although civil and political equality may be constitutionally required, the Court stressed that the Constitution cannot elevate a racially inferior group to the level of what it viewed as a superior group.

The Court rejected arguments that official segregation was a source of official degradation, humiliation, and oppression. Its thinking was challenged by the circumstances of the time, which were characterized by widespread touting of white supremacy. As the constitutional scholar Leonard W. Levy has noted, official segregation was a cornerstone of white supremacy, and the notion that "blacks were inherently inferior was a conviction being stridently trumpeted by white supremacists from the press, the pulpit, and the platform, as well as from the legislative halls of the South." The true nature of official segregation, however, was sensed by Justice John Harlan, Sr., in a dissenting opinion. Harlan warned that the majority's decision eventually would prove to be "as pernicious as the decision made . . . in the *Dred Scott Case*." Piercing the pretense that separate could be equal, Harlan observed that "every one knows . . . its origin and the purpose was not so much to exclude white persons from railroad cars occupied by blacks, as to exclude colored people from coaches occupied or assigned to white persons."

Harlan, who had been a slaveowner before the Civil War, reasoned that "the destinies of the two races, in this country, are indissolubly linked together, and the interests of both require that the common government of all shall not permit the seeds of race hate to be planted under the sanction of law." Dissatisfied with the Court's rationale that segregation promoted public harmony and order, Harlan maintained that racial hatred and distrust were exacerbated by laws that assumed "that colored citizens are so inferior and degraded that they cannot be allowed to sit in public coaches occupied by white citizens." From his perspective, "the sure guarantee of the peace and security of each race is the clear, distinct and unconditional recognition . . . of every right that inheres in civil freedom, and of the equality before the law of all citizens . . . without regard to race." The bottom line for Harlan was that "there is in this country no superior, dominant, ruling class of citizens . . . [and] no caste." On the contrary, he noted, "our Constitution is color-blind."

The Court's determination that official segregation did not imply racial inferiority provided extensive breathing room for a system of racial separation. Despite formal insistence that separate conditions had to be equal, attention to the equality requirement was more pretense than reality. This fact of life was illustrated three years later in Cumming v. Board of Education (1899), in which the Court upheld a school board's decision to shut down a black high school and keep open a white high school. The school board's action, which was justified on grounds of limited economic resources, indicated that the real meaning of separate but equal was separate, period.

Constitutional review over the next half century consistently reaffirmed the separate but equal doctrine. Consistent with the *Plessy* decision, constitutional challenges to dominant racial attitudes were viewed as futile exercises. This sense of powerlessness was graphically illustrated when Alabama, in seeming violation of the Fifteenth Amendment, refused to register nonwhite voters. Despite the obvious conflict with an amendment that prohibits deprivation of the right to vote on the basis of race, the Court in Giles v. Harris (1903) concluded that it had "little practical power to deal with the people of the State in a body. The bill imports that the great mass of the white population intends to keep the blacks from voting." To overcome such racially inspired resistance, the Court concluded that its own orders would be inadequate. Rather, "relief from a great political wrong, if done, or alleged by the people of a state and the state itself, must be given them by the legislature and the political department of the United States." As the *Plessy* Court recognized, any chance of relief from a hostile political system was illusory.

At a time when the judiciary was developing the Fourteenth Amendment as a source of rights and liberties that blunted social and economic reforms, as discussed in part IV of this volume, the Court was particularly deferential toward legislative policy that managed race relations by means of official segregation. During the first few decades of the twentieth century, constitutional review consistently supported official separation on the basis of race. Although the Court eventually would rethink and defeat the separate but equal doctrine, constitutional law over the first half of the twentieth century largely reflected the ideology of white supremacy and secured its agenda.

Bibliography

Leonard W. Levy, "Plessy v. Ferguson," in Leonard W. Levy, Kenneth L. Karst, and Dennis J. Mahoney, eds., *Civil Rights and Equality* (1989). Focuses on the racist ideology of the *Plessy* decision.

Leon F. Litwack, *North of Slavery* (1961). Examines segregation and other racially restrictive policies in the North.

Gunnar Myrdal, *An American Dilemma* (1944). One of the most comprehensive studies of the separate but equal era.

Paul Oberst, "The Strange Career of Plessy v. Ferguson," 15 *Arizona Law Review* 389 (1973). Examines the *Plessy* case's background, arguments, and consequences.

C. Vann Woodward, *The Strange Career of Jim Crow* (1955). Studies the basis, nature, and impact of racial segregation.

Korematsu v. United States

When the Supreme Court first interpreted the equal protection clause, it announced that the clause was aimed exclusively at "discrimination against the Negroes as a class." This observation in the *Slaughter-House Cases* (1873) proved to be heavier on rhetoric than on reality. The emergence of official segregation as a deeply embedded and defining cultural phenomenon effectively demonstrated the equal protection guarantee's lack of vitality through the middle of the twentieth century. The equal protection clause during this period presented itself in terms that accommodated the ideology of racial superiority. As Justice John Harlan, Sr., put it in his dissenting opinion in *Plessy v. Ferguson* (1896), the net result was a "superior, dominant, ruling class of citizens" in the face of a Constitution that allowed "no caste."

Evolution toward equal protection principles that prohibited rather than permitted official racial discrimination was a slow process. During the first few decades of the twentieth century, challenges to

Citation:	323 U.S. 214.
Issue:	Whether the forced relocation of American citizens of Japanese descent from their homes to detention centers during wartime violated the Fifth Amendment.
Year of Decision:	1944.
Outcome:	The relocation and detention processes were reasonable measures in a national emergency and thus were not unconstitutional.
Author of Opinion:	Justice Hugo Black.
Vote:	6–3.

segregation routinely were dismissed. Indications of doctrinal change began to appear, however, as the Court in the late 1930s experienced extensive turnover in its personnel. The death or resignation of several justices within a few years brought new attitudes and the suggestion of heightened interest in developing a more rigorous equal protection doctrine. In *United States v. Carolene Products Co.* (1938), the Court dropped a strong hint of its growing interest in official discrimination on the basis of race. The *Carolene Products* ruling expressly noted the possibility of "searching judicial inquiry" for the purpose of determining "whether prejudice against discrete and insular minorities may be a special condition, which tends seriously to curtail the operation of those political processes ordinarily to be relied upon to protect minorities." Although the *Carolene Products* decision itself did not directly concern racial discrimination, it signaled the Court's developing interest in scrutinizing the constitutional legitimacy of laws that burdened historically marginalized and disadvantaged racial groups.

Several years later, the Court announced a new and invigorated theory of equal protection review. The triggering event for this change was a federal order to relocate American citizens of Japanese descent from the west coast to inland detention camps during World War II. The relocation decree was authorized by President Franklin D. Roosevelt and reflected concern that Japanese Americans presented a national security risk. The presumption was that persons of Japanese descent might engage in espionage or cooperate with a military invasion of the United States. The order, which did not apply to German Americans or Italian Americans (Germany and Italy were also at war with the United States), singled out Japanese Americans without regard to whether they individually had been or likely would be disloyal. It was challenged by Toyasaburo Korematsu who was convicted for refusing to leave his home in a community subject to the exclusionary order.

The Court rejected claims that the relocation order was unconstitutional. Although this result might seem to suggest otherwise, the Court's ruling represented a significant energizing of the equal protection clause. Writing for the majority, Justice Hugo Black established the basis for searching judicial inquiry into laws that classify on the basis of race. As Black put it for the Court, "[A]ll legal restrictions which curtail the civil rights of a single racial group are immediately suspect." By regarding racial classifications as suspect, the Court did not mean that they necessarily are unconstitutional. Courts, however, "must subject them to the most rigid scrutiny." If the law disadvantages a particular racial group, it must be justified on the basis of "[p]ressing public necessity" rather than "racial antagonism."

Despite its avowed readiness to scrutinize the relocation order closely, the Court determined that the measure was motivated by "real military dangers" rather than "racial prejudice." Deferring to the judgment of military authorities, the Court accepted that the relocation was justified by wartime urgencies. Because "the properly constituted military authorities feared an invasion of our West Coast and felt constrained to take proper security measures," the Court was unwilling to second-guess their judgment. Such a deferential posture typifies constitutional review when questions of national security are at stake. In this particular instance, however, critics argued that the relocation order swept far beyond the need for protecting the nation.

In his dissenting opinion, Justice Frank Murphy maintained that the military action passed beyond " 'the very brink of constitutional power' and falls into the ugly abyss of racism." In his opinion, the relocation and detention orders constituted "one of the most sweeping and complete deprivations of constitutional rights in the history of this nation." Although Murphy acknowledged the special need to respect military judgment during national emergencies, he argued that constitutional rights could not be compromised by unsubstantiated and unsupported claims of military necessity. From his perspective, the inquiry should have focused upon whether the deprivation of a right is reasonably related to an "immediate, imminent, and impending" public danger. Searching review would have demonstrated that the basis for the relocation and detention orders was "misinformation, half-truths and insinuations that for years have been directed against Japanese-Americans by people with racial and economic prejudice." Murphy thus objected forcefully to what he characterized as "this legalization of racism . . . [that] is utterly revolting among a free people who have embraced the principles set forth in the Constitution of the United States."

Justice Robert Jackson, dissenting in terms similar to Murphy's, viewed the Court's ruling as "a far more subtle blow to liberty than the promulgation of the order itself." Because the Court rationalized the order as constitutional, Jackson asserted that it had endorsed for "all time . . . the principle of racial discrimination in criminal procedure and of transplanting American citizens." Particularly disturbing to him was what he described as a "principle [which] then lies about like a loaded weapon ready for the hand of any authority that can bring forward a plausible claim of an urgent need." From Jackson's perspective, the Court had approved an egregious constitutional breach without fully appreciating that this "passing incident becomes the doctrine of the Constitution."

Postwar inquiry has indicated that Murphy's concern with the justification for relocation and detention was well founded. His belief that the orders were based "upon questionable racial and sociological grounds," rather than demonstrable military risk, has been affirmed by the findings of historians and the federal government. A congressional inquiry four decades after *Korematsu* determined that civilian authorities within the executive branch knew that there was no credible evidentiary basis for the internment of Japanese Americans. Rather, "race prejudice" and "war hysteria" fueled what investigators characterized as a "grave injustice." American citizens were deprived of their liberty and property without any individualized findings of risk to national security. Congress eventually enacted legislation that provided reparations for the victims of forced relocation.

Despite its unfortunate political legacy, the *Korematsu* decision distinguished itself by ushering in a new era of heightened attention to laws that imposed restrictions or burdens on a particular racial group. By characterizing laws classifying on the basis of race as "suspect," the Court established the basis for searching judicial review of racial segregation and discrimination. This standard of "strict judicial scrutiny" became the basis for constitutional review that consistently has invalidated laws that intentionally impose burdens on the basis of race. As the Court described the standard of review for laws that discriminate on the basis of race in Palmore v. Sidoti (1984), racial classifications must be "subject[ed] to the most exacting scrutiny; to pass constitutional muster, they must be justified by a compelling governmental interest and must be 'necessary . . . to the accomplishment' of their legitimate purpose." So consistently did the Court invalidate racially discriminatory laws in subsequent decades that equal protection review, as described by constitutional scholar Gerald Gunther, had become "strict in theory and fatal in fact."[1] By increasing the rigor of constitutional review, the Court created what became the essential analytical tool for dismantling official segregation.

Note

1. Gerald Gunther, "Evolving Doctrine on a Changing Court: A Model for a Newer Equal Protection" 96 *Harvard Law Review* 1, 8 (1972).

Bibliography

Allan R. Bosworth, *America's Concentration Camps* (1967). Examines the forces of prejudice, wartime hysteria, and national security interests.

Peter Irons, *Justice at War: The Story of the Japanese American Internment Cases* (1983). A detailed review of the *Korematsu* decision and related cases.

Personal Justice Denied: Report of the Commission on Wartime Relocation and Internment of Civilians (1982). Reports the findings of the congressional commission that inquired into the wartime internment of Japanese Americans.

Brown v. Board of Education

As originally justified in *Plessy v. Ferguson* (1896), official segregation was "in the nature of things" and an appropriate means of ensuring public comfort, tradition, and order. This apparently benign cast to the "separate but equal" doctrine ignored the reality that segregation was a cornerstone of a social system based on racial supremacy. The true nature of the separate but equal doctrine was illustrated better by reality than by rhetoric.

Spending on South Carolina public schools in 1915, for example, was ten times more for white students than for black students. By 1954, when southern states were increasing funding for black schools in an effort to ward off constitutional challenges to official segregation, public school spending was 40 percent more for white students than for black students.

In the late 1930s, the National Association for the Advancement of Colored People (NAACP) began what proved to be a long-term but eventually successful strategy for defeating official segregation in public schools.

Citation:	347 U.S. 483.
Issue:	Whether official segregation of schools on the basis of race violated the Fourteenth Amendment.
Year of Decision:	1954.
Outcome:	Public schools segregated on the basis of race are inherently unequal and thus unconstitutional.
Author of Opinion:	Chief Justice Earl Warren.
Vote:	9–0.

Under the leadership of Charles Houston and Thurgood Marshall, the NAACP initiated litigation designed to achieve full equalization of facilities, curricula, and faculty in black and white schools. The NAACP believed that the costs of absolute equalization in separate educational facilities, would be unbearable and sought to unveil the true nature of the separate but equal doctrine by showing this. Over the course of nearly two decades, the NAACP strategy was successful in obtaining court orders requiring states to build professional and graduate schools for blacks or integrate those that had been reserved for whites. Having achieved judicial support for equalization of separate facilities, the NAACP took aim at the separate but equal doctrine itself. In Sipuel v. Board of Regents (1948), Marshall thus argued that "segregation in public education helps to preserve a caste system which is based upon race and color. It is designed and intended to perpetuate the slave tradition. . . . 'Separate' and 'equal' can not be used conjunctively in a situation of this kind; there can be no separate equality."

As the separate but equal doctrine came under increasing attack, southern states attempted to shore it up by channeling increasingly large amounts of money into black schools. In Sweatt v. Painter (1950), the Supreme Court signaled that equalization of funding and facilities might be insufficient to meet constitutional requirements. Noting that the all-white University of Texas School of Law had advantages with respect to faculty reputation, alumni status and influence, institutional traditions, and prestige and professional opportunities for graduates, the Court ordered the institution to admit a black student. The order effectively required the school to integrate.

The chipping away of official segregation at the graduate and professional level did not necessarily mean that the separate but equal doctrine was at risk across the board. Under the leadership of Chief Justice Fred M. Vinson, the Court was reluctant to extend its mandate beyond an application to "specialized institutions" of higher education. The appointment of Earl Warren as chief justice brought a desire to reexamine the separate but equal doctrine in all contexts. Reflecting the issue's highly controversial nature and profound societal stakes, the Court spent four terms reviewing and deciding the challenge to official segregation in public schools. After hearing arguments in 1952, it invited rearguments in 1953, announced a decision in 1954, and provided for relief in 1955. The decision in *Brown v. Board of Education* addressed segregated public education in Delaware, Kansas, South Carolina, and Virginia. The *Brown* case itself arose in Topeka, Kansas, where, as in other segregated communities, students were assigned to schools on the basis of their race. One student's father, Oliver Brown, believed that his daughter should be allowed to attend the elementary school closest to the family's home. When school authorities refused to enroll her at the neighborhood school, he sued.

A key question for the Court was whether official segregation was consistent with the expectations of those who framed and ratified the Fourteenth Amendment. Because the amendment's framers in Congress simultaneously provided for segregation of District of Columbia schools, and many ratifying states maintained segregated schools or denied education to blacks altogether, history provided little support for desegregation. The Court, however, noted that public education was neither pervasive nor well developed at the time of the Fourteenth Amendment's framing and ratification. Because public education had become so crucial to economic opportunity and personal development since then, the Court concluded that the intent of the framers and ratifiers was not sufficiently clear.

Having determined that it could not "turn the clock back to 1868 when the Amendment was adopted, or even to 1896 when *Plessy v. Ferguson* was written," the Court shifted to an emphasis upon the importance of education. Describing education as "perhaps the most important function of state and local governments," the Court stressed its importance to "our democratic society." It observed that education is required in the performance of our most basic public responsibilities. . . . It is the very foundation of good citizenship. Today it is a principal instrument in awakening the child to cultural values, in preparing him for later professional training, and in helping him to adjust normally to his environment. In these days, it is doubtful that any child may reasonably be expected to succeed in life if he is denied the opportunity of an education.

Having abandoned its interest in determining what the Fourteenth Amendment's framers contemplated, the Court rested its decision upon the critical role education plays in determining personal opportunity and development.

The Court then turned to whether official segregation adversely affected educational quality. It referred to social science data that suggested that separation on the basis of race negatively affected the self-esteem of minority children. The validity of these psychological findings remains disputed. They nonetheless facilitated a conclusion that racial segregation of schoolchildren "generates a feeling of inferiority as to their status in the community that may affect their hearts and minds in a way unlikely ever to be undone." Borrowing from the opinion of the trial judge in Kansas, the Court observed that

> [s]egregation of white and colored children in public schools has a detrimental effect upon the colored children. The impact is greater when it has the sanction of the law; for the policy of separating the races is usually interpreted as denoting the inferiority of the negro group. A sense of inferiority affects the motivation of a child to learn. Segregation with the sanction of law, therefore, has a tendency to [retard] the educational and mental development of negro children and to deprive them of some of the benefits they would receive in a racial[ly] integrated school system.

Because of these findings, the Court abandoned the premise that official segregation did not cause harm or racial stigmatization. In repudiating the *Plessy* decision, the Court concluded that "the doctrine of 'separate but equal' has no place" in public education. Contrary to six decades of case law that had supported and fortified official segregation, the Court found that "[s]eparate educational facilities are inherently unequal." It thus determined that racially segregated public education violated "the equal protection of the laws guaranteed by the Fourteenth Amendment."

The conclusion that segregation was unconstitutional led to the even more difficult question of how to implement integration of schools. This decision was postponed until the Court's next term. To help it in framing a viable remedy for the constitutional violation, the Court invited suggestions from those states that would be ordered to desegregate their schools.

A year later, in Brown v. Board of Education II (1955), the Court assigned to federal district courts the responsibility for ensuring "good faith" efforts to desegregate. The lower courts thus were relied upon to eliminate obstacles to desegregation "in a systematic and effective manner and to obtain relief as soon as practicable." States were required to make "a prompt and reasonable start toward full compliance." The standard established by the Court required affected schools to desegregate "with all deliberate speed." This standard reflected the Court's sense that constitutional change must proceed, but on an orderly basis. By encouraging state participation in the framing and implementation of relief, the Court hoped for cooperation rather than opposition.

The Court's decision against demanding immediate change was not without risk. The "deliberate speed" standard, as the aftermath of *Brown* showed, invited widespread resistance, evasion, and delay. Some states introduced desegregation plans that actually would maintain the status quo. Others ignored the order or declared it invalid. The Arkansas legislature, for instance, enacted a law that declared the Court's desegregation ruling "unconstitutional." For several years, constitutional change did not make any appreciable difference in the segregated status of public schools throughout the South. Even so, the Court spread the desegregation principle to all public corners of society, including beaches, parks, public transportation, and other settings. Achievement of the basic goals of desegregation in public education, however, would require further effort by the Court and eventually by Congress.

Bibliography

Alexander Bickel, *The Supreme Court and the Idea of Progress* (1970). Explores the Supreme Court's role as an agent of social change.

Robert Bork, *The Tempting of America* (1990). Challenges the *Brown* Court's theory, but not its result.

Richard Kluger, *Simple Justice* (1976). A comprehensive examination of *Brown v. Board of Education* (1954), including its background, the Court's resolution of the case, and the decision's impact.

Carl T. Rowan, *Dream Makers, Dream Breakers* (1993). Documents the NAACP's challenge to official segregation, particularly the roles of Charles Houston and Thurgood Marshall.

Cooper v. Aaron

The Supreme Court's declaration in *Brown v. Board of Education* (1954), that racially separate public schools were unconstitutional was easier to announce than to enforce. In *Brown*, the Court insisted upon the eradication of segregation "with all deliberate speed." Actual progress toward desegregation over the next decade was minimal. School districts that wished to ignore *Brown* essentially could maintain segregated conditions if they were not challenged in court. The National Association for the Advancement of Colored People (NAACP) continued to play the same leadership role it had performed prior to the *Brown* ruling. It was hobbled, however, by limited financial resources and efforts to restrict its desegregative activity. Many states adopted policies that appeared to comply with the desegregation mandate but were actually designed to maintain racially separate schools. Strategies of this nature included altered school-district lines, freedom-of-choice plans, school closings, funding of private schools for whites, and other methods that the Court struck down as inadequate.

Citation:	358 U.S. 1.
Issue:	Whether a state could delay desegregation of public schools because of concern about public opposition.
Year of Decision:	1958.
Outcome:	Desegregation was the supreme law of the land and could not be obstructed by state or local government.
Author of Opinion:	*Percuriam*.
Vote:	9–0.

While some communities attempted to avoid the impact of the desegregation ruling by delay or evasion, others confronted it more directly. The state of Arkansas, for instance, contested the constitutionality not only of desegregation but of the Court's power to order it. A state constitutional amendment was adopted that required the legislature to "approve in every Constitutional manner the Unconstitutional desegregation decisions . . . of the United States Supreme Court." Under that provision, the legislature enacted a law that relieved students from having to attend racially mixed schools. The state's action and position presented significant challenges to the Court's resolve and ultimately to its power to interpret the Constitution in a binding fashion.

The Arkansas law was passed after school officials in Little Rock had proposed a desegregation plan. In response to the possibility of desegregation, Governor Orval Faubus ordered the National Guard to block black students from entering the city's all-white high school. This resort to military resistance further dramatized the challenge to the Court's authority and the Constitution's meaning. It also placed President Dwight Eisenhower in a bind reminiscent of President Abraham Lincoln's a century before. Responding to the *Dred Scott* decision, which upheld slavery shortly before his election to the presidency, Lincoln ignored the ruling on grounds that it did not bind him or the nation. Eisenhower himself viewed the desegregation decision as misguided and counterproductive. Believing that court-ordered desegregation would cause the South to harden its resistance to racial change and progress, Eisenhower characterized the appointment of Chief Justice Earl Warren as his "biggest mistake." The president's disappointment in Warren was not entirely warranted and was certainly not a basis for claimed betrayal. Eisenhower had nominated Warren as chief justice less because of his political philosophy than as a reward for the help that Warren had given him in securing the Republican presidential nomination in 1952. The nomination of Warren also represented a means of defusing strife in the California Republican Party between bitterly divided factions loyal, respectively, to Warren and Richard Nixon. Despite his lack of enthusiasm for the desegregation mandate, Eisenhower nonetheless responded to the constitutional challenge by sending in federal troops to enforce the Court's order. Against the backdrop of tension and conflict, the Little Rock school board sought judicial approval to delay implementation of its desegregation plan.

John Aaron and other parents of African-American schoolchildren originally had sued William G. Cooper and other school board members on grounds that a gradual desegregation plan was constitutionally deficient. Although a federal trial court upheld the plan, the Governor of Arkansas declared historically white schools off limits to black students. He also called up the National Guard to enforce his decree. After the guardsmen turned away black students who had enrolled under the desegregation plan, the school board sought court approval to suspend its operation. Although the Court acknowledged that the educational process might suffer from the unfriendly climate in Arkansas, it refused to delay desegregation.

One issue before the Court was reminiscent of those that had confronted it soon after the republic's founding. Sensing a challenge to its own power in *Cooper*, the Court reasserted the notion that the Constitution is the supreme law of the land and the judiciary has the ultimate power to interpret it. Reaching back to *Marbury v. Madison* (1803), the Court stressed that the Constitution is "the fundamental and paramount law of the nation" and reaffirmed its own authority "to say what the law is." Critics have maintained that the Court's reference to *Marbury* exaggerates its own power in relationship to the Constitution. Attorney General Edwin Meese, three decades after the *Cooper* decision, criticized the Court for thinking that its "decisions are on a par with the Constitution."[1] Consistent with Lincoln's reasoning following the *Dred Scott* decision, Meese maintained that the Court's ruling bound the parties to the case but did not mean "that everyone would have to accept its judgments uncritically." He thus objected to reasoning that "reduce[d] the Constitution to the status of ordinary constitutional law, and . . . equate[d] the judge with the lawgiver."

Despite Meese's criticism that its logic was "at war with the basic principles of democratic government," the Court was emphatic in its position.[2] To indicate their resolve, all nine justices fixed their names to an opinion that unanimously reaffirmed *Brown*. In so doing, the Court proclaimed that "[t]he constitutional rights of respondents are not to be sacrificed or yielded to the violence and disorder which have followed upon the actions of the Governor and Legislature." By passing a law that challenged the Court's authority and using military force to prevent desegregation, the state was responsible for increasing tension, strife, and opposition in the community. The Court emphasized that "law and order are not here to be preserved by depriving the Negro children of their constitutional rights." Backed up by the bayonets of federal troops, the Court thus asserted its will over the resistance of Arkansas officials.

Two years after the Court's order in Brown v. Board of Education II (1955) that desegregation must proceed "with all deliberate speed," the Arkansas experience revealed the significant barriers that the desegregation mandate confronted. Reaction in states affected by the Court's ruling was profoundly negative. The Court had anticipated the possibility of an unfavorable response to desegregation. By encouraging state and local officials to participate in developing strategies for undoing official segregation, it sought to defuse opposition. In vesting lower federal courts with oversight responsibility for the implementation of desegregation, the Court hoped to distance itself from the process. The need for military intervention to enforce the Court's will suggested that the desegregation process would be a source of continuing challenge to constitutional authority and principle. Developments in subsequent years verified this premise.

Notes

1. Edwin Meese III, "The Law of the Constitution," 61 *Tulane Law Review* 979, 983–84 (1987).
2. Ibid. at 987.

Bibliography

Richard Hodder-Williams, *The Politics of the U.S. Supreme Court* (1980). Discusses President Eisenhower's reaction to the Warren Court's undoing of segregation and his disappointment in the Chief Justice.

Anthony Lewis, *Portrait of a Decade: The Second American Revolution* (1964). Focuses on the aftermath of the Court's initial desegregation ruling, including intense southern opposition to it.

A. T. Mason, *The Supreme Court from Taft to Warren* (1968). Examines the South's "electric" response to the Court's desegregation demands.

Bernard Schwartz, *Super Chief* (1983). Recounts Chief Justice Warren's tenure and achievements on the Supreme Court.

Green v. County School Board of New Kent County, Virginia

The first decade of the desegregation experience, which began in 1954, was characterized by widespread noncompliance with the Supreme Court's order and will. Despite the Court's efforts to remain in the background and leave desegregation enforcement to the lower courts in affected communities, challenges to its authority kept the Court on the front line. School desegregation also remained at the top of the Court's agenda because many lower courts were sympathetic to the interests of state and local officials in avoiding or delaying implementation. An example of this attitude was the response of the federal court in South Carolina that, in reviewing one of the cases reviewed by the *Brown* Court, asserted that a constitutional prohibition upon official discrimination "does not require integration."

Consistently in the decade following the *Brown* decision, the Court struck down desegregation plans on grounds that they were inadequate. In Rogers v. Paul (1965), it invalidated a plan for desegregating schools one year at a time. A county's closure of its entire public school system and funding of private white schools were found at odds with the equal protection guarantee in Griffin v. County School Board of Prince Edward County (1964). The persistence of sham or ineffective remedies suggested that the standard of "all deliberate speed" for achieving desegregation had become a basis for foot dragging and contrivance. Further evidencing the futility of "all deliberate speed" was the gross underachievement of integration throughout the South. During this time, the racial makeup of southern schools remained largely unchanged. In 1964, only 2 percent of black students in states with a history of segregated education attended schools that could be characterized as biracial. The reason for this lack of progress was the limited means of enforcing constitutional compliance. State and local officials were able to ignore or minimize the impact of the desegregation mandate as long as desegregation advocates lacked resources for litigation and enforcement.

Citation:	391 U.S. 430.
Issue:	Whether a desegregation plan that allowed students to choose the school they would attend satisfied the constitutional requirement of racially unitary schools.
Year of Decision:	1968.
Outcome:	A desegregation plan is impermissible if a speedier and more effective alternative is available.
Author of Opinion:	Justice William Brennan.
Vote:	9–0.

Because many of desegregation's potential beneficiaries were poor and disenfranchised, leverage for change and compliance was minimal. Enactment of the Civil Rights Act of 1964 represented a key turning point for the desegregation process. This law authorized the attorney general of the United States to sue segregated school districts. The Department of Health, Education, and Welfare was authorized to deny federal funding to school districts that did not comply with the requirements of *Brown*. The federal government's entry into the litigation arena and the use of fiscal pressure on noncomplying school districts significantly accelerated the rate of desegregative progress.

Typical of the underachieving models of desegregation advanced in the early years after *Brown* was a plan adopted by school officials and challenged in *Green v. County School Board of New Kent County, Virginia*. The policy at issue provided each student with the freedom to choose the school that he or she wished to attend. On its face, the plan was racially neutral. It was challenged by Calvin C. Green and Mary O. Green, parents of three African American students, on grounds that compulsory desegregation was necessary to eliminate segregated conditions. The Court agreed with them and struck down the freedom of choice policy on grounds that it did not meet the constitutional demand for "admission to the public schools on a nonracial basis." Critical to the Court's finding that the policy was unconstitutional was a history of segregation that preceded the new plan's adoption. Adoption of a freedom-of-choice provision in 1965 had enabled students through the eighth grade to select the school they preferred to attend throughout their primary education. Students at secondary schools had the opportunity to choose their school annually. In the event that they did not make a selection, students continued at the institution in which they were enrolled.

Under this plan, no real movement toward desegregation had occurred. No white students had sought admission to traditionally all-black schools, and only a handful of black students had transferred to historically all-white schools. From these circumstances, the Court discerned an interest in maintaining rather than changing the status quo. Although the Court did not reject the validity of a freedom-of-choice plan per se, it found that the plan at issue was constitutionally deficient under the circumstances. Because there were "speedier and more effective" means for achieving unitary status, the plan was found "unacceptable."

Beyond just determining that the freedom-of-choice model was inadequate on the immediate heels of prescriptive segregation, the Court expressed its impatience with the generally slow pace of desegregation. The Court thus seized the opportunity to demand greater responsiveness and achievement. Faced with persistent evasion and resistance, the Court announced that "[t]he time for 'all deliberate speed' has run out." In place of the standard that the Court had hoped would achieve desegregation in a measured but effective and collaborative way was a new demand for plans "that promise[d] realistically to work and promise[d] realistically to work *now*."

The heightened demand for real and prompt progress proved to be a high point of the desegregation era. School officials in communities affected by the desegregation mandate were put on notice that they had the "affirmative duty to take whatever steps might be necessary to convert to a unitary system in which racial discrimination would be eliminated root and branch." As the Court's resolve and authority were tested in the fifteen years following *Brown*, a defining hallmark during that period was the unanimity of its opinions. Although the Court unanimously supported the demand for swifter and more effective compliance, its solidarity on the desegregation front was nearing an end.

Even as the Court fortified the standards for constitutional compliance, changes in the Court's composition and in national politics were creating circumstances for limitations on desegregation doctrine. As the country became increasingly aware that busing was emerging as a primary methodology for desegregation plans that would "work now," opposition to the Court's work began to spread. George Wallace, who had defined his gubernatorial career in Alabama as an archsegregationist, attracted support throughout the West and South for his presidential campaign in 1968. The eventual winner of that year's presidential election, Richard Nixon, ran a campaign that stressed the need to appoint Supreme Court justices who would be less aggressive in their interpretation of the Fourteenth Amendment. Both tapped into mounting popular disaffection with the methods and potential reach of desegregation. Taken together, Nixon's and Wallace's appeal indicated mounting discomfort with the desegregation mandate and the dislocations that it imposed.

Viewed from a historical perspective, the emerging second thoughts about the reach of the *Brown* ruling paralleled the reservations soon after Reconstruction about the wisdom and desirability of devoting extensive political and constitutional attention to the problem of racial discrimination. In 1883, fifteen years after the Fourteenth Amendment was framed and ratified, the Supreme Court in the *Civil Rights Cases* observed that the time had come when a previously oppressed group must "cease to be the special favorite of the laws." Fifteen years after finding racially separate education "inherently unequal," the Court was holding fast to its insistence upon compliance with *Brown* but was on the verge of some important reconsiderations.

Bibliography

Derrick Bell, Jr., *Race, Racism, and American Law*, 2d ed. (1980). A critical perspective on *Brown* and its aftermath.

Donald E. Lively, *The Constitution and Race* (1992). Examines southern response and the Supreme Court's reaction during the first decade of the *Brown* era.

Swann v. Charlotte-Mecklenburg Board of Education

The judiciary's role in dismantling racially separate public schools represented the primary source of friction between the Supreme Court and states and localities affected by desegregation requirements. One initial response to the desegregation order set forth in *Brown v. Board of Education* (1954) was that the Fourteenth Amendment did not require racial mixing. This interpretation rested on the premise that the elimination of formal racial barriers did not require affirmative steps to achieve a racially integrated condition. The Court's demand in Brown v. Board of Education II (1955) for desegregation "with all deliberate speed," however, imposed an obligation that not only invalidated racially segregative attendance policies but required plans for achieving unitary schools.

Citation:	402 U.S. 1.
Issue:	What is the scope of a federal court's powers in desegregating public schools?
Year of Decision:	1971.
Outcome:	Federal courts have broad and extensive power to frame effective relief.
Author of Opinion:	Chief Justice Warren Burger.
Vote:	9–0.

Without the Court's demand for action, custom, tradition, and fear would have facilitated maintenance of segregated conditions. These cultural forces, as the Court in *Green v. County School Board* (1969) suggested, were powerful enough to maintain racial separation even without the force of law. Initially in Brown II, the Court attempted to avoid conflict with state and local authorities by announcing that they had primary responsibility for achieving desegregation. To minimize perceptions of judicial intrusiveness, the Court delegated to lower federal courts the role of determining whether desegregation was being implemented in "good faith." This distribution of function and authority reflected a sense that the lower courts were closer to local conditions and would interact more effectively and harmoniously with local officials.

In originally describing the lower courts' power to achieve desegregation, the Court spoke in generalities rather than specifics. It noted that courts had traditional equitable powers that could be exercised in framing relief and eliminating "obstacles in a systematic and effective manner." Equitable power enables courts to enter injunctions which prohibit or mandate action to achieve relief from a legal wrong. Although this breakdown and definition of responsibility were designed to minimize resistance, the Court's demands typically were perceived as intruding upon state law, custom, and autonomy. For two decades after the *Brown* case initially was argued, the conflict between federal judicial authority and state policy was at the core of the constitutional debate. By the late 1960s, the Court's resolve, coupled with federal legislation and policy that increased pressure for compliance, had resulted in significant desegregative progress. The judiciary's heightened involvement, however, also generated mounting outcries against and resistance to methods for achieving desegregation. As desegregation plans consistently were struck down in the years after *Brown*, and the Court demanded remedies that "work now," the primary means for achieving immediate results became the most debatable and unpopular. Busing of students, in particular, although it was a remedy that met the constitutional requirement for prompt relief, emerged as a lightning rod for debate over whether the Court had overreached its role and authority. Along with other methods for achieving prompt desegregation, busing brought the role of the judiciary squarely into the forefront of the constitutional debate.

In response to one state's effort to prohibit busing and bar pupil assignment on the basis of race, the Court in North Carolina State Board of Education v. Swann (1971) concluded that "state policy must give way when it operates to hinder vindication of constitutional guarantees." Just as states could not pass laws that negated the Court's desegregation order, therefore, they could not enact legislation that limited the remedies necessary to achieve racially unitary schools. An action to desegregate public schools in Charlotte initially was filed in 1965 by James E. Swann. At issue, among other things, was the means by which desegregation could be achieved. In *Swann v. Charlotte-Mecklenburg Board of Education*, a companion case that concerned desegregation of a metropolitan school district in Charlotte, North Carolina, the Court provided an expanded description of a federal court's power to frame relief. For a court to assume the role of framing and implementing a desegregation plan, the Supreme Court established two conditions. First, a constitutional violation must be identified. Second, school officials must have failed to adopt an effective plan for eradicating all vestiges of official segregation. Having premised the authority of lower courts to frame and impose desegregation plans upon the inadequacy of plans proposed by local authorities, the Court assessed "four problem areas" in the remedial process.

The first source of controversy was the use of racial quotas as a standard for compliance. The district court had imposed a racial-balance requirement of 71 percent white students and 29 percent black students for each school, consistent with the distribution of racial groups within the entire community. The Supreme Court observed that the requirement to desegregate schools does not mandate "as a matter of substantive constitutional right" that every school must reflect the racial composition of the community as a whole. However, it viewed "mathematical ratios" as a useful starting point in developing remedies to correct identified violations of the Constitution. Use of such ratios on a "very limited" basis thus was found to be within the scope of a court's equitable powers to remedy segregation.

The Court noted that Charlotte, like many metropolitan areas, was residentially segregated. Especially because minorities tended to be clustered in particular neighborhoods, the question was whether some "one-race, or virtually one-race schools within a district" might be inconsistent with constitutional requirements. Although the Court noted that a "small number" of such schools was not necessarily fatal, it emphasized that school authorities have the burden to demonstrate "that their racial composition is not the result of present or past discriminatory action on their part."

Because many schools had been built during the separate but equal era, and siting decisions reflected the imperative of segregation, the Court determined that school construction and closure policies would be significant factors for determining compliance. In reviewing and, if necessary, revising desegregation plans, courts were to ensure that "construction and abandonment are not used and do not serve to perpetuate or reestablish a dual system." Redrawing school-district lines and assigning students to distant rather than nearby schools had become a particularly controversial method of dismantling dual school systems. The Court acknowledged that "[a]ll things being equal," it might be preferable to assign students to schools nearest their home. Because "all things are not equal in a system that has been deliberately constructed and maintained to enforce racial segregation," however, the Court reserved an option for remedies that may be "awkward, inconvenient and even bizarre." From the Court's perspective, these burdens were unavoidable during the "interim period" necessary to eliminate all vestiges of official segregation.

Implicit in the power to alter attendance zones is the need for transportation of those students who must travel outside their neighborhood. On the thorny subject of busing, the Court observed that transportation has been a traditional aspect of public education and that nearly 40 percent of the nation's students were bused annually. Although the Court refused to set any fixed guidelines for busing, it upheld the Charlotte plan, which provided for average trips of seven miles lasting no more than thirty-five minutes. Stressing that desegregation plans cannot be restricted to "walk-in" schools, the Court found "no basis for holding that busing could not be a required means for desegregation." Even so, the Court indicated that the use of busing was not without limits. Transportation of students was permissible to the extent that neither time nor distance presented risks to children affected or significantly interfered with the educational process.

Although the Court's decision delineated the scope of a federal court's power to frame relief in desegregation cases, it previewed an impending redirection of desegregation principles. Until *Swann*, the Court had focused upon the dismantling of dual school systems. Once unitary status was achieved, the question invariably raised was whether integration had to be preserved. The Court's response was that unless desegregation was caused by official action, no constitutional duty existed for preserving the results of desegregation. Decisions in the years immediately following *Swann* reinforced an understanding that elimination of segregation did not necessitate the maintenance of integration.

Bibliography

Abram Chayes, "The Role of the Judge in Public Law Litigation," 89 *Harvard Law Review* 1281 (1976). An inquiry into the role of federal courts in desegregation and other contexts.

Lino A. Graglia, *Disaster by Decree* (1976). Criticizes the role of the judiciary in requiring desegregation as inappropriate and counterproductive.

Gerald N. Rosenberg, *The Hollow Hope: Can Courts Bring About Social Change?* (1991). Expresses doubts about the ability of federal courts to effect meaningful social change.

Bernard Schwartz, *Swann's Way: The School Busing Case and the Supreme Court* (1986). A detailed examination of the *Swann* decision.

Keyes v. School District No. 1, Denver, Colorado

Desegregation of public schools through the early 1970s was ordered in communities that by law had separated students on the basis of race. Constitutional attention thus was directed largely toward those southern states that historically had operated dual school systems. Segregated schools, however, were not unique to the South. In the North and West, racially separate schools typically reflected patterns of residential segregation. Even if segregated schools were not directly required by law in the North and West, as was the case in the South, they eventually became a focal point of constitutional review. Two decades after *Brown v. Board of Education* (1954), the question that confronted the Supreme Court was whether racially identifiable schools were constitutionally impermissible under any circumstance. Crucial to the resolution of this issue, as the Court announced in *Keyes v. School District No. 1, Denver, Colorado*, was the cause of segregation.

Citation:	413 U.S. 189.
Issue:	Whether segregation of public schools is unconstitutional only if it is required by law.
Year of Decision:	1973.
Outcome:	De jure but not de facto segregation violates the Constitution.
Author of Opinion:	Justice William Brennan.
Vote:	6–2.

In reviewing segregated public schools in Denver, Colorado, the Court introduced the first significant principle that limited desegregation's reach. At issue were school-board decisions regarding school siting, district boundaries, and pupil placement. These decisions were challenged by parents of Denver school children. Although segregated schools were not the result of formal legislation, as in the South, they were caused by racially discriminatory school-board actions. The Court found that the board's decision making represented "a *prima facie* case of intentional segregation." Despite having the opportunity to prove that their policies were not motivated by race, officials were unable to show that segregation of Denver's schools did not flow from their policies. The Court established a purpose to segregate as the keystone for a constitutional violation, regardless of the form of official action. If segregation was the consequence of actions other than those attributable to the government, no constitutional wrong existed. The Court thus distinguished between de jure segregation, which was constitutionally offensive, and de facto segregation, which was not. De facto segregation refers to racial separation viewed as having no linkage to intentional state action. As the Court put it, "the differentiating factor between *de jure* segregation and so-called *de facto* segregation . . . is *purpose* or *intent* to segregate." Because segregation of Denver schools resulted from official actions intended to achieve racially separate conditions, the school system was ordered to desegregate. Without governmental involvement in creating them, segregated circumstances would have been characterized as de facto and thus beyond the reach of the Constitution.

The distinction between de jure and de facto segregation is not a precise one. Segregated neighborhoods in the North and West reflect private decisions on where to live, but these often have been facilitated by government policy. Restrictive covenants that forbade a homeowner from selling his or her house to a nonwhite were a popular method through the first half of the twentieth century for protecting segregated neighborhoods. Although they represented agreements by private parties, restrictive covenants had no effect unless they were enforced by courts. The Supreme Court eventually found them unconstitutional in Shelley v. Kraemer (1948) because their efficacy was dependent on state action. The residential segregation that they achieved, however, lasted long after their constitutional invalidation. Further contributing to segregated neighborhoods were federal lending policies that precluded Federal Housing Administration loans that would create racially mixed living conditions. Residential segregation also has been caused by official decisions regarding the location of schools and public housing and the distribution of urban development funds. Despite these linkages to state action, however, the Court held fast to its distinction between de jure and de facto segregation.

Differentiation of segregation based on perceptions of cause did not sit well with critics. Justice Lewis Powell, who concurred in part and dissented in part, considered the distinction unprincipled and even hypocritical. He bridled over the fact that the South was being shouldered with desegregative responsibilities while the North and West avoided any comparable obligation. From his perspective, the cause of segregation in public schools was less significant than the adverse effect on educational opportunity. Noting that "the *de jure–de facto* distinction" established a standard of change in the South, but accommodated the status quo in the North, Powell would have abolished it.

The *Keyes* decision conditioned the constitutional duty to desegregate upon proof that racially separate schools were a result of purposeful official action. This requirement was not difficult to satisfy in the separate but equal era, because segregation laws overtly manifested their purpose to discriminate on the basis of race. Once segregation was outlawed, however, discriminatory intent became more difficult to identify. Discernment of a motive to segregate, as Powell put it, necessitated a "tortuous effort." Powell noted that segregation could be established and maintained by various methods that might appear neutral in their purpose but were capable of hiding discriminatory intent.

Among the devices for achieving segregation subtly rather than visibly are the construction, location, and size of new schools, how attendance zones are drawn, how faculty are recruited and assigned, the nature of the curriculum, and tracking that leads some students to college and others in alternative directions such as vocational school.

Despite the concerns of the dissenters, the de jure–de facto principle has become established as a primary limitation on desegregation. By disregarding or minimizing the connection between official action and segregation, the Court diminished the desegregation mandate's significance in the North and West. Although a finding of unconstitutional conditions was not impossible outside the South, proving a connection between racially separate schools and official action was more difficult in those communities where the law's purpose did not speak for itself. Such linkage was demonstrable in some northern and western communities where school boards had created racially identifiable schools but had not dismantled them following the Court's decision in *Brown v. Board of Education* (1954). In Columbus Board of Education v. Penick (1979), the Court rejected the argument that segregated schooling had to be "commanded by state law," as in the South. Noting that segregation was the "direct result of cognitive acts or omissions" by the school board that resulted in "an enclave of separate, black schools," the Court found a constitutional violation.

Emergence of the de jure–de facto distinction represented a significant limitation upon the potential for desegregation. Although racial segregation is a defining feature of communities throughout the nation, the Court in *Keyes* determined that desegregation would be required on a selective basis. Critics, as noted previously, maintain that the distinction between de jure and de facto segregation is artificial. It is a line that the Court has drawn, however, that separates constitutional responsibility from permissibility. The de jure–de facto distinction represented a turning point in the desegregation experience. Following two decades of decision making that consistently stressed the need to dismantle segregated school systems, the *Keyes* ruling ushered in an era of review that was less likely to result in findings of constitutional violations. Viewed from a historical perspective, the de jure requirement in *Keyes* defined the outer limits for the law of desegregation.

Bibliography

Frank I. Goodman, "De Facto School Segregation: A Constitutional and Empirical Analysis," 60 *California Law Review* 275 (1972). Examines the concept and nature of de facto segregation.

Kenneth L. Karst, "Not One Law at Rome and Another at Athens: The Fourteenth Amendment in Nationwide Application," 1972 *Washington University Law Quarterly* 383 (1972). Criticizes the de jure–de facto distinction.

Donald E. Lively, *The Constitution and Race* (1992). Examines the significance of the *Keyes* decision.

Milliken v. Bradley

A dominant cause of racially separate schools in the North and West was residential segregation. Limited opportunities and harsh attitudes toward blacks in the South, along with the need for labor in the nation's industrial belt, fueled a major northward migration of African Americans during the first half of the twentieth century. The advent of World War II increased this exodus from the South as factories rapidly expanded their productive capacities to meet wartime demand. Although economic opportunity was greater in their new communities, transplanted blacks also encountered significant prejudice and hostility. Even though they were not confronted with the formality of segregation by law, they faced a dominant culture that preferred to keep its distance. Racially separate housing was achieved and enforced by restrictive covenants and intimidation of those who otherwise might have crossed color lines. Consistent with the attitudes behind these methods, school districts and

Citation:	418 U.S. 717.
Issue:	Whether suburban schools could be included in a plan to desegregate schools in a major city.
Year of Decision:	1974.
Outcome:	A metropolitan desegregation plan was permissible only if suburbs intentionally contributed to the segregation of city schools.
Author of Opinion:	Chief Justice Warren Burger.
Vote:	5–4.

attendance zones typically were designed to facilitate a system of public education based upon racial separation. The great waves of black migrants from the South thus fed into communities that defined themselves by an aversion to racial integration.

Desegregation requirements were introduced not only against the backdrop of a massive geographical shift of the black population but at a time of significant demographic change. In the years following World War II, American society was becoming increasingly mobile. Automobiles and postwar prosperity led to the formation of suburbs that surrounded cities and created metropolitan areas. By the 1970s, new school districts had emerged in communities that had not even existed when *Brown v. Board of Education* (1954) was decided. Even if residents in those communities had helped shape or had supported segregated school systems in their previous hometowns, newly created suburbs had no official role in creating the segregated conditions that preceded them. Demographic circumstances by the 1970s had changed so much that Justice Lewis Powell observed that "[t]he type of state-enforced segregation that *Brown* condemned no longer exists in this country." As the social landscape changed, however, conditions in major cities remained mired in the legacy of racial prejudice and discrimination. Particularly as whites fled to the suburbs, city schools became increasingly and in some instances almost exclusively black. By the early 1970s, schools in major urban centers such as Baltimore, Detroit, New York, and Washington, D.C., ranged from 70 percent to more than 90 percent black. In the context of this demographic reality, a desegregation remedy would be meaningless unless it included both cities and suburbs.

The issue of interdistrict desegregation remedies presented itself to a Supreme Court that had experienced significant personnel turnover since desegregation demands had peaked in the late 1960s. By 1974, when the question reached the Court in *Milliken v. Bradley*, President Richard Nixon had appointed four justices (Harry Blackmun, Warren Burger, Lewis Powell, and William Rehnquist) whose attitude toward desegregation was less aggressive than that of their Warren Court counterparts. The action was brought by parents and children of Detroit public schools and the NAACP against Governor William Milliken, the State Board of Education, Detroit Board of Education, and other state and city officials. Eventually a plan for desegregating public schools in the Detroit metropolitan area was approved by a federal district court, which made findings to the effect that municipal and state officials intentionally had segregated the city's schools. Specifically, the trial court found that the school board had created optional attendance zones that facilitated racially identifiable schools, had transported students to one-race schools, and had built schools in locations that facilitated segregation. The state's role consisted of nullifying a voluntary desegregation plan, providing transportation to such an extent that it promoted segregation, and approving segregative pupil-assignment plans.

Although the Supreme Court acknowledged that local and state officials had contributed to a segregated city school system, it held that an interdistrict desegregation plan exceeded the scope of the constitutional violation. Writing for a 5–4 majority, Chief Justice Warren Burger maintained that the actions that caused segregation extended no further than the city itself. The majority determined that an interdistrict desegregation plan was impermissible unless state or suburban officials actively participated in a scheme or action to segregate the city's schools. Although the Court did not preclude the possibility that desegregation remedies might incorporate more than one community, that prospect was greatly limited by the Court's determination that one district's actions must have been intentionally designed to have a segregative influence beyond its own boundaries. Interdistrict relief thus was eliminated from the potential arsenal of desegregation remedies unless there was a finding that the racially discriminatory actions of one district had segregative consequences upon another.

The basic principle that emerged from *Milliken* was that the scope of desegregative relief must not exceed the nature of the constitutional violation. Applied in the context of predominantly black urban communities, this rule effectively immunized predominantly white communities from the demands of *Brown*. Even though urban segregation might have been induced intentionally by official action, remedies could be designed only within the demographic framework of the affected community in isolation from its surroundings. Meaningful school desegregation in predominantly black communities thus became a largely futile undertaking.

In a dissenting opinion, Justice Byron White complained that intentionally caused segregation was being left unremedied. Noting that state public school officials had taken steps to effect segregation in Detroit public schools over a period of many years, he believed that responsibility for correcting the condition extended beyond the city. Because the problem was caused in part by official forces outside of Detroit, White thought it only proper that the state and its political subdivisions be part of the solution.

Reversal of the trial court's decision contrasted sharply with the Supreme Court's problems with lower courts during the first two decades of desegregation. Previously, lower courts had been criticized for not achieving enough with respect to desegregation. This point was illustrated in *Green v. County School Board of New Kent County, Virginia* (1969) when the Court, impatient with the results achieved under the standard of "all deliberate speed" for desegregation, demanded remedies that "work now." Striking down the interdistrict desegregation plan in *Milliken* five years later, the Court indicated that the desegregation process was being pushed too far. From Justice Thurgood Marshall's dissenting perspective, however, the decision meant "no remedy at all . . . guaranteeing that Negro children . . . will receive the same separately and inherently unequal education in the future as they have in the past."

The Court's ruling defined the desegregation principle's limits with respect to geography and prefaced a similar restriction with respect to time. Two years later, in Pasadena City Board of Education v. Spangler (1976), the Court determined that school districts that had achieved desegregation were not obligated to maintain an integrated condition. Because white flight or other factors may cause resegregation, and unless official action intentionally re-creates a dual school system based upon race, no constitutional duty exists to preserve the fruits of desegregation. From Justice William Rehnquist's perspective, demographic change that unsettled the results of desegregation was attributable to the "quite normal pattern of human migration." Dissenting as he did in *Milliken*, Justice Marshall argued that a state's creation of "a system where whites and Negroes were intentionally kept apart so that they could not become accustomed to learning together, is responsible for the fact that many whites will react to the dismantling of that segregated system by attempting to flee to the suburbs."

The curtailment of desegregation demands during the 1970s reflected a growing attitude that conditions addressed by the *Brown* Court in 1954 either had been dealt with or had changed. As Justice Powell saw it, segregated schools had become a function of "familiar segregated housing patterns . . . caused by social, economic, and demographic forces for which no school board is responsible." Despite the Court's initial resolve to have its desegregation orders obeyed, the marking of desegregation's boundaries two decades after *Brown* indicated a growing sense of limits to the judiciary's own influence. Consistent with this perspective, Justice Rehnquist observed that "[e]ven if the Constitution required it, and it were possible for federal courts to do it, no equitable decree can fashion an 'Emerald City' where all races, ethnic groups, and persons of various income levels live side by side." By the twentieth century's final decade, the Court itself had downscaled not just the principle but the rhetoric of desegregation. No longer were school systems required to eliminate all vestiges of racial discrimination "root and branch." Rather, as noted in Board of Education of Oklahoma City Public Schools v. Dowell (1991), good-faith compliance with desegregation requirements was to be measured by whether those "vestiges" had been eradicated "to the extent practicable."

Bibliography

St. Clair Drake and Horace R. Cayton, *Black Metropolis* (1945). Examines the massive migration of blacks from the South to the North and West and its sociological implications.

Paul Jacobs, *Prelude to Riot: A View of Urban America from the Bottom* (1967). Discusses official action that contributed to segregation of public schools in the North and West.

William Tuttle, Jr., *Race Riot: Chicago in the Red Summer of 1919* (1970). Studies private and sometimes violent action that deterred racial integration in the North.

Loving v. Virginia

Racial segregation in the United States historically was maintained by the dominant culture's ideology of racial supremacy that was the source of discriminatory and exclusionary laws. So pervasive was this mind-set that even critics of official segregation manifested it in their own thinking. Although Justice John Harlan, Sr., dissented from the separate but equal doctrine in *Plessy v. Ferguson* (1896), he disclosed his underlying sense of white supremacy. Harlan referred to whites as "the dominant race in this country . . . in prestige, achievements, in education, in wealth and in power" and "doubt[ed] not, [they] will continue to be for all time." If Harlan's views on race did not define the law, they still were not entirely inconsistent with it.

The system that separated persons on the basis of race and was premised upon the notion of white supremacy was alert to potential sources of destabilization or disruption of a strict racial hierarchy.

Citation:	388 U.S. 1.
Issue:	Whether a state law that prohibited interracial marriage violated the Constitution.
Year of Decision:	1967.
Outcome:	The prohibition on interracial marriage violated the equal protection clause and unconstitutionally interfered with the right to marry.
Author of Opinion:	Chief Justice Earl Warren.
Vote:	9–0.

One of the more obvious threats to racial purity was the possibility of intimate interracial relationships that might blur the clarity of racial distinctions. Laws against interracial marriage dated back to colonial times and were a common accompaniment of slavery. Even before the separate but equal era, which commenced in the late nineteenth century, many states prohibited interracial marriage and imposed stiff penalties for adultery or fornication between persons of different races. In addition to criminalizing interracial marriage, such laws typically included detailed safeguards for the interests of racial purity. Licensing officials, for instance, were obligated to perform background checks to verify an applicant's racial ancestry and maintain a system of certificates of "racial composition" in their public records.

Antimiscegenation laws (statutes that prohibited interracial marriage) were a cornerstone of official segregation that remained intact for more than a decade after segregation in public schools was declared unconstitutional in 1954. As late as 1967, approximately one-third of the states outlawed interracial marriage. In Pace v. Alabama (1875), the Supreme

Court reasoned that sanctions against interracial adultery and fornication were permissible as long as white and black offenders were treated the same. This attitude began to change in the years after *Brown v. Board of Education*. In McLaughlin v. Florida (1964), the Court struck down a state law that prohibited persons of different races from living together. The decision did not focus on whether the law applied evenly to all races, but on whether conduct was prohibited merely because of its interracial nature.

A more forceful statement to this effect was made in *Loving v. Virginia*, in which the Court invalidated Virginia's antimiscegenation law. The case arose when Richard Loving and Mildred Jeter were married in Washington, D.C., and, upon returning to their Virginia home, were convicted for violating the state's ban on interracial marriage. Loving was white and Jeter was African-American. As a condition for suspending a one-year prison sentence, the couple was required to leave Virginia for twenty-five years. Several years later, the couple brought an action to set aside the judgment on grounds that the state prohibition of interracial marriage violated the equal protection clause of the Fourteenth Amendment. Writing for the Court, Chief Justice Earl Warren found that the Virginia statute violated "the central meaning" of the amendment and could not stand.

The nature and aim of the Virginia law were easy to discern. Quoting from an earlier interpretation of the statute by the Virginia Court of Appeals, Warren noted that the state's purpose was "to preserve the racial integrity of its citizens," protect against "the corruption of blood" and "a mongrel breed of citizens," and safeguard against "the obliteration of racial pride." Even though the law imposed the same disabilities on all racial groups, the Court determined that it "rest[ed] solely upon distinctions drawn according to race." Noting that racial classifications are suspect in nature, the Court reaffirmed the principle that they must "be subjected to the 'most rigid scrutiny' " and can be upheld only if they are necessary to achieve some important interest unrelated to racial discrimination. Under this standard of searching judicial inquiry, the law was struck down on grounds that no basis for it other than "invidious racial discrimination" could be identified. Particularly because the Virginia law pertained only to relationships that included a white person, an impermissible aim of preserving "White Supremacy" was manifest.

The violation of equal protection was not the only constitutionally fatal flaw in the Virginia law. Although the right to marry is not mentioned specifically in the Constitution, it historically has been viewed as a fundamental right. In the Court's words, "[F]reedom to marry has long been recognized as one of the vital personal rights essential to the orderly pursuit of happiness by free men." A state law that denied "one of the 'basic civil rights of man,' fundamental to our very existence and survival," violated not only the equal protection clause but also the due process clause of the Fourteenth Amendment. The Court thus affirmed that "the freedom to marry, or not marry, a person of another race resides with the individual and cannot be infringed by the State."

The Court's ruling effectively demolished one of the fundamental pillars of law based upon principles of racial superiority. It extended the equal protection guarantee beyond traditional methods of discrimination to the ideology that generated them. As the Court initially had suggested in *Strauder v. West Virginia* (1880), before the separate but equal era unfolded, legislation "implying inferiority in civil society" was at the core of the Fourteenth Amendment's concern. By striking down laws that prohibited interracial marriage, the Court returned to an early premise of equal protection thinking that largely had remained dormant during the separate but equal era.

The *Loving* decision frequently is cited in support of the proposition that racial classifications under any circumstances are constitutionally indefensible. In a concurring opinion, Justice Potter Stewart argued that "it is simply not possible for a state law to be valid under our Constitution which makes the criminality of an act depend upon the race of the actor." Although racial classifications are a basis for searching judicial review, and there are strong presumptions against them, the case for constitutional color blindness has not emerged as an absolute. Arguments for affirmative action policies that establish preferences in admissions or hiring policies have been based upon the notion that racial classifications in these contexts serve compelling or important social interests. One year after the *Loving* decision, in Lee v. Washington (1968), three justices including Stewart argued that inmates could be segregated, at least temporarily, in response to racial tensions within a prison. These examples confirm rather than undermine the logic and values behind the Court's thinking. Racial classifications in such circumstances may promote important interests that are independent of racial prejudice.

Bibliography

Alexander Bickel, *The Least Dangerous Branch* (1972). Discusses the Court's response to laws against interracial marriage and sensitivity to their emotional underpinnings.

Peter Irons, *Justice at War* (1983). Examines the experience of various racial groups with antimiscegenation laws throughout the United States.

Winthrop Jordan, *White over Black: American Attitudes toward the Negro, 1550–1812* (1968). A historical inquiry into attitudes that inspired prohibitions of interracial marriage and relationships.

Washington v. Davis

A turning point in the evolution of desegregation principles was the Supreme Court's announcement that the Constitution concerned itself with de jure but not de facto segregation. Under this distinction, desegregation was required only in those school districts where racial separation had been officially mandated. As discussed in *Keyes v. School District No. 1, Denver, Colorado*, (1973), this distinction dramatically reduced the potential reach of school desegregation. The de jure–de facto distinction was established in the context of education but inevitably had implications for other equal protection controversies. The determining factor in ascertaining whether segregation was de jure or de facto was whether government intentionally caused it. This focal point was the basis for a general inquiry into whether racial segregation or disadvantage was the result of a discriminatory purpose or was an unintended effect of discrimination.

Citation:	426 U.S. 229.
Issue:	Whether a test for police officer applicants that was failed by a disproportionate number of black candidates violated equal protection principles.
Year of Decision:	1976.
Outcome:	Proof of intent to discriminate is necessary to establish a violation of the equal protection clause.
Author of Opinion:	Justice Byron White.
Vote:	7–2.

The requirement that discriminatory purpose must be established to prove an equal protection violation was announced in *Washington v. Davis*. At issue was a qualifying test for police officer candidates in Washington, D.C. that black applicants failed four times more often than whites. Two candidates who failed the test brought suit against the Mayor of Washington, D.C., Walter Washington, claiming that it was discriminatory. The examination was created by the federal Civil Service Commission and was designed to "test verbal ability, vocabulary, reading and comprehension." The trial court found that the examination was reasonably related to police training and performance and was neither designed nor used to discriminate on the basis of race. The court of appeals determined that the question of discriminatory purpose was irrelevant. It found that the test's racially "disproportionate impact" established a constitutional violation. The Supreme Court reversed the appeals court and found that official action is not "unconstitutional *solely* because it has a racially disproportionate impact."

The Court noted that racially disparate impact was not entirely irrelevant in assessing government action. Laws that appeared to be even-handed, for instance, might be applied in a discriminatory fashion. For illustrative purposes, the Court referred to its decision in Yick Wo v. Hopkins (1886). In that case, the Court struck down a San Francisco ordinance that prohibited the operation of laundries in wooden buildings. Although the law was general in its application, it was enforced exclusively against persons of Chinese descent. The Court also suggested that discriminatory purpose might be inferred from "the totality of relevant facts," including disproportionate impact, or from circumstances in which "the discrimination is very difficult to explain on nonracial grounds." Even so, the Court stressed that disproportionate impact by itself does not justify the searching judicial review that is triggered when discrimination is intentional. The Court thus viewed the police qualifying test as a legitimate means for ascertaining whether a candidate had sufficient verbal skills. To question government action merely because of its effects, the Court warned, would imperil "a whole range of tax, welfare, public service, regulatory, and licensing statutes" that are not intentionally discriminatory even if they have a disproportionate impact.

The decision imposed a significant limitation on the equal protection guarantee that was reaffirmed a year later. In Arlington Heights v. Metropolitan Housing Development Corp. (1977), the Court upheld a community's decision against rezoning land from single-family to multiple-family use. The action responded to an application for construction of racially integrated housing. Although the Court acknowledged that the decision might bear more heavily on racial minorities, it found no evidence of discriminatory purpose. It thus reaffirmed the premise that "impact alone is not determinative."

Proof of discriminatory intent is difficult to establish. Because discrimination is illegal, it typically is not done openly. The Court has identified certain factors that may be useful in discerning a discriminatory purpose. Relevant considerations include departures from normal governmental procedures, changes in standards for decision making, and any contemporaneous remarks by officials. The Court also suggested that the background of a decision may indicate a wrongful purpose. Taken together, these factors suggest that history is especially relevant in a discriminatory-purpose inquiry. It became a primary focal point in the review of a state's death penalty that was challenged on grounds that the law operated on a racially discriminatory basis. In McCleskey v. Kemp (1986), the Court was presented with significant statistical disparities in the operation of Georgia's capital punishment law. Evidence demonstrated that the death penalty was sought "in 70% of the cases involving black defendants and white victims; 32% of the cases involving white defendants and white victims; 15% of the cases involving black defendants and black victims; and 19% of the cases involving white defendants and black victims." Capital punishment was carried out "in 22% of the cases involving black defendants and white victims; 8% of the cases involving white defendants and white victims; 1% of the cases involving black defendants and black victims; and 3% of the cases involving white defendants and black victims." Despite these disparities, the Court found no basis for purposeful discrimination. Rather, it viewed the racial discrepancies as "an inevitable part of our criminal justice system."

In a dissenting opinion joined by three of his colleagues, Justice William Brennan argued that the decision could be justified only if the Court turned a blind eye to historical reality. In particular, he noted the long legacy of a dual criminal justice system in Georgia and how a defense attorney's advice would vary according to the race of his or her client. Particularly in the context of plea bargaining, a black defendant would have more inducement to settle on less attractive terms. As Brennan put it "At some point in his case, [the defendant] doubtless asked his lawyer whether a jury was likely to sentence him to die." A candid assessment by the attorney invariably would include "the information that cases involving black defendants and white victims are more likely to result in a death sentence than cases featuring any other racial combination of defendant and victim."

Although discriminatory purpose has become an entrenched aspect of equal protection jurisprudence, its critics have not vanished. Detractors maintain that the equal protection guarantee should not, in the words of constitutional scholar Laurence Tribe, simply be a means for "stamping out impure thoughts."[1] Rather, it should prohibit government action that in the light of "history, context, source, and effect" is likely to "perpetuate subordination" of or reflect "hostility," "blindness," or "indifference" toward a group that traditionally has been subjugated. Others have noted that the focus upon motive is obsolete because it does not address modern realities of subtle discrimination and unconscious racism.

The Court itself has noted the risks of motive-based inquiry in other constitutional contexts. In *United States v. O'Brien* (1968), the Court refused to consider whether Congress intended to punish free speech when it passed a law that prohibited the burning of draft cards. It observed, in particular, that an otherwise constitutional law should not be struck down because of an allegation that the motive was illicit. This disinterest in probing official motivation reflects an understanding of how difficult it is to ascertain a legislature's collective intent. Because legislators may support a law for different reasons, the Court concluded that an inquiry into motive essentially is an exercise in guesswork.

A classic argument against inquiry into official motive was set forth by Justice Antonin Scalia, who, in Edwards v. Aguillard (1987), described it as "almost always an impossible task." The many reasons for a legislator to vote one way or another on a bill include not only the merits of the legislation but whether it "would provide jobs for his district," might enable him or her "to make amends with a [previously alienated political] faction," was sponsored by "a close friend," presented an opportunity to "repay[ ] a favor" to another politician, earned him appreciation from influential colleagues or wealthy contributors, represented the strong will of his or her constituency, was a way of getting even with a political nemesis or even a spouse who had made him or her "mad," or was voted on while he or she was "intoxicated and [thus] utterly *un*motivated." Because a legislature may be affected by combinations of these and other motivations, Scalia warned that looking "for *the sole purpose* of even a single legislator is probably to look for something that does not exist."

Despite the criticism of discriminatory-purpose standards in other constitutional circumstances, proof of motive remains a key fixture of equal protection doctrine. Given the difficulties of establishing discriminatory purpose, it is not surprising that successful equal protection claims since *Washington v. Davis* have been scarce. The purpose requirement is easily satisfied in the case of laws that overtly discriminate on the basis of race. Such policies largely have vanished from the political landscape, but the subtleties and complexities of discrimination in a race-conscious society continue to pose challenges. Constitutional review has yet to address these realities effectively.

Note

1. Laurence H. Tribe, *American Constitutional Law* 1520 (2d ed. 1988).

Bibliography

Paul Brest, "*Palmer v. Thompson*: An Approach to the Problem of Unconstitutional Legislative Motive," 1971 *Supreme Court Review* 95 (1971). Argues the case for inquiry into legislative motive.

Charles R. Lawrence III, "The Id, the Ego, and Equal Protection: Reckoning with Unconscious Racism," 39 *Stanford Law Review* 317 (1987). Contends that discriminatory-purpose criteria are inadequate in a society that trades more in subtle than in overt discrimination and is affected by unconscious racism.

Daniel R. Ortiz, "The Myth of Intent in Equal Protection," 41 *Stanford Law Review* 1105 (1989). Develops the notion that inquiries into discriminatory intent are futile.

Girardeau A. Spann, *Race against the Court* (1993). Develops a critical perspective on motive-based standards on grounds that they protect majoritarian preferences.

David A. Strauss, "Discriminatory Intent and the Taming of *Brown*," 56 *University of Chicago Law Review* 935 (1989). Sets forth the argument that discriminatory-purpose standards dilute the meaning of equal protection in the era after *Brown*.

Regents of the University of California v. Bakke

The idea of a "color-blind" Constitution originally was touted by Justice John Harlan, Sr., who, in *Plessy v. Ferguson* (1896), argued that the Constitution permits "no caste" system. Although Harlan's dissenting opinion was never mentioned in *Brown v. Board of Education* (1954), its rhetoric was central to the spirit of that decision. During the 1970s, as racial discrimination became increasingly subtle, proving discrimination in Court became more difficult. New methods for addressing the nation's legacy of racial discrimination emerged. Affirmative action was advanced as a means for undoing the wrongs attributable to a history of racial prejudice and disadvantage. "Affirmative action" is a broad term that has many meanings. It may mean programs to eliminate barriers that traditionally have confronted minorities, increase efforts to seek out qualified minorities, or establish quotas or preferences on the basis of race. Among these programs, race-conscious policies that set aside opportunities or positions for members of a particular racial group have been the most controversial.

Citation:	438 U.S. 265.
Issue:	Whether a medical school's admission policy of preference for minorities violated the Fourteenth Amendment.
Year of Decision:	1978.
Outcome:	A state medical school's admissions policy may take race into account provided it is not the exclusive factor.
Author of Opinion:	No majority opinion.
Vote:	5–4.

Policies that take race into account as a means of remedying the consequences of prejudice and discrimination initially were introduced because of constitutional necessity. Desegregation is a classic example of a policy that uses race as a factor in addressing official discrimination. The term "affirmative action" was first officially used in an executive order by President John Kennedy, who announced a policy that federal contractors must be hired without regard to race. In 1965, President Lyndon Johnson signed an executive order that created the Office of Federal Contract Compliance and authorized it to develop guidelines for compliance with federal anti-discrimination policy in contracting. Three years later, the office announced guidelines that referred to "goals and timetables for the prompt achievement of full and equal employment opportunity." In 1970, the office established "results-oriented procedures." One year later, the office modified its policy to emphasize "goals and timetables for the prompt and full achievement of full and equal employment opportunity." Similar transitions from antidiscrimination policy to affirmative action policy occurred in the private sector.

As educational and business institutions began to incorporate preferences for disadvantaged minorities into their admission and hiring policies, affirmative action plans became a subject of constitutional debate. The constitutionality of racial preferences initially presented itself to the Supreme Court when the University of Washington School of Law was sued by a white male who claimed that he was denied admission because of a racially preferential admissions policy. After a lower court ordered his admission to the school, and the university indicated that he would graduate, the Supreme Court in DeFunis v. Odegaard (1974) concluded that the case was moot. Four dissenting justices asserted that the Court was "side-stepping" a subject of intense public debate.

Not surprisingly, the issue of the constitutionality of racial preferences soon returned. Four years later, in Regents of the University of California v. Bakke, the Court ruled on a preferential admissions program at the University of California at Davis School of Medicine. The policy, which set aside a fixed number of seats in each entering class for designated minorities, was challenged by Allan Bakke, a white male, who alleged that it was the basis for his not being admitted. The California Supreme Court found the admissions program unconstitutional. The United States Supreme Court affirmed this ruling, and Bakke was admitted to the medical school. However, the Court split on the question of whether race was a legitimate consideration when attempting to rectify past wrongs.

Chief Justice Warren Burger and Justices William Rehnquist, Potter Stewart, and John Paul Stevens concluded that the medical school's policy violated Title VI of the Civil Rights Act of 1964, barring discrimination in educational programs, and refused to address the constitutional question. Justices William Brennan, Byron White, Thurgood Marshall, and Harry Blackmun determined that the program violated neither the equal protection clause nor Title VI. Writing separately, Justice Lewis Powell maintained that the policy violated the Constitution and the federal statute. He left open the possibility, however, that attention to race was permissible under certain circumstances. Powell's opinion, combined with the position of those who found no constitutional or statutory violation, provided support for using race as a factor if it was not the exclusive criterion for diversification.

The first question confronting the Court was whether it should adopt the standard of review—strict scrutiny—that had been used for assessing racial classifications that burdened minorities since Korematsu v. United States (1944). Justice Powell maintained that any racial classification, even if it was designed to benefit traditionally disadvantaged minorities, should be subject to searching judicial inquiry. Having adopted the least forgiving standard for reviewing government policy or action, Powell proceeded to indicate why the official reasons for the admissions policy were inadequate. With respect to the school's interest in setting aside seats for minorities, Powell maintained that racial quotas or goals were categorically invalid. He rejected the state's interest in eliminating discrimination on grounds that there were no findings of prior wrongdoing by the school. The institution's argument that it sought to improve health care in disadvantaged communities fared no better. Powell criticized the premise that minority students necessarily would practice in those communities. The final contention, that the objective of diversification by itself was a compelling need, satisfied Powell to a point. Although he emphasized that a diversification policy could not focus on race or ethnicity exclusively, he acknowledged the value and legitimacy of broader considerations that included these factors. As he put it, "An otherwise qualified medical student with a particular background—whether it be ethnic, geographic, culturally advantaged or disadvantaged—may bring to a professional school of medicine experiences, outlooks, and ideas that enrich the training of its student body and better equip its graduates to render with understanding their vital service to humanity."

Justice John Paul Stevens, joined by Chief Justice Burger and Justices Rehnquist and Stewart, adopted the position that the Constitution was color-blind for all purposes. This faction refused to distinguish racial classifications on the basis of their intention to benefit rather than burden a disadvantaged group. The Stevens group refused even to delve into the constitutional question and found a violation of Title VI of the Civil Rights Act of 1964, which was viewed as requiring strict racial neutrality in federally supported programs.

As author of an opinion joined by Justices White, Marshall, and Blackmun, supporting the notion that policies benefitting minorities should be viewed differently than those burdening them, Justice William Brennan argued that the Court's standard of review should be less strict. The Brennan plurality thus would have been more receptive to initiatives designed to eliminate or undo the consequences of discrimination against minorities. Searching judicial review tends to be highly restrictive of the legislative process, and Brennan believed that the judiciary should not be an impediment to policy making that sought to eliminate the consequences of racial discrimination. He proposed looking at whether policies styled as a means of remedying discrimination actually were based on harmful stereotypes. From his perspective, a preferential admissions program was not a source of stigma. Moreover, he viewed policies aimed at remedying societal discrimination as a sufficient justification that outweighed any negative impact on "members of the majority race."

In separate opinions, Justices Thurgood Marshall and Harry Blackmun argued that the nation's legacy of racial discrimination justified policies that were race-conscious in nature. Blackmun succinctly observed that "in order to get beyond racism, we must first take account of race." A majority of the Court did not foreclose the possibility of taking race into account for remedial purposes. However, the extent to which such methods would be allowed remained unclear for several years. Two years after the *Bakke* decision, the Court in Fullilove v. Klutznick (1980) upheld a federal program setting aside 10 percent of public works projects for minority contractors. Opinions of the justices were fragmented, however, to such an extent that it was difficult to identify a unifying principle. In Wygant v. Jackson Board of Education (1986), the Court struck down a preferential layoff program that was part of a collective bargaining agreement between school officials and teachers. Justice Powell authored an opinion, joined by Chief Justice Warren Burger, Justice William Rehnquist, and in part by Justice Sandra Day O'Connor, that rejected the notion that "alleviating the effects of societal discrimination" was an adequate justification. From Powell's perspective, such a rationale was too rough and the burden of laying off "innocent individuals" was too severe.

Through most of the 1980s, the constitutionality of affirmative action was uncertain. During this period, no standard of review commanded a majority of justices, nor did a consensus emerge on the permissible grounds for racially preferential policies. When the Court avoided the question of racial set-asides in DeFunis v. Odegaard, critics complained that "few constitutional questions in recent history have stirred as much debate." In years after *Bakke*, it became increasingly evident that few constitutional issues had generated as much discord within the Court.

Bibliography

Vincent Blasi, "*Bakke* as Precedent: Does Mr. Justice Powell Have a Theory?" 67 *California Law Review* 21 (1979). A critical perspective on the *Bakke* decision.

John Hart Ely, "The Constitutionality of Reverse Racial Discrimination," 41 *University of Chicago Law Review* 723 (1974); Richard Posner, "The *DeFunis* Case and the Constitutionality of Preferential Treatment of Racial Minorities," 1974 *Supreme Court Review* 1 (1974). Notable commentaries on affirmative action before the *Bakke* decision.

Thomas Sowell, *Race and Culture* (1994). Sets forth the argument that cultural values and productive skills are more essential than affirmative action to group progress.

Jared Taylor, *Paved with Good Intentions* (1992). Focuses on the perceived shortcomings of affirmative action.

Richmond v. J. A. Croson Co.

Justice Harry Blackmun, who in *Regents of the University of California v. Bakke* (1978) favored the use of racial preferences in a university medical school's admissions policy, was optimistic that the "time will come when an 'affirmative action' program is unnecessary . . . [and] . . . we could reach this stage within a decade at the most." A decade after *Bakke*, affirmative action remained the subject of intense constitutional debate. The Supreme Court itself remained fragmented in its thinking, and a majority position had yet to evolve.

Amid this doctrinal debate and uncertainty, the Court reviewed a Richmond, Virginia, set-aside program that required that at least 10 percent of the city's building contracts be given to minority business enterprises. The policy replicated a preferential scheme adopted by Congress and upheld in Fullilove v. Klutznick (1980). Municipal officials based the program upon the same evidence used by Congress to demonstrate nationwide discrimination in the

Citation:	488 U.S. 469.
Issue:	Whether a municipal plan that set aside 10 percent of city building contracts for minority businesses was unconstitutional.
Year of Decision:	1989.
Outcome:	Racial preferences, even if they are intended to rectify societal discrimination, violate the equal protection clause of the Fourteenth Amendment.
Author of Opinion:	Justice Sandra Day O'Connor.
Vote:	6–3.

construction industry. They also cited a study of local conditions that showed that blacks constituted 50 percent of Richmond's population, but minority businesses received less than 1 percent of the city's building contracts. The plan was adopted as a means of redistributing opportunity in an industry that historically had been heavily underpopulated by minorities. J. A. Croson Co., a majority owned business, objected to the set-aside program on grounds it was discriminatory.

Although the Court noted the city's "recitation of a benign or compensatory purpose," it found that the set-aside plan was inadequately justified and unconstitutional. In the decision, a majority of justices for the first time embraced the notion that racial classifications intended to remedy the nation's heritage of racial discrimination should be subject to strict judicial scrutiny. Under this standard of review, racial preferences are permissible only if they promote a compelling governmental objective, necessarily will achieve their aim, and represent the least burdensome way of doing so. Writing for a plurality of four, Justice Sandra Day O'Connor stated that "searching judicial inquiry" was an essential tool for purposes of "determining what classifications are 'benign' or 'remedial' and what classifications are in fact motivated by illegitimate notions of racial inferiority or simple racial politics." Strict scrutiny thus was viewed as a necessary means to "smoke out" illegitimate uses of race by assuring that government "is pursuing a goal important enough to warrant use of a highly suspect tool."

From O'Connor's perspective, distinctions between good and evil racial classifications were difficult if not impossible to make. She viewed them as a source of stigmatic harm, regardless of the race they burdened or benefitted. Even classifications with benign intentions may "promote notions of racial inferiority and lead to a politics of racial hostility" unless they are strictly reserved for specific and proven instances of discrimination. O'Connor warned that without searching inquiry into such methods, "race will always be relevant in America." Noting that half of the city's population was black, and that African Americans had a majority on the city council, she also intimated that a system of set-asides under the circumstances wrongly might represent a political entitlement based upon race.

Although O'Connor acknowledged the nation's "sorry history of both private and public discrimination," she rejected the idea that this legacy by itself supported remedial policies based upon race. Unless there was proof of discrimination in a particular instance, she saw a risk of policies that would have no ending point in establishing a system of race-conscious benefits and burdens. The city had the power to remedy proven acts of discrimination with policies that took race into account, but pursuit of racial balancing as a general policy objective was declared impermissible. As O'Connor saw it, racial preferences might be allowable only to the extent that they were "necessary to break down patterns of deliberate exclusion." To allow more than that would compromise "[t]he dream of a Nation of equal citizens in a society where race is irrelevant to personal opportunity." In its place, she argued, "achievement would be lost in a mosaic of shifting preferences based on inherently unmeasurable claims of past wrongs."

Justice Antonin Scalia, in a significant concurring opinion, also embraced the strict scrutiny standard of review. However, he challenged the O'Connor plurality's allowance of racial preferences even in narrow circumstances. In his view, overcoming the effects of past discrimination was much less of a challenge than eradicating their source, "the tendency—fatal to a nation such as ours—to classify and judge men on the basis of their country of origin or the color of their skin." In reply to those who offered racial preferences as a solution to discrimination, Scalia regarded them "as no solution at all." For Scalia, racial classifications were justifiable only when they were necessary to dismantle a segregated school system or in "a social emergency rising to the level of imminent danger of life and limb." In the absence of such exigent circumstances, he maintained that "[w]here injustice is the game . . . turn-about is not fair play."

Combined with the position of the O'Connor plurality, Scalia's opinion established a Court majority in support of strict scrutiny of racial classifications regardless of their aim. This result generated a lengthy and sharp dissent by Justice Thurgood Marshall, joined by Justices William Brennan and Harry Blackmun, who criticized the Court for "a deliberate and giant step backward." Marshall found it ironic that the Court would "second-guess the judgment" of a city that "as the former capital of the Confederacy . . . knows what racial discrimination is." He characterized the Court's work as cynical, blind to the realities of discrimination, and "a grapeshot attack on race-conscious remediation." From his perspective, the set-aside program was justified on grounds that it was designed to eradicate the consequences of racial discrimination and ensure that city spending did not reinforce and perpetuate that legacy. Disputing the determination that evidence of specific discrimination was inadequate, Marshall cited federal and local studies and the absence of any challenge to Richmond's discriminatory past. As he saw it, the Court's position "simply blinks credibility" and demonstrated a failure "to come to grips with why" the contracting industry had minuscule numbers of minorities.

The Court's adoption of a strict scrutiny standard for racially preferential remedial policies was a source of dismay for Marshall. He found "[a] profound difference separat[ing] governmental actions that themselves are racist, and governmental actions that seek to remedy the effects of prior racism or to prevent neutral governmental activity from perpetuating the effects of such racism." Marshall chastised the Court for what he considered to be an exercise in evading and denying "the tragic and indelible fact that [racial] discrimination . . . has pervaded our Nation's history and continues to scar our society." In closing, he expressed disappointment that a majority of the Court "signals that it regards racial discrimination as largely a phenomenon of the past, and that government bodies need no longer preoccupy themselves with rectifying racial injustice."

Impressions that the Court had closed the door on methods that, in Justice Blackmun's words, "take account of race . . . to get beyond racism" soon were cast into doubt, at least momentarily. A year after the *Croson* ruling, the Court in Metro Broadcasting, Inc. v. Federal Communications Commission (1990) upheld racial preferences in the process of licensing radio and television broadcasters. It overturned that decision, however, in Adarand Contractors, Inc. v. Pena (1995). By so doing, the Court reaffirmed the principle that racial classifications regardless of aim are subject to strict scrutiny. Justices Scalia and Clarence Thomas adopted the position that racial classifications can never be justified. The Court has reduced the issue of the constitutionality of affirmative action to whether this methodology is permissible to a limited extent or never.

Bibliography

Stephen L. Carter, *Reflections of an Affirmative Action Baby* (1991). A critical perspective on affirmative action by a self-described beneficiary of it.

Randall Kennedy, "Persuasion and Distrust: A Comment on the Affirmative Action Debate," 99 *Harvard Law Review* 1327 (1986). Argues that affirmative action policies have been effective, and that criticism of them is exaggerated.

Shelby Steele, *The Content of Our Character* (1990). Sets forth the view that affirmative action policies actually are harmful to their intended beneficiaries.

Patricia J. Williams, "*Metro Broadcasting, Inc. v. FCC*," 104 *Harvard Law Review* 525 (1990). Upholds the value of race-conscious methods for promoting cultural diversity.

10

Gender Issues

The Constitution originally was written by and spoke to the interests of men. This reality did not change with Reconstruction and passage of the Fourteenth Amendment. The amendment's provision for apportionment of federal legislators referred specifically to "male citizens." Constitutional challenges to laws that diminished the status of women or limited their opportunities generally were unsuccessful. Opinions typically referred to biological differences between men and women and their "natural" roles. In Bradwell v. Illinois (1873), the Supreme Court upheld a law that prohibited women from practicing law. The ruling was supported by the observation that "[t]he paramount destiny of and mission of woman are to fulfill the noble and benign offices of wife and mother. This is the law of the Creator. And the rules of civil society must be adapted to the general constitution of things." Nearly half a century later, the Nineteenth Amendment conferred upon women the right to vote. Not until recent decades, however, has gender been taken seriously under the equal protection clause. In the 1970s, the Court began to take a closer look at laws that discriminated on the basis of gender. Although state action that discriminates on the basis of gender is not as strictly scrutinized as racial classifications, the Court in Craig v. Boren (1976) established that review of such practices and policies would not be lenient.

Craig v. Boren

Within five years after the ratification of the Fourteenth Amendment, the Supreme Court described the equal protection clause as having just one purpose. In the *Slaughter-House Cases* (1873), the Court doubted whether the equal protection clause ever would be applied to discrimination that was not based on race. What the *Slaughter-House* Court characterized as "so clearly a provision for that race" was quickly reinforced. In Bradwell v. Illinois (1873), the Court upheld an Illinois law that prohibited women from practicing law. This result was explained on grounds that "[i]n the nature of things it is not every citizen of every age, sex and condition that is qualified for every calling and position." Evident in the Court's reasoning was the sense that the legislature, like "nature itself," could recognize "a wide difference in the respective destinies of man and woman." Among these differences in destiny was that "the family institution is repugnant to the

Citation:	429 U.S. 190.
Issue:	Whether a law that prohibited underage drinking by males violated the equal protection clause of the Fourteenth Amendment.
Year of Decision:	1976.
Outcome:	The law was invalid because it discriminated on the basis of gender.
Author of Opinion:	Justice William Brennan.
Vote:	6–2.

idea of a woman adopting a distinct and independent career from that of her husband." Consequently, the Court concluded, "the nature of things indicates the domestic sphere as that which properly belongs to the domain and functions of womanhood." A similar tone evidenced itself a year later in Minor v. Happersett (1874), in which the Court upheld the power of states to deny women the right to vote.

As the twentieth century unfolded, the law's attitude toward gender evolved beyond the thinking reflected in the Court's early opinions. The Nineteenth Amendment, ratified in 1920, prohibits states from denying or abridging the right to vote "on account of sex." The Civil Rights Act of 1964 prohibited employment discrimination on the basis of gender. Despite changes achieved through the political process, traditional attitudes toward the role of women continued to drive constitutional case law. In Goesart v. Cleary (1948), the Court upheld a law that prohibited women from tending bar unless they were related to the establishment's owner. Although the Court recognized "the vast changes in the social and legal position of women," it refused to preclude legislative line drawing on grounds of gender.

Nearly two decades after the determination in *Brown v. Board of Education* (1954) that racially segregated public schools were unconstitutional, the Court began taking official gender distinctions more seriously. In Reed v. Reed (1971), it struck down an Idaho law that established a preference for males as administrators of estates in probate. Two years later, in Frontiero v. Richardson (1973), the Court invalidated a federal law that presumed that the female spouse of a serviceman was dependent upon him but required a servicewoman to prove the dependency of her male spouse. Justice William Brennan, joined by Justices William Douglas, Byron White, and Thurgood Marshall, argued in support of the proposition that gender-based classifications, like race-based ones, should be regarded as suspect and should be subject to searching judicial inquiry. Justice Lewis Powell, in a concurring opinion joined by Chief Justice Warren Burger and Justice Harry Blackmun, agreed with the result but rejected a strict scrutiny standard. Because a proposed equal rights amendment to the Constitution had been submitted for ratification by the states, they believed that a decision on the general standard of review for gender classifications at least should be deferred.

The proposed equal rights amendment, which would have prohibited official discrimination on the basis of gender, eventually failed to attract enough support for ratification. The Court, however, continued to develop its standards for reviewing laws that classified on the basis of sex. In *Craig v. Boren* (1976), the Court adopted a new standard of review that was not strict but also was not entirely deferential toward legislative judgment. At issue was an Oklahoma law that prohibited the sale of 3.2 percent beer to males under the age of twenty-one and females under the age of eighteen. The statute was challenged by Curtis Craig, a male between the age of 18 and 21 years old, who claimed it constituted a gender-based discrimination that denied him equal protection of the laws. David Boren, who was named as a defendant, was Governor of Oklahoma. The state's argument for singling out males between the ages of eighteen and twenty-one was a gender-based statistical disparity with respect to arrests for driving while intoxicated. Within the relevant age group, 2 percent of the males and .18 percent of the females were arrested for drunk driving.

Under the traditional rational basis standard of review used in examining social and economic classifications that are not within the equal protection guarantee's scope of interest, the Court would have upheld the law. The Court, however, operated on the premise that statutory classifications of males and females are "subject to scrutiny under the Equal Protection Clause." It thus adopted a standard of review that reflected a heightened interest in classifications on the basis of gender. This standard, as announced by the Court, provides "that classifications by gender must serve important governmental objectives and must be substantially related to achievement of those objectives."

Reviewing the Oklahoma law and its underlying justification in these terms, the Court found that it violated the equal protection clause. The majority opinion, authored by Justice William Brennan, stated that the male-specific restriction on purchasing 3.2 percent beer did not adequately serve the state's regulatory objective. As the Court pointed out, the correlation between gender and traffic safety was minimal, and the law did not prohibit consumption if beer was purchased by another party. Other shortcomings in the legislative scheme included the failure to determine whether 3.2 percent beer in particular or liquor generally presented an increased risk to highway safety. The statistical evidence itself was criticized for inadequately documenting an age-sex distinction with respect to risks. Although the Court did not doubt the legitimacy of the state's interest, it concluded that the legislature had chosen a constitutionally impermissible means of achieving its objective.

Justice William Rehnquist dissented. From his perspective, the only classifications prohibited by the equal protection guarantee were those based upon race. Rehnquist also criticized the constitutional protection afforded males. Unlike traditionally burdened groups to whose interests the equal protection clause spoke, men as a general category were among those least needing protection from the political process and the will of the people.

The significance of this case is that it opened up new equal protection territory. Inclusion of gender within the scope of the equal protection guarantee reflects a phenomenon associated with the creation of any equality principle. The noted constitutional scholar Charles Fairman has observed that "equal protection as it spreads out tends to lift all to the level of the most favored."[1] The eventual determination that race required special attention under the equal protection clause established a model that, two decades later, largely was replicated for gender. In both instances, historical experiences of exclusion from the political process, disadvantage based upon membership in a group, and immutable characteristics provided a basis for special constitutional attention. Some critics maintain that because women have achieved a substantial level of influence in the political process and are a slight demographic majority, no sound basis exists for heightened judicial interest in policies that affect them. The standard of review in gender-classification cases is not as strict as that reserved for racial classifications. Still, review has reflected a heightened alertness to intolerance of classifications reflecting traditional stereotypes of women and their roles.

Note

1. Charles Fairman VII, *History of the Supreme Court of the United States* 168 (1971).

Bibliography

Ruth Colker, "Anti-Subordination above All: Sex, Race, and Equal Protection," 61 *New York University Law Review* 1003 (1986). Argues that equal protection principles should protect persons who traditionally have been subordinated by more dominant groups.

Sylvia Law, "Rethinking Sex and the Constitution," 132 *University of Pennsylvania Law Review* 955 (1984). Criticizes equal protection theory that fails to acknowledge certain biological differences.

Catharine A. MacKinnon, *Toward a Feminist Theory of the State* (1991). A critical view of equal protection doctrine as it relates to gender and of many alternative theories.

Joan C. Williams, "Deconstructing Gender," 87 *Michigan Law Review* 797 (1989). Examines competing arguments for developing gender-related equal protection doctrine.

11

Fundamental Rights

The equal protection clause of the Fourteenth Amendment provides two bases for a constitutional challenge to governmental action. An equal protection claim may arise when government classifies persons on the basis of their membership in a group. Discrimination on the basis of race and gender, and to a lesser extent alienage and illegitimacy, thus are actionable under the equal protection clause. A separate track of equal protection case law, concerned not with group status, provides for constitutional relief when a fundamental right is abridged. An equal protection claim may be raised by the member of any group who is denied a fundamental right. In *Reynolds v. Sims* (1964), the Supreme Court considered whether a legislative apportionment plan that gave rural voters more influence in the political process denied urban voters equal protection of the laws. In *Shapiro v. Thompson* (1969), it assessed whether a state's welfare eligibility requirements denied equal protection to indigent persons. At issue was whether a one-year waiting period for new residents interfered with their right to travel. In *San Antonio Independent School District v. Rodriguez* (1973), the Court addressed the question of whether disparities in the funding of a state's school districts violated the equal protection clause.

Reynolds v. Sims

Among the most fundamental guarantees in a system of representative government is the right to vote. Even though the Constitution does not specifically establish a right to vote, it protects the franchise in several ways. The Fifteenth Amendment prohibits states from denying the right to vote on grounds of race. The Seventeenth Amendment establishes that the people shall elect United States senators. The Nineteenth Amendment prohibits abridging the right to vote on grounds of gender. The Twenty-Fourth Amendment forbids poll taxes as a means of determining eligibility to vote. The Twenty-Sixth Amendment prohibits abridging the right to vote on grounds of age for citizens eighteen years of age or older. Despite the lack of any affirmative enumeration of a right to vote in the Constitution, the Supreme Court consistently has determined that the Constitution protects a citizen's franchise. As the Court observed in Westberry v. Sanders (1964), "No right is more precious in a free country than that of having a voice in the election of those who make the laws under which . . . we live. Other rights, even the most basic, are illusory if the right to vote is undermined."

Citation:	337 U.S. 533.
Issue:	Whether a state legislative apportionment plan that gave more weight to rural than urban voters violated the equal protection clause.
Year of Decision:	1964.
Outcome:	The plan was struck down on grounds that it violated the equal protection guarantee's command of one person, one vote.
Author of Opinion:	Chief Justice Earl Warren.
Vote:	8–1.

Although the right to vote may be inferred from a system of representative self-government, less certain has been the question of whether every citizen's vote must have the same weight. This issue dates back to the Republic's founding. A primary impediment to the framing of the Constitution was the debate between large and small states on the question of whether political representation should be based on a state's population or each state should have the same influence regardless of its population. Compromise was achieved by establishing a popularly elected House of Representatives based upon proportional representation and a Senate that gave each state two senators.

Many states adopted a similar formula or some other model of nonproportional representation. Despite significant demographic change, particularly the increase in urban population over the course of the twentieth century, many apportionment plans remained tied to the realities of a by-gone era. One example was an Alabama apportionment plan that was based on the 1900 federal census. Despite significant demographic change, the state for decades made no adjustments to reflect its population's redistribution. In statewide elections, ballots cast in rural districts, which had smaller populations, counted increasingly more than those in more heavily populated urban areas. Urban voters whose ballots effectively carried less weight in the political process argued that their rights had been diluted "just as effectively as by wholly prohibiting the free exercise of the franchise."

The Court confronted this problem in *Reynolds v. Sims*. At issue was an Alabama legislative apportionment plan challenged by M. O. Sims and other Alabama voters. They sued several state officials on grounds that the plan was not based on population and thus violated the equal protection clause. The Court's review of the Alabama apportionment plan commenced with an understanding "that the fundamental principle of representative governance in this country is one of equal representation for equal numbers of people, without regard to race, sex, economic status, or place of residence within a State." Noting that legislators represent people rather than "trees or acres" and are elected by voters instead of "farms or cities or economic interests," the Court was unimpressed with arguments that locale was a permissible basis for determining voting strength. Just as a state could not pass a law that doubled the weight of votes by citizens in a particular community, an apportionment plan could not dilute and undervalue ballots on the basis of where they were cast. In a majority opinion authored by Chief Justice Earl Warren, the Court determined that weighting of votes differently on the basis of residence was impermissible under the United States Constitution.

In a society grounded in representative government, the Court believed that each vote must be weighted equally. This premise, in the Court's view, was consistent with the legislature's basic function, which is to enact laws that govern all citizens. Within this framework, the Court stressed that each voter must be afforded "equal protection . . . in the election of state legislators." Despite arguments that apportionment is complex, and states may vary in their political philosophies, the Court insisted that population nonetheless must be "the starting point for consideration and the controlling criterion for judgment." As the Court put it, "The clear and strong command of our Constitution's Equal Protection Clause" is that a citizen is no more or less qualified "because he lives in the city or on the farm." The fundamental requirement of the equal protection guarantee, from the Court's perspective, was "substantially equal state legislative representation for all citizens, of all places as well as of all races." Put simply, as the Court had indicated in Baker v. Carr (1961), the Constitution secures the principle of "one person–one vote."

Unlike the federal system of political representation, state legislative systems since *Reynolds* must be apportioned entirely on the basis of population. The refusal to allow copying of the federal model reflects a perception that it emerged from "unique historical circumstances." As the Court noted, the original thirteen states surrendered some of their autonomy "to form a more perfect Union." Political subdivisions of states were not conceived, nor have they functioned, as sovereign entities. Rather, they represent "subordinate governmental instrumentalities created by the State to assist in the carrying out of state governmental functions." The federal model of nonproportionality was driven by considerations unique to the nation's founding. Compromise between large and small states resulted in a proportionately elected House of Representatives and nonproportionately elected Senate. At the state level, where these considerations were not present, the Court determined that a citizen's right to equal representation and equal weighting of his or her vote must be prioritized. As a consequence, it concluded that the equal protection clause requires "an honest and good faith effort to construct districts, in both houses of [a state legislature], as nearly of equal population as is practicable."

Although the Court determined that votes cannot be weighted on the basis of where a person lives, it did not preclude the possibility that the two bodies of a state legislature may be characterized by differences in structure and representation. The requirement of substantial equality of population among voting districts would not necessarily be undermined, for instance, by differences with respect to geographical size, terms of office, number of members, use of single-member or multimember districts, and constituencies. Moreover, the requirement of apportionment on the basis of population does not foreclose periodic revision of whatever plan the state adopts. Although Alabama's failure to reapportion since the early part of the century had compounded the constitutional damage of its system of representation, the Court noted that states were not required to readjust on a "daily, monthly, annual or biennial" basis. Although the Court did not demand reapportionment every ten years, it observed that "compliance with such an approach would clearly meet the minimal requirements for maintaining a reasonably current scheme of legislative representation."

The majority's opinion was criticized by Justices John Harlan, Jr., and Potter Stewart. Harlan believed that the federal judiciary had no constitutional right to supervise state political processes. From his perspective, apportionment of state legislatures was beyond the reach of all provisions of the federal Constitution except for Article IV, Section 4. This passage, commonly referred to as the republican form of government clause, establishes that "the United States shall guarantee to every State in this Union a Republican Form of Government." In Justice Harlan's view, this clause does not prohibit states from defining their political systems in accordance with their own priorities and values. In a similar vein, Justice Stewart maintained that the equal protection guarantee allows any rational allocation plan and only precludes those that work to defeat the will of a majority of state voters. Apart from that requirement, Stewart saw no basis in the United States Constitution for overriding the diverse traditions, preferences, and concerns of the states.

The *Reynolds* decision firmly established the Court's interest in what until the early 1960s had been regarded as a purely political question. By striking down a law that determined voting strength on the basis of residence, it demonstrated a commitment to monitoring the legitimacy and fairness of state legislative apportionment plans. The result has been a transfer of power not only from the state to the federal level but from the legislative to the judicial branch. Perhaps incongruously to some, therefore, it was the unelected branch of government that stepped forward to ensure that the will of the people is accurately and effectively expressed by the political process.

Bibliography

Carl Auerbach, "The Reapportionment Cases: One Person, One Vote—One Vote, One Value," 1964 *Supreme Court Review* 1 (1964). Criticizes opponents of the Court's decision in *Reynolds v. Sims*.

Robert H. Bork, *The Tempting of America* (1990). Argues that the Court's ruling in *Reynolds v. Sims* exemplified disregard for the Constitution.

Lani Guinier, *The Tyranny of the Majority* (1994). Expresses concern with simple majoritarianism as the basis for reapportionment.

Nelson Polsby, ed., *Reapportionment in the 1970s* (1971). Sets forth competing views on the Supreme Court's role in reapportioning state legislatures.

Shapiro v. Thompson

The right to travel freely from one state to another historically has been viewed as fundamental, even though it is not mentioned specifically in the Constitution. Even before the Constitution was framed and ratified, the Articles of Confederation recognized the right to "have free ingress and regress to and from any other State." Consistent with traditional understanding, but without indicating precisely what the constitutional source of the guarantee was, the Supreme Court in Crandall v. Nevada (1867) observed that American citizens "have the right to pass and repass through every part of" the nation.

Over the course of the Republic's history, the Supreme Court has discussed a right to travel in the context of the commerce clause and the privileges and immunities clause. The commerce clause, as discussed in Part II, responded to protectionist state economic policies that undermined a viable and efficient nation. The privileges and immunities clause of Article IV, Section 2[1], of the Constitution responded to state tendencies to favor their own citizens in distributing opportunities, advantages, and resources. State responses to problems of indigency have been a particularly fertile breeding ground for right-to-travel issues. In Edwards v. California (1941), the Supreme Court struck down a California law that prohibited anyone from helping indigent persons to migrate to the state. Such regulation, as the Court viewed it, created a barrier to trade. Although the Court recognized the state's interest in protecting its economic well-being and fiscal interests, which were burdened by large numbers of Dust Bowl refugees fleeing to California during the Great Depression of the 1930s, it determined that the law undermined the basis for a coherent and efficient national union. Four justices supported this decision, citing the Fourteenth Amendment's privileges and immunities clause. In the words of Justice Robert Jackson, federal citizenship meant nothing if by itself it was not "enough to open the gates of California. . . . Rich or penniless, . . . citizenship under the Constitution pledges [the citizen's] strength to the de-

Citation:	394 U.S. 618.
Issue:	Whether a state law that denied welfare benefits to persons who did not satisfy a one-year residence requirement was unconstitutional.
Year of Decision:	1969.
Outcome:	The one-year residence requirement violated the equal protection clause of the Fourteenth Amendment.
Author of Opinion:	Justice William Brennan.
Vote:	6–3.

fense of California as a part of the United States, and [the citizen's] right to migrate to any part of the land he must defend is something she must respect under the same instrument."

In Edwards, Jackson noted that a person's material worth "cannot be used by a state to test, qualify, or limit his rights as a citizen of the United States." Nearly three decades later, the Court's attention turned to a New Hampshire law that limited welfare benefits to persons who had resided in the jurisdiction for at least one year. The state justified this residence requirement on the grounds that persons who needed welfare assistance during their first year of residence were likely to become long-term burdens on the state's treasury. At issue in *Shapiro v. Thompson* (1969), therefore, was not whether the state could directly prohibit a person's right to travel but whether the person would be eligible for welfare. Writing for the majority, Justice William Brennan found a violation of equal protection. The basis for the constitutional wrong was a waiting period that established two classes of needy resident families, one eligible for benefits and the other not. Because such classifications had the intent of discouraging migration by poor persons, the Court determined that they were constitutionally impermissible. Although the Court acknowledged that states may attempt to limit their expenditures for welfare assistance and other programs, it emphasized that they may not do so "by invidious distinctions between classes of [their] citizens." It also rejected a differentiation between old and new residents on the basis of contributions each group had made through payment of state taxes. As the Court noted, such a distinction would allow "the State to bar new residents from schools, parks, and libraries or deprive them of police and fire protection" or to apportion all benefits and services on the basis of past tax contributions. From the Court's viewpoint, such a system would be at odds with the equal protection clause.

Typically, the equal protection guarantee only operates when official classifications are made on grounds that by their nature are suspect. Laws that distinguish on the basis of race or gender are primary examples of government line drawing that triggers more searching judicial review. Generally, the Court has repudiated the notion that distinctions on the basis of indigency require close or careful attention by the judiciary. In Dandridge v. Williams (1970), the Court rejected the argument that indigency provides a basis for stricter scrutiny of legislative acts. The one-year residence period for welfare benefits drew a close look in *Shapiro*, therefore, not because the classification itself was suspect, but because it "touche[d] on the fundamental right of interstate movement," and it was found unconstitutional for this reason. Given its impact on a fundamental right, and the Court's finding that it served no compelling interest, the waiting period could not stand.

Chief Justice Earl Warren and Justice Hugo Black dissented on grounds that the Court had departed from its traditional understanding of the right to travel. Because the state had not prohibited travel, and no other fundamental rights were implicated, they found no constitutional basis for striking down the waiting period. Warren and Black also maintained that Congress, under its commerce power, had the authority to establish residence requirements for federal public assistance programs.

Justice John Harlan, Jr., expressed particular concern with the equal protection guarantee's expansion so that it applied not only to suspect classifications but to fundamental rights. From his perspective, extension of the scope of the equal protection guarantee to a broad range of rights "would go far toward making this Court a 'super-legislature.'" Harlan believed that particularly when legislation affects concerns not mentioned in the United States Constitution, the Court should not "pick out particular human activities, characterize them as 'fundamental,' and give them added protection under an unusually stringent equal protection test." Although Harlan accepted the right to travel as a fundamental guarantee secured by the Fifth Amendment's due process clause, he concluded that the residence requirement did not impose an unreasonable burden on it. From his perspective, the state had valid fiscal and deterrent interests, and the law's impact on the right to travel was indirect and insubstantial.

The majority's rhetoric, particularly its focus upon classifications that deny "food, shelter, and other necessities of life," suggested the possibility that the Court would protect a new set of fundamental rights never enumerated by the Constitution. Indigency, however, has not become an independent basis for searching judicial review. Arguments that it should be a basis for strict scrutiny were rejected not only in Dandridge but in *San Antonio Independent School District v. Rodriguez* (1973). Indigency is a factor in constitutional review, however, when it is a basis for determining access to certain basic rights. In Douglas v. California (1963), the Court invalidated a law that denied counsel for indigent defendants in their first appeal from a criminal conviction. With respect to the right to travel itself, the Court in Memorial Hospital v. Maricopa County (1974) determined that residence requirements that barred persons from receiving county-subsidized health care violated the equal protection clause. A one-year waiting period for a divorce was upheld in Sosna v. Iowa (1975), however, on grounds that a divorce decree and provisions for custody and support required a "modicum of attachment to the State." These differing results indicate that although the right to travel is not absolute, it will be the basis for striking down laws and regulations that seriously burden the freedom to move from one state to another.

Bibliography

Chester James Antieau, *The Intended Significance of the Fourteenth Amendment* (1997). Explores the views of the Fourteenth Amendment's framers, as they relate to the right to travel.

Robert Bork, "The Impossibility of Finding Welfare Rights in the Constitution," *Washington University Law Quarterly* 695 (1979). Criticizes efforts to identify a right to the necessities of life.

Norman Dorsen, ed. *The Rights of Americans* (1971). Sets forth a friendlier view toward meeting the needs of indigents under the Constitution.

Peter Edelman, "The Next Century of Our Constitution: Rethinking Our Duty to the Poor," 39 *Hastings Law Journal* 1 (1987). Argues for constitutional doctrine that accounts more aggressively for the interests of indigents.

Bernard Harvith, "The Constitutionality of Residence Tests for General and Categorical Assistance Programs," 54 *California Law Review* 567 (1966). Examines the legitimacy of residence requirements.

San Antonio Independent School District v. Rodriguez

Over the course of the twentieth century, education has come to be regarded as the linchpin for individual development and societal progress. The value that the culture attaches to education is evident in laws that mandate schooling for children at least through high school. Although free public education through the secondary level is a national reality, this circumstance is a relatively recent phenomenon. When the Fourteenth Amendment was framed, public education was so underdeveloped and erratic that its potential as a fundamental right was not even considered. As public education and society's prioritization of it have evolved, so too have arguments that it is a basic right. The importance of education became a critical departure point for analysis that concluded with the finding that racially segregated schools are "inherently unequal" and unconstitutional. As the Supreme Court observed in *Brown v. Board of Education* (1954), education is "perhaps the most important

Citation:	411 U.S. 1.
Issue:	Whether a state school system that had funding disparities among districts violated the equal protection clause of the Fourteenth Amendment.
Year of Decision:	1973.
Outcome:	Disparities in a state's funding of school districts did not violate the equal protection clause.
Author of Opinion:	Justice Lewis Powell.
Vote:	5–4.

function of state and local governments," a fact that reflects "our recognition of the importance of education to our democratic society." The *Brown* Court stated that education is "the very foundation of good citizenship" and doubted whether "any child may reasonably be expected to succeed in life if he is denied the opportunity of an education."

Education's fundamental importance was restated in Bolling v. Sharpe (1954), in which the Court struck down official segregation of public schools in Washington, D.C. The *Brown* ruling had been based on the equal protection clause of the Fourteenth Amendment. This provision applies only to the states, and the Constitution sets forth no equivalent passage relating to the federal government. To claim jurisdiction over congressional action that resulted in the segregation of Washington, D.C., schools, therefore, the Court in Bolling read an equal protection guarantee into the due process clause of the Fifth Amendment. In so doing, it found that segregation artificially invaded a "liberty" that was protected by due process. By equating education with a constitutionally protected interest, the Bolling Court suggested that schooling was a fundamental right.

Two decades after the *Brown* and Bolling decisions, desegregation doctrine had reached its outer limits. In rulings announced during the early 1970s, the Court determined that (1) desegregation was required only to undo segregation that was caused by official government action; (2) interdistrict remedies generally were not allowable; and (3) integration did not have to be maintained unless the state caused segregation to recur. These restrictions upon desegregation indicated that the potential of the *Brown* decision for addressing disparities in educational opportunity was limited to circumstances in which racial prejudice was a central factor. Although desegregation dealt with racial inequality, it did not address other disparities in educational opportunity. Among the sources of inequality untouched by *Brown* were funding differences among school districts in a state, the issue in *San Antonio Independent School District v. Rodriguez.* Efforts to address these disparities through the Constitution focused upon Texas's system of financing public education through state contributions and local property taxes. This formula resulted in significant disparities in funding among schools statewide and even in the same community. In San Antonio, pupil expenditures for the most affluent school district were $594. For the least wealthy district, they were $356. These disparities provoked the claim by Demetrio P. Rodriguez and others on behalf of schoolchildren in economically disadvantaged school districts. They argued that the funding plan violated the equal protection clause of the Fourteenth Amendment.

The Court identified its "task" as having to determine whether Texas's method of financing its schools discriminated against indigent persons and, if so, "whether the resulting classification may be regarded as suspect." Citing prior case law, the Court noted that wealth discrimination was constitutionally significant only when a person was completely unable to pay for a particular benefit and thus was absolutely deprived of a meaningful opportunity to enjoy it. In support of this point, the Court cited its ruling in Griffin v. Illinois (1956), which struck down state laws that denied indigent criminal defendants access to trial transcripts necessary for filing an appeal. Because no showing was made that the Texas system "operate[d] to the peculiar disadvantage of the poor," and because education was not "absolutely deprived," the Court found no basis for identifying a "disadvantaged class" that merited close judicial attention.

On behalf of a five-justice majority, Justice Lewis Powell acknowledged the Court's recognition of education's value to the individual and society, but he asserted that "the importance of a service performed by the State does not determine whether it must be regarded as fundamental for purposes of examination under the Equal Protection Clause." This observation reflected the influence of those who doubted the Court's wisdom in developing as fundamental any rights not enumerated by the Constitution. Citing the dissenting opinion of Justice John Harlan, Jr., in *Shapiro v. Thompson* (1969), the Court warned that "[v]irtually every state statute affects important rights." Building further on Harlan's views, Powell stressed that judicial review driven by the Court's own understanding of what was important would transform the Court into a "super-legislature."

Consistent with these concerns, the Court stressed that "the key to discovering whether education is 'fundamental' " was not to be found in comparing its relative importance to other interests. Rather, "the answer lies in assessing whether there is a right to education explicitly or implicitly guaranteed by the Constitution." Education is not among the rights explicitly protected by the Constitution. The argument for recognizing education as a fundamental right was based in significant part upon its bearing "a peculiarly close relationship to other rights and liberties accorded protection under the Constitution." Although the Court acknowledged the relationship of education to freedom of expression and voting, which are constitutionally protected, it noted that it had no authority to guarantee "the most *effective* speech or the most *informed* choice." From the majority's point of view, methods for increasing the quality of expression or electoral choices needed to be developed by the legislature rather than "by judicial intrusion." The Court thus rejected the argument that the Constitution implied a fundamental right to education. Left open was the possibility "that some identifiable quantum of education is a constitutionally protected prerequisite to the meaningful exercise of either right." The Court found insufficient evidence, however, in support of a linkage between funding disparities and "an education that falls short." Because there was no suspect classification or fundamental right, the Court found no basis for searching review of the state's funding system and no grounds for an equal protection violation. Even if the financing method was imperfect, the Court viewed the plan as rationally related to a legitimate state purpose of facilitating local control of education.

A decade later, in Plyler v. Doe (1982), the Court reexamined the question of education as a fundamental right. At issue was a Texas law that denied state funds to educate children of illegal aliens. Although the Court acknowledged that education is not a right established by the Constitution, it noted that it also was not a mere benefit indistinguishable from other forms of social-welfare legislation. Stressing the importance of education to the individual and "our basic institutions," the Court reasoned that it could not "ignore the significant social costs borne by our Nation when selected groups are denied the means to absorb the values and skills upon which our social order rests." Having previously reserved the possibility that "some identifiable quantum of education" might be constitutionally significant, the Court prohibited the state from denying access to basic education on a categoric basis.

The question of funding disparities among Texas schools eventually was reassessed by the state's highest court. The Texas Constitution provides that the state has a duty to establish, support, and maintain "an efficient system of public free schools." The state also is obligated to provide for a "general diffusion of knowledge" that is "essential to the preservation of the liberties and rights of the people." In Edgewood Independent School District v. Kirby (1989), the Texas Supreme Court observed that the amount of money expended on a student's schooling "has a real and substantial impact on the educational opportunity offered that student." The Texas court thus held that the financing system was efficient neither financially nor in generally diffusing knowledge statewide. At the time of the Kirby decision, courts in nine other states had struck down similar funding systems for comparable reasons. Because a state supreme court is the ultimate authority on the law of the state in which it sits, the Kirby ruling was not subject to review by the United States Supreme Court. Consequently, students in Texas and similarly situated states have educational rights that are broader than those defined by federal constitutional law. The Kirby decision is a reminder that in a system of dual sovereigns, guarantees that do not exist under the law of one government may be enjoyed under the law of another government.

Bibliography

William Brennan, Jr., "State Constitutions and the Protection of Individual Rights," 90 *Harvard Law Review* 489 (1977). Notes the importance of state constitutions as a means of securing rights that are not protected by the United States Constitution.

John Coons, William Clune III, and Stephen Sugarman, *Private Wealth and Public Education* (1970). Examines funding of education and issues of wealth and disparities among districts.

Philip Kurland, "Equal Educational Opportunity: The Limits of Constitutional Jurisprudence Undefined," 35 *University of Chicago Law Review* 583 (1968). A critical inquiry into the role of the judiciary in ensuring educational opportunity.

IV

Individual Rights and Liberties

The United States Constitution, as originally framed, primarily established a scheme for assigning and distributing power among the branches of government. As the original states debated whether to ratify the Constitution, a key concern was the perceived dangers that would be presented by the new federal government. Fear that a centralized government would be a threat to individual rights and freedoms generated a movement to specify rights and liberties that the federal government could not abridge. Although many of the framers and supporters of the Constitution believed that such an itemization was unnecessary, and that the political process itself would safeguard personal liberty, support for a Bill of Rights grew from a sense of necessity and as a concession to secure ratification.

Although the Bill of Rights was initially conceived as a check against federal power, in many instances it has been made applicable to the states. This result has been achieved by the judiciary's determination that most provisions of the Bill of Rights are incorporated into the Fourteenth Amendment. In addition to being a vehicle for extending the scope of constitutionally enumerated rights and liberties, the Fourteenth Amendment has emerged as an independent source of fundamental rights. Constitutional review in the early twentieth century established economic liberty as a basic freedom that often defeated governmental efforts to regulate conditions in the workplace. Over the past few decades, the right of privacy has emerged as the basis for procreational liberty, a woman's freedom to obtain

an abortion, the right to marry, and the liberty to refuse unwanted medical treatment.

Part IV begins with an examination of decisions concerning the
First Amendment. Many regard its guarantee of freedom of
speech and of the press as our most fundamental liberty. This
right traditionally has been regarded as the foundation of self-
government. Without it, citizens would be less able to perform
their function as the ultimate decision maker in a representative
democracy. The First Amendment is focused upon not only as a
guarantee of freedom of expression but as a safeguard of freedom of association and freedom of religion.

Cases concerning the criminal justice system are another prolific
source of constitutional landmarks. Among the most prominent
decisions are rulings on searches and seizures under the Fourth
Amendment, police interrogation under the Fifth Amendment,
the right to counsel under the Sixth Amendment, and cruel and
unusual punishments under the Eighth Amendment. Finally, attention is directed to the nature of fundamental rights not enumerated by the Constitution and the debate over whether their
creation by the judiciary is legitimate.

12

The First Amendment:
Freedom of Speech

Freedom of speech has been defined by many as the most essential constitutional liberty. Without this freedom, other rights and liberties would have
less meaning. Although the freedom of speech clause is part of the First
Amendment, it did not become a subject of serious constitutional litigation
until the twentieth century. Like other constitutional provisions, its meaning has evolved from debate over its underlying values and the contexts in
which freedom of expression should be protected. Much of this conflict
might have been avoided if freedom of speech had been considered an
absolute right, as Justice Hugo Black held it to be. The Supreme Court,
however, persistently has rejected this premise. As the Court has defined
and amplified the guarantee of freedom of speech, it has become clear that
the First Amendment has different meanings in different settings. A hierarchy of speech freedom thus has emerged that is more protective of some
types of expression than others. Within this order, speech pertaining to
governance is most favored. Commercial expression and certain types of
defamatory speech are less protected. Some forms of expression, such as
obscenity and fighting words, are entirely unprotected by the First Amendment. Constitutional analysis of speech that is within the scope of the First
Amendment's meaning largely is an exercise in balancing the interests of
freedom of expression against the significance of official regulatory concerns.

Speech That Advocates Illegal Action

Much of what defines freedom of speech has emerged from challenges
to government's ability to suppress or punish political protest. In *Schenck*

v. United States (1919), Justice Oliver Wendell Holmes, Jr., introduced the concept that government may not regulate speech that advocates overthrow of the political order or other illegal action unless there is a "clear and present danger" that the evil will occur. The limited security that this test afforded to freedom of expression, at least in its early years, was evident in early Supreme Court decisions such as *Schenck* that imposed harsh sentences upon those who merely articulated and acted upon their disagreement with government policy. Even as this tendency persisted in the early years of doctrinal development, the framework for principles that provided more protection to dissent and protest was emerging. Among the most eloquent statements on the value of freedom of expression and the need to tolerate and protect speech that challenges the very foundations of the political system is the concurring opinion of Justices Louis Brandeis and Holmes in Whitney v. California (1927). Their views, which trumpeted the virtues of the marketplace of ideas and the need for government to allow free competition among political views, ideologies, and programs, ultimately prevailed. The Court's ruling in *Brandenburg v. Ohio* (1969) reflects Holmes's and Brandeis's influence in framing contemporary understanding of freedom of speech.

Schenck v. United States

The most fundamental constitutional right is that of freedom of speech and of the press. More than two centuries before the Constitution was drafted, John Milton wrote that "the liberty to know, to utter, and to argue freely according to conscience, [w]as above all liberties." The Supreme Court, in Palko v. Connecticut (1937), described freedom of expression as "the matrix, the indispensable condition of every other form of freedom."

Despite the First Amendment's profundity, the Supreme Court did not resolve any cases under the freedom of speech clause until the twentieth century. The absence of litigation on this front did not indicate a lack of official censorship or other efforts to suppress expression. Within a decade of the First Amendment's ratification, Congress enacted the Sedition Act, which criminally punished persons who criticized the national legislature or president "with intent to defame . . . or to bring them . . . into contempt or disrepute." The enactment represented a political

Citation:	249 U.S. 47.
Issue:	Whether a conviction for distributing antiwar leaflets to military personnel violated the First Amendment guarantee of freedom of speech.
Year of Decision:	1919.
Outcome:	Freedom of speech does not protect speech that creates a clear and present danger that government has a valid interest in preventing.
Author of Opinion:	Justice Oliver Wendell Holmes, Jr.
Vote:	9–0.

strategy to silence Jeffersonian critics of the John Adams administration. Several years later, after Thomas Jefferson was elected president, the law was repealed, but not before it was used against his own critics. Although the Supreme Court never reviewed the Sedition Act, it later observed that "the attack upon its validity had carried the day in the court of history." In *New York Times Co. v. Sullivan* (1964), it referred to "a broad consensus that the Act, because of the restraint it imposed upon criticism of government and public officials, was inconsistent with the First Amendment."

The Court's first step toward developing doctrine on freedom of speech responded to arguments that the Espionage Act of 1917 was unconstitutional. This law, reviewed in *Schenck v. United States* (1919), prohibited distribution of antidraft literature that was "calculated to cause . . . insubordination and obstruction" of military recruiting. Charles Schenck, who was general secretary of the Socialist Party, had overseen the printing of 15,000 leaflets that characterized the draft as a violation of the Thirteenth

Amendment, criticized World War I as a "monstrous wrong against humanity in the interest of Wall Street's chosen few," and urged recipients to assert their rights. Writing for the Court, Justice Oliver Wendell Holmes, Jr., observed that the literature "in many places and in many times" would have been constitutionally protected. Given wartime conditions and the increased need for protection of national security, however, the Court emphasized the need to take "circumstances" into account. Noting that the documents would not have been disseminated unless they were intended to have an effect, the Court found that they were calculated to promote resistance to and obstruction of the war effort.

After reiterating that the expression "in ordinary times" would have been constitutionally protected, the Court observed that "the character of every act depends upon the circumstances in which it was done." At this point, Holmes introduced what has become a classic illustration of the First Amendment's limits. As he put it, "[t]he most stringent protection of free speech would not protect a man in falsely shouting fire in a theater and causing a panic." In every case, therefore, the question "is whether the words used are used in such circumstances and are of such a nature as to create a clear and present danger that they will bring about the substantive evils that Congress has a right to prevent."

Holmes's formulation of the clear and present danger test focused upon the harm that might result from expression. Because the ruling criminalized political dissent, it generated significant criticism. Detractors maintained that the clear and present danger test, as Holmes originally conceived it, punished expression not on the basis of predictable, real, or imminent harm but because of its potentially evil consequences. Contemporaneous decisions demonstrated the aptness of such criticism. In Frohwerk v. United States (1919), the Court upheld Espionage Act convictions of antidraft protesters who published literature that criticized American participation in the war and praised Germany. As author of the Court's opinion, Justice Holmes noted that these "words of persuasion" were not within the First Amendment's scope of protection. In Debs v. United States (1919), the Court upheld the conviction of a prominent politician and socialist for expressing opposition to the war in a public speech. The First Amendment scholar Harry Kalven, Jr. described Eugene V. Debs's imprisonment as comparable to putting 1972 Democratic Party presidential nominee George McGovern "in prison for his criticism of the [Vietnam] War."[1] From his prison cell in 1920, Debs garnered nearly one million votes in an unsuccessful candidacy for the presidency.

As initially applied, the clear and present danger test showed little potential for protecting freedom of expression. The formula, however, soon evolved into a much more protective regimen. Within a year of the aforementioned decisions, Justice Holmes dissented from the Court's affirmation of convictions for encouraging resistance to the war effort. The majority opinion in Abrams v. United States (1920) made no mention of clear and present danger principles. It merely concluded that speech with a harmful tendency could be prohibited. In a dissenting opinion joined by Justice Louis Brandeis, Holmes advocated a more effective standard for freedom of expression. Building upon the clear and present danger formula of *Schenck*, he urged a distinction between expression that was aimed toward imminently producing an illegal action and speech that merely had a dangerous but remote tendency. Holmes thus introduced the "marketplace of ideas" theory that has become a foundation of First Amendment analysis. This concept reflects the sense "that the ultimate good desired is better reached by free trade in ideas—that the best test of truth is the power of the thought to get itself accepted in the competition of the market." Knowing that "time has upset many fighting faiths," Holmes offered a clear and present danger test that precluded any abridgment of expression except in emergency circumstances. Only when time was insufficient to allow the marketplace of ideas to work because a threat was imminent did Holmes support a restriction on speech. From his perspective, the twenty year prison terms affirmed in Abrams for violation of the Espionage Act were imposed for exercising "the same right to publish as the Government has to publish the Constitution of the United States."

Despite indications in *Schenck* that wartime circumstances were unique factors that militated against freedom of expression, postwar cases were no friendlier to political dissent. In Gitlow v. New York (1923), the Court upheld convictions of persons who disseminated publications that advocated political strikes. As the Court saw it, speech was punishable if it was aimed toward a "substantive evil" regardless of the chance that the evil would materialize. The Court in Whitney v. California (1927) affirmed convictions under a law that prohibited "advocating, teaching or aiding and abetting . . . crime, sabotage . . . or unlawful acts of force or violence" as a means of achieving economic or social change. At issue was whether a member of the Communist Labor Party could be convicted for her assistance in organizing a group that was dedicated to change through illegal action, attendance at a party meeting, and membership in the group. Finding that "united and joint action involves even greater danger to the public peace and security than the isolated utterances and acts of individuals," the Court was unmoved by a First Amendment claim.

However, evolution continued toward a doctrine that was more protective of expression. Justice Brandeis's concurring opinion, joined by Justice Holmes, in Whitney criticized the Court for failing to develop standards for determining "when a danger shall be deemed clear; how remote the danger may be and yet be present; and what degree of evil shall be deemed sufficiently substantial to justify resort to abridgment of free speech and assembly as the means of protection." To fill in this perceived void, Brandeis began with the premise that "[t]hose who won our independence by revolution were not cowards . . . [and] did not fear political change . . . or exalt order at the cost of liberty." In Brandeis's words,

> No danger flowing from speech can be deemed clear and present, unless the incidence of the evil apprehended is so imminent that it may befall before there is opportunity for full discussion. If there be time to expose through discussion the falsehood and fallacies, to avert the evil by the processes of education, the remedy to be applied is more speech, not enforced silence. Only an emergency can justify repression. . . . [Even then], imminent danger cannot justify resort to prohibition of these functions essential to effective democracy, unless the evil apprehended is relatively serious.

Although the Holmes-Brandeis model of First Amendment analysis did not prevail in Gitlow and Whitney, case law soon began to move in their direction. In DeJonge v. Oregon (1937), the Court struck down a law on grounds that freedom of expression could not be abridged without "incite[ment] to violence and crime." The influence of Holmes and Brandeis was even more noticeable in Herndon v. Lowry (1937), in which the Court struck down the conviction of a Communist Party organizer for inciting insurrection by promoting "equal rights for the Negroes and self-determination of the Black Belt." In doing so, the Court emphasized that speech could not be punished merely for its harmful tendencies without considering the probability that a harm or evil would result. A few more decades passed before the Court fully committed itself to the doctrinal legacy of Holmes and Brandeis. Eventually, their imprint on First Amendment case law became indelible, and freedom of expression became more secure.

Note

1. Harry Kalven, Jr., "Professor Ernst Freund and Debs v. United States," 40 *University of Chicago Law Review* 235, 237 (1973).

Bibliography

Zechariah Chafee, Jr., *Free Speech in the United States* (1948). One of the earliest and most influential works on freedom of expression.

Leonard Levy, *Legacy of Suppression* (1960). Explores the nation's experience under the Sedition Act.

Robert K. Murray, *Red Scare: A Study of National Hysteria, 1919–1920* (1955). A study of the political and social context of the early freedom of speech cases.

William Preston, Jr., *Aliens and Dissenters: Federal Suppression of Radicals, 1903–1933* (1983). Examines governmental efforts to punish dissenters in the early part of the twentieth century.

Brandenburg v. Ohio

Free speech doctrine in its early stages demonstrated a serious vulnerability to the nation's temper at a given time. During the Red Scare of the 1920s, when anxiety and hysteria over aliens and radicals were at a peak, First Amendment jurisprudence upheld punishment of speech that challenged or criticized established authority. Although the clear and present danger test formulated by Justices Oliver Wendell Holmes, Jr., and Louis Brandeis evolved into a mainstream principle in the late 1930s, sensitivity toward freedom of expression continued to vary with the times. The Holmes-Brandeis model initially was approved in Bridges v. California (1941), in which the Supreme Court observed that the " 'clear and present danger' cases [reflect] a working principle that the substantive evil must be extremely serious and the degree of imminence extremely high before utterances can be punished."

The Court's fidelity to clear and present danger principles

Citation:	395 U.S. 444.
Issue:	Whether a state law that prohibited advocacy of political change by means of violence abridged freedom of speech.
Year of Decision:	1969.
Outcome:	The freedom of speech clause prohibits government from punishing mere advocacy of illegal action.
Author of Opinion:	*Per curiam.*
Vote:	9–0.

was tested by the Cold War atmosphere of the 1950s. In Dennis v. United States (1951), it considered the constitutionality of a federal law that prohibited "knowingly or willfully advocat[ing], abet[ting], advis[ing], or teach[ing] the duty, necessity, or propriety of overthrowing or destroying any government in the United States by force or violence." In upholding the convictions of Communist Party organizers under the statute, the Court raised doubts about the nature and vitality of the clear and present danger test. Although the Court stated that it was employing the clear and present danger test, it actually used a diluted version of it. Writing for a plurality, Chief Justice Fred Vinson maintained that it was necessary to focus on "whether the gravity of the 'evil,' discounted by its improbability, justifies such invasion of free speech as is necessary to avoid the danger." This standard of review essentially discounted the need for showing that any harm was imminent. The key factor for the Court was whether the possibility of harm in the near or distant future was of sufficient magnitude. To prohibit speech that presented a risk of harm, proximate or remote, government was not required to wait until the "*putsch* is to be executed."

The Dennis decision suggested a reversion to the "bad tendency" standard that had governed early free speech decisions in the post–World War I era. Decisions after Dennis, however, reflected an increasingly rigorous application of First Amendment principles. In Yates v. United States (1957), the Court refused to affirm convictions of Communist Party members who had been tried on charges of advocating and teaching forcible overthrow of the government. The Yates ruling reclaimed some lost constitutional ground by stressing that the Dennis decision had not "obliterated the traditional dividing line between advocacy of abstract doctrine and advocacy of action." The Court observed that "those to whom the advocacy is addressed must be urged to *do* something, rather than merely to *believe* in something." In Scales v. United States (1961), however, the Court rejected arguments that a risk of harm must be proximate before speech can be punished. It thus attempted to quell any doubt that "present advocacy of *future* action for violent overthrow satisfies . . . constitutional requirements equally with advocacy of *immediate* action to that end." Under this reasoning, the Court upheld a conviction that was based upon a defendant's knowing membership in an organization dedicated to violent overthrow of the United States.

Despite the Court's insistence upon proof of a specific intent to incite violent insurrection, uncertainty about the vigor of free speech doctrine persisted. The possibility that First Amendment standards would be strengthened further manifested itself in Bond v. Floyd (1966). At issue in this case was whether a state legislator's criticism of the Vietnam War constituted incitement of illegal conduct. Because of this expression, the Georgia legislature had denied the legislator the seat to which he had been elected. The Court found a First Amendment violation and ordered the legislature to administer the oath of office to him.

The most crucial doctrinal event with respect to clear and present danger principles was the Court's ruling in *Brandenburg v. Ohio*. At issue in *Brandenburg* was the conviction of a Ku Klux Klansman under an Ohio law that prohibited advocacy of "the duty, necessity, or propriety of crime, sabotage, violence, or unlawful methods of terrorism as a means of accomplishing industrial or political reform." From the earliest First Amendment interpretation in the 1920s, criminal syndicalism laws like these routinely had been upheld. The basis for the conviction in *Brandenburg* was a statement that "[w]e are marching on Congress on July Fourth, four hundred thousand strong. From there we are dividing into two groups, one group to march on St. Augustine, Florida, the other group to march into Mississippi." Audience response to the speech included such comments as "[t]his is what we are going to do to the niggers," "[s]end the Jews back to Israel," "[s]ave America," "[b]ury the niggers," "[w]e intend to do our part," and "[f]reedom for the whites."

In striking down the Ohio statute, the Court formally abandoned decades of case law that had enabled government periodically to prohibit and punish speech based upon mere advocacy. Citing its recent First Amendment decisions, the Court embraced "the principle that the constitutional guarantees of free speech and free press do not permit a State to forbid or proscribe advocacy of the use of force or of law violation except where such advocacy is directed to inciting or producing imminent lawless action and is likely to incite or produce such action." Particularly fatal to the Ohio law was its punishment of mere advocacy. Under *Brandenburg*, speech may not be punished unless it is connected with "incitement to imminent lawless action."

The *Brandenburg* decision conclusively rejected the premise that speech may be punished merely because it has a harmful tendency. The Court expanded its constitutional inquiry beyond asking whether speech is intended to incite illegal action. Punishment of speech that advocates illegal action is permissible only if the harm is imminent and likely. The imminence requirement, in particular, introduced a significantly higher level of protection of speech into First Amendment doctrine. Its impact was soon evidenced. In Hess v. Indiana (1973), the Court considered the proximity of harm in reversing a disorderly conduct conviction of an antiwar protester who had screamed to a police officer that "[w]e'll take the fucking street later." Because the defendant's statement at worst urged illegal action at some future time and was not addressed to any group in particular, the Court found no evidence of an intent and likelihood to produce imminent disorder.

Despite its strengthening of free speech doctrine, the Court was criticized for not making it rigorous enough. Justice Hugo Black maintained that clear and present danger principles had "no place in the interpretation of the First Amendment." Similarly, Justice William O. Douglas saw "no place in the regime of the First Amendment for any clear and present danger test." From their perspectives, clear and present danger doctrine was too easily warped by society's mood, temperament, and sense of security. Given a history of uneven and often harsh results over the course of half a century, Black and Douglas doubted whether standards of imminence and likelihood of harm could withstand the fears and paranoia that accompany war or perceived threats to the social order. Their point is reinforced by First Amendment scholar Thomas Emerson, who observed that the clear and present danger test permits suppression of political speech whenever it presents the possibility of becoming effective. Both Douglas and Black would have rejected the clear and present danger test in favor of absolute protection for speech that was not coupled with actual illegal action. From their viewpoint, doctrine that fell short of absolute protection ignored the reality that "[e]very idea is an incitement."

Although reality since *Brandenburg* has been characterized by more consistent protection of political dissent, the clear and present danger test also has demonstrated its vulnerability to social passions. Incidents of flag burning during the 1980s triggered prosecutions that raised First Amendment concerns. By the barest of margins, the Court reversed convictions and invalidated the flag-desecration laws. Such episodes suggest that freedom of expression is not served just by the formality of tests for protection of speech. Rather, effective protection requires an appreciation of the value speech has for a society characterized by diverse ideas and people and predicated upon informed self-governance.

Bibliography

Thomas Emerson, *The System of Freedom of Expression* (1970). Sets forth a comprehensive theory of freedom of speech.

Harry Kalven, Jr., *A Worthy Tradition* (1987). Examines the issues related to speech that advocates illegal action.

Hans Linde, " 'Clear and Present Danger' Reexamined," 22 *Stanford Law Review* 1163 (1970). Assesses clear and present danger principles from a critical perspective.

Frank Strong, "Fifty Years of 'Clear and Present Danger:' From *Schenck* to *Brandenburg*," 1969 *Supreme Court Review* 41 (1969). Traces the history of the clear and present danger test over the half century preceding *Brandenburg*.

Defamation

Defamation, or injury to reputation, can result from the spoken word (slander) or the written word (libel). Slanderous or libelous expression historically has been subject to regulation and punishment. Criticism of the king or queen at one time in England was punishable by death. Truth was not a defense but an aggravating factor. Although penalties for defamation became less severe, such speech nonetheless remained beyond the protection of the First Amendment. Beginning in the 1960s, the Supreme Court extended constitutional protection to certain types of defamation. Recognizing the value of speech that was essential for informed self-government, the Court in *New York Times Co. v. Sullivan* (1964) established an "actual malice" standard that required public officials to prove that a false statement about them was made with knowledge of its falseness or in reckless disregard of the truth. In *Gertz v. Robert Welch, Inc.* (1974), the Court determined that this standard, although applicable to public figures, did not extend to private persons.

New York Times Co. v. Sullivan

Defamation historically has been beyond the scope of First Amendment protection. Defamatory speech is expression that injures reputation by means of falsehood in the form of the spoken word (slander) or the written word (libel). The traditional view of defamatory speech is that it has slight, if any, social value. This understanding was confirmed in Beauharnais v. Illinois (1952), in which the Supreme Court upheld an Illinois law that prohibited speech that por-trayed any group in terms of "depravity, criminality, un-chastity, or lack of virtue ... [because] of any race, color, creed or religion" or subjected any class of citizens "to con-tempt, derision, or obloquy" or that produced "breach of the peace or riots." The Court thus affirmed a conviction based upon dissemination of a leaflet that urged "white men and women" to "preserve and protect white neighborhoods from the constant and contin-uous invasion, harassment and encroachment by Negroes." A

Citation:	376 U.S. 254.
Issue:	Whether defamation of a public official is protected speech under the First Amendment.
Year of Decision:	1964.
Outcome:	The First Amendment protects statements that defame a public official provided they are not made with "actual malice."
Author of Opinion:	Justice William Brennan.
Vote:	9–0.

central theme of the circular was that "forced mongrelization" of neigh-borhoods was "degrad[ing] the white race" and subjecting it to the criminal "aggressions ... of the Negro." Despite the state's interest in reducing ra-cial tension and degradation, Justice Hugo Black warned of the risks in-herent in regulating even harmful speech. Stressing that a law that protects group reputation has particularly oppressive possibilities when it is used by a majority group against a minority group, Black commented that "any minority groups who hail this holding as their victory, ... might consider the possible relevancy of this ancient remark: 'Another such victory and I am undone.' "

Justice Black's concerns about regulating harmful speech materialized into reality when the elected police commissioner of a southern city sued civil rights activists and the *New York Times* for publishing an advertise-ment that criticized Montgomery, Alabama, police for their handling of a protest on a state college campus. Demonstrators had assembled to protest official acts of intimidation and violence aimed at deterring peaceful civil rights protests led by Dr. Martin Luther King, Jr. The editorial, signed by

64 persons who were prominent in public affairs, religion, organized labor, and the arts, contained some minor inaccuracies. Typifying the factual errors were statements that

> [t]he students sang The Star Spangled Banner, not My Country 'Tis of Thee; nine students were expelled, not for leading the demonstration, but for demanding service at a lunch counter in the county courthouse; the dining hall was never padlocked; police at no time ringed the campus though they were deployed nearby in large numbers; they were not called to the campus in connection with the demonstration; Dr. King had been arrested only four times; and officers disputed his account of the alleged assault.

Based upon the editorial, which described a "wave of terror" against nonviolent civil rights demonstrators, the city Commissioner of Public Affairs, L. B. Sullivan, sued for libel. Sullivan's responsibility included supervising city police. A jury found that the false statements were libelous and awarded him half a million dollars in damages. These damages were not based on any proof of reputational injury but, as state law allowed, an injury presumed by the jury. Left untouched, this ruling would have been an effective weapon for blunting the civil rights movement. Because defamation was entirely unprotected by the First Amendment, the result was consistent with constitutional understanding at the time. To undo the state court decision, it was necessary to redefine the First Amendment. This result was achieved when the Supreme Court declared in *New York Times Co. v. Sullivan* that defamatory expression was constitutionally protected under certain circumstances.

The Court's analysis commenced with reference to "a profound national commitment to the principle that debate on public issues should be uninhibited, robust, and wide-open, and that it may well include vehement, caustic, and sometimes unpleasantly sharp attacks on government and public officials." Given the particular importance of an informed citizenry in a system of representative government, the Court stressed the need for political expression to have ample breathing space, at least when public officials are concerned.

Writing for the majority, Justice William Brennan referred to a "general proposition that freedom of expression upon public questions is secured by the First Amendment." The principle of freedom of expression, as Brennan explained it, was designed to guarantee "unfettered interchange of ideas for the bringing about of political and social changes desired by the people." Quoting from Judge Learned Hand, whose writings and rulings had been a significant influence on the development of free speech theory during the first half of the twentieth century, the Court observed that the First Amendment "presupposes that right conclusions are more likely to be gathered out of a multitude of tongues, than through any kind of authoritative selection. To many this is, and always will be, folly; but we have staked upon it our all." As an expression of "grievance and protest," the editorial was viewed as the type of speech that most deserved First Amendment protection.

In defamation cases, truth typically is a defense. Because sharp differences may arise with respect to what the truth is, and it may elude discovery altogether, the Court reasoned that truth by itself was an insufficient basis for constitutional protection. Acknowledging that advocacy of a point of view often includes exaggeration, vilification, and even falsehood, the Court nonetheless noted that freedom of expression is so essential to enlightened opinion that abuse and excess must be tolerated. In a society premised upon free debate, the Court further observed that erroneous statements not only are inevitable but must be protected if freedom of expression is to have a sufficient margin of tolerance for survival. Protection of speech that injures official reputation, therefore, reflected a sense that the benefits for informed self-governance outweighed the harm to individuals.

The Court feared inevitable self-censorship if critics of official conduct were required to prove the truth of their factual assertions. Because of doubt with respect to whether the truth could be proved in court or because of the cost associated with litigation, critics might mute their criticism to avoid the risk of liability. As the Court put it, such a rule would induce critics "to make only statements which steer far wide of the unlawful zone." If truth was the only defense to defamation, at least when public officials were the victims, the Court viewed the risk to vigorous public discourse as excessive. In addition to the defense of truth, therefore, the Court established a new First Amendment standard for defamation actions. Under *Sullivan*, a public official may not obtain "damages for a defamatory falsehood relating to his official conduct unless he proves that the statement was made with 'actual malice.' "

The actual malice standard speaks not to spite but to degree of knowledge by the defendant. Actual malice exists when a defamatory statement is made "with knowledge that it was false or with reckless disregard of whether it was false or not." Dimensions of the actual malice standard have been defined by case law since *Sullivan*. As the Court observed in Harte-Hanks Communications, Inc. v. Connaughton (1989), reckless disregard requires "a high degree of awareness of probable falsity" or a showing that the speaker or publisher "entertained serious doubts as to the truth of the publication." Mere negligence, such as a failure to check sources or investigate the basis for an assertion, thus does not suffice to establish actual malice.

Two key terms in the Court's opinion are "public official" and "official conduct." Decisions since *Sullivan* generally have identified public officials as persons who exercise significant responsibility in the conduct of state affairs. Official conduct has been defined broadly to include not only actions in office but actions that reflect upon a person's qualifications for office. The net result is a privilege for defamation of public officials that is roughly congruent with the immunity that they enjoy against being sued personally for acts committed in the scope of their official duties.

Adoption of the actual malice standard imposed a major disability upon public officials, who traditionally had been able to sue for statements that defamed them. The decision reflected prioritization of First Amendment values, especially the theory that political expression must be particularly safeguarded as a means for ensuring informed government by the people. Enthusiasm for the actual malice standard, however, has not been universal. Justice Byron White, who participated in the majority decision, eventually came to regret and criticize it. Two decades later, in Dun & Bradstreet, Inc. v. Greenmoss Builders, Inc. (1985), White concluded that "the Court struck an improvident balance . . . between the public's interest in being informed about public officials and public affairs and the competing interests of those who have been defamed in vindicating their reputation." In his view, the Court's tolerance of falsehood had created conditions that compromised the information marketplace. Because the actual malice standard allows certain lies to stand and the public to be misinformed, White maintained that it was a source of unacceptable harm to society.

Regardless of the debate the actual malice standard has engendered, its adoption represented a significant rebalancing of regulatory and constitutional interests. Defamation had traditionally been so strongly censured that until the mid-eighteenth century, truth was not a defense and actually was an aggravating factor in determining damages. Injury to reputation, whether based on a true or a false statement, was a basis for recovery. Official power to protect reputation, as the *Sullivan* case evidenced, provided a significant opportunity for abuse and repression. Defamation actions by public officials could be and have been weapons for silencing voices of change, protest, and dissent. Without the Court's intervention, Alabama defamation law would have operated as a mechanism against those who challenged the systematic deprivation of civil rights and official disregard of human equality. Regardless of the criticism it has generated, the *Sullivan* ruling represents a classic statement of the central values associated with a system of free expression.

Bibliography

Anthony Lewis, "*New York Times v. Sullivan* Reconsidered: Time to Return to 'The Central Meaning of the First Amendment,' " 83 *Columbia Law Review* 603 (1983). Examines the importance of the *Sullivan* decision in enabling civil rights groups to protest and the media to cover southern resistance to racial change.

Alexander Meiklejohn, *Free Speech and Its Relation to Self-Government* (1948). Upholds the need to protect expression necessary for informed self-governance.

John Stuart Mill, *On Liberty* (1859). A classic statement of the value of freedom of expression, regardless of its truth or falsity.

Gertz v. Robert Welch, Inc.

The Supreme Court's determination in *New York Times Co. v. Sullivan* (1964) that public officials must meet a higher standard of proof to prevail in a defamation action represented a significant First Amendment advance. Because the Court protected speech that pertained to self-government even though that speech was false and damaging to reputation, it was widely applauded for vindicating the First Amendment's central meaning. Because the higher standard of proof reflected an appreciation of the value that political speech has in a democracy, the logic that singled out public officials potentially was extendable to other persons or contexts that might be relevant to informed self-government. Four years after the *Sullivan* decision, in Curtis Publishing Co. v. Butts (1968), the Supreme Court introduced the concept of "public figures" and asserted that they too should have to prove more than the ordinary person in a defamation action. The Court described public figures as those persons who are "intimately involved in the resolution of important public questions or [who], by reason of their fame, shape events in areas of concern to society at large." Given their roles and a public interest similar to what exists with public officials, the Court extended the actual malice standard to public figures.

Citation:	418 U.S. 323.
Issue:	Whether private persons, like public officials and public figures, are subject to the actual malice standard when they sue for defamation.
Year of Decision:	1974.
Outcome:	Private persons who sue for defamation are not required to establish actual malice.
Author of Opinion:	Justice Lewis Powell.
Vote:	5–4.

Expansion of the actual malice standard to another category of persons soon provoked arguments that with respect to speech that was essential for informed self-government, it was the nature of the expression rather than the status of the person to whom it pertained that was relevant. Four justices in Rosenbloom v. Metromedia, Inc. (1971) thus advocated enlarging the scope of the actual malice standard so that it applied to "statements concerning matter[s] of general or public interest." Only Justice Hugo Black's insistence that freedom of speech was absolute, and that defamation laws were barred by the First Amendment, prevented the public interest standard from becoming adopted as the law of the land. Pressure continued for further broadening of the actual malice standard, however, and the Court eventually confronted again whether the actual malice standard should refer to the status of the plaintiff or the nature of the controversy. The issue was raised when Elmer Gertz, an attorney who had brought a wrongful-death action on behalf of a family whose son had been shot by a Chicago police officer, claimed that he had been defamed by a publication of the John Birch Society. The suit was brought against Robert Welch, Inc., which published *American Opinion*—a monthly magazine disseminating the John Birch Society's anti-Communist views. The article inaccurately described Gertz as the "architect [of a] Communist frame-up" and the subject of an extensive police file. If applicability of the actual malice standard turned upon whether the story pertained to an issue of general or public concern, the speech would be protected. It would also be safeguarded if the Court, as it was asked to do, extended the actual malice criterion to private persons.

Writing for a majority of the Court, Justice Lewis Powell concluded that the actual malice standard applied only to public officials and public figures. Recognizing that some tension is inevitable between the need for "vigorous and uninhibited" expression and valid interests in redressing reputational injury, the Court noted its recent history of providing some "strategic protection" to defamatory speech. It found no logic, however, for stretching the actual malice standard beyond defamation of public persons. Only public officials and those persons "who by reason of the notoriety of their achievements or the vigor and success with which they seek the public's attention are properly classified as public figures" were found subject to a higher standard of proof in a defamation action. Public figures, like public officials, thus have to demonstrate that a defamatory statement "was made with knowledge of its falsity or with reckless disregard for the truth."

The Court acknowledged that the standard, although it was a "powerful antidote" to self-censorship, exacted "a correspondingly high price from the victims of defamatory falsehood." The greater burden was justified, however, on grounds that significant differences existed between public and nonpublic defamation plaintiffs and the First Amendment concerns that were involved. A primary distinction, for instance, is the relative ability of public and nonpublic persons to obtain a defamation remedy by "self-help." The Court noted that public officials and figures typically command greater access to the channels of communication than private persons. They thus "have a more realistic opportunity to counteract false statements than private individuals normally enjoy."

Even more important than this disparity in vulnerability based on status was the Court's sense that public officials and figures, by their decisions to seek government office or the limelight, assume greater risks of public scrutiny. Either as a candidate for government office or as a result of having assumed "especial prominence in the affairs of society," public persons "invite attention and comment." Even if these perceptions are not valid in every instance, the Court determined that the "media are entitled to act on the assumption that public officials and public figures have voluntarily exposed themselves to increased risk of injury from defamatory falsehood concerning them." No such assumption, the Court found, was warranted with respect to private individuals. Having neither sought public office nor assumed a role of influence, such a person relinquished no interest in protecting his or her "good name." The Court thus concluded that private persons not only were more vulnerable to defamatory injury but more deserving of relief.

The line between public figures and private persons may not always be easy to draw. The Court observed that public figures actually consist of three types. What it characterized as "involuntary public figures" are persons who attain that status through no purposeful action of their own. They constitute an "exceedingly rare" category. A second group of public figures consists of persons who "occupy positions of such pervasive power and influence that they are deemed public figures for all purposes." What the Court characterized as the most common type of public figure consists of those who "have thrust themselves to the forefront of particular public controversies in order to influence the resolution of the issues involved." Given these choices, the essential task for the Court was identifying the category into which Gertz fit.

As a member of various government commissions and because he served as an attorney and thus was an officer of the court in which he litigated the wrongful death action, Gertz arguably might have been characterized as a public official. The Court found that the defamatory statements did not pertain to his general government service, and the actual malice standard would be extended too far if every attorney was subject to it. The Court rejected the notion that Gertz was a public figure who had attained that status involuntarily or on the basis of any pervasive power or influence. Despite Gertz's numerous community service activities, the Court determined that he had not voluntarily thrust himself into the public eye. From the Court's perspective, therefore, Gertz was a private person who did not have to be bound by the actual malice standard in seeking relief. The net result was a double standard in defamation actions—one that subjects public officials and figures to the actual malice standard and another that allows states to define the appropriate standard for private persons provided that the law does "not impose liability without fault."

In a dissenting opinion, Justice Byron White complained that the decision catered too much to the media. As he saw it, the press was strong enough to accept responsibility and pay for any defamatory harm to a private citizen even if liability was imposed without fault. Justice Brennan was concerned that the ruling left significant gaps in the First Amendment's coverage. In particular, he warned that self-censorship would result when matters of public interest concerned persons who had no public status. The

White and Brennan perspectives typify critical reaction that has argued, respectively, that the Court's decision overly indulged the law of defamation and was too insensitive toward the First Amendment.

Subsequent case law has veered more toward White's concerns than Brennan's. In Time, Inc. v. Firestone (1976), the Court found that a well-known Palm Beach socialite was not a public figure in the context of a divorce proceeding. The proceeding had attracted widespread attention because of extensive testimony that, in the trial judge's words, would have "made Freud's hair curl." Although evidence of this nature dominated the proceeding, the news article wrongly stated that a divorce had been granted on grounds of extreme cruelty and adultery. Although the process was public, and the plaintiff held news conferences throughout it, the Court concluded that she had not voluntarily injected herself into "the forefront of any particular public controversy in order to influence the resolution of the issues involved in it." Three years later, in Wolston v. Reader's Digest Association (1979), the Court found that the passage of time had transformed a former public figure into a private person. Taken together, the Firestone and Wolston decisions suggest that conscious entry into the definition of a public issue is essential for purposes of qualifying as a public figure. Achievement of that status, however, does not necessarily create a public figure for all time.

Bibliography

Gerald Ashdown, "*Gertz* and *Firestone*: A Study in Constitutional Policy-Making," 61 *Minnesota Law Review* 645 (1977). Explores the consequences of the *Gertz* decision.

Steven Shiffrin, "Defamatory Non-media Speech and First Amendment Methodology," 25 *UCLA Law Review* 915 (1978). Examines the logic of distinguishing between categories of plaintiffs and defendants in defamation actions.

Obscenity

Like defamatory expression, obscenity historically has been regarded as beyond the scope of the First Amendment. Unlike defamation, which in recent decades has achieved qualified constitutional protection when the plaintiff is a public official or figure, obscenity remains categorically unprotected by the First Amendment. During the colonial era and during and after the framing and ratification of the Constitution, laws prohibiting blasphemy and vulgar, profane, and obscene language were widespread. Their enforcement, however, tended to be spotty. By the late nineteenth century, the federal government had become a primary source of antiobscenity statutes. The Comstock Act, passed in 1873, made it a crime to disseminate obscene materials through the mail. This enactment led to confiscation not only of commercial pornography but of scientific and philosophical works and information about contraceptives. Such enactments were based upon Congress's power to regulate commerce among the several states. As the Supreme Court saw it in Ex parte Jackson (1877), Congress's power to regulate what could be mailed included the power to exclude material from the mail. Such a result would be constitutionally intolerable if the expression at issue was political rather than obscene. In *Roth v. United States* (1957), however, the Supreme Court referred to a "universal judgment that obscenity should be restrained." Consistent with its determination in *Roth*, the Court consistently has refused to give constitutional currency to claims that obscene expression should be protected by the First Amendment. Through the first half of the twentieth century, determinations of what constituted obscenity were made under a test originally adopted in England. Borrowing from Queen v. Hepburn (1868), federal courts typically inquired "[w]hether the tendency of the matter charged as obscenity is to deprave and corrupt those whose minds are open to such immoral influences." Although it has struggled to define obscenity, the Court has not wavered in its resolve to view obscenity as beyond the margins of constitutionally protected speech. This determination was evident in *Miller v. California* (1973), a decision that defines contemporary obscenity doctrine.

Roth v. United States

In 1957 the Supreme Court squarely confronted the question of whether obscenity is protected by the First Amendment. At issue was the conviction of Samuel Roth for mailing obscene materials in violation of California and federal law. Drawing upon a history of extensive regulation dating back to the nation's founding, the Court identified sufficient evidence "to show that obscenity . . . was outside the protection intended for speech and press." Despite the First Amendment's "unconditional phrasing," the Court observed that the free speech and press clauses were "not intended to protect every utterance." Their purpose, as the Court saw it, was "to assure unfettered interchange of ideas for the bringing about of political and social changes desired by the people." Constitutional security thus was limited to "ideas having even the slightest redeeming social importance." Although unorthodox, controversial, and even hateful expression was protected, the First Amendment's history had rejected obscenity as being "utterly without redeeming social importance." Citing *Chaplinsky v. New Hampshire* (1942), the Court reaffirmed the proposition that "[t]here are certain well-defined and narrowly limited classes of speech" beyond the First Amendment's purview. Obscene speech is one of these classes of expression that, from the Court's perspective, "are no essential part of any exposition of ideas, and are of such slight social value as a step to truth that any benefit that may be derived from them is clearly outweighed by the social interest in order and morality." Finding no value in obscenity, the Court held that it "is not within the area of constitutionally protected speech or press."

Citation:	354 U.S. 476.
Issue:	Whether obscene expression is protected by the First Amendment.
Year of Decision:	1957.
Outcome:	Obscenity is not protected by the freedoms of speech and the press.
Author of Opinion:	Justice William Brennan.
Vote:	6–3.

The determination that obscenity is categorically without First Amendment protection meant that its harm need not be demonstrated on a case-by-case basis or balanced against constitutional interests. In *Roth v. United States*, obscenity laws were challenged on grounds that they punished "incitation to impure *thoughts*, not shown to be related to any overt antisocial conduct." The argument was that persons should not be convicted without proof that obscene expression creates "a clear and present danger of antisocial conduct." The case for inquiry into specific harm was foreclosed, however, by the determination that obscenity is not constitutionally protected speech. Nor was the Court impressed with arguments that sex and obscenity are synonymous. Noting that sex is "a great and mysterious motive force in human life" and a subject of "absorbing interest to mankind through the ages," the Court distinguished obscenity as material "which deals with sex in a manner appealing to prurient interest." Although the Court stressed that the portrayal of sex in art, literature, and scientific works was within the scope of the First Amendment, such protection did not extend to material that appealed to "prurient interest[s]." To distinguish between protected and unprotected sexually explicit materials, therefore, a definition of obscenity was crucial. The Court noted that traditional standards for determining obscenity focused upon the effect of isolated passages in materials and risked encompassing material that legitimately dealt with sex. To avoid that problem, it adopted a test that asked "whether to the average person, applying contemporary community standards, the dominant theme of the material taken as a whole appeals to the prurient interest."

The ruling generated two significant dissenting opinions. Justice John Harlan, Jr., objected to the federal role in prohibiting obscenity. Noting that Congress has no power over sexual morality, he asserted that the interests addressed by federal obscenity laws are primarily entrusted to the care of the states. Harlan viewed a federal presence in the field as particularly dangerous to free thought and expression. Although states might vary in their attitudes toward a particular work of literature, a "blanket ban" of a given work would destroy the prerogative of states to "differ on their ideas of morality." Justice William O. Douglas, joined by Justice Hugo Black, found the decision troubling because it made "the legality of a publication turn on the purity of thought which a book or tract instills in the mind of the reader." From their perspective, the majority's standard was not "faithful to the command of the First Amendment."

Douglas's dissent reflects many of the arguments that have been articulated by critics of the *Roth* decision. If obscenity convictions could be obtained for the "arousing of sexual thoughts," Douglas believed that censorship could operate freely "over a vast domain." Without the need to prove unlawful action, laws regulating obscenity merely on the basis of "an *undesirable* impact on thoughts" represented to him a drastic curtailment of First Amendment freedom. Although Douglas conceded that a nexus between impure sexual thoughts and action might put obscenity laws on less dangerous footing, he argued that no "dependable information" established such a connection. In the absence of such evidence, he stressed the importance of avoiding "the losses to society that result from interference with literary freedom."

Douglas was particularly troubled by tying a determination of offensiveness to community standards. His concern was that juries would use criteria of "sexual impurity" or identify tendencies "to incite lustful thoughts" as a cover for decisions to censor, suppress, or punish expression that they merely disliked. As Douglas put it, "community censorship . . . creates a regime where in the battle between the literati and the Philistines, the Philistines are certain to win." From his perspective, the lesson of history was "that censorship of obscenity has almost always been both irrational and indiscriminate." Finding "no special historical evidence" that literature concerning sex was to be excluded from the First Amendment, he also warned of the constitutional risks associated with the Court's judging whether a particular form of expression has "redeeming social importance." Douglas regarded the First Amendment as an absolute prohibition designed to preclude the judiciary and legislature from weighing the value of speech under any circumstance. If a test may suppress "a cheap tract today," Douglas warned that it "can suppress a literary gem tomorrow." The opportunities for judges or juries to outlaw books because they incite or arouse lascivious thoughts or lustful desires, in Douglas's view, were endless.

Douglas's dissent illuminated the primary point of division within the Court. Future case law would refocus on the question of whether government could punish mere thoughts or, as Douglas urged, must demonstrate that they are "so closely brigaded with illegal action as to be an inseparable part of it." The Court effectively avoided the question in *Roth* by asserting that any constitutional inquiry was foreclosed once it was determined that the speech at issue in a particular case was without First Amendment protection. In Stanley v. Georgia (1969), the Court noted that obscenity's unprotected status did not foreclose the possibility of constitutional protection in all instances. Although the Court identified an important government interest in regulating commercial distribution of obscenity, it found that the First Amendment was violated by a law that prohibited possession of obscene material in the privacy of one's home. Justice Thurgood Marshall concluded that the rationales for obscenity's unprotected status did not "reach into the privacy of one's own home." Writing for the majority, he reasoned that the First Amendment means nothing unless "it means that a State has no business telling a man, sitting alone in his own house, what books he may read or what films he may watch. Our whole constitutional heritage rebels at the thought of giving government the power to control men's minds." Despite this reservation of First Amendment security for in-home possession of obscene materials, the Court reaffirmed government's general power to regulate obscenity as a constitutionally unprotected form of expression.

Bibliography

Harry Clor, *Obscenity and Public Morality* (1969). Examines the premise of the *Roth* decision and the Court's reasoning.

Richard Posner, *Sex and Reason* (1992). Argues that pornography is not without social value and actually advances First Amendment interests.

Frederick Schauer, *Free Speech: A Philosophical Inquiry* (1982). Proposes the notion that obscenity is not speech and is more akin to sexual acts.

Miller v. California

Obscenity, as the Supreme Court determined in *Roth v. United States* (1957), is among the categories of speech that lack any constitutional protection. By excluding obscenity on a wholesale basis from the First Amendment's scope of concern, the Court established a model for review that was relatively simple in nature. If expression is found obscene, no further inquiry is necessary into whether government is justified in punishing it. Reality, however, has been more complex. A prerequisite for any finding of obscenity is a definition of what constitutes it and how it is distinguishable from other forms of sexually explicit expression.

A decade after *Roth*, the Court had yet to adopt a definition of obscenity that commanded majority support. In Memoirs v. Massachusetts (1966), three justices proposed a test for determining whether material was obscene. Under their suggested standard, government had to establish

that (a) the dominant theme of the material taken as a whole appeals to a prurient interest in sex; (b) the material is patently offensive because it affronts contemporary community-

standards relating to the description or representation of sexual matters; and (c) the material is utterly without redeeming social value.

Citation:	413 U.S. 15.
Issue:	Whether expression must be utterly lacking in redeeming social value to be found obscene.
Year of Decision:	1973.
Outcome:	Expression is obscene when (1) the average person applying contemporary community standards finds that it appeals on the whole to prurient interests; (2) it depicts in a patently offensive way sexual conduct specifically defined by state law; and (3) taken as a whole, it lacks serious literary, artistic, political, or scientific values.
Author of Opinion:	Chief Justice Warren Burger.
Vote:	5–4.

Justice Potter Stewart perhaps best illustrated the vexing nature of the task of definition. Stewart candidly suggested that efforts to capture the meaning of obscenity required "trying to define what may be undefinable." Consistent with his sense that attempts to define obscenity were futile, Stewart operated on the premise that "I know it when I see it." As the Court continued to decide obscenity cases without a settled standard of review, it provoked criticism that its decisions were merely subjective. In *Miller v. California* (1973), the Court acknowledged that the concern had merit. As the Court stated, it had adopted "the role of an unreviewable board of censorship for the 50 states, subjectively judging each piece of material brought before us." Chief Justice Warren Burger conceded that standards for determining obscenity were inadequate and stressed the Court's interest in eliminating the "strain" that a steady flow of obscenity cases had created for the court system. To address these concerns, the Court thus sought to formulate a viable definition of obscenity.

At issue was the conviction of Marvin Miller, who had mailed advertisements consisting primarily of pictures and drawings "very explicitly depicting men and women in groups of two or more engaging in a variety of sexual activities, with genitals often prominently displayed." Mailing of such materials violated a California law that prohibited the knowing distribution of obscene materials. Writing for the majority, Chief Justice Burger commenced his analysis with the premise that state regulation of obscenity "must be carefully limited" and confined "to works which depict or describe sexual conduct." The conduct that is the basis for an obscenity finding, Burger noted, must be defined specifically. Against this backdrop, the Court defined obscenity as "works which, taken as a whole, appeal to the prurient interest in sex, which portray sexual conduct in a patently offensive way, and which, taken as a whole, do not have serious literary, artistic, political, or scientific value." By themselves, these standards offered general guidance. Recognizing a need for amplification, the Court provided more specific instructions on how juries should apply them. "Prurient interest," according to the Court, had to be determined from the perspective of "the average person, applying contemporary community standards." Whether a work was "patently offensive" had to be measured against a law that "specifically defined" the relevant sexual conduct. As the Court noted, the "serious literary, artistic, political, or scientific value" standard was less rigorous than the "utterly without redeeming social value criterion."

Instead of announcing a single formula, the Court left to each state the task of defining obscenity in specific terms. Although the Court noted that its function was not "to propose regulatory schemes for the States," it nonetheless provided a model that would satisfy the requirement for "specifically defined acts" presented in a "patently offensive way." State law was sufficient if it barred "[p]atently offensive representations or descriptions of ultimate sexual acts, normal or perverted, actual or simulated," and "[p]atently offensive representation or descriptions of masturbation, excretory functions, and lewd exhibition of the genitals." Material of this nature qualifies as obscene if it does not have "serious literary, artistic, political, or scientific value." Cited as an example of protected expression were "medical books for the education of physicians." Although their "graphic illustrations and descriptions of human anatomy" may reflect a scientific value, it also might be argued that they neither appeal to the prurient interest nor are patently offensive representations of sexual acts or other specifically described sexual conduct.

The use of contemporary community standards as the benchmark for assessing prurient interest and patent offensiveness represented an effort by the Court to steer the question of obscenity from a national to a local forum. It also reflected a sense that uniform standards for what constitutes obscenity are impossible for a nation that "is simply too big and too diverse." The Court considered it neither realistic nor constitutionally wise to require "that the people of Maine or Mississippi accept public depiction of conduct found tolerable in Las Vegas, or New York City." In formulating its standards, the Court was driven by an understanding that "[p]eople in different States vary in their tastes and attitudes, and this diversity is not to be strangled by the absolutism of imposed uniformity." Defending itself from criticism that it was siding with the forces of "repression," the Court maintained that historical experience with obscenity control had not impaired serious literary, artistic, political, or scientific expression. Because the First Amendment was designed to protect free and robust exchange of ideas and political debate, the Court saw no harsh hand or repression of political liberty "lurking" behind state efforts to regulate "commercial exploitation of human interest in sex." On the contrary, the majority maintained that equating political speech with commercial trading in obscenity actually cheapened "the grand conception of the First Amendment and its high purposes in the historic struggle for freedom."

Although Justice William O. Douglas described the majority's opinion as "earnest and well intentioned," he held fast to his general view of the First Amendment as an absolute guarantee. As he saw it, the First Amendment was unconditional in its protection of expression and did not allow the Court to remove categories of speech from its scope. Douglas maintained that to implement what he described as "a regime of censorship," a "constitutional amendment after full debate by the people" was necessary. A judge's or jury's power to punish ideas because they are offensive represented a development that Douglas found "astounding." This development represented "a sharp and radical break with the traditions of a free society" that keep debate open to "offensive" as well as "staid" people. Douglas acknowledged that the material before the Court "may be garbage," but he observed that "so too is much of what is said in political campaigns, in the daily press, on TV, or over the radio." Because much of this "garbage" may not be sexual in nature, Douglas's concern was that speech regulation on grounds of offensiveness had the potential to expand and eventually to ensnare expression that historically has been valued and protected. Douglas concluded that judges were without constitutional power to define obscenity, and until the people by constitutional amendment decided whether and what to ban as obscene, the Court had no guidelines "except our own predilections."

Justice William Brennan wrote a particularly notable dissent. Brennan had authored the Court's opinion in *Roth* that determined that obscenity was constitutionally unprotected. He abandoned that position, however, because the problem of defining obscenity was too great and the constitutional costs of applying vague standards were too high. Brennan, whose dissent in *Miller* actually was published in another obscenity decision, Paris Adult Theater I v. Slaton (1973), adopted a position that was more attentive to constitutional interests. Specifically, he argued that sexually oriented materials could be prohibited only when necessary to protect juveniles and unconsenting adults.

Despite the pleas of dissenting justices, the *Miller* test continues to operate in the context of obscenity. Questions persist with respect to whether obscenity can be precisely defined. Justice Antonin Scalia has suggested that "[j]ust as there is no use arguing about taste, there is no use litigating about it." While some have questioned the extent to which the Court has foreclosed attention to the First Amendment issues that obscenity regulation might present, other theorists maintain that standards should be based not upon obscenity's lack of value but upon the harm that it causes to women. During the 1980s, some municipalities adopted antipornography ordinances that prohibited sexually explicit materials. These laws were based on the theory that pornography facilitates society's traditions of subordinating women by characterizing them as sex objects, diminishing their worth, and reinforcing harmful ways of viewing women. The Supreme Court, in American Booksellers, Inc. v. Hudnut (1985), reviewed an Indianapolis law of this nature. It affirmed a federal appeals court decision that had struck down the law. The appeals court stressed that freedom of speech assumes the risk that insidious expression may "influence the culture and shape of our socialization." It further noted that "if a process of [cultural] conditioning were enough to permit governmental regulation, that would be the end of freedom of speech." Unsatisfactory as the obscenity experience has been for the Court and its various critics, who have objected for different reasons, the *Miller* test has survived a quarter of a century of challenge to its presence on the constitutional landscape.

Bibliography

Susan Brownmiller, *Against Our Will: Men, Women, and Rape* (1976). Explores the notion that pornography is a source of affirmative harm to women, rather than merely lacking in value.

Final Report of the Attorney General's Commission on Pornography (1986). A government study that found a relationship between pornography and aggression toward women.

Report of the Commission on Obscenity and Pornography (1970). This federal
   commission, which published its report a few years before the *Miller* decision, found no linkage between obscenity and antisocial behavior.
Nadine Strossen, *Defending Pornography* (1995). Argues that freedom even for
   pornographic expression advances women's interests more effectively than
   suppression.

Fighting Words

   Like obscenity, fighting words historically have been beyond the scope
of the First Amendment. Both have been placed beyond the scope of constitutional concern because, as the Supreme Court observed in *Chaplinsky
v. New Hampshire* (1942), they are viewed as inessential to "the exposition
of ideas" and have "such slight social value as a step toward truth." Obscenity and fighting words also have similar characteristics because both
are difficult to define. This problem has been much more of a barrier to
enforcement of laws prohibiting fighting words than to obscenity prosecutions. Decisions by the Supreme Court since *Chaplinsky* largely have
overturned convictions on grounds that regulation does not adequately distinguish fighting words from otherwise sharp, provocative, but protected
speech. Efforts to expand the fighting words concept generally have been
repulsed by First Amendment principle. In *Cohen v. California* (1971), the
Court drew a line between speech that induces individualized violent reactions and expression that is simply offensive. The Court in *R.A.V. v. City
of St. Paul* (1992), however, added a somewhat unexpected twist to the
concept of unprotected speech. Striking down an ordinance that regulated
hate speech as fighting words, it nonetheless referenced First Amendment
safeguards against content and viewpoint discrimination.

Chaplinsky v. New Hampshire

Protection of expression tends to be most grudging when speech is offensive or provocative. Constitutional guarantees tend to be less imperative when expression is orthodox or unchallenging. The First Amendment is far more crucial for defending speech that unsettles or disturbs its audience.

Tension between society's interest in maintaining public order and its commitment to freedom of speech has manifested itself historically in codes that regulate decorum and propriety. Speech control in colonial America maintained not only protocol but social hierarchy. In New England, the law provided sanctions for servants who spoke disrespectfully of their masters and wives who characterized their husbands in negative terms. The value assigned to formality, appearance, and civility is manifested by official record and anecdote. Among the numerous revealing incidents of the time was a "falling out" between a Virginia couple. A witness found the wife with "her hair about her ears" and upset with what she characterized as her "base rascal" of a husband. For this verbal indiscretion, a Virginia court ordered her "tied to the back of a boat and dragged up and down the James River."

Citation:	315 U.S. 568.
Issue:	Whether fighting words are protected by the First Amendment.
Year of Decision:	1942.
Outcome:	Fighting words are not protected by the First Amendment.
Author of Opinion:	Justice Frank Murphy.
Vote:	9–0.

Not surprisingly for a society that traditionally has been mistrustful or skeptical of authority, government has been a primary target of antagonistic and offensive expression. Because of colonial resentments toward England, contact with government officials frequently strained the interests of civility. Expressions of anger or disrespect toward government generated regulation that reflected an interest in maintaining peace, order, and the integrity of governmental institutions. The colonial experience is replete with instances of persons being sentenced or fined for visiting verbal indignities upon government officials. Although amusing in retrospect, these examples demonstrate how fragile the concept of freedom of expression was. Similar episodes of more recent vintage indicate how brittle the guarantee remains.

The value of speech that is annoying, derisive, or insulting was considered in *Chaplinsky v. New Hampshire* when a city marshal in Rochester, New Hampshire, attempted to stop Walter Chaplinsky, a Jehovah's Witness, from distributing religious literature on a street corner. The defendant responded to this effort by calling the marshal a "God damned racketeer," telling him that he was "a damned Fascist and the whole government of Rochester are Fascists or agents of Fascists." As a consequence of his verbal tirade, he was prosecuted under a state law providing that "[n]o persons shall address any offensive, derisive or annoying word to any other person who is lawfully in any street or other public place, nor call him by any offensive or derisive name, nor make any noise or exclamation in his presence and hearing with intent to deride, offend or annoy him, or to prevent him from pursuing his lawful business or occupation."

Responding to arguments that the state's punishment of "fighting words" violated freedom of speech, the Court commenced its analysis with the observation that the free speech guarantee "is not absolute at all times and under all circumstances." Among those categories of expression that find no shelter in the First Amendment are "the lewd and obscene, the profane, the libelous, and the insulting or fighting words." The Court characterized "fighting words" as expression that by its "very utterance inflict[s] injury or tend[s] to incite an immediate breach of peace." Consistent with the then-contemporary view of obscenity and defamation, the Court dismissed fighting words as having "no essential part of any exposition of ideas" and possessing "slight social value as a step toward truth." The low value assigned to fighting words reflected the Court's sense that any social benefit resulting from them was outweighed by society's "interest in order and morality." Also revealed was a belief system with respect to what constituted valid ways of communicating opinions and thoughts. Citing Cantwell v. Connecticut (1940), the Court noted that "[r]esort to epithets or personal abuse is not in any proper sense communication of information or opinion safeguarded by the Constitution."

Like the problem of identifying obscenity, which is discussed in *Miller v. California* (1973), the primary challenge to the concept of fighting words is defining it. For definitional purposes, the Court referred to the state law and its focus on words tending directly "to cause acts of violence by the person to whom, individually, the remark is addressed." It did not enumerate or provide examples specifically of what these words or expressions might be. It noted, however, that there are numerous terms commonly understood as " 'fighting words' when said without a disarming smile." Words that persons of "common intelligence" know are likely to cause a fight are actionable when they have the plain tendency "to excite the addressee to a breach of peace." Without such an "excitement," the Court indicated that annoying and derisive words by themselves are not actionable. From the Court's perspective, it was evident that terms such as "damned racketeer" and "damned Fascist" were likely triggers for retaliation by the average person and thus an evil that the state could regulate.

Exclusion of fighting words from the First Amendment's scope of protection has generated extensive critical commentary and questions about the Court's underlying theory. Even if fighting words are viewed as having slight value in society's effort to discern truth, they are a means of self-expression that may divert anger and hostility from conduct to expression. It is not inconceivable that such speech may be the essence of political expression. Calling a policeman a "fascist," for instance, may be a short-hand way of drawing attention to oppressive attitudes, policies, or actions. The characterization, even if it provokes a hostile reaction, also may be true. The narrow line between fighting words and political expression requires a high level of sensitivity in distinguishing between provocative and offensive speech in isolation and such expression with political overtones.

In cases in which offensive expression has political implications, the Court consistently has reversed fighting words convictions. In Gooding v. Wilson (1972), the Court struck down a state law that had been applied to a defendant who, among other things, said to a police officer, "white son of a bitch, I'll kill you" and "[y]ou son of a bitch, if you ever put your hands on me again, I'll cut you to pieces." In Lewis v. New Orleans (1974), the Court noted that vulgar and offensive speech is protected by the First Amendment. It thus found a statute used to convict a defendant for saying "you goddamn mother fucking police" vague and overbroad because it punished constitutionally protected expression. Although the Court has never eliminated the fighting words doctrine, case law over the past half century has narrowed its operation. Unless fighting words are used in a face-to-face confrontation, modern case law is unfriendly toward regulation that punishes such expression. Because Supreme Court review is discretionary rather than a matter of right, it is worth noting that many convictions have not been subject to review at the highest level. Even though fighting words doctrine is concerned with a narrow category of unprotected speech, it persists as a potential if not regular source of conflict with First Amendment values.

Bibliography

Larry D. Eldridge, *A Distant Heritage* (1994). A historical perspective on regulating insulting, offensive, or disrespectful expression.

Stephen W. Gard "Fighting Words as Free Speech," 58 *Washington University Law Quarterly* 531 (1980). Explores the vitality and impact of fighting words doctrine in the lower courts.

Martin Redish, *Freedom of Expression* (1984). Propounds a First Amendment theory that is friendly to fighting words and emphasizes not just informed self-governance, but also the individual's interest in self-realization.

Cohen v. California

Speech has the capacity to offend in a variety of ways and for a variety of reasons. Expression that is sexually explicit, for instance, may unsettle some people's sense of morality. If speech is found obscene, it may be prohibited. Burning of a flag or a draft card may upset those who feel strongly about what these symbols represent. Speech that effectively makes a point to certain segments of society may be regarded as blasphemous, appalling, and distressful in other quarters.

The extent to which taste should be a factor in determining constitutional protection has been a persistent theme of First Amendment debate. When a pornographic magazine depicted a well-known evangelist in morally depraved but fanciful terms, the Supreme Court considered how far the First Amendment's boundaries extend when taste or lack of taste is concerned. At issue in Hustler Magazine v. Falwell (1988) was a parody of a popular liquor advertisement titled "Jerry Falwell

Citation:	403 U.S. 15.
Issue:	Whether the First Amendment prohibits regulation of expression that offends public morality.
Year of Decision:	1971.
Outcome:	The First Amendment prohibits regulation of words merely because they offend.
Author of Opinion:	Justice John Harlan, Jr.
Vote:	5–4.

Talks about His First Time." Included in the takeoff was a fabricated interview in which Falwell stated that his "first time" was during an incestuous encounter with his mother in an outhouse. Doubtless, the magazine's contempt for Falwell could have been expressed in less shocking terms. Reversing a jury award for damages based upon intentional infliction of emotional distress, the Court noted that "many things done with motives that are less than admirable are protected by the First Amendment." The risk of punishing expression on the basis of its outrageousness, the Court reasoned, is too great because "it would allow a jury to impose liability on the basis of the jurors' tastes or views, or perhaps on the basis of their dislike of a particular expression."

The Falwell decision illustrates the First Amendment maxim "that one man's vulgarity is another's lyric." This premise reflects an understanding that results from a vigorous and extended debate over society's interest in civil discourse. It was at the heart of the constitutional controversy that arose when Paul Robert Cohen entered Los Angeles County Courthouse wearing a jacket that bore the words "Fuck the Draft" on its back. Upon entering the courtroom, Cohen removed his jacket and stood with it folded over his arm. A policeman sent the presiding judge a note that suggested that Cohen be arrested for contempt of court. Although the judge refused, the policeman arrested Cohen when he left the courtroom. For the way in which he expressed opposition to the Vietnam War, Cohen was convicted under a state law that prohibited "maliciously and willfully disturb[ing] the peace or quiet of any neighborhood or person . . . by . . . offensive conduct." Because Cohen engaged in no act other than wearing the jacket and generated little if any risk of a violent response, his conviction rested "solely upon 'speech.' " As Justice John Harlan, Jr., observed for a majority of the Supreme Court, the state had no power to punish Cohen for the message that he conveyed. The Court observed that if he could be convicted at all, it could only be for the manner in which he exercised his freedom. This possibility, however, proved to be more theoretical than real under the circumstances of the case.

Noting that neither obscenity nor fighting words were at stake, and the speech at issue thus was not without First Amendment protection, the Court considered the argument that "Cohen's distasteful mode of expression was thrust upon unwilling or unsuspecting viewers." Although the Court noted that the rule may be different when unwanted expression invades the privacy of the home, it observed that "we are often 'captives' outside the sanctuary of the home and subject to objectionable speech." Without a significant privacy interest at stake as a basis for shutting off discourse, government authority to control offensive speech would "empower a majority to silence dissidents simply as a matter of personal predilections." Unlike the plight of a captive audience, those who would be exposed to and offended by the message could "avoid further bombardment of their sensibilities simply by averting their eyes." The privacy interest of persons in a public courthouse, as the Court saw it, fell short of "the interest in being free from unwanted expression in the confines of one's own home."

From the Court's perspective, the issue was reducible to whether California, "acting as guardians of public morality, may properly remove this offensive word from the public vocabulary." In assessing whether the state possessed such power, the Court stressed that the First Amendment aims to remove governmental restrictions from the arena of public discussion and put "the decision as to what views shall be voiced largely into the hands of each of us, in the hope that use of such freedom will ultimately produce a more capable citizenry and more perfect polity." For many persons, the Court acknowledged, such freedom generates "only verbal tumult, discord, and even offensive utterance." As the Court saw it, the fact that "the air may at times seem filled with verbal cacophony is . . . not a sign of weakness but of strength." Even though speech may seem annoying or trifling, the Court noted that it also may serve fundamental societal values.

Further leading the Court toward the First Amendment interest was its sense that the state's interest in regulating offensive speech seemed "inherently boundless." Because it could not distinguish Cohen's message "from any other offensive word," the Court viewed the state law as an effort "to cleanse public debate to the point where it is grammatically palatable to the most squeamish among us." Even if Cohen's chosen terminology might have been distasteful, the Court believed that government officials could not make principled distinctions with respect to what constitutes proper expression. As a consequence, the better and constitutional choice was to leave "matters of taste and style . . . largely to the individual."

The Court also noted the "dual communicative purpose" that much expression serves. As Harlan observed, speech conveys not only ideas but otherwise inexpressible emotions. Words sometimes are chosen not just for their cognitive force but for their emotional impact. Because this emotive function may even be the more important aspect of expression, the Court was particularly reluctant to interpret the First Amendment in a way that diminished this dimension. Quoting Justice Felix Frankfurter in Baumgartner v. United States (1944), the Court added that a "prerogative[ ] of American citizenship is the right to criticize public men and measures—and that means not only informed and responsible criticism but the freedom to speak foolishly and without moderation." Consistent with this perspective, the Court refused to "indulge the facile assumption that one can forbid particular words without also running a substantial risk of suppressing ideas in the process." Without a compelling or particularized reason for punishing Cohen's speech, the Court concluded that the state could not make his four-letter expletive a criminal offense.

In a dissenting opinion joined by Chief Justice Warren Burger and Justice Hugo Black, Justice Harry Blackmun described the "absurd and immature antic" as "mainly conduct and little speech." This characterization put the expression into the category of fighting words and thus would have upheld the conviction.

The decision in the *Cohen* case represents a particularly forceful statement on behalf of expressive pluralism and cultural tolerance. The notion that persons can avert their eyes from unwanted expression was reaffirmed in Erznoznik v. Jacksonville (1975), in which the Court struck down a city law that prohibited offensive motion pictures on outdoor movie screens visible from a public street. Considerations of privacy prevailed, however, when the Court upheld the Federal Communications Commission's determination that it could prohibit profane language on radio and television. In *Federal Communications Commission v. Pacifica Foundation* (1978), the Court emphasized that broadcasting "confronts the citizen, not only in public, but also in the privacy of the home, where the individual's right to be left alone plainly outweighs the First Amendment rights of an intruder." This decision was not unfaithful, however, to the *Cohen* ruling, which had noted the special privacy interest affecting the home. As the Court put it in *Pacifica*, when government "finds that a pig has entered the parlor, the exercise of its regulatory power does not depend on proof that the pig is obscene."

Bibliography

William Cohen, "A Look Back at *Cohen v. California*," 34 *UCLA Law Review* 1595 (1987). A retrospective view of the Court's ruling in *Cohen*.

Nat Hentoff, *The First Freedom* (1980). Discusses the background and context of the *Pacifica* case.

Robert C. Post, "The Constitutional Concept of Public Discourse: Outrageous Opinion, Democratic Deliberation, and *Hustler Magazine v. Falwell*," 103 *Harvard Law Review* 601 (1990). Examines the competing interests of expressive freedom and civilized discourse.

Michael J. Sandel, *Democracy's Discontent* (1996). A view of *Cohen v. California* as indicating a shift from self-government to self-fulfillment as grounds for First Amendment protection.

Suzanna Sherry, "An Essay Concerning Toleration," 71 *Minnesota Law Review* 963 (1987). Explores the imperative of tolerance in a culturally diverse society.

R.A.V. v. City of St. Paul

Civil rights and freedom of expression historically have been mutually re-inforcing. During the 1950s and 1960s, the First Amendment was an essential weapon in the struggle for civil rights. As protesters marched, demonstrated, and organized against racial segregation and discrimination, southern states frequently responded with arrests, censorship, and other repressive methods. Amid systematic intimidation, the First Amendment provided shelter from official efforts to silence the voices of change. So critical was freedom of expression to the civil rights movement in the face of official repression and suppression that constitutional scholar Harry Kalven, Jr., credited "the Negro with reclaiming the First Amendment freedom of all Americans."[1]

Despite the First Amendment's crucial role during the civil rights era, the 1980s brought arguments that racial justice in some instances might be served better by suppressing rather than protecting speech. Concern with the impact of hate speech on minorities generated speech codes in numerous communities and on college campuses. The case for prohibiting hate speech is predicated upon the notion that it verbally assaults and seriously injures its victims. Such expression has been described as an "instantaneous slap in the face"[2] that chills rather than facilitates dialogue. It also has been described as an "implement" of racism that works "in coordination, reinforcing conditions of domination."[3]

Citation:	505 U.S. 377.
Issue:	Whether a city ordinance that prohibited symbols arousing resentment on the basis of race, color, creed, religion, or gender violated the First Amendment.
Year of Decision:	1992.
Outcome:	The ordinance discriminated on the basis of content and viewpoint and thus violated the First Amendment.
Author of Opinion:	Justice Antonin Scalia.
Vote:	9–0.

Advocates of regulation maintain that hate speech deters members of historically subordinated groups from living where they choose, traveling freely, fully participating in the political process, and exercising their full range of constitutional liberties. Speech-code critics, however, express concern that regulation chills important expression and ineffectively promotes racial equality. These issues eventually made their way to the Supreme Court in *R.A.V. v. City of St. Paul* (1992). At issue was a city ordinance making it a crime to place on public or private property a symbol or object, such as a swastika or burning cross, with reason to know that it would cause anger, alarm, or resentment on grounds of race, religion, color, creed, or gender. Several teenagers who burned a cross inside the fenced yard of a black family's home were convicted under the law. Use of the petitioner's initials, R.A.V., reflected the state's interest in protecting the identity of minors. The Minnesota Supreme Court found that the ordinance legitimately prohibited fighting words, which, as determined in *Chaplinsky v. New Hampshire* (1942), are constitutionally unprotected. It thus upheld the law.

In a majority opinion authored by Justice Antonin Scalia, the United States Supreme Court decided that the ordinance was unconstitutional. The Court restated its long-held view that fighting words can be prohibited because of their "slight social value." It noted that despite their categorically unprotected status, however, fighting words are not "entirely invisible to the Constitution." Government, the Court noted, may not single out and punish certain words or views even though they otherwise may be unprotected uncategorically. Just as an ordinance could not reserve defamation actions for a favored group, it "may not regulate use based on hostility—or favoritism—toward the underlying message expressed." This wrinkle altered traditional understanding that unprotected speech does not fall within the scope of the First Amendment.

The Court's emphasis on the law's selective focus reflected a concern that government power, if not restrained, could drive certain thoughts or perspectives from the information marketplace. With respect to the St. Paul ordinance, the majority determined that it applied only to symbols or displays that insulted or provoked violence on several specified grounds. Left unchecked were "displays containing abusive invective, no matter how vicious or severe, . . . [not] addressed to one of the specified disfavored topics." The Court thus determined that the city unconstitutionally had discriminated on the basis of content by imposing "special prohibitions on those speakers who express views on disfavored subjects." The Court also found the ordinance objectionable because it established a preferred viewpoint. Under the regulatory scheme, fighting words could be punished only when they were uttered toward, rather than by, a minority. The Court accordingly refused to uphold the city's "authority to license one side of a debate to fight freestyle, while requiring the other to follow Marquis of Queensbury rules."

The Court acknowledged that culturally diverse communities had the responsibility to reckon with racism when it manifested itself. Such efforts, however, had to be through strategies that did not impose a "selective limitation upon speech." The Court stressed that fighting words are categorically excluded from the First Amendment's protection, not because they communicate a particular idea, but because they represent "a particularly intolerable (and socially unnecessary) mode of expressing whatever idea the speaker wishes to convey." Because the city had not singled out a particularly offensive "mode" of expression, but had focused upon a particular message, the Court discerned an unconstitutional effort "to handicap the expression of particular ideas." The city attempted to persuade the Court that the law was an essential means of "ensuring the basic human rights of members of groups that have historically been subjected to discrimination, including the right of such group members to live in peace where they wish." Although the Court did not doubt the compelling nature of these interests, it stressed that content or viewpoint discrimination were not acceptable regulatory methods. As the Court reiterated, special hostility "is precisely what the First Amendment forbids." The city thus was left to achieve its goals through regulation that was categorical rather then selective.

Justice Byron White, in a concurring opinion joined by Justices Harry Blackmun, Sandra Day O'Connor, and John Paul Stevens, criticized the Court for making the case more complicated than necessary. White favored striking the ordinance on grounds that "it criminalized not only unprotected expression but expression protected by the First Amendment." Noting the law's focus on speech that created "anger, alarm or resentment," White maintained that such generalized reactions are not sufficient to deny speech its constitutional protection. Traditionally, as White further observed, the tendency of speech to cause "hurt feelings, offense, or resentment" does not leave it unprotected.

In a separate concurrence, Justice Harry Blackmun expressed "fear that the Court has been distracted from its proper mission by the temptation to decide the issue over 'politically correct speech' and 'cultural diversity.' " Blackmun argued that neither of these considerations was present in the case. Blackmun perceived "great harm" in preventing a community from specifically punishing race-based fighting words that result from prejudice. Although Blackmun found no First Amendment values compromised by an ordinance that prohibited "hoodlums from driving minorities out of their homes by burning crosses on their lawns," he agreed with Justice White that the St. Paul law reached beyond fighting words and regulated protected speech.

The Court's decision left open the possibility of a fighting words ordinance that did not focus on a particular group or message. Critics maintain that such two-way regulation discounts the historical experience of racially subordinated groups. The ruling itself had little effect on the debate over speech codes that continued to rage among scholars and politicians. Many, including those who oppose hate speech control, acknowledge that racist expression is a source of real harm to groups that historically have been disadvantaged. The source of disagreement between traditional civil libertarians and advocates of speech codes is not with respect to the reality of but the remedy for hate speech. The case for regulating such expression reflects the sense that it causes or reinforces stigmatization in such a way that it compromises equality and warrants punishment. Competing against that notion is the argument that speech control diverts attention from the root causes of racism and undervalues the ability of freedom of expression to promote the interests of equality.

Notes

1. Harry Kalven, Jr., *The Negro and the First Amendment* 4 (1965).
2. Mari Matsuda, et al., *Words That Wound* 68 (1993).
3. Ibid. at 23–24.

Bibliography

Henry Louis Gates, Jr., Anthony P. Griffin, Donald E. Lively, Robert C. Post, William B. Rubenstein, and Nadine Strossen, *Speaking of Race, Speaking of Sex* (1994). Presents arguments against speech codes as a means of dealing with racism.

Harry Kalven, Jr., *The Negro and the First Amendment* (1965). Explores the connection between freedom of expression and progress in civil rights and racial equality.

Mari Matsuda, Charles R. Lawrence III, Richard Delgado, and Kimberle Crenshaw, *Words That Wound* (1993). Argues the case for speech codes as a means of combating racially stigmatizing and dehumanizing expression.

Commercial Speech

Commercial speech traditionally has been regarded as a form of expression that is beyond the First Amendment's pale. This perspective was based upon the sense that speech driven by the economic interests of the speaker did not raise constitutional issues. Modern commercial speech doctrine reflects an understanding that even the most protected forms of expression, including political speech, may be motivated by economic considerations. The fact that advertising may be prompted by an interest in commercial gain, moreover, does not necessarily minimize the value of such expression to the public. These points were not lost on the Supreme Court when it determined in Bigelow v. Virginia (1975) that restrictions on abortion advertising were unconstitutional. In *Virginia State Board of Pharmacy v. Virginia Citizens Consumer Council, Inc.* (1976), commercial speech was elevated on a wholesale basis from a constitutionally unprotected status to a position in the First Amendment order.

Virginia State Board of Pharmacy v. Virginia Citizens Consumer Council, Inc.

First Amendment case law traditionally has divided speech into protected and unprotected expression. Even on the scale of protected speech, however, not all expression is assigned equal weight. Using the sun as a metaphor for the First Amendment, obscenity and fighting words would exist in a different universe. Within the constitutional solar system, political speech would be in an orbit closest to the First Amendment. Other categories of expression, operating in more distant orbits, would be less subject to the First Amendment's gravitational influence. Differentiation among protected types of speech requires line drawing that defines the various categories of expression.

Speech essential for informed self-government traditionally has been afforded the highest level of First Amendment protection. Since the 1960s, the Supreme Court has recognized that other types of speech have value that may be

Citation:	425 U.S. 748.
Issue:	Whether commercial expression is protected by the First Amendment.
Year of Decision:	1976.
Outcome:	Speech does not lose First Amendment protection because of its commercial nature.
Author of Opinion:	Justice Harry Blackmun.
Vote:	7–1.

less than what is associated with political speech but nonetheless merits constitutional shelter. Defamation of public officials and of public figures was afforded First Amendment protection in *New York Times Co. v. Sullivan* (1964) and Curtis Publishing Co. v. Butts (1968), respectively. Some decisions have indicated that sexually explicit but not obscene speech is protected by the First Amendment. As the Court noted in *Federal Communications Commission v. Pacifica Foundation* (1978), however, it is more vulnerable to regulation. Although commercial speech is pervasive in a free-market society, it historically has been excluded from the protection of the First Amendment. Until the 1970s, the status of commercial speech was defined by the Supreme Court's decision in Valentine v. Christensen (1942). In that case, the Court determined that the First Amendment did not preclude governmental regulation of "purely commercial advertising."

In the 1970s, the Court began to reexamine the constitutional status of commercial speech. In Pittsburgh Press Co. v. Pittsburgh Commission on Human Relations (1973), it upheld a city ordinance that prohibited newspapers from listing help-wanted advertisements by gender. The Court indicated that states could restrain advertising only when the underlying activity was illegal. Two years later, in Bigelow v. Virginia (1975), the Court applied this logic in striking down a state law that banned advertisements for abortion. The primary constitutional breakthrough for commercial speech occurred in *Virginia State Board of Pharmacy v. Virginia Citizens Consumer Council, Inc.* (1976). At issue was a Virginia law that prohibited the advertisement of prescription drug prices. The state's justification for the regulation was that it preserved professional standards of pharmacists, ensured that the intensified competition would not induce them to cut corners and endanger the public's health, and helped maintain the viability of small pharmacies against chains and larger operations. Consumers maintained that they would benefit from advertising that would provide them with information on retail drug prices.

Writing for the majority, Justice Harry Blackmun acknowledged that the speech at issue did not concern a cultural, philosophical, or political interest and only stated the basis for a commercial transaction. The basic question was whether speech that "does 'no more than propose a commercial transaction' is so removed from any 'exposition of ideas' and from 'truth, science, morality, and arts in general' that it lacks all protection." From the majority's standpoint, the answer was no. In support of its position, the Court observed that a consumer's interest in free-flowing commercial information is "as keen, if not keener by far, than his interest in the day's most urgent political debate." Although the Court conceded the legitimacy of the concerns that were the basis for the law, it viewed the advertising restriction as inconsistent with the needs of a free-market economy and the imperative of individual decision making. As the Court put it, the allocation of resources in a free-market economy is driven by numerous private decisions that must be "intelligent and well informed." In that setting, "the free flow of commercial information is indispensable." Rather than relying upon what it characterized as the state's "highly paternalistic approach," the Court preferred to "assume . . . that people will perceive their own best interests only if they are well enough informed, and that the best means to that end is to open the channels of communication rather than to close them."

Although the Court stressed that the First Amendment assumes the risk that freedom of expression will be abused, it indicated that commercial speech might be more vulnerable to regulation than political speech. Advertising of illegal services or activities, for instance, might be entirely prohibited without any constitutional consequences. Requirements for disclosure of information or disclaimers to guard against consumer fraud, injury, or similar perils also might be imposed. This regulatory leeway reflects the Court's sense that commercial expression presents unique dangers that government may seek to prevent through appropriate methods of control. The "commonsense differences" that support "a different degree of protection" for commercial speech are that it is a "hardier" and "more easily verifiable" form of expression. These rationales have not been immune to debate. The premise that commercial expression is hardier may overlook the vigor of and force behind political speech when candidates or agendas compete with each other. A politician's interest in being elected or a lobbying group's pursuit of a pet interest may be at least as powerful as the motive to make money. The notion that commercial expression is easier to verify also raises questions. Deception in either the commercial or political context may have profoundly negative consequences for the public. Misrepresentation of a product, agenda, or candidate may be as intentional in one setting as the other. A politician who lies about a plan to cut taxes, for instance, knows his or her deceit as well as an automobile salesperson who turns back the odometer on a vehicle.

The decision to protect commercial expression on a categoric but diminished basis raises questions about the speech-classification process itself. Advertising or speech that invites a commercial transaction can include political or social fund raising. Although the Court has not viewed such efforts as commercial in nature, Justice William Rehnquist's dissenting opinion in Schaumburg v. Citizens for a Better Environment (1980) saw it otherwise, at least in the context of charitable fund raising. From his perspective, this activity was purely commercial. He thus rejected the Court's understanding that such solicitation "does more than inform private economic decisions and is not primarily concerned with providing information about the characteristics and costs of goods and services."

By finding that restrictions on prescription advertising were impermissible, the Court cleared the way for deregulation of commercial speech in other settings where it traditionally had been prohibited or strictly regulated. The ruling triggered a series of successful challenges of regulations that barred or restricted lawyer advertising and solicitation. Although the *Virginia Pharmacy* decision redefined the First Amendment's meaning in relationship to commercial speech, subsequent case law established the formal standards that govern analysis of commercial speech regulation. In Central Hudson Gas and Electric Co. v. Public Service Commission (1984), the Court announced a multipoint test for assessing the permissibility of commercial speech regulation. Under this formula, commercial expression may be protected under the First Amendment only if it neither is misleading nor promotes an unlawful activity. Even then, it may be regulated to the extent justified by an important governmental interest if the regulation directly advances that interest and the law is no more extensive than necessary to serve that interest. Political speech, in contrast, can be regulated only for the most compelling reasons. These standards of review demonstrate that although commercial speech is more valued than unprotected forms of expression, it does not rise to the top of the First Amendment pecking order.

Bibliography

C. Edwin Baker, *Advertising and a Democratic Press* (1994). Examines the risks of advertising in a society rooted in principles of freedom of expression.

Sylvia Law, "Addiction, Autonomy, and Advertising," 77 *Iowa Law Review* 909 (1992). Studies the logical extent of commercial speech protection.

Steven H. Shiffrin, "The First Amendment and Economic Regulation: Away from a General Theory of the First Amendment," 78 *Northwestern University Law Review* 1212 (1984). Explores the implications of commercial speech doctrine for efforts to develop a comprehensive theory of the First Amendment.

Symbolic Speech

Speech in its purest form consists of articulation of words and thoughts through human physiological processes. Actual communication is dependent upon factors external to the speaker, including laws of physics. Effective expression is determined not just by content but by method of presentation. The spoken word thus may be enhanced by body language, amplification, and imagery. Political protest typically makes its impression not just on the basis of the basic message but through actions that rivet the audience's attention or make a point more compelling than simple words would allow. Hanging a government official in effigy, pouring tea into Boston Harbor, or picketing a segregated lunch counter represent ways of expressing a position not just by word but by deed. Because of its efficacy, symbolic speech has particular value under the First Amendment. Delicate questions arise with respect to separating conduct from speech for purposes of regulation. The Court in *United States v. O'Brien* (1968) considered Congress's ability to punish draft-card burning on grounds unrelated to suppression of speech. In *Texas v. Johnson* (1989), the Court's review of a law that prohibited flag desecration reaffirmed the principle that punishment of conduct is unconstitutional if its aim is to suppress speech.

United States v. O'Brien

Defining speech is not always an easy task. It is essential, however, for purposes of determining what is protected by the First Amendment. Speech is easily discernible when words are spoken or printed on a placard. Picketing, silent protests, and other symbolisms also have been recognized as speech. When speech is mixed with conduct, some fine lines have to be drawn between what is constitutionally protected and what is not.

Speech, especially expression designed to persuade, often is accompanied by action that goes beyond the body movements required to articulate or gesticulate. Conduct, such as burning a flag or hanging a government official in effigy, may convey by its symbolism the speaker's message or enhance its force and the attention it receives. Given the nature and consequences of conduct, it is understandable that not every symbolic statement is protected by the First Amendment. Although words typically do not kill directly, conduct may. An argument that the bombing of an abortion clinic is protected by the First Amendment, for instance, is unlikely to receive a serious hearing. The question that typically presents itself when speech is combined with conduct, therefore, is whether the action creates an independent basis for regulation or prosecution. Not surprisingly, such issues have presented the greatest challenge during times of social turmoil or unrest when the potential for divisiveness and intolerance is especially acute.

Citation:	391 U.S. 367.
Issue:	Whether prohibition of and punishment for burning a draft card violate the First Amendment.
Year of Decision:	1968.
Outcome:	Government may punish action that is combined with speech, provided that it can show a substantial justification and is not trying to suppress expression.
Author of Opinion:	Chief Justice Earl Warren.
Vote:	8–1.

A seminal and defining decision on symbolic expression arose during the 1960s, when sharp divisions existed over the nation's participation in the Vietnam War, and antiwar and antidraft protests pervaded the social landscape. Typical methods of expressing opposition to the war included rallies on university and college campuses, demonstrations on city streets and in parks, blockages of induction centers, flag desecration, and draft-card burning. Amid this social unrest, Congress in 1965 enacted a law that prohibited the mutilation of draft cards. A year after the law's enactment, federal agents arrested David Paul O'Brien and three companions on the steps of a Boston courthouse for publicly burning their draft cards. During the police interrogation, O'Brien told officers that he burned his card "because of his beliefs, knowing that he was violating federal law." At trial and on appeal, O'Brien did not contest the fact that he had destroyed the card. Relying on the First Amendment, he maintained that his action was intended to influence others in their thinking about the war. O'Brien testified that he wanted others to "reevaluate their positions with Selective Service, with the armed forces, and reevaluate their place in the culture of today, to hopefully consider my position." In appealing his case to the Supreme Court, O'Brien argued that the burning of his draft card constituted "symbolic speech" protected by the First Amendment.

The Court, in an opinion authored by Chief Justice Earl Warren, rejected O'Brien's argument. It began by repudiating the notion that "an apparently limitless variety of conduct can be labeled 'speech' whenever the person engaging in the conduct intends thereby to express an idea." Although the Court acknowledged that the "communicative element" in O'Brien's conduct might be protected by the First Amendment, it found no basis for concluding that the destruction of a draft card was constitutionally protected activity. The Court determined that when speech and nonspeech elements are combined in the same course of conduct, the nonspeech aspect can be regulated with less constitutional concern. Such regulation that imposes incidental limitations on First Amendment freedoms is justifiable when it is supported by "a sufficiently important governmental interest."

To determine when government regulation of such conduct is permissible, the Court set forth a three-part test. Regulation is permissible insofar as it (1) is based upon a legitimate governmental power, (2) furthers an important or substantial governmental interest unrelated to suppressing expressive freedom, and (3) imposes no more of a restriction on First Amendment freedom than is necessary to further the regulatory purpose. With respect to the first criterion, the Court noted Congress's power to raise and support armies and to make all laws necessary and proper to that end. The power to classify and conscript "manpower," from the Court's perspective, was "beyond question." The issuing of draft cards was a "legitimate and substantial aid in the functioning" of the Selective Service System.

O'Brien argued that the certificate was a meaningless restatement of information already known to the cardholder. The Court, however, upheld the government's interests in protecting the integrity of draft cards. As the Court noted, a draft card serves as proof that the individual has registered for the draft as required by law, provides information that facilitates communication between registrants and draft boards, reminds the registrant to notify his draft board in the event of any change in address or status, and safeguards against their deceptive use. For the Court, these functions established "beyond doubt" that Congress had not only a legitimate but a "substantial" interest in preventing their destruction. For this substantial interest to be achieved, the Court also saw "no alternative means that would more precisely and narrowly assure the continuing availability of" issued draft cards. Despite arguments that the law abridged protected speech, the Court determined that its operation was limited to the noncommunicative aspect of O'Brien's conduct. It thus determined that O'Brien's burning of his draft card "wilfully frustrated th[e] governmental interest" in a Selective Service System that functioned smoothly and efficiently.

The Court also addressed the argument that the law was unconstitutional because it was intended to suppress expressive freedom. In rejecting this contention, it referred to "a familiar principle of constitutional law that this Court will not strike down an otherwise constitutional statute on the basis of an alleged illicit legislative motive." As the Court put it, inquiries into legislative motives or purposes "are a hazardous matter." To void a statute on the basis of what some legislators said about it, the Court indicated, was ill advised. It pointed out that "[w]hat motivates one legislator to make a speech about a statute is not necessarily what motivates scores of others to enact it, [so] the stakes are sufficiently high to eschew guesswork." The Court's reluctance to probe the "actual" purpose of the law may have reflected the sense that motive-based inquiry is perilous and often fruitless. This concern, however, tends to be selective. Standards that govern equal protection review in the context of race and gender, as discussed in the entry on *Washington v. Davis* (1976), require proof of illicit purpose to establish a constitutional violation. This seeming inconsistency has never been effectively explained by the Court.

In a concurring opinion, Justice John Harlan, Jr., argued against foreclosing the First Amendment's applicability when an "incidental" restriction on expression has the effect of precluding the speaker's ability to reach an audience. From Harlan's perspective, this concern did not apply to O'Brien, who had other means for communicating his message. Implicit in Harlan's view is the premise that the First Amendment does not guarantee speakers the freedom to use the communicative means that they believe are most effective.

Justice William O. Douglas authored a dissenting opinion that acknowledged that Congress's power to draft personnel into the military was far-reaching during wartime. Because the United States had never formally declared war on Vietnam, he urged "reargument on the question of the constitutionality of a peacetime draft." Although Douglas generally bypassed the First Amendment issues, he pointedly addressed them in retrospect a year later. In *Brandenburg v. Ohio* (1969), Douglas criticized the *O'Brien* decision on grounds that it was inconsistent with the First Amendment. As Douglas explained it, "Action is often a method of expression and within the protection of the First Amendment." Using picketing as an example to make his point, he observed that it is "free speech plus [conduct]." Douglas acknowledged that the "plus" aspect of picketing can be regulated for valid reasons that include the time, place, or manner of the protest. From Douglas's point of view, these needs were not involved when a draft card was burned as a political statement. This argument is supported by O'*Brien*'s critics, who note that the reason for burning the draft card was to make a political point rather than merely to destroy a piece of cardboard.

Despite its origins in the context of political protest and demonstration, the O'*Brien* test has been extended to less passionate settings where the First Amendment stakes are no less significant. A federal law that required cable television operators to set aside channels for local broadcasters, for instance, was evaluated from a perspective that it regulated activity unrelated to speech. Rejecting the argument that the expressive freedom of cable operators was being abridged, the Court in Turner Broadcasting System, Inc. v. Federal Communications Commission (1994) used the O'*Brien* test to review the law. The ruling reflected the Court's findings that the regulation was based on an important government interest, and no less restrictive regulatory method existed. The O'*Brien* formula emanated from a context of controversy and has been a source of controversy itself. It also has become a settled principle for limiting the First Amendment's scope.

Bibliography

C. Edwin Baker, *Human Liberty and Freedom of Speech* (1989). Includes a critical perspective on the O'*Brien* decision and some of its critics.

Steven Shiffrin, *The First Amendment, Democracy, and Romance* (1990). Argues that the O'*Brien* standard devalues political dissent.

Texas v. Johnson

Symbolic speech, because of its nature, design, and impact, has generated some of the First Amendment's greatest drama. Although words may be powerful and intense, symbols typically are chosen for their graphic, provocative, or even inflammatory effect. Some of the most incendiary cases that the Supreme Court has considered over the years have resulted from prosecutions for desecrating the American flag. This symbol of the nation traditionally has been a focus of holidays, ceremonies, pledges, and other rituals that are a source of cultural identity and appreciation. Because of its meaning and stature, the flag has been a favored target for dissidents and protesters wishing to vent their dissatisfaction with government action or policy.

To secure the flag's physical and symbolic integrity, many states punished desecration of the American flag. For many years, the Court generally avoided the constitutional questions that challenges to these laws presented. In Street v. New York (1969), the Court reversed the conviction of a protester who burned a flag while he declared, "[w]e don't need no damned flag." Finding that the conviction might have been based upon the defendant's use of protected speech, rather than desecration of the flag, the Court upheld the First Amendment interest. In Spence v. Washington (1974), the Court reviewed the conviction of a college student for taping a black peace symbol to a flag that he displayed to protest the Vietnam War. Because the tape did not permanently disfigure the flag, the Court reversed the conviction. In Smith v. Goguen (1974), the Court reversed the conviction of a person who had been prosecuted for wearing a flag on the seat of his trousers. The statute, which prohibited "contemptuous" treatment of the flag, was declared overbroad and vague. None of these cases resolved whether flag desecration was protected by the First Amendment. Finally, in *Texas v. Johnson* (1989), the Court squarely confronted this issue.

The case arose from a political protest at the 1984 Republican National Convention. As a participant in the demonstration outside the convention

Citation:	491 U.S. 397.
Issue:	Whether a conviction for burning the American flag violates the First Amendment.
Year of Decision:	1989.
Outcome:	Burning an American flag to make a political statement is protected by the First Amendment.
Author of Opinion:	Justice William Brennan.
Vote:	5–4.

hall in Dallas, Gregory Lee Johnson unfurled an American flag, doused it in kerosene, and set it afire. As the flag burned, protesters chanted, "America, the red, white, and blue, we sit on you." Johnson was prosecuted under a Texas law that prohibited intentional or knowing desecration of "a state or national flag. Desecration, as defined by the enactment, meant to deface, damage, or otherwise physically mistreat in a way that the actor knows will seriously offend one or more persons likely to observe or discover his action." At Johnson's trial, several witnesses testified that the flag burning had "seriously offended" them. The state acknowledged that Johnson's conduct was expressive in nature. Johnson himself testified that the flag was burned because "Ronald Reagan was being nominated as President. And a more powerful statement of symbolic speech, whether you agree with it or not, couldn't have been made at that time. It's quite a juxtaposition. We had new patriotism and no patriotism."

Although this case was seemingly akin to *United States v. O'Brien* (1968), which concerned a protester's burning of his draft card, the Court viewed the issue differently. In *O'Brien*, it found that government had an interest in maintaining the integrity of the military draft that was separate from any concern with speech content. The *Johnson* court determined, however, that the burning of a flag was speech itself, and the Texas law must be viewed as an exercise in content control. The state thus was held to the high standard of proving a compelling justification for the statute.

In urging the Court to uphold the conviction, Texas maintained that its flag-desecration statute was justified as a means of preventing breaches of the peace. Because no disturbance of the peace occurred, the Court found the state's emphasis upon the protesters' "disorderly action . . . somewhat surprising." Nor was any showing made that a disturbance of the peace was a likely reaction to flag burning. The Court noted that it could not "countenance such a presumption." On the contrary, it pointed out, the primary function of freedom of expression is to invite dispute. Moreover, as the Court observed, freedom of speech actually may serve its purpose best "when it induces a condition of unrest, creates dissatisfaction with conditions as they are, or even stirs people to anger."

A key part of the state's case was a claimed "interest in preserving the flag as a symbol of nationhood and national unity." The Court noted that it must respond to this point with "particular care" because the case was one of "prosecution for the expression of an idea through activity." It identified as a "bedrock principle underlying the First Amendment" that government may not curb expression of ideas merely because society finds them "offensive or disagreeable." The Court also expressed concern with allowing government to advance its own view of the flag, or permit only a limited set of meanings to be communicated. To decide which symbols were sufficiently special to warrant such a unique status, it reasoned, would force the Court "to consult our very own political preferences, and impose them on the citizenry, in the very way that the First Amendment forbids us to do." Noting further that those who framed the Constitution and authored the First Amendment "were not known for their reverence for the Union Jack," the Court determined that freedom of speech does not guarantee that concepts sacred to the nation "will go unquestioned in the marketplace of ideas." It thus declined "to create for the flag an exception to the joust of principles protected by the First Amendment."

The Court perceived the Texas law as an overreaction to the actual likelihood of harm. Although the state assumed a high likelihood that flag burning would cause a breach of peace, circumstances actually confirmed for the Court that the flag's special role and stature were not endangered. If they were at risk, the Court noted, "no one would riot or take offense because a flag had been burned." The Court even suggested that the flag's "cherished place" in the national community was strengthened by a holding that reaffirmed principles of freedom, inclusiveness, and "the conviction that our toleration of criticism such as Johnson's is a sign and source of our strength." Rather than punish those who burn flags, the Court proposed that the best response was waving one's own flag or saluting the flag that is being destroyed. This method represents the classic premise upon which the First Amendment is based—that the best remedy for speech is more speech.

Chief Justice William Rehnquist, in a dissenting opinion joined by Justices Byron White and Sandra Day O'Connor, would have allowed the state to regulate the marketplace of ideas when flag desecration was concerned. As the dissenters saw it, the American flag was not "just another symbol." Rather, it was "the visible symbol embodying our Nation" that transcended the views of any political party or philosophy. Because Rehnquist viewed the flag as not simply another idea or viewpoint competing for attention in the information marketplace, he could not agree that the First Amendment required the invalidation of federal law and the laws of forty-eight of the fifty states that criminalized public burning of the flag. As Rehnquist saw it, burning the flag in protest "was no essential part of any exposition of ideas." Johnson could have denounced the flag verbally, burned it in private, and desecrated other government symbols or effigies of political leaders without a basis for arrest or prosecution. Like fighting words, which are constitutionally unprotected, Rehnquist believed that flag burning has "such slight social value as a step to truth that any benefit that may be derived from [it] is clearly outweighed" by the public's interest in avoiding a probable breach of the peace.

Justice John Paul Stevens also dissented. He viewed the flag as "an important national asset" that could be protected for the same reason that political graffiti could be banned on the facade of the Lincoln Memorial. Although the value of the flag as a symbol might not be capable of measurement, Stevens maintained that the interest in preserving its value for the future was both significant and legitimate. If "ideas of liberty and equality" are worth fighting for, Stevens reasoned that the flag that "uniquely symbolized their power is . . . itself worthy of protection from unnecessary desecration."

The flag-burning decision has been viewed by supporters as a quintessential statement of the First Amendment's central meaning. They maintain that it is precisely because Johnson demeaned a revered political symbol that First Amendment protection was so essential. Others have pointed out that the concept of a common national purpose and values of unity set the flag apart and justify a unique status that distances it from traditional First Amendment norms. The Court's ruling actually stirred more outcry and outrage than the flag-burning incident itself. Within a year of the decision, Congress passed a federal law that criminalized mutilation, defacement, burning, or trampling of the American flag. For reasons similar to those expressed in *Johnson*, the Court in United States v. Eichman (1990) struck down the enactment as a violation of the First Amendment. Reaction to the Court's rulings has included efforts to propose a constitutional amendment to ban flag desecration. To date, such an amendment has not been adopted.

Bibliography

Lee Bollinger, *The Tolerant Society* (1986). Examines the value of tolerance as a basis for defining First Amendment principles.

George Fletcher, *Loyalty* (1993). Explores the nature of patriotism and loyalty to a society.

13

The First Amendment: Freedom of Association

Unlike freedom of speech and of the press or the right to peaceably assemble and petition government for redress of grievances, freedom of association is not specifically itemized by the First Amendment. In its rulings, however, the Supreme Court has recognized how dependent these textually explicit guarantees are upon the ability of individuals to organize, mobilize, or join on the basis of shared views. The constitutional standing of the right to associate thus derives from an understanding that it is essential for guaranteeing freedom of speech and the press, and rights of assembly and petition. This premise is the foundation of the Court's decision in *NAACP v. Alabama* (1958) that the state could not compel disclosure of a civil rights organization's membership list.

NAACP v. Alabama

The ability to organize is crucial for any individual or group dedicated to promoting political or social change. This lesson was demonstrated early in the twentieth century when the labor movement pressed increasingly for reform in the workplace. A legal environment that was unfriendly to collective action by employees effectively slowed the development of unions as a counterbalance to management. Not until the 1930s, when Congress enacted the National Labor Relations Act, did labor have the opportunity to organize freely and be an effective force in defining employment practices and conditions.

The civil rights movement is another significant example of how organization is essential to effective advocacy of ideas and agendas. The campaign to end segregation was waged at significant peril to the lives and well-being of those associated with the National Association for the Advancement

Citation:	357 U.S. 449.
Issue:	Whether a state can compel disclosure of an organization's membership list.
Year of Decision:	1958.
Outcome:	Disclosure can be required only if a compelling justification exists.
Author of Opinion:	Justice John Harlan, Jr.
Vote:	9–0.

of Colored People (NAACP). This organization conceived and implemented the legal strategy for challenging and eventually undoing the separate but equal era. Lawyers who traveled into hostile communities to challenge segregation regularly encountered threats to life, limb, or property. Also threatened were those who were subject to intimidation and violence if they were identified with the forces of change in their own communities.

The Supreme Court's determination in *Brown v. Board of Education* (1954) that racially separate schools were "inherently unequal" did not terminate public and private pressure on persons and groups that advocated racial change. Until 1964, when the Department of Justice was authorized to initiate desegregation lawsuits, the NAACP was the primary source for bringing court actions that would dismantle segregated school systems. The more that resources were strained during the early years of desegregation, the less the NAACP accomplished. Aware of this reality, and in an effort to neutralize the NAACP as a force for charge, Virginia enforced a regulation that prohibited solicitation of legal business. In NAACP v. Button (1963), the Court held that the organization's efforts to litigate constituted "a form of political expression" designed to achieve "the lawful objectives of equality of treatment by all government." It thus found the NAACP's efforts to organize litigation protected under the First Amendment.

The Button decision reaffirmed the principle of freedom of association. Although freedom of association is not enumerated in the Constitution, it has been established by rulings that view it as essential to meaningful First Amendment protection. The principle initially was articulated in *NAACP v. Alabama*, in which the Court repulsed Alabama's effort to oust the NAACP from doing business in the state. The state had brought an action against the organization for not complying with a corporate registration law. During the course of the proceeding, the Alabama attorney general moved to have the NAACP produce various records, including its membership list. The organization resisted disclosure on grounds that this would "abridge the rights of its rank-and-file members to engage in lawful association in support of their common beliefs."

Although the state's effort to secure membership information did not constitute a direct restraint upon freedom of association, the effect was the same. Writing for the majority, Justice John Harlan, Jr., identified a close connection between group association and the freedoms of speech and assembly. As he put it, "[e]ffective advocacy of both public and private points of view, particularly controversial ones, is undeniably enhanced by group association." So important is the freedom to associate for purposes of advancing beliefs and ideas that the Court defined it as "an inseparable aspect" of the liberty "which embraces freedom of speech." Given the significance of the liberty interest, the Court stated that any attempt to curtail it must be "subject to the closest scrutiny." Careful evaluation was required because, as the Court noted, "compelled disclosure of affiliation with groups engaged in advocacy may constitute [an] effective . . . restraint on freedom of association." Realistically, loss of privacy in group association may undermine freedom of association, "particularly where a group espouses dissident beliefs." Given the animus toward the NAACP at the time, the case for privacy was particularly strong. The organization demonstrated that identification of rank-and-file members in the past had exposed them "to economic reprisal, loss of employment, threat of physical coercion, and other manifestations of public hostility." Because of this history of intimidation, the Court determined that compelled disclosure of the organization's membership list likely would undermine the organization's and its members' ability "to pursue their collective effort to foster beliefs which they admittedly have the right to advocate."

The Court observed that, like other rights and liberties, the freedom to associate is not absolute. However, it could be abrogated only by a state interest that was compelling in nature. Alabama's asserted reason for seeking the membership list was to determine whether the NAACP was violating the state's foreign corporation registration statute. The issues were whether the organization was subject to the registration law, and whether the extent of its activities without being registered supported its ouster from the state. Given the nature of these concerns, the Court failed to see how disclosure of the identities of rank-and-file members had any bearing on their resolution. It indicated, however, that a different result might have followed if the nature of the NAACP's activities had been different. Because prior case law had upheld compelled disclosure of the Ku Klux Klan's membership in New York, the Court indicated that it was appropriate to take into account whether an organization participates in "acts of unlawful intimidation and violence."

The Court's ruling demonstrated appreciation of the nexus between associational freedom and the ability to speak and advocate effectively. The value of this freedom was reaffirmed a quarter of a century later in NAACP v. Claiborne Hardware Co. (1982). This case concerned a boycott of white businesses that resulted in significant business losses and acts of violence. Holding that liability did not extend beyond those persons who actually committed unlawful acts, the Court rejected the idea of group liability under the circumstances. For the entire group to be liable, the Court found that the organization must have illegal goals and the individual specifically intended to further those unlawful objectives. In so ruling, the Court restated the significance of associational freedom to the achievement of political or social change. As the Court put it, "[c]oncerted action is a powerful weapon. History teaches that special dangers are associated with conspiratorial activity. And yet one of the foundations of our society is the right of individuals to combine with other persons in pursuit of a common goal by lawful means."

Subsequent case law also has refined and expanded the meaning of associational freedom. In Roberts v. United States (1984), the Court indicated that freedom of association breaks down into two categories. Freedom of intimate association safeguards the ability of persons to establish and maintain close personal relationships. It is a guarantee that relates to relatively small groups that have a high degree of selectivity in determining affiliation and detaching themselves from others. Freedom of expressive association facilitates First Amendment purposes of speech, assembly, and petitioning for redress of grievances. Although such freedom implies a freedom not to associate, the liberty is not absolute. The Court in Roberts held that a state law that prohibited gender discrimination constituted a compelling justification, and therefore the United States Jaycees could not restrict membership to men. This decision reveals the inherent tension in such associational freedom cases between the interests of exclusion and those of inclusion.

Bibliography

Thomas Emerson, *The System of Freedom of Expression* (1970). Examines the emergence of freedom of association as a constitutionally protected interest.
David Fellman, *The Constitutional Right of Association* (1963). Discusses the right of association as essential to constitutional democracy.
Carl Rowan, *Dream Makers, Dream Breakers* (1993). Documents the repressive and suppressive tactics experienced by NAACP lawyers and their clients in challenging official segregation.

14

The First Amendment: Freedom of the Press

Freedom of the press in the United States emerged against a centuries-old backdrop of official suppression. Introduction of the printing press in the fifteenth century in Europe presented a threat to established political and religious orders accustomed to controlling the stream of information. Responding to the perils they perceived in uncontrolled dissemination of information to the masses, authorities strictly limited access to print technology and imposed harsh sanctions for criticism of church or state. Although intolerance of speech that challenged established centers of power carried over to the American colonies, resentment of royal policies and privileges fueled and facilitated interest in a system of press liberty. Before and during the American Revolution, the press played a critical role in defining and mobilizing anti-British sentiment. Widespread mob violence against pro-British publishers, however, demonstrated that appreciation of a free press was often selective rather than universal.

This tension between freedom of the press and suppressive instincts continued after the colonial experience. Abolitionists were largely unheard from in the South, for instance, where they were subject to punishment if they distributed antislavery literature. Publications that criticized American participation in World War I triggered prosecutions and resulted in harsh sentences under federal espionage laws. During the 1950s, anti-Communist fervor similarly daunted mass dissemination of expression that advocated radical political change. Although the terms of the freedom of the press clause of the First Amendment have remained unchanged since the Republic's founding, the press itself has redefined itself dramatically. Communications technologies, such as broadcasting, cable, satellites, and networked computers, did not exist when the First Amendment was framed and ratified. A constitutional response to their emergence has become a primary preoccupation of modern First Amendment review.

Prior Restraint

Few principles are as central to the First Amendment's meaning as the doctrine of prior restraint. Official censorship is perhaps the rawest and most fundamental method of suppressing expression. In seventeenth-century England, it was the primary means for the state to control what was published and disseminated to the public. The English Licensing Act authorized the Crown to select and limit the number of printers who could engage in the publishing trade. This regulatory scheme was abandoned in 1694. Its legacy was an understanding that advance screening of what is spoken or published is a particularly intolerable form of speech control. This historical understanding became the basis of the Supreme Court's decision in *Near v. Minnesota* (1931) that invalidated a state law that prohibited publication of a "malicious, scandalous and defamatory" publication. The strong presumption against prior restraint's constitutionality and the heavy burden that government has in justifying such a restriction were reaffirmed in *New York Times Co. v. United States* (1971).

Near v. Minnesota

Although freedom of expression is now a constitutional norm, it has not always been a societal tradition. For most of the world's history, official suppression and control have typified response to speech and publication. The advent of movable type in Europe in the late fifteenth century presented significant challenges to cultures that until then had not confronted the possibility of mass dissemination of information and ideas. Although the printing press provided both church and state authorities an opportunity to propagate their thoughts and agendas more effectively, it also exposed them to the risk that new ideas might compete for public acceptance. To minimize the dangers to established authority, the Crown in England introduced a system of licensing. A special printing company was established to produce works that were approved by royal authorities. Official control was maintained by a system of prepublication review that censored information that did not satisfy the interests or needs of authorities.

Citation:	283 U.S. 697.
Issue:	Whether the state may restrain publication of a newspaper that published defamatory and scurrilous stories.
Year of Decision:	1931.
Outcome:	The First Amendment prohibits prior restraint of expression except under extraordinary circumstances.
Author of Opinion:	Chief Justice Charles Evans Hughes.
Vote:	5–4.

Although the English Licensing Act was repealed in 1694, traditions of suppression persisted and were exported to the American colonies. Systems of prior restraint that enabled government to prevent publication of information or ideas were widespread throughout prerevolutionary America, as were taxation of publishers and criminal libel laws that deterred criticism of church and state. These methods effectively preserved the established order's interest in control of the media. Early concepts of press freedom were nourished by grievances with colonial rule and an emerging case for independence. Amid these circumstances, the English jurist William Blackstone declared that "liberty of the press is . . . essential to the nature of a free state . . . [but] consists in laying no previous restraints upon publications." Blackstone's statement eventually worked its way into the mainstream of First Amendment jurisprudence, which has established this concept as a basic premise.

Prior restraint consists of prepublication silencing of expression by government command. The First Amendment is hostile toward systems of prior restraint, whether they manifest themselves as a censorship board, a park permit, or an injunction that forbids expression. In Thomas Emerson's words, "They contain within themselves forces which drive irresistibly toward unintelligent, overzealous, and usually absurd administration."[1] Underlying this observation is the concern that when editorial content is reviewed by officials empowered to decide what is fit to publish, institutional agendas may be prioritized over First Amendment imperatives. As Emerson viewed it, official content control endangers "the innocent and borderline as well as the offensive, the routine as well as the unusual," and creates the risk that valuable information will not enter the information marketplace. This concern has been acknowledged by the Supreme Court, which, in Freedman v. Maryland (1965), observed that "the censor's business is to censor."

The seminal case on prior restraint in the United States, *Near v. Minnesota* (1931), required the Court to examine a Minnesota nuisance law that empowered the state to obtain an injunction against the publication of any "malicious, scandalous and defamatory newspaper, magazine or other periodical." The initial target of this law was a weekly Minneapolis newspaper, *The Saturday Press*, that was dedicated to muckraking and characterized by a persistent and overtly anti-Semitic tone. Jay M. Near was its publisher. The newspaper published several stories alleging that the police chief and other city officials had relationships with organized crime and were engaged in various corrupt activities. Each of the stories was punctuated with anti-Semitic rhetoric. Although the state succeeded in obtaining an injunction against the publication, which was found to be "malicious, scandalous and defamatory," the publisher was successful in obtaining a hearing from the Supreme Court.

The majority opinion, authored by Chief Justice Charles Evans Hughes, embraced Blackstone's view of prior restraints. As the Court put it, "the chief purpose of the guaranty [of liberty of the press] is to prevent previous restraints upon publication." Although the Court emphasized the First Amendment's resistance to prior restraint, it noted that expression or publication was not necessarily without consequence. Citing Blackstone directly, the Court observed that "[e]very freeman has an undoubted right to lay what sentiments he pleases before the public; to forbid this, is to destroy the freedom of the press; but if he publishes what is improper, mischievous or illegal, he must take the consequence of his own temerity." Put simply, it may not be permissible to deny a person the opportunity to express himself or herself. However, liability or punishment may follow if the words are actionable. Although it may not be possible to obtain an injunction that restrains a person from uttering a defamation, for example, a libelous or slanderous statement may be the basis for a subsequent determination of legal liability.

Even if the Minneapolis publication was "malicious, scandalous and defamatory," the Court was unwilling to establish a rule that would have risked suppression of information. Despite questions of taste, bias, and subsequent liability, the publication had a record of identifying and exposing corruption in local government. If the newspaper were to have been silenced, that result would have followed from its publication of stories alleging official misconduct. Given what the Court described as the increasing complexity of government and expanding opportunities for corruption and malfeasance, it determined that the need for "a vigilant and courageous press" was profound even if the liberty was abused.

Although the Court found that the Minnesota law constituted an impermissible system of censorship, it emphasized that the constitutional barrier against prior restraint was not insurmountable. Even so, any exception to the rule against prior restraint had to be justified by extraordinary circumstances. For example, the Court noted that "government might prevent actual obstruction to its [military] recruiting service or the publication of the sailing dates of transports or the number and location of troops." What the Court characterized as the "[r]equirements of decency" may justify censorship of obscene publications. Moreover, "security of the community life may be protected against incitements to acts of violence and the overthrow by force of orderly government." Although these examples of circumstances that warrant departure from the rule against prior restraints were not presented under a unifying premise or principle, taken together they indicate that prepublication suppression would have to be based upon some demonstrably compelling or exigent need that was at the level of a national security interest.

In a dissenting opinion, Justice Pierce Butler criticized the Court for giving "to freedom of the press a meaning and a scope not heretofore recognized." Referring to a trial record that demonstrated that every edition of the newspaper was dominated by "slanderous and defamatory matter," Butler maintained that the Court was imposing upon Minnesota a federal restriction that was unprecedented. He argued that the state law technically was not a prior restraint in the sense that Blackstone and others historically had condemned. Because Minnesota had not established a system that vested an administrator with power to license or censor, but had provided a remedy for sources of malicious, scandalous, and defamatory expression, freedom of the press was not endangered by any "arbitrary and infallible judge of all controverted points in learning, religion, and government." As Butler saw it, the state merely was trying to abate a nuisance in the interest of "morals, peace, and good order." Its aim thus was to prevent "*further publication*" of a formally defined "nuisance" publication rather than to secure "*previous restraint* upon the press" by a system of licensing comparable to what concerned Blackstone. The major downside of the Court's ruling, from Butler's perspective, was that "the business and private affairs of every individual" were being made hostage "to the constant and protracted false and malicious assaults of any insolvent publisher who may have purpose and sufficient capacity to contrive and put into effect a scheme or program for oppression, blackmail, or extortion."

Dividing the Court on the issue of prior restraint was the majority's concern with what was perceived as "an immediate and irreversible sanction" at the expense of First Amendment values and the dissenters' worry that abuse of press freedom causes damage that can not always be remedied by a system of subsequent punishment. Some commentators have suggested that the debate over prior restraint focuses on a false issue. Although prior restraint may be a significant issue when timeliness of information is a factor, attention to it as a general concern has been criticized for elevating form over substance. A system of subsequent punishment resulting in an award of damages that puts a newspaper out of business, for example, may be no less effective than an injunction in silencing expression. In line with the notion that postpublication punishment generally tends to chill expression, but prior restraint invariably freezes it, resistance to prior restraint continues to be one of the First Amendment's most defining features.

Note

1. Thomas I. Emerson, "The Doctrine of Prior Restraint," 20 *Law and Contemporary Problems* 648, 655–66 (1955).

Bibliography

William Blackstone, *Commentaries on the Laws of England* (1765). Sets forth Blackstone's influential insights and views on prior restraint, as well as on the law in general.

Thomas I. Emerson, *The System of Freedom of Expression* (1970). A general assessment of prior restraint.

Fred Friendly, *Minnesota Rag* (1981). A colorful history of the newspaper and publisher that became the focal point of the *Near* case.

John C. Jeffries, Jr., "Rethinking Prior Restraint," 92 *Yale Law Journal* 409 (1983). A critical perspective on the law's particular disfavor toward prior restraint.

New York Times Co. v. United States

Constitutional rights and liberties by their nature establish limits on the exercise of government power. Justice George Sutherland, dissenting in West Coast Hotel v. Parrish (1937), stated that "the meaning of the Constitution does not change with the ebb and flow of" societal circumstances. Sutherland's dissent, offered in the context of the nation's grave economic crisis in the 1930s, objected to the Court's departure from constitutional principles that previously had barred the social and economic initiatives of president Franklin Roosevelt's New Deal. History demonstrates, in any event, that the scope and force of individual rights and liberties tend to shrink during periods of national emergency or crisis. Justice Oliver Wendell Holmes, Jr., in *Schenck v. United States* (1919), observed that during wartime "many things that might be said in time of peace are such a hindrance to [the nation's] effort that their utterance will not be

Citation:	403 U.S. 713.
Issue:	Whether publication of a classified document on the Vietnam War could be prevented.
Year of Decision:	1971.
Outcome:	The government could not suppress the government report.
Author of Opinion:	*Per curiam.*
Vote:	6–3.

endured so long as men fight and that no Court could regard them as protected by any constitutional right." Imperatives of war explain why the Supreme Court, in *Korematsu v. United States* (1944), deferred to the judgment of military authorities instead of finding that the forced relocation of Japanese Americans during World War II violated the equal protection clause. The judiciary's reluctance to second-guess military authorities also influenced the Court's thinking in Rostker v. Goldberg (1978), in which Congress's exclusion of women from registration with the Selective Service System was upheld.

Considerations of national security can outweigh even the strongest constitutional doctrines. A cardinal First Amendment principle, announced in *Near v. Minnesota* (1931), is that the First Amendment generally forbids any system of prior restraint. Even that rule, as the *Near* Court suggested, may be compromised when the nation's security interests are concerned. In assessing government arguments that national security may be imperiled, the Court typically shies away from probing deeply into official rationales. Such deference reflects an institutional conservatism perhaps driven by a reluctance to have the nation shoulder the consequences of a judicial mis-calculation.

Despite this risk-averse nature, circumstances may arise in which a national security claim leaves the Court unimpressed. Such a moment arose in the early 1970s when the federal government sought to enjoin the *New York Times* and *Washington Post* from publishing a classified report on American policy making with respect to Vietnam. In a *per curiam* opinion, the Court determined that neither newspaper could be restrained from publishing what popularly became known as *The Pentagon Papers*. The primary argument in support of an injunction was that the president, who has primary responsibility for conducting foreign affairs and ensuring the nation's safety, had inherent power to act in behalf of the country's security needs. The Court's opinion was brief, consisting of only three paragraphs, but its repudiation of the government's position was pointed. As the Court put it, "[a]ny system of prior restraints of expression comes to this Court bearing a heavy presumption against its constitutional validity." To rebut the presumption in favor of First Amendment interests, government also "carries a heavy burden of showing justification for the imposition of this restraint." These two points taken together establish a simple rule for prior restraints. There is a strong presumption against their legitimacy, but this presumption may be overcome when government presents an exceptionally strong justification.

The lack of elaboration in the Court's opinion beyond these basic points illuminated the bedrock nature of prior restraint doctrine. Each justice, however, set forth his reasoning in separate opinions that revealed some significant divisions in reasoning and rationales. Consistent with their reputations as First Amendment absolutists, Justices Hugo Black and William O. Douglas maintained that prior restraint was never permissible under any circumstance. Even in a national emergency, they were prepared to assume the risk of an entirely unfettered flow of information. Black disparaged the government's case for proposing "that the First Amendment does not mean what it says, but rather means that the Government can halt the publication of current news of vital importance to the people of this country." In a similar vein, Douglas referred to the terms of the First Amendment itself and concluded that a provision that prohibited Congress from making any "law . . . abridging freedom . . . of the press, [left] no room for governmental restraint of the press."

Justice William Brennan reached the same result as Black and Douglas, but maintained that prior restraints were not impermissible under all circumstances. From his perspective, the government failed to establish that publication of *The Pentagon Papers* would have "inevitably, directly and immediately" imperiled national security. He thus was unwilling to sacrifice constitutional interests upon a mere showing of "surmise or conjecture" that harm might result.

Like Brennan, Justice Potter Stewart was not satisfied that disclosure would "surely result in direct, immediate, and irreparable damage to our Nation and its people." He also believed that secrecy and confidentiality were essential at times for effective performance of the president's responsibilities when diplomacy and defense were concerned. Although Stewart found that the president and Congress could develop rules and laws to protect confidentiality, he was unable to find such a provision in support of the government's request. Justices Byron White and Thurgood Marshall also cited the absence of congressional action authorizing confidentiality as a basis for upholding First Amendment interests.

Each of the three dissenting justices also offered his own opinion. Chief Justice Warren Burger urged at least a temporary injunction that would enable the Court to make a thoughtful and informed judgment. He complained of the "unseemly haste" with which the Court had reviewed the case. The litigation, which commenced in two federal district courts on June 12 and 18, 1971, worked its way through the courts of appeal in less than a week. After a June 26 argument to the Supreme Court, opinions were rendered on June 30. Burger contrasted the unusual speed of the review process with the four months that editors for the newspapers had taken to study the government documents and prepare their stories. Justice John Harlan, Jr., shared Burger's concerns. Choosing even stronger rhetoric, he chastised the Court for being "almost irresponsibly feverish" in reaching a prompt resolution of the controversy. In addition to what he believed was a need for more deliberation, Harlan maintained that judicial review of the president's power over foreign affairs was "very narrowly restricted." Justice Harry Blackmun tripled the sentiment that the Court had rushed to judgment. He also criticized the Court for ignoring the fact that the First Amendment constitutes "only one part of an entire Constitution" that assigns responsibilities that sometimes may conflict with and even override freedom of expression.

Despite the dissenters' concerns, the *Pentagon Papers* decision stands as a powerful statement against any system of prior restraint. Of the various opinions presented in support of the First Amendment interest, the reasoning of Justice Brennan and of Justices Stewart, White, and Marshall probably has been the most influential.

In United States v. The Progressive, Inc. (1979), a federal district court determined that national security interests outweighed a publisher's freedom to publish a story explaining how to build a hydrogen bomb. Consistent with Brennan's "clear and present danger" formula, the trial judge found that publication would gravely, directly, immediately, and irreparably injure the national interest. The court also distinguished the case on grounds that the *Pentagon Papers* were merely historical documents, the government's only reason for restraining their publication was to prevent embarrassment, and no congressional authorization of confidentiality protected them. Although no legislative act supported confidentiality in the *Pentagon Papers* case, a provision in the Atomic Energy Act provided for injunctive relief against anyone who would communicate restricted data with reason to believe that it might harm the nation or provide an advantage to a foreign country. Justices Stewart, White, and Marshall, as previously noted, had believed that such authorization was a crucial consideration. For the trial court, it was "[a] final and most vital difference." The decision also provided insight, however, into the tendency of courts to take national security interests seriously and perhaps even overpredict harm. As the trial judge put it during the proceeding, he was not prepared to be the person who "gave the hydrogen bomb to Idi Amin."

The aftermath of the district court's ruling provides further insight into the wisdom and value of prior restraints, or the lack thereof. As the magazine pursued its appeal, the article that it was enjoined from publishing appeared in other newspapers. The case thus was dismissed and the judgment vacated as moot. The net result was a testament to Justice White's insight in the *Pentagon Papers* case that prior restraint is futile and ineffective once security is breached. This reality, even if it is not always articulated, represents a particularly cogent reason for not burdening First Amendment interests with unnecessary baggage. The logic is that a significant constitutional interest should not be traded off without assurance that suppression will achieve its essential purpose.

Another historical footnote relates to the fate of Daniel Ellsberg, a former Defense Department and Rand Corporation employee, who copied and leaked the classified documents to the newspapers. Consistent with prior restraint doctrine, the government was free to prosecute Ellsberg for violating the law. A criminal action for disclosing official secrets actually was brought. The judge, however, directed a verdict of acquittal because of prosecutorial misconduct, including an illegal break-in into the offices of the defendant's psychiatrist.

Bibliography

Stanley Godofsky and Howard Rogatnick, "The Pentagon Papers Case Revisited," 18 *Cumberland Law Review* (1988). A detailed study of the *Pentagon Papers* case and the various opinions it engendered.

Theodore R. Kupferman, ed., *Censorship, Secrecy, Access, and Obscenity* (1990). An anthology of essays on prior restraint and other issues concerning press freedom.

The Pentagon Papers (1971). The extensive history of American decision making in Vietnam that was excerpted by the *New York Times* and *Washington Post*.

Definition and Scope

Decisions under the freedom of the press clause typically have focused more upon the boundaries of liberty than upon what constitutes the press. How the press is defined, however, determines who benefits from its freedom and the extent of constitutional protection that is afforded. Justice Potter Stewart asserted that the press performs a unique and essential role in informing a public. Because individuals may not have time or opportunity to access the information they need for intelligent self-government, Stewart urged special constitutional attention to the news-gathering function. Supreme Court decisions have not responded favorably to his arguments. In *Branzburg v. Hayes* (1972), the Court rejected a claim that reporters have a First Amendment privilege that protects them from having to testify and reveal confidential sources to a grand jury. The special role of the press also was discounted in *Zurcher v. Stanford Daily* (1979), in which the Court determined that newsrooms were not immune from police searches and seizures that otherwise were reasonable under the Fourth Amendment. Although the Court noted that judicial proceedings generally must be open, it stressed in *Globe Newspaper Co. v. Superior Court* (1982) that the press had no greater rights of access to them than the public.

Branzburg v. Hayes

The First Amendment does not safeguard against all abridgments of freedom of expression. Certain types of speech, such as obscenity, fighting words, and defamation of nonpublic persons, are entirely beyond the First Amendment's purview. Expression also can be controlled when compelling societal interests, such as the need to protect against imminent and likely violence, are demonstrated. When the First Amendment collides with other constitutional interests, moreover, difficult choices sometimes have to be made with respect to which provision or value must prevail.

The Fifth Amendment provides that "[n]o person shall be held to answer for a capital, or otherwise infamous crime, unless on a presentment or indictment of a Grand Jury." The grand jury was incorporated into the federal constitutional scheme and is provided for by many state constitutions as a primary instrument of the criminal justice system. By reviewing evidence prior to prosecution, the grand jury protects oppressive or unfounded prosecutions. If evidence is inadequate or prosecution is perceived as unjust, a grand jury may refuse to indict. At the same time, the grand jury serves the needs of the criminal justice system by conducting inquiries and obtaining evidence that may support prosecution. Although grand-jury powers are not unlimited, they reflect Justice Felix Frankfurter's understanding that "the public . . . has a right to every man's evidence." This basic principle operates in the grand-jury context unless a person is protected by a constitutional, common-law, or statutory privilege. The constitutional protection against self-incrimination and traditional immunities such as the attorney-client privilege thus may be a basis for not testifying.

Typically, grand juries, like any decision-making tribunal, benefit from the most information possible. Privileges against testifying are recognized because they promote some overarching societal goals. The privilege against self-incrimination represents a belief that the criminal justice system should not be relieved of its responsibility to prove guilt. The attorney-client privilege is designed to ensure an open and honest flow of information between

Citation:	408 U.S. 665.
Issue:	Whether the First Amendment protects a news reporter from having to testify before a grand jury.
Year of Decision:	1972.
Outcome:	Reporters do not have a First Amendment privilege against being compelled to testify even if they promise their sources confidentiality.
Author of Opinion:	Justice Byron White.
Vote:	5–4.

lawyers and their clients. Consistent with the premise that testimony should not be required when higher interests are at stake, advocates of a First Amendment privilege for news reporters have argued that the public's stake in a free flow of information at times outweighs the needs of the criminal justice system. The Supreme Court addressed this issue directly in *Branzburg v. Hayes*. The case arose when Paul M. Branzburg, a reporter for the *Louisville Courier-Journal*, refused to testify to a grand jury with respect to the identities of persons he had observed processing, possessing, and using marijuana. Branzburg had obtained this information in the course of writing a story and maintained that disclosure of his confidential sources and information would undermine his effectiveness as a reporter. When ordered to testify, Branzburg sought an order compelling the trial judge, John P. Hayes, to recognize a First Amendment privilege against testifying. At the Supreme Court, Branzburg's case was joined with those of two other reporters who faced similar circumstances in Providence, Rhode Island and New York City, cases that arose when several reporters were summoned by different grand juries and were ordered to disclose their sources. One grand jury sought information that a reporter had obtained in the course of observing illegal drug activity. The other reporters were summoned before grand juries and refused to answer questions concerning their interviews with members of the Black Panther Party, which was a target of federal and local law-enforcement investigations. In each instance, the reporters claimed that they had received information on a confidential basis and were protected by the First Amendment from having to disclose their sources.

In reviewing these claims, the Court started with the premise that news gathering qualifies for some degree of First Amendment protection. For general purposes, the Court observed that without "some protection for seeking out the news, freedom of the press could be eviscerated." When there was no direct interference with expression, no command that the press publish what it preferred not to, no penalty regarding the content of what was published, no restriction on the use of confidential sources, or no attempt to force disclosure of sources on an indiscriminate basis, the Court found no First Amendment interest. From the Court's perspective, the only issue was whether reporters must "respond to grand jury subpoenas as other citizens do and . . . answer questions relevant to an investigation into the commission of crime." More specifically, the issue was whether reporters are exempt from having to identify their sources because informants will refuse to furnish newsworthy information without assurances of confidentiality.

Responding to the argument that the First Amendment creates a reporter's privilege, the Court noted the "high place" that the grand jury has as an instrument of justice. The case for a privilege thus had to be measured against the grand jury's broad investigative powers necessary to determine

the existence of possible criminal conduct and its responsibility for protecting citizens against unfounded prosecution. Given these functions, the
Court viewed the grand jury's authority to subpoena witnesses and obtain
evidence as not only a historic but an essential function. Because of this
role's significance, the Court determined that it could not "seriously enter-
tain the notion that the First Amendment protects a newsman's agreement
to conceal the criminal conduct of his source." The Court found that a
privilege claim by a reporter who sought immunity from having to reveal
or testify about a crime that he or she witnessed presented "no substantial
question."

In reaching its conclusion, the Court rejected the argument that sources
would dry up without assurances of confidentiality and the public's interest
in a free flow of newsworthy information would suffer. It acknowledged
evidence that some reporters rely heavily upon confidential sources, and
some informants would be silenced if they risked exposure. The Court was
not satisfied, however, that "a significant constriction of the flow of news
to the public" would result if a privilege against testifying was denied. Even
if some informants who themselves were not criminals refused to talk with
reporters for fear of having their identities disclosed, the Court found that
the public interest in an effective criminal justice system outweighed First
Amendment concerns. In the Court's words, "[w]e cannot accept the argument that the public interest in possible future news about crime from
undisclosed, unverified sources must take precedence over the public interest in pursuing and prosecuting crimes reported to the press by informants
and in thus deterring the commission of such crimes in the future." Because
informants historically had not been protected by a First Amendment privilege, and the press was perceived as a flourishing institution, the Court
found no basis for such protection.

Rejection of a constitutionally based privilege for informants, as the
Court noted, did not bar Congress or state legislatures from adopting laws
that shielded reporters from having to disclose their sources. The Court
reiterated its initial point, moreover, that news gathering is not without
some First Amendment protection. Investigations that were conducted
without good faith and harassment of the press without a legitimate law-
enforcement purpose were cited as two examples of potential First Amendment violations. Because such activities would constitute abuse of
grand-jury power and process under any circumstance, the First Amendment actually added little to protection that already existed.

Despite the firm tones of Justice Byron White's opinion, the ruling actually was a source of mixed signals. In a concurring opinion, Justice Lewis
Powell supported the notion of a qualified privilege. As Powell saw it, a
grand-jury subpoena needed to be assessed against standards of good faith,
relevancy, and need. Taken together, these criteria seemed to preclude official prying into reporters' sources and information unless it could first be

demonstrated that the information sought was relevant to the investigation and was not available from other sources. Combined with the opinion of four dissenting justices who favored the idea of a broad First Amendment privilege for reporters, Powell's concurring opinion provided a basis for at least a qualified immunity from being required to testify. Several courts interpreted it in that way, consistent perhaps with Justice Potter Stewart's observation that the Court rejected the idea of a journalist privilege "by a vote of 5–4, or, considering Mr. Justice Powell's concurring opinion, perhaps by a vote of 4 ½–4 ½." The somewhat confused message of the decision has never been clarified in the context of a reporter's privilege claim. In University of Pennsylvania v. Equal Employment Opportunity Commission (1990), however, the Court indicated that First Amendment concerns were limited to "bad faith" exercises of grand-jury powers. This case concerned a First Amendment privilege claim for confidential tenure files at an institution of higher learning. Finding the case to be "in many respects . . . similar to *Branzburg*," the Court noted that "[w]e were unwilling then, as we are today," to accept the First Amendment argument. Even if this decision was not a conclusive reinterpretation of the law concerning a reporter's privilege, it suggests strongly that *Branzburg* closed rather than opened the door for a First Amendment privilege.

Bibliography

Vincent Blasi, *Press Subpoenas: An Empirical and Legal Analysis* (1971). Examines the use of confidential sources and reporters' perceptions on their utility.

David Lange, "The Speech and Press Clause," 23 *UCLA Law Review* 77 (1975). Criticizes the notion of special protection for the press.

Potter Stewart, " 'Or of the Press,' " 26 *Hastings Law Journal* 631 (1975). Argues that the press performs key societal functions that necessitate a special First Amendment status, including a reporter's privilege.

Zurcher v. Stanford Daily

The First Amendment secures freedom of speech and of the press. Whether the speech and press clauses protect different interests has been vigorously debated by courts and commentators. The notion that freedom of expression has a special position in the constitutional universe was introduced in Murdock v. Pennsylvania (1943), in which the Supreme Court stated that "freedom of press [and] freedom of speech . . . are in a preferred position."

The implications of this "preferred position" have been several and varied. It has been argued, for instance, that freedom of expression is absolute and outweighs any constitutional consideration that may compete against it. This absolutist theory of the First Amendment largely has been repudiated. More successful have been arguments that not only speech but factors facilitating its utility must be protected. Freedom of association, for instance, has been established as a constitutional liberty because the ability to organize and interact with others is understood as essential to speech and advocacy.

Citation:	436 U.S. 547.
Issue:	Whether the search of a newsroom by law-enforcement officers violated the First Amendment.
Year of Decision:	1978.
Outcome:	The First Amendment establishes no barrier to an otherwise valid search for criminal evidence.
Author of Opinion:	Justice Byron White.
Vote:	5–3.

With respect to the free press clause, the argument is made that the media require special constitutional attention to functions that enable them to perform their role of informing the public. The case for affording protection to the press beyond what is extended to speech reflects an understanding of the relationship between the mass media and the public. Justice Potter Stewart was a primary exponent of the notion that the press has a unique stature within the First Amendment order. In a 1975 law-review article, Stewart noted that the speech and religion clauses protect specific rights of individuals. The press clause, however, extends "protection to an institution." Because institutional needs of gathering information are so closely related to the public's interest in receiving knowledge that is essential for effective self-government, Stewart believed that the press clause extended protection not only to publishing but to those processes that facilitated a free and abundant flow of news.

Despite the force with which Stewart pursued his argument in dissenting opinions and essays, case law generally has rejected his premise. The Supreme Court's rulings largely are shaped by a contrary view that, as Chief Justice Warren Burger put it in First National Bank of Boston v. Bellotti (1978), no difference exists "between the right of those who seek to disseminate ideas by way of a newspaper and those who give lectures or speeches." This perspective, generally hostile to the notion that institutional media have a special status under the First Amendment, was reflected in the Court's response to claims that a police search of a newsroom was unconstitutional. The search, which became the focal issue of *Zurcher v. Stanford Daily* (1979), occurred in the wake of a demonstration at Stanford University that had been photographed by a photographer for the campus newspaper. After the publication ran an extensive story on a clash between protesters and police, law-enforcement officials obtained a warrant to search for photographs and other evidence that would enable them to identify demonstrators who had committed criminal acts. Following the search, the newspaper and its staff brought an action against James Zurcher, Chief of Police for the City of Palo Alto, and other officials for violating their civil rights. In so doing, they sought an injunction against any future newsroom searches. In an opinion authored by Justice Byron White, the Court found that the case involved not only the First Amendment but the Fourth Amendment guarantee against "unreasonable searches and seizures" of individuals' "persons, houses, papers, and effects." At issue in *Zurcher* was whether the First Amendment itself established a rule against a police search of a newspaper's offices.

The Court rejected the notion that the First Amendment provides a layer of constitutional protection beyond what the Fourth Amendment already establishes. The Court stressed, however, that when First Amendment interests are present, Fourth Amendment requirements must be followed with "scrupulous exactitude." It noted that a general warrant that enabled officers to rummage through records, documents, and papers would violate the Fourth Amendment. The Court restated the principle governing all searches and seizures that warrants should "leave as little as possible to the discretion and whim of the officer in the field." However, the Court pointed out that while the Constitution's framers were aware of the historical struggle between "Crown and press" and the need to safeguard against official intrusion into the editorial process, they did not create a First Amendment exception to the Fourth Amendment. Consequently, editorial offices are no different from corporate offices or homes for Fourth Amendment purposes. Newsrooms are afforded the same Fourth Amendment protection as any other venue that might be searched. The Fourth Amendment is not violated when (1) a search warrant is issued with probable cause that evidence will be found, (2) the warrant specifically describes the place to be searched, and (3) the warrant satisfies the requirement of overall reasonableness. The Court was satisfied that these safeguards, which are sufficient in other settings, were adequate for newsroom searches.

In a concurring opinion, Justice Lewis Powell echoed the Court's sentiment against creating a separate constitutional procedure for the press. Like the majority, Powell believed that the terms of the Fourth Amendment would read differently "[i]f the Framers had believed that the press was entitled to a special procedure." He noted, however, that a judicial officer issuing a warrant to search a newsroom "should take cognizance of the independent values protected by the First Amendment."

Those values that Powell referenced were set forth in Justice Stewart's dissenting opinion. From Stewart's perspective, it was "self-evident that police searches of newspaper offices burden the freedom of the press." One of the most obvious First Amendment harms, as he described it, was the disruption of editorial operations, including news gathering, writing, and publishing, at least during the course of the search. The possibility that confidential information or sources might be revealed struck Stewart as an ever-greater risk. Search warrants enable investigators to read "each and every document until they have found the one named in the warrant." The "end result" of such a process, in Stewart's view, was "a diminishing flow of potentially important information to the public" and injury to First Amendment interests. Particularly because there were no emergency circumstances that required prompt investigative action and there was no criminal activity on the part of the newspaper, Stewart maintained that the evidence could have been obtained by less invasive means. Rather than using a search warrant, a court could have issued a *subpoena duces tecum* requiring the newspaper to produce the photographs on a timely basis. A *subpoena duces tecum* is a judicial order requesting production of documents or other materials. Unless it is challenged on grounds of privilege or some other basis, it requires compliance. Stewart argued that such a procedure would have achieved the same result without the risk of ransacking editorial offices or chilling sources. Although Stewart's reasoning did not command a majority of the Court, it influenced development of the law governing newsroom searches. Congress enacted the Privacy Protection Act of 1980, which prohibits newsroom searches unless there is probable cause that materials to be seized are in the possession of a person who committed a crime or it is necessary to prevent death or serious bodily harm. Absent these extraordinary circumstances, information sought by law-enforcement officials must be obtained through the less disruptive method of a *subpoena duces tecum*. Unlike search warrants, subpoenas also may be challenged readily prior to their issuance on grounds that they are unconstitutional or the information sought is confidential. Although special regard for freedom of the press may not have moved the Court in *Zurcher*, the ruling precipitated a congressional accounting for the same First Amendment interest.

Bibliography

Wayne R. LaFave and Jerold H. Israel, *Criminal Procedure* 2d ed. (1992). Includes a survey of the law governing search and seizure, not just in relationship to First Amendment issues but generally.

Leonard W. Levy, *Emergence of a Free Press* (1985). A primary study of the origins of the free press clause, including discussion of whether it has meaning independent of the free speech clause.

Anthony Lewis, "A Preferred Position for Journalism?" 7 *Hofstra Law Review* 595 (1979). A detailed examination of the *Zurcher* decision.

Potter Stewart, " 'Or of the Press,' " 26 *Hastings Law Journal* 631 (1975). Expounds Justice Stewart's views on the special status and role of the press.

Globe Newspaper Co. v. Superior Court

Because information about the political process is essential for a viable system of representative government, political speech typically is afforded the highest degree of constitutional protection. The high value assigned to expression or information concerning the political process is reflected in federal and state freedom-of-information laws and open-meeting statutes. The collective self-interest of the nation's citizens requires access to government proceedings and information. However, even if open access is a norm, concerns that reflect a more important societal interest may take precedence. Exceptions to openness in government typically are allowed when national security concerns, sensitive law-enforcement records, personnel files, trade secrets, or other compelling needs require secrecy or confidentiality.

Of the three branches of government, the judiciary traditionally has been the least open to the public. Judges historically have exercised strict control over the coverage of judicial proceedings. Until the Supreme Court determined that the First Amendment limited the use of gag orders, in Nebraska Press Association v. Stuart (1976), they represented a common method of controlling the flow of information from the courtroom to the public. Such restrictions on what participants in a trial can say or the media can report typically have been sought as a means of protecting the right to a fair trial. Concern with prejudicial publicity that may impair a jury's ability to decide a case fairly is the most frequent basis for a gag order or a decision to close proceedings to the press and public. If the media disseminate information that prejudices jurors, not only the guarantee of a fair trial but the Sixth Amendment right to an impartial jury is at risk.

The Sixth Amendment guarantee of an impartial jury was the basis of the Court's determination in Gannett, Inc. v. DePasquale (1979) that pretrial hearings could be closed. The ruling reflected the Court's sense that the Sixth Amendment belonged to the defendant rather than to the press

Citation:	457 U.S. 596.
Issue:	Whether a state law that provided for closed hearing of a young sex offender's trial testimony violated the First Amendment.
Year of Decision:	1982.
Outcome:	Denial of public and press access to judicial proceedings without a compelling and narrowly defined state interest violates the First Amendment.
Author of Opinion:	Justice William Brennan.
Vote:	6–3.

or public. Because transcripts of the proceeding were made available after the risk of prejudice disappeared, the Court found that the interest in open proceedings had not been compromised. The Gannett decision sent uncertain signals about the openness of the judicial process. Although it concerned pretrial proceedings rather than trials themselves, the leeway that the ruling provided for closure and its lack of reference to First Amendment considerations raised questions about accessibility to judicial proceedings.

A year later, in Richmond Newspapers, Inc. v. Virginia (1980), the Court found that the First Amendment established a right for the public and the media to attend trials. Stressing that trials traditionally had been open, and that closure invited risks of abuse, the Court determined that the authority of judges to conduct trials in secrecy was narrow. Although First Amendment interests prevailed, the justices varied in their rationales. A majority opinion in support of access to criminal trials emerged two years later. In *Globe Newspaper Co. v. Superior Court*, the Court reviewed a Massachusetts newspaper's claim that it was unconstitutionally denied access to a rape trial. Under state law, the trial court had closed the proceedings because the alleged victims were minors. The trial court denied Globe Newspaper Co's. motion to revoke the closure order. Although the Massachusetts Supreme Judicial Court upheld the ruling, the United States Supreme Court reversed it on grounds the state law violated the First Amendment. As the Court saw it, the statute was constitutionally defective because of its mandatory nature. The law aimed to protect sex-offense victims from embarrassment and injury. By providing them with confidentiality, the law also was designed to encourage their testimony. Finding that an absolute bar to open proceedings diminished the public's and press's interest in attending trials, the Court determined that a trial judge must weigh various factors before deciding upon closure. Among these considerations were such circumstances as age, maturity, family preferences, nature of the crime, and whether testimony would be given if the proceeding was not closed. The Court acknowledged that child sex-abuse cases may create a risk that victims will experience further trauma if they are required to testify in an open court. This problem could be dealt with, however, by standards that protected vulnerable individuals such as minors when necessary.

In a majority opinion authored by Justice William Brennan, the Court found that the closure provision overreacted to the need. Mandatory closure was not shown to have encouraged victims of minor sex offense crimes to come forward or to protect effectively their confidentiality. Information about the victim could be obtained from transcripts, court personnel, and other sources. Because the mandatory closure rule was defective in purpose and reason, it failed to offset the "presumption of openness" that characterizes "our system of justice." The Court's opinion reflected the sense that the First Amendment must protect not only freedom of speech and of the press but those interests that effectively facilitate those constitutional imperatives. As the Court put it, "[T]he First Amendment is . . . broad enough to encompass those rights that, while not unambiguously enumerated in the very terms of the Amendment, are nonetheless necessary to the enjoyment of other First Amendment rights." The Court explained that access to criminal trials was constitutionally assured because the right was crucial to "free discussion of public affairs." Two particular aspects of the criminal justice system itself were cited as reasons why a right of access was secured by the First Amendment. First, criminal trials historically had been open both to the press and public. So solidly grounded were open trials that the Court was "unable to find a single instance of a criminal trial conducted *in camera* in any federal, state, or municipal court during the history of this country." Not only did this tradition of openness carry "the gloss of history," but it demonstrated "a tradition of accessibility impl[ying] the favorable judgment of experience." Second, a right of access for the public and press was an effective safeguard and facilitator of the judicial process's quality and integrity. As the Court noted, access "fosters an appearance of fairness, thereby heightening public respect for the judicial process." A factor particularly relevant to a system of self-governance was that access provides an opportunity "to participate in and serve as a check upon the judicial process."

In striking down the provision for closed trial proceedings, the Court did not foreclose all possibilities for denying access. Rather, it determined that any denial of access to a trial must be based upon "a compelling governmental interest" that is "narrowly tailored" to protect a minor. The courtroom thus might be closed if the government, in a particular case, demonstrated that the alleged victim would be harmed if he or she was required to testify with the press or public in attendance. Left unanswered by the decision was whether openness extended to judicial proceedings other than trials. Given a criminal justice system in which most resolutions are achieved through plea bargains rather than trials, this question is particularly significant. In Press Enterprise Co. v. Superior Court (1986), the Supreme Court established a First Amendment right of access to preliminary hearings. In so doing, it stressed the historical and pervasive preference for open proceedings. It also affirmed, despite contrary indications in Gannett, that the First Amendment interest in access extended to criminal proceedings generally and not just to a particular stage of such proceedings.

In a complex society in which time, opportunity, and distance prevent many persons from observing and assessing government on a firsthand basis, the press performs a critical role in facilitating an informed citizenry. The Court, however, has not accepted this premise as a basis for giving the press any privileged access to government proceedings or facilities. The right to attend criminal trials thus extends equally to the press and the public. Decisions regarding access to government proceedings or facilities consistently acknowledge that the press performs an essential role in facilitating informed self-government. Despite the significance of that function, the Court largely has adhered to the premise that the media are entitled to no special constitutional standing above and beyond that of the public that it serves.

Bibliography

Wayne R. LaFave and Jerold H. Israel, *Criminal Procedure*, 2d ed. (1992). Examines the conflict between the interests of a free press and fair trials.

Donald E. Lively, Allen S. Hammond IV, Blake D. Morant, and Russell L. Weaver, *Communications Law: Media, Entertainment, and Regulation* (1997). An overview of the law governing public and media access to government proceedings and information.

John E. Nowak and Ronald D. Rotunda, *Constitutional Law*, 5th ed. (1995). Includes general discussion of access to judicial proceedings.

Inger J. Sagatun and Leonard P. Edwards, *Child Abuse and the Legal System* (1995). Discusses special concerns relating to child sex-abuse cases.

Different First Amendment Standards for Different Media

Interpretations of the First Amendment guarantee of freedom of the press have been modified as new communications methodologies have evolved. Freedom of the press in its modern sense represents not a single doctrine but a variety of premises and degrees of protection that are dependent upon how the information source is perceived and understood. Rather than develop a theory of press freedom based upon a universal function of informing the public, the Supreme Court has determined that each medium presents unique problems that require a customized definition and application of the First Amendment. As Justice Robert Jackson put it in Kovacs v. Cooper (1949), "[t]he moving picture screen, the radio, the newspaper, the handbill, the sound truck and the street orator have differing natures, abuses, and dangers. Each . . . is a law unto itself." Even as cable, satellite, computer, and other telecommunications technologies have unfolded during the latter half of the twentieth century, the Court has continued to uphold medium-specific standards. Its decision in *Miami Herald Publishing Co. v. Tornillo* (1974) exemplifies how print media are afforded the highest level of First Amendment protection. The Court's rulings in *Red Lion Broadcasting Co. v. Federal Communications Commission* (1969) and *Federal Communications Commission v. Pacifica Foundation* (1978) demonstrate that broadcasting, although it is the nation's dominant medium, is the least protected medium under the First Amendment.

Miami Herald Publishing Co. v. Tornillo

When the freedom of the press clause was adopted as part of the First Amendment, it governed a media universe far simpler than what exists in modern times. Newspaper publishers in the late eighteenth century typically were motivated by strong partisan convictions. Not surprisingly, they traded primarily in sharp political debate over government officials and policy. In addition to their fiercely political nature, early newspapers tended to reach relatively small audiences because of limited methods of distribution and the state of literacy at the time. As the Industrial Revolution ushered in new methods of mass production and dissemination, the newspaper business evolved beyond its early nature. The advent of photojournalism in the late nineteenth century expanded the dimensions and influence of newspapers, which had previously communicated through text and sketchings.

So disturbing were some changes in the newspaper industry that critics suggested the need for a legal response to its impact. Louis Brandeis in 1890 coauthored an influential law-review article that expressed concern about intrusive and sensational news reporting. At the time of the Republic's founding, media generally were vehicles of partisan debate. From Brandeis's perspective, they had become instruments of gossip that appealed to people's lower instincts. This trend, as Brandeis saw it, diverted space from "matters of genuine community concern" to the interests of "the indolent." Because the press was "overstepping in every direction the obvious bounds of propriety and decency" through "[i]nstantaneous photographs" and "newspaper enterprise," Brandeis believed the law must shore up the individual's "right 'to be let alone.' "

Change was not limited to the medium's interests, the tone of its coverage, and the means of reporting. A primary trend of the newspaper industry, especially over the course of the twentieth century, has been the emergence of chains in which many publications are operated by group ownership. Another phenomenon has been the decline of the total number of daily newspapers. In 1910, a total of 2,600 daily newspapers were pub-

Citation:	418 U.S. 241.
Issue:	Whether a state law that gave political candidates the right to space in a newspaper that criticized them was unconstitutional.
Year of Decision:	1974.
Outcome:	A candidate has no right to space enabling him or her to reply.
Author of Opinion:	Chief Justice Warren Burger.
Vote:	9–0.

lished in American metropolitan areas. By the final decade of the twentieth century, that number had diminished to fewer than 1,750. Cities with more than one newspaper, which were common at the beginning of the century, were a rarity by its end. As the Supreme Court observed in the early 1970s, one-newspaper towns "have become the rule, with effective competition operating in only four percent of our large cities." With increasingly concentrated ownership of newspapers and a shrinking market for them, concern emerged that power to inform the American people and influence public opinion rested in the hands of a relative few.

The question of whether concentrated ownership necessitated a redefinition of press freedom presented itself in *Miami Herald Publishing Co. v. Tornillo*. At issue was a Florida "right to reply law" that was designed to ensure a fair and balanced flow of information. Pat Tornillo, a candidate for public office, had been harshly criticized in a *Miami Herald* editorial. Under the terms of the statute, he had "a right to equal space to reply to criticism and attacks on [his] record by a newspaper." In determining whether this provision undermined press freedom, the Court acknowledged that the newspaper industry increasingly had become characterized by concentrated ownership and diminished competition. Because editorial output had become a function of centralized and homogenized opinion, commentary, and analysis, the argument for the law was that "the public has lost any ability to respond to or contribute in a meaningful way to the debate on issues." The state presented the law as a means to ensure broad and balanced coverage of important public concerns and as a constitutional check against "the vast accumulations of unreviewable power in the modern media empires."

The Court noted that economic facts had altered the right of free public expression as experienced when the nation was founded. Editorial competition over the course of the twentieth century became difficult if not impossible to maintain because entry into the publishing business had become prohibitively expensive. Despite these changes and their impact on First Amendment circumstances, the Court rejected the notion that the state could force a publisher to be fair, accurate, or accountable. Writing for the majority, Chief Justice Warren Burger indicated that "a responsible press" might be a "desirable goal," but it could not be achieved by constitutional interpretation without violating the First Amendment. The core issue presented by Florida's right-to-reply law was whether government could force "editors to publish that which 'reason tells them should not be published.' " Such a requirement, from the Court's point of view, intruded into the very essence of the editorial process. As the Court observed, a public right of access requires a setting aside of "space that could be devoted to other material the newspaper may have preferred to print." The Court not only viewed the law as impermissible because it compromised editorial autonomy, which is the essence of press freedom, but noted that it might encourage editors to shy away from controversy so that they would not trigger a right to reply. Such a result would be detrimental not only to editorial freedom but to the needs of the information marketplace.

Because the law compelled printing of a reply, it was viewed as extracting a penalty on the basis of content. These costs included "printing and composing time and materials and . . . space" that might be used for other stories. Even if the law did not impose additional costs, a right of reply was unacceptable because it intruded into the function of editors. As the Court described them, newspapers are "more than a passive receptacle of conduit for news, comment, and advertising." The content of a newspaper and decisions concerning size and attitude toward persons and policy "constitute the exercise of editorial control and function." Whether editorial judgment is "fair or unfair," it is a central aspect of press freedom. Recognizing the importance of editorial autonomy, the Court stressed that it had not been demonstrated how governmental regulation of this process could be upheld without ignoring the First Amendment.

The Court's decision shows an appreciation of the role that the press plays as a check on government and how that function might be undermined if the state assumed responsibility for fairness and balance. It reflects a philosophy faithful to founding sentiments expressed by John Adams, who drafted the free press clause of the Massachusetts Constitution. Adams observed that "liberty of the press is essential to the security of the state, . . . [and] the relevant metaphor . . . is the metaphor of the Fourth Estate." The Fourth Estate is a term that referred to the "Reporters' Gallery" of the British Parliament. From this vantage point, journalists observed the three traditional estates of Parliament, which included the clergy, nobility, and commons. Today, the term refers to the press generally. Justice Byron White in a concurring opinion reinforced the value of this role by referring to "the unhappy experiences of other nations where government has been allowed to meddle in the internal editorial affairs of newspapers." No matter how noble or beneficial the purpose of regulation was, White stressed the need to "remain intensely skeptical about those measures that would allow government to insinuate itself into the editorial rooms of this Nation's press." For him, a right-to-reply law advanced an important interest but ignored how "[w]oven into the fabric of the First Amendment is the unexceptional, but nonetheless timeless, sentiment that 'liberty of the press is in peril as soon as the government tries to compel what is to go into a newspaper.'" As media ownership has become more highly concentrated, and the number of newspapers has fallen, concern has been expressed about the press's ability to provide fair and balanced coverage. This concern may be offset, however, by the emergence of new media technologies such as the internet that are sources of information, opinion, and dialogue. By striking down Florida's right-to-reply law, the Court conclusively repudiated the notion that the First Amendment either permits or requires government to promote fairness and even-handedness through official regulation. It established the basic premise governing all print media that the First Amendment requires not a fair but a free press.

Bibliography

Louis D. Brandeis and Samuel D. Warren, "The Right to Privacy," 4 *Harvard Law Review* 193 (1890). A critical reaction to the increasingly intrusive methods of newspaper reporters and sensationalized stories in the late nineteenth century.

Zechariah Chafee, *Government and Mass Communications* (1947). A seminal work on the constitutional relationship between government and the media.

Edwin Emery, *The Press and America* (1962). Examines the history of American newspapers.

Cass Sunstein, *Democracy and the Problem of Free Speech* (1993). A critical view of the *Tornillo* decision and its rationale.

Red Lion Broadcasting Co. v. Federal Communications Commission

The First Amendment, as interpreted, provides different levels of protection for speech depending upon the nature of the expression. Political speech is especially valued and thus is afforded the highest measure of constitutional security. Obscenity and fighting words are perceived as having such slight value that they are categorically without First Amendment protection (see the discussions of *Roth v. United States* [1957]; *Miller v. California* [1973];

Chaplinsky v. New Hampshire [1942]. Paralleling this hierarchy of speech are variable levels of constitutional stature for the press. Although print, broadcasting, cable, and other media have the same function of disseminating information, the First Amendment regards each of them differently. Newspapers and other publications historically have been ranked at the top of the First Amendment order. Regulation that would interfere with editorial autonomy, as the Supreme Court noted in *Miami Herald Publishing Co. v. Tornillo* (1974), is inimical to the core meaning of the freedom of the press clause.

Citation:	395 U.S. 367.
Issue:	Whether a federal rule requiring broadcasters to balance points of view on controversial issues is constitutional.
Year of Decision:	1969.
Outcome:	Requiring broadcasters to provide balanced points of view does not violate the First Amendment.
Author of Opinion:	Justice Byron White.
Vote:	8–0.

Over the course of the twentieth century, broadcasting has emerged as the nation's dominant medium, yet it is more susceptible to content regulation than newspapers and other print media. Federal regulation historically has imposed upon broadcasters regulatory obligations that would be constitutionally impermissible if they were applied to publishers. The Communications Act of 1934 prohibits radio or television broadcasting without a license that, among other things, is granted upon a finding that the broadcaster will serve the public interest. Because of the notion that broadcasters have special obligations to the public, they have been governed by rules that require them not only to inform the public about important issues but to ensure that their coverage is balanced. One example of these rules was the fairness doctrine, which the Federal Communications Commission (FCC) set forth in 1949 as a duty to "[1] devote a reasonable percentage of . . . broadcast time to the . . . consideration of public issues . . . [and] (2) make sufficient time available for full discussion thereof."

The fairness doctrine was attacked on First Amendment grounds two decades later when Red Lion Broadcasting Co., which operated a Pennsylvania radio station, refused to provide free reply time following a program that characterized an author as antipatriotic and sympathetic to communism. The FCC found that the broadcast constituted a personal attack and that the radio station must provide free reply time. In so doing, it affirmed the constitutionality of fairness regulation in broadcasting and determined that such rules actually promoted First Amendment interests. Historical experience, from the Court's perspective, supported the need for government regulation that achieved rational use of the broadcast spectrum. Without such control, as Justice Byron White stated for a unanimous Court, "the medium would be of little use because of the cacophony of competing voices, none of which could be clearly and predictably heard." This observation referred to what the Court viewed as a unique characteristic of broadcasting—spectrum scarcity. The number of frequencies available for broadcasting is less than the number of broadcasters who would like to use them. Under these circumstances, the Court found it "idle to posit an unabridgeable First Amendment right to broadcast comparable to the right of every individual to speak, write or publish." The FCC's authority to establish fairness requirements derived from its general power to regulate in the public interest. As the Court observed, "[t]he 'public interest' in broadcasting clearly encompasses the presentation of controversial issues of importance and concern to the public."

The broadcaster argued that an official requirement of full and fair coverage of important issues interfered with its freedom to use and exclude from its frequencies whomever it wanted. The point paralleled the successful contention of a publisher in *Miami Herald Co. v. Tornillo* (1974) that newspaper publishers could not be required "to publish that which 'reason tells them should not be published.' " Although the Court acknowledged that broadcasting was protected by the First Amendment, it emphasized the medium-specific nature of the free press clause. It thus stressed that "differences in the characteristics of new media justify differences in the First Amendment standards applied to them." As the Court saw it, the most significant and distinguishing characteristic of broadcasting was spectrum scarcity. Because of this trait, the First Amendment stature of broadcasters was set at a level beneath that of publishers. Specifically, the Court determined that the First Amendment does not prevent government from requiring a broadcaster "to conduct himself as a proxy or fiduciary with obligations to present those views and voices which are representative of his community and which could otherwise, by necessity, be barred from the airwaves." From the Court's perspective, the idea of "100 persons" wanting to broadcast when only "10 frequencies" were available necessitated a fresh view of the First Amendment. What the Court eventually characterized as an "unusual order" of constitutional interests in the context of broadcasting was necessitated by the sense that the medium must "function consistently with the ends and purposes of the First Amendment." Because spectrum scarcity created the risk that some views and voices might not be heard, to the detriment of the public, the Court stated that "the right of the public to receive suitable access to social, political, esthetic, moral, and other ideas and experiences is crucial here."

Viewers and listeners thus were afforded a First Amendment right to receive diverse information from broadcasters, and this interest was found to outweigh the interest in editorial autonomy. Because broadcasters might prove resistant to or "timorous" in the discharge of their fairness duties, the Court emphasized that the FCC had the power to insist upon compliance with these responsibilities. Included in the range of regulatory options in the event of a fairness violation were fines and nonrenewal or revocation of a license. In reality, the FCC shied away from vigorously enforcing the fairness doctrine. A study in 1973–74 showed that out of 4,280 fairness complaints, only 19 resulted in findings against the broadcaster. This enforcement pattern generated criticism that fairness regulation was not only ineffective but a lurking threat to traditional First Amendment interests. A primary argument of critics was that spectrum scarcity, which was the premise for fairness requirements, was not a problem unique to broadcasting. At both the local and national level, the number of broadcasting outlets far exceeded the number of daily newspapers. A response to this concern was that scarcity in broadcasting is a function of physical and technological limits, while the number of newspapers is determined by what the market will bear. The distinction, as pointed out in a federal appeals court ruling by Judge Robert Bork in Telecommunications Research and Action Center v. Federal Communications Commission (1986), is "without a difference." Bork noted that "[a]ll economic goods are scarce, not least the newsprint, ink, delivery trucks, computers, and other resources that go into the production and dissemination of print journalism." As was the case in broadcasting, "[n]ot everyone who wants to publish a newspaper, or even a pamphlet, may do so." It is worth noting, moreover, that the primary obstacle to publishing or broadcasting is having or accessing the significant amount of capital necessary to run a viable business operation.

Persistent criticism of the fairness doctrine moved the FCC to abandon it. In so doing, it cited Bork's point that spectrum scarcity is an inadequate rationale. After decades of embracing the fairness doctrine, the FCC in 1987 concluded that it "disserves both the public's right to diverse sources of information and the broadcaster's interest in free expression." A doctrine that initially had been conceived and developed to facilitate First Amendment values thus was repudiated as a disservice to them.

Despite the FCC's rejection of the scarcity premise, the Court has yet to eliminate it as a unique factor in defining broadcasting's First Amendment status. In Metro Broadcasting, Inc. v. Federal Communications Commission (1990), the Court reaffirmed the notion that the scarcity of broadcast frequencies justifies official restraints "on licensees in favor of others whose views should be expressed on this unique medium." It thus restated the proposition that "the public's right to receive a diversity of views and information over the airwaves" is consistent with the First Amendment's aims and purposes. Even if broadcasting is no longer subject to fairness regulation, therefore, it is still subject to a constitutional order that effectively relegates it to second-class status under the First Amendment.

Bibliography

Erik Barnouw, *A History of Broadcasting in the United States* (1969). A comprehensive history of broadcasting.

Lucas A. Powe, Jr., *American Broadcasting and the First Amendment* (1987). A critical evaluation of the premises of modern broadcasting regulation, especially the scarcity rationale.

Benno C. Schmidt, Jr., *Freedom of the Press vs. Public Access* (1976). Examines the conflict between traditional concepts of press freedom and the public's interest in accessing diverse information.

Steven Simmons, *The Fairness Doctrine and the Media* (1978). An extensive review of the fairness doctrine's development and application.

Federal Communications Commission v. Pacifica Foundation

Since the framing and ratification of the First Amendment in the late eighteenth century, its terms have remained fixed. The media universe that it governs, however, has expanded dramatically. Publishing was the original and exclusive focus of the free press clause. Print eventually became only one of many methods of mass communication that include motion pictures, radio, television, cable, computers, and satellites.

First Amendment recognition of some of these newer media has come later rather than sooner. Motion pictures were denied First Amendment status for the first half of the twentieth century because they were perceived as a mere "spectacle" having a significant potential for "evil." The constitutional protection of motion pictures, like that of other new media, is more restricted than that of print media. These variable First Amendment standards reflect the belief, expressed in Metromedia, Inc. v. San Diego (1981), that each method of communication requires "a 'law unto itself,' reflecting the 'differing natures, values, abuses, and dangers' of each method."

Citation:	438 U.S. 726.
Issue:	Whether the First Amendment bars the Federal Communications Commission from prohibiting indecent but not obscene expression on radio or television.
Year of Decision:	1978.
Outcome:	The First Amendment does not prevent regulation of indecent expression by broadcasters.
Author of Opinion:	Justice John Paul Stevens.
Vote:	5–4.

A persistent concern with any new medium is its impact upon society. In refusing to view motion pictures as part of the press in Mutual Film Corp. v. State Industrial Commission of Ohio (1915), the Court noted that the medium offered "mere representations of events, of ideas and sentiments published and known." Although these images may be "useful and entertaining," the Court found that they had a potential for evil that was enhanced by their "attractiveness and exhibition." Particularly because children had easy access to motion pictures, the Court found their potential for "corruption" even more "insidious."

Although the Mutual Film decision eventually was overturned, the Court continued to assess a medium's potential for "evil" and its availability. These issues have become a particular focal point in broadcasting, especially when government has regulated sexually explicit or indecent programming. Such regulation was the basis for a First Amendment challenge in *Federal Communications Commission v. Pacifica Foundation* (1978). Pacifica Foundation is the licensee of radio stations known for their focus on arts, politics, and avant-garde programming. At issue was the broadcast by a Pacifica operated radio station in New York of a monologue by comedian George Carlin that used "words you couldn't say on the public . . . airwaves." The presentation, titled "Filthy Words," had been recorded before a live audience and later was broadcast by a New York radio station during the middle of a weekday afternoon. It was preceded by warnings that the language might offend some listeners. The complainant encountered the program while driving with his fifteen-year-old son. Despite the radio station's argument that the humorist was a "significant social satirist," the Federal Communications Commission (FCC) found that the broadcast violated its rules against patently offensive words dealing with sex and excretion.

Although the Court noted that speech cannot be regulated merely because it is "offensive," it held that there was no First Amendment violation. Patently offensive expression such as Carlin's was not without constitutional protection. The context in which it was communicated, however, determined the extent of that protection. The Court thus indicated that words acceptable in a transmission between cab drivers or in an Elizabethan comedy could be regulated and punished in another setting.

The Court then turned its attention to the context of the expression. At this point, majority sentiment vanished. Justice John Paul Stevens, supported by three of his colleagues, noted that broadcasting was the least protected medium under the First Amendment. This diminished constitutional status contrasts with the greater protection afforded print media. The Court itself published the entire Carlin monologue in its opinion. The FCC's authority to regulate such programming was justified on two grounds. First, the Stevens plurality declared that broadcasting has "a uniquely pervasive presence in the lives of all Americans." Particularly because patently offensive expression confronts viewers and listeners in the privacy of their homes, where privacy interests are at their peak, "the right to be left alone plainly outweighs the First Amendment rights of an intruder." Second, the Stevens plurality found that broadcasting "is uniquely accessible to children, even those too young to read." Although a printed message might be incomprehensible to a first-grader, exposure to the Carlin monologue would "have enlarged a child's vocabulary in an instant." In closing, the Stevens plurality grounded the basis for regulating indecent broadcasting on a nuisance rationale that "requires consideration of a host of variables." Among these factors were the time of day, the composition of the audience, and the difference between broadcasting over public airwaves and by closed circuit. Expanding upon the nuisance concept, the Stevens plurality referred to prior case law that characterized a nuisance as "merely a right thing in the wrong place—like a pig in the parlor instead of the barnyard." As the plurality stated, "[w]hen the [FCC] finds that a pig has entered the parlor, the exercise of its regulatory power does not depend on proof that the pig is obscene."

The decision elicited a sharp and lengthy dissent by Justice William Brennan, who argued that the Court misconceived the privacy interests at stake. Brennan maintained that the Court denied the interests of persons who wanted access to programming such as the Carlin monologue. His arguments reflect the concern of those who believe that privacy is better served by relying upon individuals to decide for themselves what programming is fit for their consumption. From Brennan's perspective, the decision reflected a disturbing and "depressing inability to appreciate that in our land of cultural pluralism, there are many who think, act, and talk differently from the Members of this Court, and who do not share their fragile sensibilities." The ruling for Brennan also was evidence of "an acute ethnocentric myopia that enables the Court to approve the censorship of communications solely because of the words they contain." Noting that the words that the Court found "unpalatable" were "the stuff of everyday conversations" in many communities, he warned that the decision would penalize most those who disagree with or challenge the "dominant culture." By requiring conformity to a preferred "way of thinking, acting and speaking" and disregarding the value of expression as a means "to flout majoritarian conventions," the Court, in Brennan's opinion, missed the point of the First Amendment.

For nearly two decades after the *Pacifica* ruling, the courts wrestled with the scope of federal power to regulate indecent expression. Following a series of procedural twists and turns, changes in its position, and remands by reviewing courts, the FCC issued rules that restricted indecent programming to the hours between 10 P.M. and 6 A.M. This "time channeling" provision for sexual expression that falls short of obscenity was upheld by a federal appeals court in Action for Children's Television v. Federal Communications Commission (1995) on grounds that government had a compelling interest in protecting children under the age of eighteen. Also relevant was the fact that adult viewers and listeners were not entirely denied access to a constitutionally protected form of expression.

Sexually explicit expression continues to be a source of controversy not only in broadcasting but in other settings. Children's access to websites trading in sexually explicit words and graphics has generated legislative efforts to control them. In Reno v. American Civil Liberties Union (1997), the Court struck down provisions of the Communications Decency Act prohibiting indecent communications through the Internet. In so doing, the Court noted that sexual expression, even if indecent as opposed to obscene, is protected by the First Amendment. It concluded that, despite a valid governmental interest in protecting children, this concern did "not justify an unnecessarily broad suppression of speech addressed to adults." As with other telecommunications methodologies, parents can prevent their children from accessing inappropriate materials by purchasing software or using other blocking devices. Against this backdrop, at least when technology affords parents adequate control, the Court has refused to reduce the level of "discourse . . . to that which would be suitable for a sandbox."

Bibliography

Nat Hentoff, *The First Freedom* (1980). Delineates the background and circumstances of the *Pacifica* case.

Alexander Meiklejohn, *Free Speech and Its Relation to Self-Government* (1948). An early view of broadcasting as not deserving First Amendment protection because it does not cultivate taste, reasoned judgment, integrity, and other qualities.

Lucas A. Powe, Jr., *American Broadcasting and the First Amendment* (1987). Assesses efforts to regulate indecency over the airwaves.

Matthew Spitzer, *Seven Dirty Words and Six Other Stories* (1986). Criticizes the *Pacifica* decision as a product of false distinctions.

15

The First Amendment:
Freedom of Religion

Many provisions of the Bill of Rights grew out of colonial experience with abuses of power under British authority. Attention to freedom of religion reflects an appreciation of the historical reality that colonization in large part was driven by persons who were seeking to escape religious persecution. The constitutional guarantee of religious freedom is twofold. Under the establishment clause, Congress may not enact laws "respecting an establishment of religion."

Under the free exercise clause, it may not prohibit "the free exercise" of religion. Taken together, these provisions prevent Congress from imposing a particular creed by law and from interfering with an individual's chosen set of religious beliefs. The Supreme Court's incorporation of the establishment and free exercise clauses into the due process clause of the Fourteenth Amendment has extended their application to state governments. The establishment clause and free exercise clause, however, are not always easy to reconcile with each other. State aid to religious schools, for instance, may be viewed as an unconstitutional support of religion. At the same time, denial of such assistance may be regarded as interference with the free exercise of religion. Such conflicting perceptions illuminate a tension between the clauses that is reflected throughout the relevant case law.

The Establishment Clause

Review of the establishment clause by the Supreme Court has been a source of striking metaphors but uncertain doctrine and results. Central to many of the Court's decisions in the field is a notion that the establishment clause erects "a wall of separation between church and State." This understanding, drawn from the writings of Thomas Jefferson and James Madison in support of religious freedom in Virginia, suggests more clarity than relevant case law actually has generated. The concept of a wall between church and state suggests a clear dividing line between politics and religion. It is a barrier, however, that has many holes and leaks in it. One example of this reality was the Court's ruling in *Everson v. Board of Education* (1947). Although the Court stressed the existence of a wall between church and state, it determined that state reimbursement of transportation costs for students (including those who attended parochial schools) did not violate the establishment clause. Since the *Everson* decision, the Court has grappled with the task of developing standards of review that are perceived as principled and effective. This effort has been complicated because many critics, including some justices, do not subscribe to the wall metaphor. In *Lemon v. Kurtzman* (1971), the Court nonetheless settled on establishment clause standards that generally define the field even as they continue to be sources of debate. As evidenced by its ruling in *Lynch v. Donnelly* (1984), the Court remains sensitive to the possibility that the finding of an establishment clause violation may burden free exercise interests.

Everson v. Board of Education, Township of Ewing

The First Amendment contains two significant passages that account for religious freedom. The "establishment clause" provides that "Congress shall pass no law respecting an establishment of religion." The amendment also denies Congress the ability to make any law "prohibiting the free exercise of religion." The common command of these provisions is that government must be neutral toward religion. Although both of these clauses intend to guarantee religious liberty, an inherent tension exists between them. A law that permitted any group except a religious organization to use a public park, for instance, would avoid promoting religion. Such an enactment would be susceptible to claims, however, that it was interfering with free exercise interests.

The historical record has played a significant role in analysis of the freedom of religion clause, particularly in the context of establishment clause cases. Primary influences have been the writings of Thomas Jefferson and James Madison, who, one year before the framing of the Constitution, spearheaded the effort to establish complete separation between religion and government in Virginia. Their arguments are the source of one of the most durable metaphors in the field— the notion that the First Amendment creates a "wall" between church and state. History provides mixed signals about original purpose because the Virginia experience was not consistent with attitudes in other states. Efforts to identify a consensual understanding of the establishment clause based on attitudes and practices contemporaneous with the framing of the Constitution are common but futile. Those who drafted and ratified the First Amendment supported the establishment clause for different reasons. Delegates from South Carolina, Massachusetts, Connecticut, Maryland, and New Hampshire, for instance, had official churches that they wished to protect from possible federal interference. The

Citation:	330 U.S. 1.
Issue:	Whether a state law that reimburses parents for transportation costs of public and private school students violates the First Amendment.
Year of Decision:	1947.
Outcome:	The First Amendment does not prohibit the state from reimbursing transportation costs incurred by all students.
Author of Opinion:	Justice Hugo Black.
Vote:	5–4.

Pennsylvania delegation supported the provision because it believed that religious diversity was desirable. Pennsylvania, however, extended rights and liberties only to those persons who professed a Christian faith. Virginia pushed the notion of separation of church from both the federal and state governments.

The seminal case under the establishment clause was *Everson v. Board of Education, Township of Ewing*. As a taxpayer in the township, Arch R. Everson challenged the school board's authorization of reimbursement to parents for the costs of sending their children to school on public buses. The Board's action, authorized by state law, extended to parents whose children attended Catholic schools. It thus was challenged on grounds it violated the establishment clause. In a 5–4 majority opinion, Justice Hugo Black examined events that preceded the First Amendment's adoption. Black stressed that many of the nation's early settlers left Europe "to escape the bondage of laws which compelled them to support and attend government-favored churches." Many of the Old World's practices, including punishment of those who criticized, did not attend, or failed to pay tithes or taxes to support government-established churches, were transplanted to the English colonies. Use of tax monies to pay clerical salaries and to build and maintain official churches generated indignation in many quarters that helped fuel support for the establishment clause. Focusing upon the Virginia experience, the majority referred to Jefferson's and Madison's effort to defeat a tax levy in support of the state-established church. Madison's influential document, the Memorial and Remonstrance, asserted that true religion does not need the law's support, no person should be taxed to support a religious institution, society's best interests are served by free minds, and "cruel persecutions were the inevitable result of government-established religions." Because these sentiments were a foundation for the First Amendment, the Court determined that the establishment clause "means at least this: Neither a state nor the Federal Government can set up a church. Neither can pass laws which aid one religion, aid all religions, or prefer one religion over another." Nor, as the majority observed, can any person be forced or influenced to attend or avoid church or profess a belief or disbelief in any religion, or be taxed to support any religious activities or institutions. Citing Jefferson, the Court concluded that "the clause against establishment of religion by law was intended to erect 'a wall of separation between church and State.' "

Having identified the standards for its analysis, the Court observed that a state could not contribute monies directly to a religious institution without violating the establishment clause. It noted further, however, that a state cannot exclude persons from a general welfare program without abridging their free exercise interests. Although it acknowledged "that children are helped to get to church schools," it found this assistance indistinguishable from the use of state police officers to protect those same students from traffic hazards on the way to and from school. To deny parents of parochial school students reimbursement of transportation costs, from the majority's perspective, would represent the use of state power to burden religion. It would be no different than cutting off parochial schools from "such general government services as ordinary police and fire protection, connections for sewage disposal, public highways and sidewalks." As the Court noted, such an outcome would discourage parents from sending their children to parochial schools, and "such is obviously not the purpose of the First Amendment." Although the establishment clause requires the state to be neutral in its relations with believers and nonbelievers, the Court stressed that "it does not require the state to be their adversary." On the contrary, "State power is no more to be used so as to handicap religions than it is to favor them." Because the state contributed no money to parochial schools and did not support them, the Court found that the legislation merely provided a general program of support for all parents of schoolchildren regardless of religion.

The essence of the Court's decision was that the wall between church and state "must be kept high and impregnable," and that it would not "approve the slightest breach." Four dissenting justices were unable to reconcile this seemingly unforgiving standard with the result. In his separate dissent, Justice Robert Jackson found the majority's rhetoric "utterly discordant with its conclusion." As he put it, "[t]he case which irresistibly comes to mind as the most fitting precedent is that of Julia who, according to Byron's reports, whispering 'I will ne'er consent,'—consented." Jackson disputed the Court's analogy of transportation reimbursement plans to police and fire protection. From his viewpoint, no parallel existed because police protect persons and firefighters protect property. Neither is obligated to ask whether an individual or a building is, for instance, Catholic. However, school authorities must confront directly the question of whether the school is religious before they draw a check to reimburse parents for student bus fares. Jackson maintained that religious freedom "was first in the Bill of Rights because it was first in the forefathers' minds." It represented an effort to keep government out of religion and religion out of government and, most important, to make sure that bitter religious disputes did not spill over into the political realm. These "great ends," Jackson observed, had been "immeasurably compromised" by a decision that sought to "have it both ways." Despite the seeming harshness of prohibiting public aid to religious education, Jackson stressed that "it is the same Constitution" that affords Catholics and other groups the right to maintain their schools. He warned that if the state could aid religious schools, it could regulate them. Given the historical struggle associated with separating political from ecclesiastical affairs, Jackson concluded with a sense that the Court was "giving the clock's hands a backward twist."

Although the *Everson* decision generated criticism, it established the

"wall" between church and state as a defining criterion for future establishment clause analysis. Inevitably, given the Court's selective focus on the
Virginia experience, other versions of history have vied for the Court's
attention. In Wallace v. Jaffree (1985), Justice William Rehnquist challenged the "wall" on grounds that "[i]t is impossible to build sound constitutional doctrine upon a mistaken understanding of constitutional
history." Citing the metaphor as a "misguided analytical concept," Rehnquist urged its abandonment. In its place, he advocated an understanding
of the establishment clause that is limited to prohibiting a national religion
and discrimination among denominations. Although the Madison-Jefferson
model continues to be a vital force in establishment clause review, decisions
since *Everson* have expanded the grounds for public aid to parochial education in a variety of settings. These results extended the scope of the
Court's seminal reasoning and suggest that the wall between church and
state, even if it has not been breached, is not as insurmountable as its
strongest advocates might wish.

Bibliography

Robert S. Alley, ed., *James Madison on Religious Liberty* (1985). Describes Mad-
    ison's role in drafting the First Amendment.
Thomas E. Buckley, *Church and State in Revolutionary Virginia: 1776–1787*
    (1977). Explores the Virginia experience that led to the creation of a wall
    between church and state.
Leonard W. Levy, *The Establishment Clause* (1986). Examines the history of the
    establishment clause of the First Amendment.

Lemon v. Kurtzman

The establishment clause of the First Amendment prohibits Congress from making any "law respecting an establishment of religion." Establishment clause doctrine largely reflects the notion, introduced by James Madison and Thomas Jefferson, that a "wall" separates church and state. Early decisions that struck down laws on grounds that they violated the establishment clause were based upon findings that government policy was intended to promote a religious purpose or had the primary effect of advancing religion. These considerations were manifest in Engel v. Vitale (1962), the Court struck down a New York law that provided for student recitation of a nondenominational prayer in public schools at the beginning of the school day. The Court found that the establishment clause represented "an awareness of the historical fact that governmentally established religions and religious persecutions go hand in hand." It further observed that the

Citation:	403 U.S. 602.
Issue:	Whether state supplementation of salaries for parochial school teachers is unconstitutional.
Year of Decision:	1971.
Outcome:	Partial subsidization of salaries for teachers at religious schools is unconstitutional.
Author of Opinion:	Chief Justice Warren Burger.
Vote:	8–1.

clause's "most immediate purpose rested on the belief that a union of government and religion tends to destroy government and to degrade religion."

The impermissible purpose and primary effect of advancing religion emerged as primary focal points in Abington School District v. Schempp (1963), in which the Court struck down Maryland and Pennsylvania laws that required Bible readings and recitation of the Lord's Prayer at the beginning of the school day. In so doing, it observed that an enactment violated the establishment clause unless its purpose was not religious and its primary effect neither advanced nor inhibited religion. Although the Court allowed study of religion or even of the Bible as part of a secular program of education, it found that compulsory Bible reading and prayer were inconsistent with the First Amendment. For similar reasons, the Court in Stone v. Graham (1980) found that posting the Ten Commandments in classrooms was unconstitutional. So too was a law, struck down in Epperson v. Arkansas (1968), that prohibited the teaching of evolution in public schools and universities.

Attention to a law's purpose and effect soon was joined by another important but controversial element of establishment clause review. This new facet of First Amendment analysis was introduced in *Lemon v. Kurtzman.* This case, which consolidated actions brought in Rhode Island and Pennsylvania, concerned laws that provided state aid to church-related elementary and secondary schools. The Pennsylvania action was brought by Alton J. Lemon, other state citizens and taxpayers, and the Superintendent of Public Instruction, David H. Kurtzman. The Rhode Island case also was initiated by citizens and taxpayers. Unlike the Pennsylvania plaintiffs, they were successful in convincing a federal district court that the state had violated the establishment clause. At issue specifically were teacher salary supplements that each state provided to teachers in nonpublic elementary schools. Because each statute clearly indicated an intent to enhance the quality of secular education in all schools, the Court in an opinion by Chief Justice Warren Burger was unable to identify a purpose of advancing religion. Nor was there a basis for discerning that the primary effect of the provision was not to advance a secular aim. Beyond purpose and effect, however, the Court announced that it was necessary to demonstrate that the provision did not cause "excessive government entanglement with religion." To make this determination, the Court stated that it "must examine the character and purposes of the institutions that are benefitted, the nature of the aid that the State provides, and the resulting relationship between the government and the religious authority."

Teacher salary supplements, from the Court's perspective, excessively entangled church and state. Even if teachers in parochial schools would not function in bad faith or consciously evade the establishment clause's dictates, the Court believed that they would find it difficult to avoid a total separation between secular teaching and religious doctrine. Teaching the requirements of "good citizenship," for instance, might be influenced by religious doctrine or belief.

Even with the best efforts of teachers to avoid mixing religious and secular instruction, the Court determined that the state could not guard against breaches without excessively entangling itself in religion. As safeguards against this possibility, the state had conditioned its aid upon what the Court characterized as "pervasive restrictions." Eligible recipients, for instance, could teach only courses offered in public schools and use only texts and materials used in public schools. They were specifically prohibited from teaching any course in religion. The Court noted that to monitor compliance, it would be necessary for the state to establish "[a] comprehensive, discriminating, and continuing state surveillance . . . to ensure that these restrictions are obeyed and the First Amendment otherwise respected." With respect to salary supplements, the Court observed that the instructor cannot be inspected just once to safeguard against crossing an unconstitutional line. Necessary measures to ensure compliance, from the Court's perspective, necessitated excessive entanglement of the state with religion. The entanglement was compounded, moreover, by a provision of the law that exempted teachers at nonpublic schools whose per pupil expenditures exceeded those at public schools. To determine qualification and compliance, government would have to examine school records to assess school expenditures. Such inspection and evaluation of a religious organization, as the Court put it, was "fraught with the sort of entanglement that the Court forbids."

The primary significance of the ruling was its creation of a three-part test for determining an establishment clause violation. The Court announced that "[f]irst, the statute must have a secular legislative purpose; second, its principal or primary effect must be one that neither advances nor inhibits religion; finally, the statute must not foster 'an excessive government entanglement with religion.' " Although this standard appears to be compact and orderly, it has been a source of significant unpredictability and criticism. In a dissenting opinion, Justice Byron White described "[j]udicial caveats against entanglement" as a "blurred, indistinct and variable barrier." The Court itself, in upholding federal grants to build physical facilities at universities and colleges, acknowledged that it could "only dimly perceive the boundaries of permissible governmental activity in this sensitive area of constitutional adjudication." In Tilton v. Richardson (1971), the Court allowed a system of governmental aid on grounds that students at religiously affiliated universities and colleges are "less impressionable and susceptible to religious indoctrination" than pupils at the primary and secondary levels.

The uncertainty created by the test of purpose, effect, and excessive entanglement is evidenced by its legacy. The Court has upheld tax deductions for educational costs, government funding of standardized testing, subsidized physical and psychological diagnostic services and counseling, and publicly financed construction at sectarian colleges and universities. It has struck down loans of instructional materials to parochial schools, government-subsidized field-trip transportation, tax credits for educational costs, reimbursement for nonstandardized testing, and special educational programs for students and adults. These variable outcomes have been a source of criticism by those who seek doctrine that generates more predictability than turmoil. Despite the inadequacies of establishment clause analysis, the Court persists with it. A primary theme of establishment clause review, expressed in Zorach v. Clauson (1952), is that "[w]e are a religious people." Free exercise principles reinforce that understanding. A possible response to that premise that does not necessarily detract from it is that "we are a diverse people." To ensure that analysis does not turn away from appreciation of diversity, some critics suggest that attention to excessive entanglement may be the best safeguard. Efforts to safeguard government and religion from entanglement with each other aim to ensure that persons are not required to accept or support what they find objectionable. When politics and religion are mixed, they undermine each other's integrity and independence. These risks must be managed regardless of the direction establishment clause doctrine ultimately takes.

Bibliography

Jesse H. Choper, "The Establishment Clause and Aid to Parochial Schools," 56 *California Law Review* 260 (1968). Focuses on the subject of public aid to parochial schools.

Kenneth F. Ripple, "The Entanglement Test of the Religion Clauses—A Ten Year Assessment," 27 *UCLA Law Review* 1195 (1980). Examines the consequences of attention to excessive entanglement.

Steven D. Smith, *Foreordained Failure: The Quest for a Constitutional Principle of Religious Freedom* (1995). Explores efforts to structure effective First Amendment standards in the area of religion.

Lynch v. Donnelly

Tension between the First Amendment's establishment and free exercise clauses historically has been a source of constitutional difficulty and uncertainty. The establishment clause prohibits government from establishing any religion. The free exercise clause is interpreted as barring government from "prohibiting the free exercise" of religion. State support for education in the form of subsidized transportation, construction, textbooks, or teacher salaries advances a legitimate societal interest. If such assistance is provided to parochial schools, it raises establishment clause concerns. If religious institutions are excluded from general assistance programs, it may be argued that the free exercise clause is violated. This conflict between the establishment and free exercise clauses has created a doctrinal dilemma. Resolving it requires a standard of review that upholds each constitutional interest without violating the other.

Citation:	465 U.S. 668.
Issue:	Whether a city-funded nativity scene in a park owned by a nonprofit organization violated the establishment clause, which prohibits government from establishing any religion.
Year of Decision:	1984.
Outcome:	The nativity scene did not violate the First Amendment.
Author of Opinion:	Chief Justice Warren Burger.
Vote:	5–4.

Toward that end, the Supreme Court has introduced the principle of accommodation. Under this concept, official action that otherwise might constitute an establishment clause violation may be allowed as an accommodation of free exercise interests. In Marsh v. Chambers (1983), the Court rejected a constitutional challenge to prayer at the opening of legislative proceedings. Although the state paid for the chaplain's services, the Court found that religious invocations were "simply a tolerable acknowledgement of beliefs widely held among the people of this country." The concept of accommodation, which potentially could offset findings of a religious purpose or effect or of excessive entanglement between church and state, was instrumental in the review of a city-supported religious display during the Christmas season. At issue in *Lynch v. Donnelly* was a nativity scene paid for by the city of Pawtucket, Rhode Island and erected in a park owned by a nonprofit organization. Included in the display were decorations and figures associated with the Christmas season, such as Santa Claus, reindeer, a Christmas tree, and a banner that read "Season's Greetings." The scene also contained a creche consisting of "the Infant Jesus, Mary and Joseph, angels, shepherds, kings, and animals." Cost and maintenance of the nativity scene were insubstantial.

In a majority opinion authored by Chief Justice Warren Burger, the Court noted that it must reconcile the conflict between prevention of intrusions of church and state into each other's affairs and the impossibility of total separation of government and religion. It also suggested that the traditional concept of a "wall" between church and state was somewhat overstated. Although the metaphor was useful as a "figure of speech," it was "not a wholly accurate description of the practical aspects of the relationship that in fact exists between church and state." Noting that no institution can live in a vacuum or in total isolation from other aspects of society, the Court found that the First Amendment does not "require complete separation of church and state." Rather, to avoid "callous indifference" to free exercise interests, establishment clause principles must provide breathing room for free exercise concerns.

The requirement of accommodation, from the Court's perspective, reflected a historical understanding "of the role of religion in American life from at least 1789." Specific examples of traditions that officially have reflected the nation's religious heritage include the celebration of Thanksgiving, which, like Christmas, originated as a religious holiday before being declared a national holiday. Further examples include the national motto "In God We Trust," which is stamped on coinage, inclusion of the passage "one nation under God" in the Pledge of Allegiance, federal support for art galleries that include religious paintings, and a presidentially proclaimed annual National Day of Prayer. Because of this heritage, the Court has refused to interpret the establishment clause as a barrier to all government action that may benefit or recognize religion. The necessary inquiry, as the Court described it in *Lynch v. Donnelly*, is whether official conduct or policy "in reality . . . establishes a religion or religious faith, or tends to do so." In pursuing this analysis, the Court restated that it typically drew lines on the basis of whether government action had a secular purpose, had a principal or primary effect of advancing religion, or excessively entangled church and state. The Court determined, however, that it need not be confined to this analysis and in reviewing the creche scene would not be so restricted.

Because the display was designed to celebrate the holiday, the Court concluded that its purpose was secular. With respect to the creche, the Court was not satisfied that it had the primary effect of promoting religion. The majority further concluded that the city's support for the nativity scene did not excessively entangle government with religion. No evidence was identified to support any finding of government contact with church authorities concerning the content, design, or presentation of the creche. Although the creche might have "special meaning" to certain religious groups, the Court viewed it as the source of "a friendly community spirit of goodwill in keeping with the season." The majority would have found it ironic if the creche's presence "would so 'taint' the city's exhibit as to render it violative of the Establishment Clause." Such a result, the Court noted, would be "a stilted overreaction contrary to our history and to our holdings." It accordingly dismissed "[a]s far-fetched indeed" the argument that such symbols "pose a real danger of establishment of a state church."

Justice Sandra Day O'Connor wrote a concurring opinion that offered "a clarification of our Establishment Clause doctrine." O'Connor asserted that the establishment clause could be violated only when church and state were excessively entangled or when religion was officially approved or endorsed. From her perspective, the central issue was whether the city had endorsed Christianity by displaying the creche. Because the religious display had neither the purpose nor primary effect of advancing religion, she found no endorsement. For O'Connor, it constituted a mere acknowledgement of religion rather than official approval of a particular religious belief.

Justice William Brennan, joined in dissent by Justices Thurgood Marshall, Harry Blackmun, and John Paul Stevens, viewed the creche "as a recreation of an event that lies at the heart of the Christian faith." Brennan expressed concern with what he characterized as "the Court's less-than-vigorous application" of establishment clause standards. From his perspective, the secular setting of the nativity scene did not dilute its "singular religiosity." On the contrary, he viewed official support for the display as inconsistent with "our remarkable and precious religious diversity as a Nation, which the Establishment Clause seeks to protect." Brennan argued that "it blinks reality to claim, as the Court does, that by including such a distinctively religious object as the creche in its Christmas display," the city had purged it of its religious content. The creche, from Brennan's perspective, retained its Christian religious significance. He refused to believe that non-Christians, when confronted with "the chief symbol" of Christian belief in a divine savior, would view it any other way. Far from being "a mere representation" of a certain historic religious event, the creche in Brennan's view represented a central aspect of "Christian dogma—that God sent His Son into the world to be a Messiah." To equate it with such traditional symbols as reindeer and Santa's house, Brennan argued, actually insulted those who viewed "the story of Christ" in religious terms. He urged recognition of the city's action "for what it is," a small but coercive "step toward establishing the sectarian preferences of the majority at the expense of the minority, accomplished by placing public facilities and funds in support of the religious symbolism and theological tidings that the creche conveys."

The use of accommodation principles as a means of defusing tension between establishment and free exercise values has not eliminated the high level of uncertainty that still exists in the field. Distinguishing between allowable accommodation and impermissible endorsement is a difficult exercise. This phenomenon manifested itself in another case that concerned seasonal religious displays. In County of Allegheny v. American Civil Liberties Union, Greater Pittsburgh Chapter (1989), the Court determined that the display of a creche in a county courthouse was an unconstitutional endorsement of religion. Placement of a Chanukah menorah outside a city-county building, adjacent to a Christmas tree and a sign saluting liberty, was found to be a permissible "recognition of cultural diversity." The decision generated a dissenting opinion by Justice Anthony Kennedy, joined by Chief Justice William Rehnquist and Justices Byron White and Antonin Scalia, who questioned whether the traditional focus on purpose, effect, and excessive entanglement between church and state should persist as the "primary guide" for establishment clause review. As he put it, "[S]ubstantial revision of Establishment Clause doctrine may be in order."

Establishment clause decisions continue to reflect significant doctrinal turmoil. Several justices have criticized establishment clause standards for their unpredictability. As Justice Antonin Scalia observed in Lee v. Weisman (1992), "[J]urisprudence has become bedeviled . . . by reliance on formulaic abstractions that are not derived from, but positively conflict with, our long-accepted constitutional traditions." A majority in Lee, however, refused the invitation "to reconsider our decision in *Lemon*" (which established the three-part test). Even so, Justice Scalia and Justice Clarence Thomas in Lamb's Chapel v. Center Moriches Union Free School District (1993) announced that they were abandoning the formula of purpose, effect, and excessive entanglement. The Court's continuing use of it has prompted Scalia to observe that "[l]ike some ghoul in a late-night horror movie that repeatedly sits up in its grave and shuffles abroad, after being repeatedly killed and buried, [the test continues to] stalk our Establishment Clause jurisprudence." Despite the fact that six justices had authored or joined opinions that had "personally driven pencils through the creature's heart," as Scalia put it, no replacement test has commanded a majority. As a consequence, or perhaps by default, a test widely criticized for its inadequacy continues to be the primary analytical tool of establishment clause review.

Bibliography

Jesse H. Choper, *Securing Religious Liberty* (1995). A critical perspective on establishment clause principles.

Daniel O. Conkle, "Toward a General Theory of the Establishment Clause," 82 *Northwestern University Law Review* 1113 (1988). Proposes a reformulation of establishment clause standards.

Leo Pfeffer, "Freedom and/or Separation: The Constitutional Dilemma of the First Amendment," 64 *Minnesota Law Review* 561 (1980). Examines tensions between the establishment and exercise clauses, which accommodation principles seek to mitigate.

William Van Alstyne, "Trends in the Supreme Court: Mr. Jefferson's Crumbling Wall—A Comment on *Lynch v. Donnelly*," 1984 *Duke Law Journal* 770 (1984). Argues that the *Lynch* decision reflects a trend toward reestablishing government under religious auspices.

The Free Exercise Clause

The free exercise clause, like the free speech clause, safeguards against governmental action that would interfere with a protected constitutional interest. Defining precisely what that interest is, however, is not always easy. Early case law attempted to distinguish between religious belief and action. This distinction created risks to meaningful religious freedom when government restricted actions that were motivated by religious belief but did not officially prohibit belief. Over the course of the twentieth century, free exercise clause analysis has evolved into a balancing process. The Supreme Court typically considers whether religious freedom has been impaired, and, if so, whether the impairment is justified by a compelling governmental interest. This method of review was demonstrated in *Wisconsin v. Yoder* (1972), in which the Court considered whether Amish parents had to comply with a state law that required children to attend school until the age of sixteen.

Wisconsin v. Yoder

The free exercise clause of the First Amendment, which prohibits government from interfering with the free exercise of religion, addresses concerns shared by other provisions of the First Amendment. Like freedom of speech and of the press, the free exercise clause protects persons who otherwise may be the victims of official disfavor. As the Supreme Court observed in Church of Lukumi Babalu Aye, Inc. v. City of Hialeah (1993), the right to worship freely reflects the lesson of "historical instances of religious persecution and intolerance." At a minimum, the free exercise clause safeguards against official action that "discriminates against some or all religious beliefs or prohibits conduct because it is undertaken for religious reasons."

Like all constitutional principles, security for religious freedom has its limits. In Reynolds v. United States (1878), the Court upheld a congressional act that prohibited polygamy. Although the Court noted that the free exercise clause protected reli-

Citation:	406 U.S. 205.
Issue:	Whether a state law requiring children to attend school until they reach the age of sixteen violated the free exercise clause of the First Amendment.
Year of Decision:	1972.
Outcome:	The compulsory-attendance law violated the free exercise clause insofar as it was applied to Amish families.
Author of Opinion:	Chief Justice Warren Burger.
Vote:	6–1.

gious belief and opinion, it concluded that it does not necessarily safeguard "practices." If such protection was to be extended, the Court observed, human sacrifices might be beyond the reach of government control. More than a century later, in Employment Division, Department of Human Resources of Oregon v. Smith (1990), the Court determined that use of an illegal drug for religious purposes was not constitutionally protected. Among other things, these decisions demonstrate that otherwise unlawful conduct may not be protected by the free exercise clause.

Free exercise analysis requires a balancing of constitutional and governmental interests. This method of review was evidenced in the Court's analysis in *Wisconsin v. Yoder* of a Wisconsin law that required children to attend school until they reached the age of sixteen. The statute was challenged by Jonas Yoder and other members of the Old Order Amish religion who refused to send their offspring to school after the eighth grade. Amish parents maintained that their children's enrollment in high school was contrary to their religion and way of life. If they were required to send their children to high school, they believed that the church community would censure them and their salvation would be imperiled. No dispute existed with respect to the sincerity of these beliefs.

In commencing its analysis, the Court in an opinion by Chief Justice Warren Burger announced two criteria governing free exercise clause review. First, the state may not impose a requirement that interferes with a religious belief. Second, a strong state interest must be identified as a basis for overriding any free exercise interest. The Court found that the law constituted an interference with Amish religious beliefs and subordinated them to contemporary society's "insistence on conformity to majoritarian standards." Although elementary schooling in rural areas could be provided within the context of Amish life, modern secondary education typically was remote from the student's home and "alien to his daily home life." Such schooling removed Amish families from their protected environment and exposed them "to the worldly influence they reject." Compulsory secondary education thus interfered with basic tenets and principles of the Amish faith by exposing "children to worldly influences in terms of attitudes, goals, and values contrary to beliefs." Mandatory schooling also complicated their "integration into the way of life of the Amish faith and community at the crucial adolescent stage of development." Because the Amish religion had existed for nearly three centuries and there was strong evidence that a sustained faith pervaded the Amish way of life, the Court was convinced that the compulsory-education law would "gravely endanger if not destroy the free exercise of religious beliefs."

The state maintained that its interest in compulsory education was so compelling that the religious concerns must give way. It identified two primary arguments in support of its educational requirement. First, the state maintained that some degree of education is essential to prepare citizens for effectively and intelligently participating in the nation's political system. Second, the state contended that education instills important social skills of self-reliance and self-sufficiency. With respect to the first point, the Court observed that an education's value must be assessed in relationship to its capacity to equip a child for life. It distinguished between the need for another year or two of education for a child who was preparing "for life in modern society as the majority live" and the training "for life in the separated agrarian community that is the keystone of the Amish faith." Although the Court acknowledged the state's interest in protecting children from ignorance, it noted that the Amish had been a highly successful social unit, even if they lived apart from society's mainstream. The Court was particularly impressed with the productivity and law-abiding ways of the faith's members and with a degree of self-sufficiency and independence that had prompted Congress to exempt them from having to pay Social Security taxes. Despite the Amish way of isolating themselves from the general community to avoid worldly influences, the Court was unwilling to make an assumption that the majority's practices were right and the Amish were wrong. Particularly because the amount of additional schooling in question was relatively slight, the Court believed that only a "speculative gain" could be achieved if the compulsory-attendance law was enforced.

The Court also rejected arguments that the state had an interest in extending the benefits of secondary education to children despite the wishes of their parents. Such a basis was inadequate, from the Court's perspective, because no evidence existed of harm to a child's physical or mental health or to public health, peace, safety, or order. Nor was there any theory that children were being denied schooling against their wishes. Even if parents were preventing their children from attending high school, the Court indicated that it would be reluctant to intrude into family decisions concerning religious training. In support of this point, it stressed how the "history and culture of Western civilization reflect a strong tradition of parental concern for the nurture and upbringing of their children." The "primary role" of parents in the upbringing process had been "established beyond debate as an enduring American tradition." When constitutionally protected concerns of parenthood were combined with a free exercise claim, the state was obligated to demonstrate a powerful reason to overcome them. The Court concluded that the state had failed to make this showing.

Justice William O. Douglas dissented from the ruling because it reserved the decision on school attendance for parents. Douglas criticized the Court for assuming that the only interests at stake were those of the parents and the state. He believed that an opportunity should be afforded for the children to be heard. It was not inconceivable that an Amish child might wish to be a "pianist," "astronaut," or "oceanographer." To achieve these goals, it would be necessary for that child to break with Amish tradition. Whether the child wished to follow the dictates of his or her parents or not, Douglas believed that the student's opinion should be heard before an exemption from compulsory education was granted. Without knowing what that interest might be, he found it impossible to determine whether an exemption from compulsory education should be honored.

The vindication of Amish religious interests represented a significant triumph of free exercise values, perhaps, as Justice Douglas noted, at the expense "of the right of students to be masters of their own destiny." Subsequent case law, however, has not always been charitable toward free exercise values. A decade later, the Court in United States v. Lee (1982) upheld a federal law that required an Amish employer to pay Social Security taxes. Despite the religion's requirement to care for "fellow members," the Court concluded that the federal interest in a viable Social Security system was more important. The decision also reflected concern that protecting the Amish from such requirements would generate "myriad exceptions flowing from a wide variety of religious beliefs." However, in Hobbie v. Unemployment Appeals Commission of Florida (1987), the

Court upheld free exercise claims in striking down a law that denied unemployment benefits to a Seventh Day Adventist who, consistent with her religious beliefs, refused to work on Saturdays.

Case law also has limited the free exercise clause to government action or policy that directly prohibits, indirectly coerces, or penalizes free exercise of religion. Laws of general application, even if they make it more difficult to practice certain religions, raise no constitutional concern. The Court in Bowen v. Roy (1986) thus rejected a parental claim that having to use a Social Security number would "rob the spirit" of their two-year-old daughter. In Lyng v. Northwest Indian Cemetery Protection Association (1988), a claim that national timber and road-construction policies interfered with sacred Native American grounds also did not rise to the level of constitutional significance. Free exercise clause interests were upheld in Church of the Lukumi Babalu Aye, Inc. v. City of Hialeah (1993), however, when the Court determined that a city ordinance that prohibited animal sacrifice was aimed at persecuting a particular religion. This case was found to present the rather rare phenomenon of state action that manifestly discriminated against a particular religion.

Free exercise analysis increasingly has been criticized for providing less protection to religious freedom than it should. Modern rulings limit free exercise principles to instances in which government singles out a particular religious group. Under these standards, government may enact and enforce laws that apply to the general population but incidentally burden religion. Measured against a historical backdrop that inspired a commitment to protect marginal as well as mainstream groups, such an understanding is criticized for departing from a free exercise clause that protects religious diversity in all its shapes and stripes.

Bibliography

Robert S. Alley, ed., *James Madison on Religious Liberty* (1985). Examines the views of James Madison, who was the primary drafter of the First Amendment.

John H. Garvey, "Freedom and Equality in the Religion Clauses," 1981 *Supreme Court Review* 193 (1981). A study of free exercise principles and equality interests.

Paul G. Kauper, *Religion and the Constitution* (1964). Details the history and nature of the free exercise clause.

16

The Fourth Amendment: Search and Seizure

The Fourth Amendment, like many other provisions of the Bill of Rights, emerged in response to colonial experiences with abusive police practices. Under English rule, the king's agents in the colonies were empowered to search dwellings and other places on the basis of mere suspicion or whim. Typically, these searches were conducted for the purpose of finding publications that criticized colonial rule. From this historical experience, the Fourth Amendment emerged as a guarantee against unreasonable searches and seizures. Consistent with the Bill of Rights generally, the Fourth Amendment initially was conceptualized as a safeguard against abuse by the federal government. Eventually, it was made applicable to the states through the Fourteenth Amendment.

The primary remedy for a violation of the Fourth Amendment is exclusion from trial of any evidence illegally obtained. The Supreme Court adopted the exclusionary rule as a federal remedy in Weeks v. United States (1914). In Wolf v. Colorado (1949), it refused to extend this rule to the states through the Fourteenth Amendment due process clause. Twelve years later, after evidence suggested that illegal searches and seizures could not be effectively deterred otherwise, the Court in *Mapp v. Ohio* (1961) held that the exclusionary rule also governed illegal searches and seizures at the state level. Although the Fourth Amendment was initially viewed as a means of protecting private property interests, it eventually came to be understood in broader and deeper terms. In *Katz v. United States* (1967), the Court emphasized that the primary concern of the Fourth Amendment was with a person's reasonable expectation of privacy in his or her self, dwelling, papers, and effects. Determining when police investigative activity constitutes a search or seizure is not always an easy task. The Court in *Terry v. Ohio* (1968) considered not only what constitutes a search but how the degree of intrusiveness may influence Fourth Amendment requirements.

Mapp v. Ohio

The Bill of Rights has more provisions pertaining to the criminal justice system than to any other concern. The Eighth Amendment prohibits cruel and unusual punishments and excessive bail or fines. The Sixth Amendment provides for the right to a speedy, public, and jury trial, the right to confront witnesses, compulsory process for purposes of obtaining the testimony of witnesses, and assistance of counsel. The Fifth Amendment demands that infamous crimes be prosecuted under a grand-jury indictment, prohibits double jeopardy, and provides safeguards against self-incrimination. Before these guarantees come into action, however, the Fourth Amendment establishes the basic premises that must be satisfied to trigger the criminal justice system's operation. The Fourth Amendment prohibits unreasonable searches and seizures and precludes issuance of warrants without probable cause. Specifically, it provides that

Citation:	367 U.S. 643.
Issue:	Whether an unauthorized search of a residence requires exclusion of evidence found there from a criminal trial.
Year of Decision:	1961.
Outcome:	Evidence obtained from an illegal search is subject to exclusion from a criminal trial.
Author of Opinion:	Justice Tom Clark.
Vote:	6–3.

> [t]he right of the people to be secure in their persons, houses, papers, and effects, against unreasonable searches and seizures, shall not be violated, and no Warrants shall issue, but upon probable cause, supported by Oath or affirmation, and particularly describing the place to be searched, and the persons or things to be seized.

Despite the security the Fourth Amendment provides against illegal searches and seizures, it contains no mechanism for enforcement. Nearly a century after the Fourth Amendment's ratification, the Supreme Court in Boyd v. United States (1886) ruled that documents that were evidence of a crime but had been obtained through illegally coerced disclosure could not be used in criminal proceedings against the defendant. Two decades later, in Adams v. New York (1904), the Court announced that courts typically should not inquire into how otherwise admissible evidence was obtained. In Weeks v. United States (1914), it adopted the exclusionary rule which prohibited use of illegally seized evidence in federal criminal trials. Noting that use of illegally seized evidence would "affirm by judicial decision" a violation of the Constitution, the Court determined that such evidence could not be used at trial.

The Bill of Rights as adopted restricted only the powers of the federal government. The Fourteenth Amendment, which prohibited states from "depriv[ing] any person of life, liberty, or property without due process of law," eventually became the basis for making many provisions of the Bill of Rights applicable to the states. Inevitably, the question with respect to whether the Fourth Amendment was incorporated into the Fourteenth Amendment presented itself as a constitutional issue. The Court in Wolf v. Colorado (1949) determined that the "core of the Fourth Amendment," which protects an individual's privacy against arbitrary intrusion, was enforceable against the states. Despite its determination in Weeks that the exclusionary rule governed federal criminal proceedings, the Court in Wolf concluded that it did not apply to state proceedings. The Court also noted that the exclusionary rule was not subscribed to by "most of the English-speaking world," had been rejected by a majority of the states, and was not the exclusive remedy against police misconduct. In accordance with what it perceived as the interests of federalism, the Court viewed each state as a laboratory for testing different methods for protecting Fourth Amendment privacy interests. Among these possibilities were civil actions for damages, internal disciplinary procedures against police violators, and informed public opinion.

Pressure for the Court to reconsider its position in Wolf mounted in the years following that decision. In Rochin v. California (1952), the Court ordered exclusion of evidence that had been obtained when police had used a stomach pump on the defendant. It did so on grounds that the method was one that "shocks the conscience," so the exclusionary rule was still not extended to state proceedings. That issue resurfaced, however, in *Mapp v. Ohio*. At issue was a police search of a home without a search warrant. Police obtained access to the home by forcible entry and against the defendant's expressed wishes. Although the search was conducted to find evidence related to a bombing, it uncovered only obscene materials. The homeowner, Dollree Mapp, was prosecuted and convicted for possession of obscene material. The state's position, based upon Wolf v. Colorado, was that the Fourth Amendment was no bar to the use of illegally seized evidence in a state criminal trial.

In an opinion authored by Justice Tom Clark, the Court abandoned previous decisions that had refused to apply the exclusionary rule to the states. The ruling in Wolf, Clark observed, was grounded in the expectation that states would create and implement effective methods for deterring illegal searches and seizures. Experience had demonstrated, however, that other remedies were "worthless and futile." Particularly influential was a

California Supreme Court ruling that had adopted the exclusionary rule because other alternatives had "completely failed to secure compliance with the" Fourth Amendment. Because of this disillusionment with other options, the Court determined that its traditional justifications against applying the exclusionary rule to the states no longer were valid.

A dozen years after its ruling in Wolf, the Court in *Mapp v. Ohio* decided to "close the only courtroom door remaining open to evidence secured by official lawlessness in flagrant abuse of" the Fourth Amendment. It held "that all evidence obtained by searches and seizures in violation of the Constitution is, by that same authority, inadmissible in a state court." Given the inadequacy of the means for deterring illegal police action, the Court noted that a contrary decision would be "to grant the right but in reality to withhold its privilege and enjoyment." Its ruling reflected a sense that "the freedom from unconscionable invasions of privacy" is intimately related to the perpetuation of "principles of humanity and civil liberty." The decision also sought to avoid potential violations of constitutional and common sense that different rules for state and federal prosecutors generated. Noting that evidence illegally seized by a federal prosecutor could be turned over to a state's attorney "across the street," even if it could not be used in federal court, the Court's ruling eliminated a reality that "encourage[d] disobedience to the Federal Constitution."

A primary argument against the exclusionary rule has been that it enables criminals to go free when "the constable has blundered."[1] The Court acknowledged that this result would occur in some instances, but believed that it was a lesser evil. The greater harm was that the use of tainted evidence damaged judicial integrity. As the Court put it, "nothing can destroy a government more quickly than its own failure to observe its own laws, or worse, its disregard of the charter of its own existence." The Court was also unwilling to agree that the exclusionary rule would interfere with legitimate needs of law enforcement. Although the exclusionary rule had operated in the federal system for nearly half a century, no showing or suggestion had been made that it diminished the efficacy of the Federal Bureau of Investigation or disrupted the administration of criminal justice. In sum, the Court was moved by a sense that it could no longer permit the right to be secure against "rude invasions of privacy by state officers . . . to remain an empty promise." The Court believed that its decision afforded "the individual no more than that which the Constitution guarantees him, to the police officer no less than that to which honest law enforcement is entitled, and, to the courts, that judicial integrity so necessary in the true administration of justice."

The ruling and its rationale were not persuasive to Justice John Harlan, Jr., who, joined by Justices Felix Frankfurter and Charles Whittaker, noted that the factual grounds for established case law had not changed as dramatically as the majority suggested. As Harlan pointed out in his dissent, half of the states still rejected the exclusionary rule. The dissenters viewed the divergence of views among the states as an indication that the need for a federal rule in place of each state's judgment was still debatable. Believing that each state might have "its own peculiar problems in criminal law enforcement," they objected to a rule that empowered the Court "to suit its own notions of how things should be done."

The exclusionary rule's application not only to federal but to state criminal processes has been a source of continuing controversy. Despite the majority's belief that no other remedial alternative was workable, critics have argued that the exclusionary rule hampers police and does not deter police misconduct effectively. Such criticism eventually led to a significant modification of the exclusionary rule. In United States v. Leon (1984), the Court adopted a good-faith exception to its operation. Under this exception, the exclusionary rule does not bar evidence obtained by officers who reasonably relied on a seemingly valid search warrant that ultimately was found to lack probable cause. From the Court's perspective in Leon, police misconduct is not an issue when investigative action is taken in reliance upon the judgment of a qualified judicial officer who has issued the warrant. Critics maintain that this result effectively insulates magistrates from subsequent judicial review of their decisions. The Court viewed considerations of police deterrence as minimal under such circumstances and found the "costs" of excluding evidence unacceptably high. Critics have disagreed with this assessment. As they see it, these costs are attributable not to the exclusionary rule but to the Fourth Amendment.

Note

1. People v. Defore, 150 N.E. 585, 587 (N.Y. 1926).

Bibliography

Wayne R. LaFave and Jerold H. Israel, *Criminal Procedure* 2d ed. (1992). Includes a survey and analysis of the law of the Fourth Amendment.

Henry P. Monaghan, "Constitutional Common Law," 89 *Harvard Law Review* 1 (1975). Discusses the exclusionary rule as a departure from normal practice.

J. Harvie Wilkinson, *Serving Justice* (1974). Views the rights of criminal defendants as being particularly susceptible to "emotional reaction."

Katz v. United States

The Fourth Amendment establishes a right of privacy that protects persons from unreasonable intrusions by law-enforcement agents. By its terms, the Fourth Amendment protects "persons," "houses," and "effects." Until the mid–twentieth century, searches typically were regarded as investigations of places. As electronic methodology enhanced the ability of police to investigate crime, historical concepts of "constitutionally protected areas" were challenged on grounds that they were obsolete. The impact of communications technology upon law enforcement initially was assessed in Olmstead v. United States (1928), in which the Court considered whether wiretapping of telephone conversations violated the Fourth Amendment. The Court held that because federal agents had accessed telephone wires without entering the defendant's house or office, no search had occurred. It also found no seizure because the law-enforcement officials obtained no physical objects and thus no "things." This ruling generated a dissent by Justice Louis Brandeis, who maintained that regardless of the means employed, any "unjustifiable intrusion upon the privacy of the individual . . . must be deemed a violation of the Fourth Amendment."

Citation:	389 U.S. 347.
Issue:	Whether a telephone conversation in a public telephone booth was protected by the Fourth Amendment.
Year of Decision:	1967.
Outcome:	The telephone conversation was protected by the Fourth Amendment because the defendant had a justifiable expectation of privacy.
Author of Opinion:	Justice Potter Stewart.
Vote:	7–1.

Brandeis warned that the "progress of science in furnishing the Government with means of espionage is not likely to stop with wire-tapping." Even as electronic technology evolved toward more sophisticated methods of police surveillance, the Olmstead Court's understanding of the Fourth Amendment remained fixed for the next four decades. In Goldman v. United States (1942), the Court rejected a Fourth Amendment challenge to the use of a listening device that had been planted on the wall of an office next to the defendant's. In On Lee v. United States (1952), it found no constitutional violation when police wired an informant to enter a home with the owner's consent. Implanting a microphone so that it touched a duct that supplied heat to a home under surveillance, however, was found to be a Fourth Amendment violation. The basis for that determination in

Silverman v. United States (1961) was that the house itself had been invaded. Despite this finding of a constitutional violation, Fourth Amendment understanding remained rooted in concepts of trespass.

Under this notion, Fourth Amendment security terminated when individuals were not within the confines of a "constitutionally protected area" such as a home or office. As long as privacy was correlated to places and things, boundaries between protected and unprotected realms were rather clear. Government's ability to snoop and access information and evidence and bypass the Fourth Amendment eventually caused the Court to rethink the concept of privacy. This reevaluation occurred in *Katz v. United States*. Under review was the conviction of Charles Katz who was convicted for transmitting wagering information in violation of federal law. Evidence against him had been obtained by the FBI's use of an electronic listening device which intercepted his calls made from a public telephone booth. In conformity with established case law, the defendant framed the issue in terms of whether a public telephone booth was a constitutionally protected area. In an opinion authored by Justice Potter Stewart, the Court rejected that formulation of the issue. Writing for the majority, Stewart referred to the "constitutionally protected area" phrase as an "incantation" that did not necessarily reflect Fourth Amendment interests. He noted that the privacy concern at stake was not of a broad nature, such as a general "right to be let alone," but an interest that was uniquely protected by the Fourth Amendment from government intrusion. Attention to the telephone booth as a constitutionally protected area deflected attention from the real problem. The purpose of the Fourth Amendment, as Stewart put it, was to protect "people, not places." What a person knowingly exposes to the public from his or her office or home is not protected by the Fourth Amendment. On the other hand, what a person seeks to preserve as private even in a public place may be constitutionally protected.

One of the state's arguments was that the defendant could not have expected privacy in the context of a glass telephone booth. The Court determined that by entering the booth, the defendant sought to exclude not the "intruding eye" but the "uninvited ear." As the Court saw it, a person who occupies a phone booth, "shuts the door behind him, and pays the toll that permits him to place a call, is surely entitled to assume that the words he utters into the mouthpiece will not be broadcast to the world." The Court also abandoned the traditional correlation of Fourth Amendment protection to trespass concepts. Having shifted attention from places to people, the Court pointed out that the Fourth Amendment could not "turn upon the presence or absence of a physical intrusion into any given enclosure." It accordingly determined that use of an electronic listening device to record the defendant's words constituted a search and seizure that violated the right of privacy secured by the Fourth Amendment. Whether the device actually penetrated the wall of the booth would have been the deciding factor in previous cases. Under reformulated standards, that fact had "no constitutional significance."

The majority opinion represented a significant restructuring of Fourth Amendment principle. The concurring opinion of Justice John Harlan, Jr., has been particularly influential in the Fourth Amendment's redefinition. Harlan agreed that the amendment "protects people, not places." He offered a two-part requirement that had to be satisfied if a violation of the constitution was to be established. First, the person who asserted a constitutional claim had to demonstrate that he or she had an actual expectation of privacy. Second, that expectation had to be one that society was prepared to acknowledge as reasonable. To provide an example of the interaction between these standards, Harlan noted that a person's home for most purposes was a place where privacy was expected. If the home dweller exposed "objects, activities, or statements" to the plain view of outsiders, however, no intention of confidentiality could be inferred. Growing marijuana in a planter box that was plainly visible from the street or sidewalk, for instance, would not support a reasonable expectation of privacy. It is not inconceivable, moreover, that some of the most public places imaginable might provide the greatest privacy for certain illegal activities. As one commentator has noted, "[i]f two narcotics peddlers were to rely on the privacy of a desolate corner of Central Park in the middle of the night to carry out an illegal transaction, this would be a reasonable expectation of privacy."[1] At the same time, it would be difficult to find a Fourth Amendment violation if a police officer by chance encountered the transaction. The officer, if he or she had a lawful basis for being present, would not be prohibited from responding to whatever evidence was in plain view.

As redefined by the Court, the privacy interest protected by the Fourth Amendment became portable rather than fixed. This development has not lacked critics. In a dissenting opinion, Justice Hugo Black criticized the Court for distorting the Fourth Amendment's meaning. The advent of electronic methods of surveillance, from his perspective, did not present a risk beyond what the framers themselves might have contemplated. Wiretapping, for instance, merely constituted a more sophisticated means of eavesdropping that had been performed by the naked ear or "under the eaves of houses or their windows" in earlier times. Because the framers were aware of this practice, they could have prohibited or restricted the use of evidence obtained by such means. As Black saw it, the Court had taken constitutional language aimed directly "at searches and seizures of things that can be searched and seized" and applied it to conversations that technically "can neither be searched nor seized." Such an exercise redefined the Fourth Amendment not on the basis of principle but through "the ingenuity of language-stretching judges."

The revised focus upon "people" rather than "things" has resulted in some difficult cases. For instance, in California v. Greenwood (1988), a search of a suspected drug dealer's garbage without a warrant was upheld on grounds that "society would not accept as reasonable [the] claim to an expectation of privacy in trash left for collection in an area accessible to the public." Dissenting from the Court's opinion, Justice William Brennan argued that there was a reasonable expectation of privacy for sealed containers regardless of whether they had been discarded. In Florida v. Riley (1989), the Court upheld an aerial search of a partially covered backyard greenhouse used to grow marijuana. Because the helicopter was flying at a legal altitude, Justice Byron White, joined by Chief Justice William Rehnquist and Justices Antonin Scalia and Anthony Kennedy, concluded that the police officers were lawfully present and merely observed what they were entitled to see in plain view. Justice Sandra Day O'Connor agreed with this plurality, but noted that aerial surveillance from a lower level might be intrusive enough to violate reasonable expectations of privacy. Dissenting again, Justice Brennan framed the question not in terms of whether the police officers had a right to be where they were but whether their method of public observation was "so commonplace" that it defeated a reasonable expectation of privacy. These cases demonstrate a continuing debate over the concept of reasonableness that is unlikely to vanish. It has been and will continue to be driven by differences of opinion over whether society's best interests are served by expanding or restricting the opportunities for law-enforcement officials to identify and respond to crime.

Note

1. Note, "From Private Places to Personal Privacy: A Post-Katz Study of Fourth Amendment Protection," 43 *New York University Law Review* 968, 983 (1968).

Bibliography

Jesse Choper, Yale Kamisar, and Laurence H. Tribe, *The Supreme Court: Trends and Developments* (1979). A critical perspective upon the Court's Fourth Amendment jurisprudence.

Wayne R. LaFave and Jerold H. Israel, *Criminal Procedure*, 2d ed. (1992). Examines historical and current trends in defining the Fourth Amendment's focus.

Silas J. Wasserstrom and Christie L. Snyder, eds., *A Criminal Procedure Anthology* (1996). Includes excerpts from some of the leading commentaries on the Fourth Amendment.

Terry v. Ohio

The Fourth Amendment applies to searches and seizures performed by either criminal or civil authorities. Traditionally, the requirement for a search or seizure has been "probable cause." This standard requires law-enforcement authorities to demonstrate that they have adequate grounds for a search or seizure. In Brinegar v. United States (1949), the Supreme Court defined probable cause as "more than bare suspicion" but "less than evidence which would justify . . . conviction." Probable cause is the threshold law-enforcement agents must cross to secure a search or arrest warrant. Authorities sometimes encounter circumstances that raise suspicions short of probable cause. Under certain circumstances, it may be permissible to investigate in ways that intrude into an otherwise constitutionally protected realm of privacy.

Whether police might conduct a limited search and seizure without probable cause was at issue in *Terry v. Ohio*, in which the Supreme Court

Citation:	392 U.S. 1.
Issue:	Whether the stopping and frisking of two men standing on a street corner was an unreasonable search and seizure that violated the Fourth Amendment.
Year of Decision:	1968.
Outcome:	The procedure was justified because it was relatively nonintrusive and supported by reasonable suspicion.
Author of Opinion:	Chief Justice Earl Warren.
Vote:	8–1.

reviewed a so-called stop and frisk procedure. This investigative practice was used by a Cleveland plainclothes detective on one of two persons whom he suspected of casing a store in preparation for a robbery. Having seen these individuals walk up the street, peer in a store, confer with a third person, and repeat the process again, the officer stopped them and asked for their names. After a mumbled response from them, the officer spun one of them around, patted his breast pocket, felt a pistol, and removed it. Charged with carrying a concealed weapon, the defendant filed a motion to suppress its use as evidence on grounds that it was the fruit of a Fourth Amendment violation. Without probable cause, he argued, the search and seizure were unconstitutional.

The Court determined that, given the minimal intrusiveness of the search, probable cause did not have to be established. Rather, it was sufficient that the officer demonstrated reasonable suspicion. In a majority opinion authored by Chief Justice Earl Warren, the Court noted that it "would be less than candid if we did not acknowledge that this question thrusts to the fore difficult and troublesome issues regarding a sensitive area of police activity." In favor of a finding of a Fourth Amendment violation was the notion that police must be "strictly circumscribed" by Fourth Amendment standards that do not vary by context. Competing against this premise was the argument that police have a need for increasingly intrusive investigative measures that respond to the seriousness of risks they face in performance of their duties. The Court noted that "[s]treet encounters between citizens and police officers are incredibly rich in diversity" and range from the extremes of friendly to hostile. It was mindful that certain communities, particularly those populated by historically disadvantaged minorities, were subject to "wholesale harassment" by some elements of the police force. The majority of the Court was unwilling to find a Fourth Amendment violation, however, as a way to make a constitutional statement at the cost of "a high toll in human injury and frustration of efforts to prevent crime."

Although the Court upheld the stop and frisk procedure, it refused to dismiss the tactic as a "petty indignity." It found that when a law-enforcement officer accosts an individual and explores the outer surfaces of the person's body in public, there is "a serious intrusion upon the sanctity of the person." Because such a procedure may result in "great indignity" and generate "strong resentment," the Court refused to accept the argument that the Fourth Amendment did not apply. It also rejected the argument that the stop and frisk procedure was something short of a search and seizure. The Court concluded, however, that probable cause was not a prerequisite for such a procedure. Circumstances that necessitated swift action in response to the officer's on-the-scene observation did not lend themselves to the usual procedure of obtaining a warrant from a magistrate. Whether the officer's conduct was reasonable depended, from the Court's perspective, on whether the facts available at the time would have supported like action by a person of reasonable caution. The Court found the officer's actions in his investigation of possible criminal activity appropriate. Because the officer viewed highly suspicious activity, he performed a "legitimate investigative function." So questionable was the defendant's behavior that the majority observed that "[i]t would have been poor police work" not to have investigated it further.

The Court held that the stop and frisk procedure was justified because the police officer was "taking steps to assure himself that the person with whom he is dealing is not armed with a weapon that could unexpectedly and fatally be used against him." Noting that American criminals have a long tradition of armed violence, the Court determined that it would be unreasonable for an officer to take unnecessary risks in the performance of his or her duties. It refused to "blind" itself to the need of law-enforcement officers for self-protective action even though probable cause for an arrest was lacking. The Court believed that if an officer had reasonable suspicion that a person being investigated at close range was armed and presently dangerous, it would be wrong to deny the officer the power to determine whether the individual was carrying a weapon. The Court stated, however, that without probable cause to arrest, any search for weapons had to be restricted by the need that justified it. A search under the circumstances, therefore, could proceed no further than discovering a weapon that might be used to harm the officer or others nearby.

Applying these principles to the facts of the case, the Court determined that the stop and frisk procedure represented the "tempered act" of an officer who had to make a "quick decision" to protect himself and others from danger. The scope of the search also was appropriate. Because the officer merely patted down the defendant's clothing and reached into his pocket only after feeling a weapon, his actions did not constitute "a general exploratory search." Rather, they were only as intrusive as was necessary to determine whether the defendant was armed and to disarm him once the weapon was discovered. In sum, the Court held that when a police officer observes unusual conduct that leads him or her to determine that criminal activity is afoot and the suspect may be armed and dangerous, the officer is not necessarily bound by the usual requirement of probable cause. If the officer identifies himself or herself, makes reasonable inquiries, and experiences nothing to dispel reasonable fear with respect to safety, the interest in self-protection justifies a limited search of outer clothing to discover weapons.

Justice William O. Douglas dissented on grounds that the ruling narrowed and distorted the Fourth Amendment. Because the officer did not have probable cause to make an arrest, he would not have been able to secure a warrant from a magistrate. Consequently, the Court vested the police with power to conduct a search and seizure that a judge could not have authorized. Douglas feared that if searches on the basis of a reasonable suspicion rather than probable cause were allowed, inklings, hunches, and biases rather than objectively evaluated grounds would be sufficient to trigger intrusive police practices.

Although a stop and frisk is less invasive than a full-blown search and seizure, some police investigative methods that could be called searches may be considered even less invasive and thus be allowed under the Fourth Amendment. A request by law-enforcement officials to search the luggage of individuals on a bus, either on a random basis or because they were "vaguely" suspicious, was upheld in Florida v. Bostick (1991) because the police made no threats and indicated that the person had a right to refuse. The Court determined that the transaction did not constitute a seizure but was a mere encounter that did not fall within the scope of the Fourth Amendment. As a consequence, police were not required to demonstrate reasonable suspicion that otherwise would have been necessary to seize drugs found in the defendant's suitcase. Justice Thurgood Marshall, in an opinion joined by Justices Harry Blackmun and John Paul Stevens, dissented on grounds that the Court had focused on the wrong question. Instead of asking whether the defendant felt free not to consent, Marshall believed that the inquiry should have focused upon whether he felt at liberty to terminate the encounter.

The Court's "stop and frisk" and "encounter" rulings effectively have responded to law enforcement's interests in flexibility with respect to how officers may respond to criminal activity. Having to obtain a warrant and demonstrate probable cause prior to taking preventive or protective action imposes a significant disability when circumstances demand a timely and effective response. At the same time, relaxed standards for less intrusive search and seizure methods may be an invitation for pretext searches based upon an inkling rather than facts supporting probable cause. This risk may be magnified when prejudice or bias is a motivating factor in singling out persons who historically have been more susceptible to police harassment and victimization. An example of this peril is the conflicting testimony in Bostick with respect to whether the police actually advised the defendant that he simply could leave without consequence. "Reasonable" suspicions or "random" encounters initially may trigger a less invasive investigative methodology. The more the procedure uncovers evidence that would not have been obtainable without probable cause to search, however, the more it may be a temptation to action that is based upon pretext rather than principle.

Bibliography

Wayne R. LaFave, *Search and Seizure*, 3d ed. (1996). Sets forth the justification for and scope of stops, frisks, and encounters, and criticisms of them.

Tracey Maclin, "The Decline of the Right of Locomotion: The Fourth Amendment on the Streets," 75 *Cornell Law Review* 1258 (1990). A critical perspective on *Terry*.

Scott E. Sundby, "A Return to Fourth Amendment Basics: Undoing the Mischief of *Camara* and *Terry*," 72 *Minnesota Law Review* 383 (1988). Expresses concern that the Court has diluted Fourth Amendment standards pursuant to *Terry*, and that they require fortification.

17

The Fifth Amendment: Self-Incrimination

Police practices before the twentieth century traded significantly upon tactics of intimidation and violence. Such tactics date back to early English police methods that freely used torture and brutality to obtain confessions. Such statements were admissible at trial until the late eighteenth century, when the law began to reflect concern that confessions elicited by force or promises were unreliable and thus inadmissible. American courts generally embraced the premise that manipulation of a suspect's fears or hopes compromised the reliability and voluntariness of a confession. This understanding is manifested in interpretations of the Fifth Amendment privilege against self-incrimination that make coerced confessions inadmissible at trial on constitutional grounds. While violent methods of extracting confessions faded as a common police practice, other methods emerged for inducing confessions against a suspect's will. In *Miranda v. Arizona* (1966), the Supreme Court formulated a set of rules that were designed to offset the inherently coercive nature of police interrogation and psychological ploys designed to generate confessions less brutally but no less involuntarily than physically abusive tactics.

Miranda v. Arizona

The privilege against self-incrimination, like many features in American criminal procedure, has its roots in English tradition and experience. Through the middle of the seventeenth century, Star Chamber courts in England conducted roving inquiries to seek out and punish religious and political dissenters. The Star Chamber was a court of inquisition that provided no procedural safeguards for the accused. These tribunals had an unlimited charter to interrogate suspects and punish those who did not cooperate. Despite the harsh consequences of refusing to testify, some suspects claimed that they were not bound to provide information that would be self-accusatory. In the years following abolition of the Star Chamber, this principle became established as a judicially recognized privilege against self-incrimination. This privilege reflects not only experience with systems of persecution but a recognition that the use of torture to obtain confessions generates unreliable evidence. Infliction of physical pain or mental duress may coerce an acknowledgment of guilt. The confession, however, may reflect a desire to stop the torment rather than to tell the truth.

Citation:	384 U.S. 436.
Issue:	Whether a confession that was obtained by means of interrogation while a suspect was in police custody and without the suspect's lawyer being present violated the Fifth Amendment.
Year of Decision:	1966.
Outcome:	Unless a suspect waives his or her right of self-incrimination and right to a lawyer, a confession that is obtained in the course of interrogation while a suspect is in custody violates the Fifth Amendment.
Author of Opinion:	Chief Justice Earl Warren.
Vote:	6–3.

The privilege against self-incrimination was transplanted to the American colonies, where it made its way into state constitutions. It also was included in the Fifth Amendment of the United States Constitution, which provides that an accused person cannot be "compelled in any criminal case to be a witness against himself." Although by its terms the privilege is confined to "criminal cases," it has been expanded to protect persons in noncriminal proceedings from having to make statements that could be used against them for purposes of prosecution or conviction. This expansion has derived from a sense by the Supreme Court that "a noble principle often transcends its origins."

One of these transcendent applications has been in the context of police interrogation. This process, as the Court observed in *Miranda v. Arizona* (1966), typically "takes place in privacy," which "in turn results in a gap in our knowledge as to what in fact goes on in the interrogation rooms." The Court has struggled with this problem. In McNabb v. United States (1943), the Court ruled that a confession could not be admitted if it had been obtained during a period of "unnecessary delay" in effecting an arrest. This requirement was not imposed under the Constitution but under the federal judiciary's supervisory power over the federal criminal justice process. This rule operated in conjunction with a test that focused upon the "totality of the circumstances" and attempted to determine whether a confession was voluntary. Accurate fact-finding to establish voluntariness for confessions obtained in secrecy, however, was difficult. Given the challenges of determining what actually happened in the course of interrogation while a suspect was in custody, the Court in Escobedo v. Illinois (1964) determined that denial of access to a lawyer during a police-station interrogation, without warning of the right to remain silent, violated the Sixth Amendment right to counsel.

The Court eventually shifted from a focus on the Sixth Amendment right to counsel to one on the Fifth Amendment right against self-incrimination when, in *Miranda*, it addressed the inherently coercive nature of interrogation in custody. In *Miranda*, the Court reviewed a case in which police questioned Ernesto A. Miranda in a special interrogation room and obtained a confession that he had kidnapped and raped an eighteen year old girl. Two hours passed between the time questioning began and his oral and written confession. Miranda's case was joined with three others that were similar. Even if it was assumed that physical abuse as a means of obtaining confessions had diminished or disappeared, the Court noted that a process that takes place in privacy causes significant psychological stress. Chief Justice Earl Warren, who authored the majority opinion, determined that in such circumstances, certain safeguards were necessary to ensure that the defendant's statements "were truly the product of free choice." As a former California prosecutor, Warren was familiar with the strategies that may be used to break down a suspect and induce a confession. He referred to police manuals that train officers to manipulate a suspect's psychological state, encourage alternating friendliness and hostility toward the suspect, explain how to use trickery in the form of false witness identifications, and draw negative inferences from a desire to remain silent or seek an attorney. When such methods failed, handbooks frequently encouraged deceptive strategies that included offering false legal advice. As Warren put it, the goal was "to keep the subject off balance, for example, by trading on his insecurity about himself or his surroundings. The police then persuade, trick, or cajole him out of exercising his constitutional rights." From Warren's perspective, custodial interrogation, even without official brutality, exacted a heavy toll on individual liberty and traded on the weakness of the individual.

A particular concern for the Court was a defendant's placement in "an unfamiliar atmosphere" and exposure to "menacing police interrogation procedures." Especially because the defendants were "a seriously disturbed person with profound sexual fantasies" and the other "an indigent Los Angeles Negro who had dropped out of school in the sixth grade," Warren perceived a potential for compulsion that was "forcefully apparent." He viewed the interrogation environment as having been purposely created to "subjugate the individual to the will of his examiner." Without adequate protective devices to offset "the compulsion inherent in custodial settings," Warren maintained that "no statement obtained from the defendant can truly be the product of his free choice." He viewed the privilege against self-incrimination as especially significant in this context because government has the entire responsibility of producing evidence through its own labors "rather than by the cruel, simple expedient of compelling it from [the defendant's] own mouth."

To dispel the inherently coercive nature of custodial interrogation and offset the tactical advantage that undermines the right against self-incrimination, the Court concluded that it was necessary to adopt and enforce a set of "prophylactic" safeguards. Unless other effective means might be available to inform an accused person of the right to remain silent, the Court determined that police must provide specific warnings prior to any questioning. Thus, a "person must be warned that he has a right to remain silent, that any statement he does make may be used against him, and that he has a right to the presence of an attorney, either retained or appointed," during police questioning. The Court noted that these warnings may be waived if the suspect does so "voluntarily, knowingly and intelligently."

As many televised crime dramas demonstrate, the *Miranda* warnings have become a virtual cliché in modern police practice. Initial reaction to the Court's ruling, however, was decidedly less friendly. Police objected that their hands were being tied, and Congress enacted a law that purported to repeal the decision as it relates to federal prosecutions. Although that law remains in effect, the Department of Justice mostly has abided by the Court's ruling. Over the years, however, the judiciary's attitude about the premises and applicability of the warnings has changed. In Michigan v. Tucker (1974), the Court noted that the *Miranda* rules were not constitutional rights but procedural safeguards designed to reinforce the right against self-incrimination. If incriminating statements are made in violation of *Miranda*, the Court nonetheless has allowed their use as evidence to impeach defendants who take the stand in their own defense. Once a defendant asserts his or her right to remain silent, police must cease questioning immediately. In Michigan v. Mosely (1975), however, the Court indicated that attempts to resume the interrogation could be made provided a new set of warnings was issued. If the suspect asserts a right to counsel, as the Court determined in Edwards v. Arizona (1981), the police cannot resume questioning until an attorney is provided.

A particularly critical need for purposes of determining when warnings are required is defining when custodial interrogation commences. In Rhode Island v. Innis (1980), the Court affirmed that "the *Miranda* safeguards come into play whenever a person in custody is subjected to either express questioning or its functional equivalent." Not only express questioning but words or actions that police know are reasonably likely to elicit an incriminating response, therefore, define custodial interrogation. Under this standard, what must be examined is whether police should have foreseen that an incriminating statement would be made as a response to their methods. The Court's application of this principle has been subjected to extensive criticism. In the Innis case itself, Innis, a murder suspect, had been advised of his rights and had expressed the desire to see a lawyer. The patrolmen in the car transporting him proceeded to have a conversation in which one of them said, "there's a lot of handicapped children running around in this area, and God forbid one of them might find a weapon with shells and they might hurt themselves." The suspect interrupted the conversation and offered to lead police to the place where the incriminating weapon could be found. Both officers testified that their discussion was motivated strictly by safety concerns, and the majority of the Court adopted the position that "police surely cannot be held accountable for the unforeseeable results of their words or actions." What actually motivated the officer's comment probably requires a mind-reading exercise. The possibility that the officers may have been trying to obtain incriminating evidence, however, demonstrates that even the *Miranda* safeguards are not tamper-proof.

Of the many controversial decisions issued by the Warren Court, the one in *Miranda* was among the most debated. It nonetheless established a model for protecting the right against self-incrimination that was copied in other settings. Referring to the need for counsel at police lineups, the Court in United States v. Wade (1967) noted that such identification procedures were "riddled with innumerable dangers and variable factors which might seriously, even crucially, derogate from a fair trial." *Miranda* methods for safeguarding constitutional interests, however, generated significant political backlash. In addition to Congress's effort to repeal *Miranda*, Richard Nixon in 1968 was elected president in part on a promise to appoint justices who opposed and presumably would undo the ruling. One constitutional law scholar predicted that with the passing of the Warren Court, it was reasonable to expect that the Court would "treat *Miranda* unkindly."[1] Although case law since has narrowed the scope of the decision and created various exceptions to its operation, its core remains intact. Ernesto Miranda himself became a poignant footnote to the legacy he created. A decade after the Court's decision, he died in a barroom brawl. The person suspected of killing him received the warnings that the decision bearing Miranda's name required.

Note

1. Yale Kamisar, et al., *Modern Criminal Procedure: Cases, Comments, and Questions* 599 (1994).

Bibliography

Liva Baker, *"Miranda": Crime, Law, and Politics* (1983). Examines the political fallout from the *Miranda* decision.
Fred E. Inbau and John E. Reid, *Criminal Interrogation and Confessions* (1962). The authors of some of the police manuals, that the Court condemned in *Miranda*, explain the need for pre-*Miranda* interrogation methods.
Paul Marcus, "A Return to the 'Bright Line Rule' of *Miranda*," 35 *William and Mary Law Review* 93 (1993). Argues that the Court was not aggressive enough in extending Fifth Amendment protection to suspects.

18

The Sixth Amendment: The Right to Counsel

A defendant's ability to face the criminal justice system depends not only upon the quality of his or her case but upon the ability to secure legal representation. Without counsel, the odds increase that innocent persons will be found guilty and the defendant will not receive a fair trial. Because the average person possesses neither an attorney's legal expertise nor understanding of the criminal justice system, legal representation is crucial to that system's legitimacy and credibility. Whether a defendant may retain counsel to represent him or her in a criminal proceeding has never been a real issue. For individuals who could afford a lawyer, the question of the right to representation was academic. Less certain historically was whether indigent defendants had a right to appointed counsel. Earlier in the twentieth century, the Supreme Court determined that a right to such representation existed in federal trials. Not until *Gideon v. Wainwright* (1963) did the Court determine that indigent defendants in state proceedings had the same right.

Gideon v. Wainwright

The Sixth Amendment provides that "in all criminal prosecutions, the accused shall enjoy the right . . . to have the Assistance of counsel for his defence." The ability not only to possess but to exercise one's rights or liberties is in significant part a function of resources. Freedom of the press, for instance, is enjoyed most by persons who have the wealth to own or run a newspaper. For the individual without such resources, the liberty exists in theory rather than fact. Such disparities, as the Supreme Court has noted in several instances, are not constitutionally significant. The right to counsel, however, is an exception to this norm. When the criminal justice system proceeds against an individual, life and liberty interests are great. Defense lawyers play a crucial role in helping defendants cope with an intimidating and perilous process. The Sixth Amendment right to counsel thus has been a concern that is not just abstract but real. As Justice Hugo Black put it in Griffin v. Illinois (1956), "there can be no equal justice where the kind of trial a man gets depends on the amount of money he has."

Citation:	372 U.S. 335.
Issue:	Whether the failure of a state court to appoint counsel for a defendant charged with a felony violated the Sixth Amendment.
Year of Decision:	1963.
Outcome:	The right to counsel is so fundamental in a criminal proceeding that the cost of paying for an attorney must be incurred by the state if the defendant cannot afford one.
Author of Opinion:	Justice Hugo Black.
Vote:	9–0.

The essential role that counsel performs in a criminal trial and the consequent need to provide for it when defendants otherwise would have no access to an attorney were graphically illustrated in Powell v. Alabama (1934). The Powell case arose from an Alabama court's conviction of Ozie Powell and several other teenage defendants on charges they had raped two white girls. The defendants, described as "ignorant and illiterate," were rushed to trial within two weeks of the alleged offense. Rather than appoint a specific lawyer to represent the defendants, the trial judge turned their case over to the entire bar in the community. Although two lawyers offered to provide representation, the Court denied them a request for more time to prepare a defense. Eight of the nine defendants were convicted and sentenced to death.

In reversing the convictions, the Supreme Court determined that the complexities of a criminal trial require the right to have counsel present. Without such assistance, a "defendant faces the danger of conviction because he does not know how to establish his innocence." Critical to the outcome in Powell was the Court's sense that a defendant who is unable to hire counsel and incapable of defending himself or herself must have counsel assigned as an essential aspect of "due process of law." Within a decade of the Powell decision, the Court responded to arguments that a defendant is entitled to an attorney in any criminal proceeding. In Betts v. Brady (1942), it determined that appointed counsel was not required in every criminal case. The Court thus refused to extend the right of counsel without regard to the seriousness of the offense.

This premise was reversed in *Gideon v. Wainwright*. At issue was whether an indigent defendant accused of breaking into and entering a pool hall was entitled to appointed counsel. Because the defendant, Clarence Earl Gideon, was not charged with a capital crime, the Florida court determined that the state need not provide him with counsel. The defendant conducted his own defense, which included an opening statement to the jury, cross-examination of witnesses, refusal to testify in his own behalf, and a closing statement. Despite this effort, the jury returned a guilty verdict. Following his conviction, Gideon brought an action against Louie L. Wainwright, Director of the Florida Division of Corrections. Gideon sought release on grounds he had been denied the right to have counsel appointed for him.

For the Court, it was "an obvious truth" that "any person haled into court, who is too poor to hire a lawyer, cannot be assured a fair trial unless counsel is appointed for him." The essential role that lawyers perform is evidenced by the substantial levels of funding for the criminal justice system and, in particular, the appointment of prosecutors "to protect the public's interest in an orderly society." Noting that state constitutions and the federal Constitution from the "very beginning" have emphasized procedural and substantive safeguards as means to assure fair trials, the Court stressed that these guarantees were essential to a fair trial. The general interest in securing the best representation available with the resources at one's disposal suggested strongly to the majority "that lawyers in criminal courts are necessities, not luxuries." The guarantee of a fair trial before an impartial tribunal in which every defendant was equal before the law could not be satisfied if "the poor man charged with crime has to face his accusers without a lawyer to assist him." Because the defendant had been denied the right to counsel, the Court reversed the lower court and remanded the case for retrial. Counsel was provided at the new trial, and the defendant was found not guilty.

Because the defendant had been charged with a felony, it was unclear whether a right to appointed counsel also extended to misdemeanors. In Argersinger v. Howard (1963), the Court determined that the reason for providing assistance of counsel in a felony trial applied "to any criminal trial, where an accused is deprived of his liberty." At the same time, it qualified the scope of the Sixth Amendment guarantee. Under this new provision, the right to counsel was established if a person was charged with a crime that might result in a prison sentence of any duration. Although the Court acknowledged that petty offenses do not necessarily ensure less complex proceedings than more serious violations of the law, it nonetheless seems to have factored the defendant's stakes into the calculation of when the Sixth Amendment guarantee operates. In so doing, it also put judges in the rather unusual position of having to consider sentencing possibilities before a trial even begins. Unless a judge appoints counsel, he or she cannot impose a prison sentence regardless of what the evidence demonstrates. In Scott v. Illinois (1979), the Court reviewed and reaffirmed the line it drew in Argersinger. The Scott decision reiterated "that no indigent criminal defendant be sentenced to a term of imprisonment unless the State has afforded him the right to assistance of appointed counsel in his defense."

By its terms, the Sixth Amendment extends only to "criminal prosecutions." The Court, however, has determined that a person is entitled to the assistance of counsel when a statutory right exists for appealing a criminal conviction. Such a right of appeal in the first instance exists in all states. Assistance of counsel in the appeals context is based not upon the Sixth Amendment but upon the Fourteenth Amendment due process and equal protection clauses. As the Court put it in Douglas v. California (1963), the absence of counsel for the only appeal that an indigent person will have etches "an unconstitutional line . . . between rich and poor." The right to an attorney on appeal does not extend, as the Court held in Ross v. Moffitt (1974), to appeals that are granted on a discretionary basis. An indigent person thus might appeal to the Supreme Court but would not be afforded the assistance of counsel to do so.

Universal access to counsel for trials and the first level of appeal does not necessarily mean that interests in effectiveness and quality of representation have been equalized. The Sixth Amendment has been interpreted so that it upholds the right of a person who can pay for an attorney to obtain representation from the lawyer he or she prefers. Indigent defendants, however, have no constitutionally protected interest in choosing an attorney. Although the Sixth Amendment has been held to expect that retained or appointed counsel will provide "effective assistance," the standards for determining incompetence are relatively relaxed. As the Court described them in Strickland v. Washington (1984), these criteria focus on whether deficiencies in representation were "so serious that counsel was not functioning as 'counsel.'" The burden is put on the defendant to demonstrate that the lawyer's judgment, viewed from the attorney's perspective and under "all the circumstances," was constitutionally insufficient. Because judicial review of such claims makes "a strong presumption" that counsel's conduct is reasonable, and tactical decisions are "virtually unchallengeable," the chances of a successful claim are not great. In the Strickland case itself, the Court denied a Sixth Amendment claim even though it acknowledged that the attorney's own sense of "hopelessness" for the defendant's case caused him to function less vigorously than he might have. Even if representation is proved to be deficient, the defendant still must demonstrate prejudice to the effect that the "errors were so serious as to deprive the defendant of a fair trial."

Like any other guarantee, the right to appointed counsel is not absolute, nor is it available on equal terms to everyone. By providing counsel to indigent persons at trial and on appeals by right, modern case law has established a baseline level of representation to which any person is entitled. It follows that those who can afford to pay an attorney will have choices that the indigent defendant will not have. Despite limits to equalization and tolerance for variances in effectiveness of representation, it would be mistaken to discount the significance of the *Gideon* decision. Before the ruling, the right to counsel was essentially a hollow guarantee for indigent defendants. Since *Gideon*, basic legal representation of those who cannot afford a lawyer has become professionalized through public defender offices that operate at the federal level and in many states. Paralleling this model has been the emergence of the federal legal aid program, which provides the poor access to legal representation in certain types of civil cases. By the final decade of the twentieth century, more than eight million criminal defendants and nearly 80 percent of the nation's inmate population annually were being represented by court-appointed lawyers. Even though a double standard may exist in the quality and effectiveness of representation, depending upon whether legal representation is by choice or appointment, such numbers suggest that a right to counsel literally has made the difference between a verdict of guilt or innocence for some of these defendants.

Bibliography

William M. Beaney, *The Right to Counsel in American Courts* (1955). Documents the inadequacy of counsel for indigent defendants owing to limited availability and efficacy of state-appointed lawyers prior to *Gideon*.

Anthony Lewis, *Gideon's Trumpet* (1964). Examines the history, litigation, and immediate consequences of the *Gideon* decision.

Robert L. Spangenberg and Patricia A. Smith, *An Introduction to Indigent Defense Systems* (1986). Analyzes various models for representing the poor in the criminal justice system.

19

The Eighth Amendment: Cruel and Unusual Punishments

The Eighth Amendment's ban on cruel and unusual punishments derives from a historical tradition, that dates back to sixteenth-century England, of inhumane punishments inflicted on persons found guilty of a crime. Typically, such methods consisted of torture and resulted in death. The Eighth Amendment was included in the Bill of Rights as a safeguard against such practices. Contemporary debate over the Eighth Amendment principally focuses upon the constitutionality of capital punishment. Although many observers, including some Supreme Court justices, have argued that the death penalty per se is cruel and unusual, the Court itself has never adopted that position. Nonetheless, it has struck down some capital punishment laws on grounds that standards governing their application breach the Eighth Amendment. The Court's ruling in *Furman v. Georgia* (1972) is consistent with this premise.

Furman v. Georgia

The Eighth Amendment guarantee against "cruel and unusual punishments" arose from the experience of late sixteenth-century England. Torture was a common method then for obtaining confessions from people suspected of crimes. Some critics complained that these practices were "cruel and barbarous" and thus in violation of the Magna Carta, a document signed by King John of England in 1215 as a condition imposed by the barons for swearing their allegiance to him. This charter established the principle that the king was not above the law and it was a seminal source of rights and freedoms that eventually made their way into American constitutional law. For those convicted of an offense, punishment was even crueler. Brutality, zealously applied, typically led to death. This official "parade of horrors," as some have described it, peaked during the late seventeenth century. Excessive and sometimes barbaric methods eventually generated sufficient public outrage to spur adoption of the English Bill of Rights in 1689. Included within these guarantees was a prohibition against "cruel and unusual punishments."

Citation:	408 U.S. 238.
Issue:	Whether a state law that provided for capital punishment violated the Eighth Amendment.
Year of Decision:	1972.
Outcome:	The death penalty is unconstitutional if it is applied in an arbitrary or discriminatory manner.
Author of Opinion:	*Per curiam.*
Vote:	5–4.

This safeguard was transported to the American colonies, where it surfaced in the Virginia Declaration of Rights. Using virtually the same language that eventually would constitute the Eighth Amendment, and exactly the terms of the English Bill of Rights, the Virginia Declaration of Rights provided "[t]hat bail ought not to be required, nor excessive fines imposed, nor cruel and unusual punishment inflicted." Similar guarantees were adopted in other states. In urging Virginia's adoption of the provision, Patrick Henry argued that a defining feature of the new nation was its refusal to "admit of tortures, or cruel and barbarous punishment." His fear was that the federal government might adopt some model other than the English common law and "introduce the practice of France, Spain, and Germany—of torturing, to extort a confession of the crime." If that occurred he warned, "[w]e are then lost and undone."

Capital punishment during colonial times typically was limited to crimes that violated not just the law but religious principle. The Capital Laws of New-England drafted in 1636, for instance, included "idolatry, witchcraft, blasphemy, murder, assault in sudden anger, sodomy, burglary, adultery, statutory rape, rape, man stealing, perjury in a capital trial, and rebellion." For each of these crimes, the Old Testament was cited as a source. Through the prerevolutionary period, and in part because of the insecurity and inadequacy of jails, capital punishment, mutilation, and fines were relied upon to control the criminal population. The first organized efforts to abolish capital punishment began to surface in the late eighteenth century. In 1846, Michigan became the first state to prohibit executions. Other states followed with similar legislative action or reductions in the number of offenses that were defined as capital in nature. By the end of the nineteenth century, mandatory capital punishment almost entirely had been eliminated. States that retained the death penalty typically vested juries with discretion to decide whether it was warranted in a particular case. Following World War I, several states reenacted the death penalty. By the 1970s, the vast majority of states and the federal government authorized it for at least one crime (typically murder).

The Supreme Court's first significant decision on capital punishment responded to a death sentence imposed upon a defendant convicted of premeditated murder. In Wilkerson v. Utah (1879), the Court allowed the public execution to proceed after studying the Utah Territory's historical attitudes toward such methods, contemporary thinking on capital punishment, and practices in other countries. The ruling established a principle that has continued to govern analysis of cruel and unusual punishments. The Court observed that the Eighth Amendment "is not fastened to the obsolete, but may acquire meaning as public opinion becomes enlightened by a humane justice." This point has been reiterated in the course of subsequent decisions that have required the Court to "draw its meaning from the evolving standards of decency that mark the progress of a maturing society."

By the late 1960s, a Gallup Poll indicated that 47 percent of the nation's population opposed the death penalty and 42 percent favored it. Whether society had evolved to the point of regarding capital punishment as cruel and unusual became a question that the Court confronted in Furman v. Georgia. It did so on a criminal justice landscape that had not seen a death sentence since 1967. At issue were impositions of the death penalty on three defendants, one of whom was convicted of murder and the other two for rape. Like the other two petitioners, William Henry Furman, convicted of the murder, was African American. Each of the petitioners contended that Georgia's system of capital punishment was unconstitutional. Under state law, discretion to impose the death penalty was vested with the trial judge or jury. Although five justices voted to invalidate the law, their reasons for doing so varied.

Justice William O. Douglas argued that the death penalty law was constitutionally deficient because it gave judges and juries "practically untrammeled discretion to let an accused live or insist that he die." Of particular concern to him was that death sentences "were disproportionately imposed and carried out on the poor, the Negro, and the members of unpopular groups." What he characterized as "uncontrolled discretion" in administering the death penalty created problems of arbitrary or discriminatory application. Without standards to govern the death penalty's operation, Douglas found it unacceptable that "[p]eople live or die, dependent on the whim of one man or of 12." Particularly in a social context that included an embedded legacy of racism, Douglas was uneasy with statutes that were "pregnant with discrimination." As he viewed it, the Eighth Amendment joined with the equal protection guarantee that itself was "implicit in the ban on 'cruel and unusual' punishments." Douglas noted that a law that provided for the execution of criminal offenders if they had not been educated beyond the fifth grade, made less than $3,000 a year, or were black, unpopular, or unstable "would plainly fall." So too, he concluded, should a state statute that had the same result "in practice."

The "primary principle" of the Eighth Amendment, from Justice William Brennan's perspective, was that "punishment must not be so severe as to be degrading to the dignity of human beings." A key factor in determining whether a penalty degraded human dignity, as he saw it, was whether the state arbitrarily or without reason inflicted a severe punishment not imposed upon others. Equally important concerns for him were whether a punishment was "unacceptable to contemporary society" or "excessive." He believed these assessments should be made by asking whether other methods would serve penal ends as effectively. Describing death as "truly an awesome punishment" because, among other things, it is irrevocable, denies "membership in the human family," and in some instances will be visited upon innocent persons, Brennan concluded that capital punishment "is uniquely degrading to human dignity." Although he staked out the position that the death penalty categorically was unconstitutional, he also agreed with Douglas that it violated the Eighth Amendment because its application was arbitrary. Particularly as executions had become increasingly rare, the risk of arbitrary application had increased. Facilitating this danger was the fact that death sentence decisions were found to be wholly unguided by standards. Noting that the defendant in *Furman* accidentally shot his victim when he fell trying to escape from a home he was burglarizing, Brennan was unmoved by arguments that the death penalty was reserved for "extreme" cases. In Brennan's view, "Furman or his crime illustrated the extreme" only if all murderers and their murders were extreme. Despite the fact that many states still had death penalty laws, society's refusal to apply them suggested "a deep-seated reluctance to inflict" them. He also was not persuaded by arguments that capital punishment was an effective deterrent to crime. Because the death penalty was neither invariably nor swiftly imposed in a system of arbitrary application, a potential murderer confronted neither the certainty of speedy death nor likely execution in the distant future.

Justice Potter Stewart found that the death penalty was "cruel" because it exceeded the type of punishment necessary under the circumstances. He considered capital punishment "unusual" because it was rarely imposed when it was applicable. Most significantly, from Stewart's perspective, the death penalty was "cruel and unusual for the same reason that being struck by lightning is cruel and unusual." Of all the persons convicted for capital crimes during the same year as the defendant, many for offenses that were equally if not more "reprehensible," those sentenced to death were "among a capriciously selected handful" subject to execution. Stewart thus concluded that the Constitution could not tolerate the death penalty under a legal system that permitted its use "so wantonly and freakishly."

In his concurring opinion, Justice Byron White rejected the notion that any system of capital punishment is per se unconstitutional. He expressed his lack of confidence in the deterrence value of the death penalty when it was reserved for so few. As White noted, many who were convicted of crimes for which others were put to death received lesser sentences. Because the penalty was seldom invoked, it struck him as less than a credible deterrent. Under circumstances that inflicted "pointless and needless extinction of life with only marginal contributions to any discernible social or public purpose," White believed that capital punishment violated the Eighth Amendment.

Justice Thurgood Marshall had served with the NAACP Legal Defense Fund in the 1950s when that organization had began to challenge capital punishment on constitutional grounds. Marshall described six conceivable purposes of the death penalty: "retribution, deterrence, prevention of repetitive criminal acts, encouragement of guilty pleas and confessions, eugenics, and economy." Although he acknowledged that retribution was a legitimate social interest, he maintained that it could not be the sole objective of punishment. If capital punishment displaced aims of general deterrence and rehabilitation, he viewed it as equivalent to "vengeance," which the Eighth Amendment and a free society condemned as "an intolerable aspiration." Noting that deterrence was "the most hotly contested issue" with respect to capital punishment, Marshall cited a national study that indicated no correlation between murder rates and the presence or lack of the death penalty. Referring to other studies that supported these findings as a "massive amount of evidence" against deterrence theory, he argued that capital punishment could not be justified on the premise that it discouraged crime. After rejecting arguments that the death penalty advanced any of its claimed purposes, Marshall concluded that it represented an "excessive and unnecessary punishment that violates the Eighth Amendment."

His perception that capital punishment had become "morally unaccepta-ble" to the American people was a further argument for its unconstitution-ality.

Chief Justice Warren Burger authored a dissenting opinion, joined by Justices Harry Blackmun, Lewis Powell, and William Rehnquist in which he argued that he would abolish capital punishment or limit it to a small number of heinous crimes if he were a legislator. Proceeding from the prem-ise that constitutional inquiry must be detached from personal feelings, Burger questioned whether the Eighth Amendment's framers intended the provision against cruel and unusual punishments to have the same meaning as its English predecessor. As he viewed the early debates, the framers' exclusive aim was to prohibit the use of torture. Because Burger found no discussion of an interrelationship between the words "cruel" and "un-usual," his inclination was to view the former term as controlling. He thus rejected the argument that because capital punishment was cruel "in the everyday sense of the word, and had become unusual due to decreased use," it violated the Eighth Amendment. Noting that the framers offered no indication that they opposed capital punishment, and finding no evi-dence that the death penalty shocked the modern conscience of society, Burger refused to condemn a commonly allowed, albeit infrequently ap-plied, state practice. Regardless of whether the death penalty served penal aims, including deterrence, Burger maintained that it was a legislative rather than a judicial concern.

Taken together, the opinions in favor of striking down the Georgia law did not categorically declare the death penalty unconstitutional. Justices Brennan and Marshall, however, adopted that position and continued to articulate it over the course of their careers on the Court. The opinions of Justices Douglas, Stewart, and White thus were crucial for purposes of determining how a state's capital punishment law might conform to the Eighth Amendment. Consequently, future litigation turned on whether a legislature provided adequate standards for guiding judges and juries in determining whether to apply the death penalty.

In response to the Court's decision, many states changed their death penalty statutes. Typically, these laws limited discretion by mandating cap-ital punishment for certain crimes, identified specific considerations for the application of the death penalty, and established specific procedures for death penalty deliberations. Georgia reenacted a death penalty law that identified several aggravating factors warranting capital punishment and required juries to consider mitigating or aggravating circumstances. The Court upheld the revised law in Gregg v. Georgia (1976). At the same time, in Woodson v. North Carolina (1976), the Court struck down a state law that mandated the death penalty for all persons convicted of first-degree murder. In addition to the argument of Justices Brennan and Marshall that the Eighth Amendment categorically prohibited the death penalty, a plurality of three justices (Stewart, Powell, and John Paul Stevens) insisted that "particularized consideration of relevant information" was constitutionally required.

In reviewing the Georgia death penalty law one year after Gregg, the Court confronted massive racial disparities in executions for rape. Evidence showed that from 1930 to 1972, 89 percent of rape executions involved black men accused of raping white women. Over the course of the state's history, no man—black or white—had ever been convicted of raping a black woman. A four-justice plurality concluded that rape was a serious offense "but does not compare with murder" in its "moral depravity." Justices Brennan and Marshall weighed in with their absolute condemnation of capital punishment. In Coker v. Georgia (1977), the Court found that the death penalty was excessive punishment for rape and thus an Eighth Amendment violation. In the same year, the Court, in Lockett v. Ohio (1977), also struck down an Ohio law that required the death penalty whenever a jury identified one of several specified aggravating factors. Because a jury could not consider mitigating evidence, the Court found the Ohio statute unconstitutional.

Jurisprudence after *Furman* reflected a growing tension between requirements for limiting jury discretion and the need for individualized sentencing. Justice Blackmun concluded that because narrowed discretion made individualized decisions impossible, the death penalty could not be administered constitutionally. He eventually joined Justices Marshall and Brennan in viewing capital punishment as an Eighth Amendment violation per se. Justice Antonin Scalia, in Walton v. Arizona (1990), found no "inherent tension" between the requirement of limited jury discretion and the need for individualized sentencing. To find such a conflict, he noted, would be like "saying there was perhaps an inherent tension between the Allies and the Axis powers in World War II." Thereafter, he pledged never to find a constitutional violation when a mandatory death penalty was imposed for a crime that traditionally had been punished by execution.

With the retirement of Justices Brennan, Marshall, and Blackmun, the premise that the Eighth Amendment categorically prohibits capital punishment lost its voice. A quarter of a century after Gregg, most death penalty litigation focuses not on capital punishment as a general proposition, but on whether it is constitutional as applied to a particular defendant. Executions have become more commonplace since the end of the virtual moratorium on them during the 1960s. For both proponents and detractors, however, delay compounded by uncertainty of application continues to raise questions regarding capital punishment's efficacy as a deterrent. Legislators in states that provide for capital punishment have attempted to speed the execution process by narrowing opportunities for postconviction review. The Court generally has been friendly toward these efforts. Even so, the time between conviction and execution is characterized by an extensive and expensive process of multiple reviews by state and federal courts. Under these circumstances, modern experience with capital punishment is a source of dissatisfaction both for the death penalty's supporters and detractors, albeit for different reasons.

Bibliography

President's Commission on Law Enforcement and Administration of Justice, *Task Force Report: The Courts* (1967). Includes measures of public attitudes toward capital punishment.

Thorsten Sellin, *The Death Penalty: A Report for the Model Penal Code Project of the American Law Institute* (1959). This key study that challenged the theory that the death penalty deters crime proved to be influential for those justices who found capital punishment a violation of the constitution.

Brian Vila and Cynthia Morris, eds., *Capital Punishment in the United States: A Documentary History* (1997). This collection of primary documents traces the history of this issue in American history.

20

The Fourteenth Amendment

The power of judicial review, which establishes the judiciary as the final authority in interpreting the Constitution, was affirmed in *Marbury v. Madison* (1803). However, the *Marbury* decision did not resolve a crucial question regarding the sources of rights and liberties the judiciary may draw upon in negating executive or legislative action. The controversy over whether the Constitution sets forth the only rights and liberties that the judiciary can cite, or whether the judiciary can identify other rights as fundamental barriers to political action, persists to this day. When the Court announces a right that is not specified by the Constitution, such as the right of privacy, critics accuse it of judicial activism. Their argument is that the Court is creating rights out of its own cloth rather than from constitutional thread. These advocates of judicial restraint note that federal judges are appointed for life rather than elected. When the judiciary blocks the work of the elected branches of government on grounds that the Constitution does not specifically mention, detractors claim that the Court also is defeating the will of the people. Those who think differently maintain that the Constitution is not the exclusive bank of rights and liberties, and that the people are better served when the Court acknowledges and asserts guarantees that are rooted in the nation's traditions and conscience.

Economic Rights

The concept of economic rights presented itself as a constitutional concept in the context of slavery. Writing for the Supreme Court in *Dred Scott v. Sandford* (1857), Chief Justice Roger B. Taney asserted that "a right of property in a slave is distinctly and expressly affirmed by the Constitution."

Constitutional change through the process of Reconstruction repudiated this notion. The Fourteenth Amendment, however, soon became a focal point for economic rights advocates who argued that it secured property rights and the freedom to make contracts. In the *Slaughter-House Cases* (1873), the Court rejected the notion that the Fourteenth Amendment's privileges and immunities clause protected any economic freedoms. This ruling generated a sharp dissent by Justice Stephen Field, who maintained that the Fourteenth Amendment secured precisely such liberties. Nearly a quarter of century later, after the nation had directed its attention from Reconstruction to industrial and commercial growth and development, economic rights theory found the constitutional shelter that it initially had been denied. In Allgeyer v. Louisiana (1897), the Court concluded that the Fourteenth Amendment's due process clause secured not only a person's general liberty to use his or her "faculties . . . in all lawful ways" but the "liberty of contract." The crucial moment for economic rights doctrine, however, was the Court's decision in *Lochner v. New York* (1905). This ruling established significant limitations on governmental power to interfere with marketplace freedom and blunted legislative initiatives for social and economic reform. Not until the late 1930s, in the context of a national economic emergency and following a political crisis caused by the Court's refusal to give ground, did the judiciary relent on its commitment to economic rights. This turnabout, achieved in *United States v. Carolene Products Co.* (1938), resulted in the Court's abandonment of economic rights doctrine.

Lochner v. New York

Throughout the early part of the twentieth century, the Supreme Court consistently invalidated federal legislation that attempted to regulate conditions of employment. A primary basis for striking down minimum-wage and maximum-hour legislation was that such enactments exceeded Congress's authority under the commerce clause. In restricting federal power to regulate conditions in the workplace, the Court typically observed that matters of health and safety were within the province of the states.

Toward the end of the nineteenth century, labor began to organize in an attempt to equalize bargaining power with the forces of capital and industrialization. Responding to the concerns of organized labor, many states began to adopt laws that addressed dangerous or oppressive conditions in the workplace. Such regulations emerged in a constitutional environment that seemingly would have been hospitable to their enactment.

Citation:	198 U.S. 45.
Issue:	Whether a state law that set maximum hours of employment violated the due process clause of the Fourteenth Amendment.
Year of Decision:	1905.
Outcome:	The regulation exceeded the state's police power and violated the due process clause.
Author of Opinion:	Justice Rufus Peckham.
Vote:	5–4.

In the *Slaughter-House Cases* (1873), the Supreme Court had determined that the Fourteenth Amendment was not a bar to state laws that regulated economic opportunity. The *Slaughter-House* Court had concluded that the privileges and immunities clause, in particular, did not incorporate the Bill of Rights so as to make its provisions applicable to the states. The Court also rejected the premise that rights and liberties that were not specified by the Constitution could be established through the Fourteenth Amendment.

Over the final quarter of the nineteenth century, the Court chipped away at the *Slaughter-House* decision. During the two decades following that ruling, the due process clause emerged as a potential basis for rights and liberties that were identified by the Court even though they were not enumerated by the Constitution. This possibility became a reality when, in Allgeyer v. Louisiana (1987), the Court struck down a law that prohibited out-of-state insurers from selling policies in Louisiana. In support of its ruling, the Court found that the regulation impaired liberty of contract. Although the Constitution does not mention this freedom, the Court deemed it fundamental and protected by the Fourteenth Amendment. The

Allgeyer decision began a four-decade era of jurisprudence characterized by expanding concepts of liberty and use of the due process clause to defeat state regulations that interfered with fundamental rights. Although these rights were not mentioned by the Constitution, the Court found them basic. The era that followed became synonymous for many with the notion of antidemocratic jurisprudence that impeded social and economic change. Legislated initiatives during the late nineteenth and early twentieth centuries that sought to ban child labor, recognize labor unions, create a minimum wage, or achieve other reforms persistently were annulled by the Court's protection of contractual liberty.

The defining economic rights case of the early twentieth century was *Lochner v. New York* (1905). At issue in *Lochner* was a New York law that limited the workday and workweek for bakery employees to ten hours and sixty hours, respectively. Joseph Lochner had been convicted under the law for allowing an employee to work more than sixty hours a week. On review, the United States Supreme Court reversed the conviction and found the law unconstitutional on two grounds. First, it determined that the regulation was not a legitimate health and safety measure and thus was not within the scope of the state's police power. Traditionally, the police power enables states to provide for the public health, safety, and morals. As the Court viewed the law, it was labor legislation "pure and simple" without any demonstrated connection to police power concerns. Second, the law violated freedom to contract, which the Court identified as a protected liberty interest under the due process clause of the Fourteenth Amendment. Despite disparities in the marketplace between employers and employees, which the state legislature had attempted to equalize, the Court determined that an official restriction on work hours violated the freedom of both parties.

The Court acknowledged that states possessed the authority to protect the health, safety, and general welfare of the public. When a state exercised its police power, however, the Court emphasized that it must determine whether the regulatory objective or the burden imposed upon individual freedom was more significant. Although the state justified its maximum-hour law as a public health measure, the Court was not convinced that a public health interest was at stake. Without a demonstrated and direct connection between the regulatory method and protection of public health, the Court determined that an individual's freedom to contract was more important and must prevail. Lacking, from the Court's perspective, was a convincing basis for finding that the regulation was essential for purposes of protecting the health of bakers or the public. Put simply, the Court was unwilling to accept the legislature's judgment that the baking trade presented health risks to employees or that long hours might increase the chances for adulterated bread that would harm the public.

Invalidation of the state law provoked controversy then and later. In a dissenting opinion, Justice John Harlan, Sr., argued that the majority merely disagreed with the wisdom of the legislation. Such review, as he saw it, wrongly injected the Court into the political domain. Because a relationship between regulatory methods and aims could not be dismissed, Justice Harlan considered it wrong for the Court to substitute its assessment of public health needs for those of the legislature.

Also in a dissenting opinion, Justice Oliver Wendell Holmes, Jr., maintained that the Court had overstepped its boundaries. Holmes considered protection of contractual liberty under the Fourteenth Amendment to be a highly misguided exercise. From his perspective, the Court was using its power to interpret the Constitution as a means to achieve a preferred policy result. Protection of contractual liberty, as Holmes saw it, enabled the Court to undo the laws not because they were unconstitutional but because a majority of the justices disliked the policy or ideology that they reflected.

Over the vigorous objections of dissenting judges and commentators, the Court's emphasis upon economic freedom was a hallmark of constitutional jurisprudence during the first third of the twentieth century. Throughout this period, the Court's decisions thwarted a broad array of legislative and social reform. Regulation of the workplace was viewed suspiciously, for instance, unless the case for health and safety was overwhelming. In Muller v. Oregon (1908), the Court upheld a state law that limited the working hours of women. Critical to the outcome of this case was a detailed brief that exhaustively catalogued the "unique" risks to women of long hours in the workplace. The Court emphasized, however, that "freedom of contract is . . . nevertheless the general rule and restraint the exception." The fate of prohibiting child labor or establishing a minimum wage or maximum hours was determined by this general rule rather than the exception.

Not until the mid-1930s did the Court rethink and eventually abandon economic rights doctrine. This change was attributable to the pent-up frustration of the political branches of government, which persistently found the Court to be an unrelenting barrier to change. Massive personnel turnover on the Court in the late 1930s gave President Franklin D. Roosevelt the opportunity to appoint justices with anti-*Lochner* sentiments. This new attitude was evidenced in West Coast Hotel v. Parrish (1937), when the Court upheld a state minimum-wage law. Such a law routinely would have been struck down under the *Lochner* regime. A primary criticism of *Lochner* was that the Court generated concepts such as economic freedom to strike down laws that it merely disliked. According to this perspective, the Court assumed the role of a "superlegislature" that defeated the will of the people as expressed through their elected agents. The Court eventually agreed with its critics, at least insofar as review of economic legislation was concerned. In Olsen v. Nebraska (1941), the Court announced that it was "not concerned . . . with the wisdom, need or appropriateness of the legislation. Differences of opinion on that score suggest a choice which 'should be left where [it] was left by the Constitution—to the states and to Congress.' "

Although the Court has abandoned economic rights doctrine, it continues to use the due process clause to establish unenumerated rights and freedoms. The right of privacy, as discussed in the following section, is a primary example of modern rights development under the due process clause. This process has generated the same criticism that was directed at the *Lochner* court. Detractors maintain that the Court has merely changed its focus rather than its practice and that it makes no difference what interest the Court protects under the Fourteenth Amendment. What is crucial, and wrong from their perspective, is that the Court develops and protects rights and liberties that are not specifically enumerated by the Constitution.

It is worth noting that although the *Lochner* era is best remembered for doctrine that blunted popular social and economic reform, the Court during this period significantly expanded the constitutional menu of rights and liberties. Seminal case law emerged during this period on freedom of expression and religion and the rights of the accused. Perhaps the most expansive statement of protected liberty interests under the due process clause was set forth in Meyer v. Nebraska (1923), in which the Court characterized this clause as protecting "not merely freedom from bodily restraint but also the right of the individual to contract, to engage in any of the common occupations of life, to acquire useful knowledge, to marry, to establish a home and bring up children, to worship God according to the dictates of conscience, and generally to enjoy those privileges long recognized at common law as essential to the orderly pursuit of happiness for free men." How these guarantees should be determined, and whether, the Court should be the source of their identification, are controversies fueled by *Lochner* that survive its repudiation.

Bibliography

Edward S. Corwin, *Liberty against Government* (1948). Examines the Court's evolution toward doctrine that struck down state regulation on grounds that it violated the Fourteenth Amendment.

A. T. Mason, *William Howard Taft, Chief Justice* (1983). Includes a discussion of dominant views and attitudes of the Supreme Court during the early twentieth century.

William Nelson, *The Fourteenth Amendment: From Political Principle to Judicial Doctrine* (1988). A study of the development of the Fourteenth Amendment from its early understanding to modern interpretation.

United States v. Carolene Products Co.

Protection of economic freedom under the due process clause of the Fourteenth Amendment was a defining aspect of Supreme Court rulings during the first few decades of the twentieth century. Although the case for protecting economic freedom is largely discredited today, it is not entirely baseless. The Fourteenth Amendment was framed and ratified to ensure that persons of African descent could exercise the fundamental rights and liberties that slavery had denied them. The risk that slavery might persist in fact, if not in form, was evidenced shortly after the nation ratified the Thirteenth Amendment. Southern states, defeated in the Civil War, immediately adopted Black Codes that imposed such comprehensive restrictions on former slaves that their newfound rights and liberties were essentially negated. Responding to this development, Congress passed the Civil Rights Act of 1866, which guaranteed to "the inhabitants of every race . . . the

Citation:	304 U.S. 144.
Issue:	Whether a federal law that prohibited shipment of "filled milk" in interstate commerce violated the due process clause of the Fifth Amendment.
Year of Decision:	1938.
Outcome:	The regulation had a rational relationship to its objective and thus was constitutional.
Author of Opinion:	Justice Harlan Fiske Stone.
Vote:	6–1.

same rights to make and enforce contracts . . . [and] to inherit, purchase, lease, sell, hold and convey real and personal property." A year later, fearing that the act might be repealed when southern states regained their political influence after Reconstruction, Congress proposed and the states ratified the Fourteenth Amendment. Given Congress's emphasis upon economic freedom as a means of ensuring individual opportunity and self-development, and reaffirmation of these aims through the constitutional amendment process, the Court's protection of contractual liberty and property rights at least had some grounding in the concerns of the Fourteenth Amendment's framers and ratifiers.

Despite this connection, and as outlined in the discussion of *Lochner v. New York* (1905), the Court's championing of economic rights became increasingly discredited as the twentieth century evolved. Critics argued that the Court's rigorous review of economic regulation was driven not by constitutional considerations but by disagreement with the political wisdom and ideology of legislation. Frustrated by judicially imposed barriers to his New Deal initiatives during the mid-1930s, President Franklin D. Roosevelt, as discussed in *Wickard v. Filburn* (1942), advanced a reorganization plan for the Supreme Court. Although Congress did not adopt the plan, death and retirement soon resulted in a Court that was more deferential toward legislative initiative and reform.

A pivotal event in this doctrinal turnabout was the Court's ruling in *United States v. Carolene Products Co.* At issue was a federal law, enacted in 1923, that prohibited "the shipment in interstate commerce of skimmed milk compounded with any fat or oil other than milk fat." The law was justified on grounds that "filled" milk was injurious to health and a fraud upon the public. In reality, the measure was based upon dubious scientific evidence marshaled on behalf of lobbying efforts by the dairy industry. The law's primary effect was to protect producers of canned milk from the rigors of marketplace competition. Carolene Products Co., the producer of a condensed skim milk and coconut oil blend marketed as "Milnut," was convicted of violating the law. If *Lochner*-style economic rights doctrine still had been in vogue, the law would have been struck down on grounds that it interfered with marketplace freedom. The Court, reconstituted with justices reflecting anti-*Lochner* views, decided differently. In so doing, it made clear that the era of closely scrutinizing economic regulation had ended.

In upholding the Filled Milk Act, the Court announced that it no longer would require the legislature to demonstrate that its policies were desirable or workable. As long as they had "a rational basis," their underlying wisdom no longer was to be a judicial concern. Adoption of this "rational basis" test has become the norm for review of economic regulation. Not since the *Carolene Products* decision has the Court struck down legislation on the grounds that it impairs economic freedom in violation of due process. As a consequence, the legislative process since *Carolene Products* has been liberated from judicial review that had cramped its ability to regulate the economy.

The wholesale rejection of economic rights doctrine has not been without its critics, both on and off the Court. Justice Robert Jackson, in Day-Brite Lighting v. Missouri (1952), questioned the wisdom of abandoning all interest in how regulation might affect economic liberty. Responding to a decision that upheld a Missouri law that required employers to give workers half a day off on election day, Justice Jackson warned that the Court's refusal to give close attention to economic interests incurred the risk of legislative overreaching. Despite such concerns, the rational basis test has embedded itself as a standard that is highly deferential to the legislature.

Although the Court abandoned the concept of economic rights, it noted that "the presumption of constitutionality" afforded by rational basis review might give way under certain circumstances. Specifically, the Court reserved the possibility of closer review when legislative acts on their face fall "within a specific prohibition of the Constitution, such as the first ten amendments [i.e., the Bill of Rights]." The Court also indicated that "searching judicial inquiry" may be apt when legislation is "directed at particular religious, or national, or racial minorities" or when "prejudice against discrete and insular minorities . . . curtails the operation of those political processes ordinarily to be relied upon to protect minorities." This allowance for stricter review of laws affecting minorities became a key departure point for decisions that eventually prohibited official segregation and discrimination on the basis of race.

The Court's repudiation of "searching judicial inquiry," except when a provision of the Bill of Rights or legislation affecting minorities was at stake, soon was qualified. Despite an unbroken line of rulings that deferred to legislative judgment on economic policy, the Court four years after the *Carolene Products* decision closely scrutinized and struck down a state law that required involuntary sterilization of certain habitual criminals. No constitutionally enumerated right prohibits such action. The Court in Skinner v. Oklahoma (1942), however, found that it impaired a fundamental interest in procreation. This determination suggested a continuing judicial interest in identifying and developing rights not enumerated by the constitution. Emergence of the right of privacy in subsequent decades confirmed this tendency. The significance of the *Carolene Products* decision, therefore, is that it conclusively removed economic rights from the realm of guarantees that the court identifies as fundamental.

The fate of the Carolene Products Company itself is an absorbing historical footnote. Over the course of time, the low fat and sugar content of "filled" milk came to be better appreciated from a nutritional perspective. Apart from its wholesomeness, the commodity was less expensive than the condensed and evaporated milk products that were protected from competition with "filled" milk. The dairy industry's constitutional timing was ideal, however, and bans on filled milk survived until the early 1970s. The Carolene Products Company vanished as a business entity, at least in name, but filled milk continued to be marketed in a small number of states where it was legal. In 1972, restrictions on the sale of filled milk were struck down by a federal district court. The action was brought by the Milnot Company, which, as a just fate might have it, originally had done business as the Carolene Products Company.

Bibliography

Frank H. Easterbrook, "Substance and Due Process," 1982 *Supreme Court Review* 85 (1982). Argues that the Court's ruling in *Carolene Products* was an overreaction that set a tone for extreme deference toward legislative judgment in the area of economic regulation.

Geoffrey P. Miller, "The True Story of Carolene Products," 1987 *Supreme Court Review* 397 (1987). Recounts the story of the Carolene Products Company and goes beyond the Court's decision to include decades of political and corporate intrigue.

The Right of Privacy

Few areas of constitutional law are as controversial as the Supreme Court's development of the right of privacy. This right, which the Court has declared fundamental, is not mentioned in the Constitution. It has its roots, however, in constitutional case law. In Olmstead v. United States (1928), Justice Louis Brandeis dissented from the Court's decision that wiretapping did not violate the Fourth Amendment. In his dissenting opinion, Brandeis asserted that "the right to be let alone" was "the most comprehensive of rights and the right most valued by civilized men." Although Brandeis made his argument in a specific constitutional context governed by an enumerated constitutional right (namely, the Fourth Amendment), his basic premise evolved into a much broader understanding. Since its original formulation by Brandeis, "the right to be let alone" has been expanded into a general right of privacy broad enough to include reproductive freedom, abortion, and the ability to refuse unwanted medical care. The right of privacy emerged as a constitutionally recognized guarantee in *Griswold v. Connecticut* (1965), in which the Court struck down a state law that prohibited the dispensing or use of contraceptives. This right was extended in *Roe v. Wade* (1973) to include a woman's freedom to terminate an unwanted pregnancy by obtaining an abortion. Persistent challenges to the *Roe* decision resulted in some dilution of the right in *Webster v. Reproductive Health Services* (1989). The core meaning of *Roe* was reaffirmed, however, in *Planned Parenthood of Southeastern Pennsylvania v. Casey* (1992). In *Bowers v. Hardwick* (1986), the Court determined that the right of privacy did not extend so far as to protect homosexual intimacy. Constitutional privacy was found broad enough to include a right to refuse unwanted medical treatment in *Cruzan v. Director, Missouri Department of Health* (1990).

Griswold v. Connecticut

Few issues of constitutional law are more hotly contested than the judiciary's power to identify rights and liberties that are not constitutionally enumerated. The legitimacy of rights and liberties is not disputed when they are set forth by the Bill of Rights, but when the judiciary identifies a right or liberty as fundamental under the due process clause of the Fourteenth Amendment, critics maintain that the democratic process is violated. For the first third of the twentieth century, the Supreme Court regarded the due process clause as a source of economic rights and liberties. This provision regularly was cited in striking down federal or state laws that regulated the marketplace.

Citation:	381 U.S. 479.
Issue:	Whether a general right of privacy bars a state from prohibiting the sale of contraceptives to married persons.
Year of Decision:	1965.
Outcome:	The right of privacy is protected by the Constitution even though it is not specifically mentioned therein.
Author of Opinion:	Justice William O. Douglas
Vote:	7–2.

Contrary to its active development and vigilant protection of economic rights in the early twentieth century, the Supreme Court since the late 1930s consistently has determined that such interests are not within the Fourteenth Amendment's scope. In striking down an Oklahoma law that prohibited opticians from fitting or duplicating lenses without an ophthalmologist or optometrist's prescription, the Court in Williamson v. Lee Optical of Oklahoma (1955) observed that its function was not to invalidate laws merely because they were unwise or oppressive. When policies might be disagreeable or undesirable, the Court stressed that the remedy was in the election booth rather than the courtroom. Particularly indicative of the Court's interest in economic rights since the late 1930s was its pronouncement in Ferguson v. Skrupa (1963) to the effect that whether "the legislature takes for its textbook Adam Smith, Herbert Spencer, Lord Keynes or some other [social or economic philosopher] is no concern of ours." Summing up the Court's position, Justice Hugo Black observed that "[w]e refuse to sit as a superlegislature to weigh the wisdom of the legislation."

Although the Court discontinued use of the Fourteenth Amendment to protect economic freedom, it did not entirely abandon it as a source of other rights and liberties. A few years after terminating its use of the due process clause as a basis for striking down economic regulation, the Court determined that it still would protect certain interests as fundamental. In Skinner v. Oklahoma (1942), the Court struck down an involuntary sterilization law that applied to certain habitual criminals. The Court acknowledged that "the right to procreate" was not set forth in the Bill of Rights, but it emphasized that this was a fundamental freedom that must be protected. The Skinner decision indicated that even if economic rights were not to be protected, the Court had not closed the door on identifying freedoms that it considered fundamental even if they were not enumerated in the Constitution.

In *Griswold v. Connecticut*, the Court established the right of privacy. At issue in *Griswold* was a Connecticut law that prohibited contraceptive distribution and counseling. The case arose from the arrest of Estelle Griswold, Executive Director of the Planned Parenthood League of Connecticut. This organization operated a birth-control clinic in New Haven. Also charged was a Yale Medical School professor, who served as medical director of the Planned Parenthood League. Both were convicted of violating the state law against distributing contraceptives. Although the Constitution does not provide for a right of privacy in specific terms, the Court nonetheless found a basis for it in the Bill of Rights and determined that the state law thus was unconstitutional. As Justice William O. Douglas put it for the majority, several provisions of the Bill of Rights combine to form zones of privacy. These zones, which he referred to as "penumbras," emanate from the First Amendment right of association, the Third Amendment guarantee that forbids government from quartering soldiers in private homes, the Fourth Amendment protection against unreasonable searches and seizures, the Fifth Amendment safeguard against self-incrimination, and the Ninth Amendment, which reserves unenumerated rights for the people. Taken together, these guarantees were sufficient to embrace a right of privacy that protected what the Court referred to as "the sacred precincts of the marital bedroom." This right, as defined by the Court, enabled married persons to decide for themselves issues of such a personal and intimate nature. The right of privacy thus protected a married couple's right to purchase contraceptives.

The Court's opinion generated a sharp and significant dissent by Justice Hugo Black. In his words, Black professed to "like my privacy as much as the next one, but I am nevertheless compelled to admit that government has a right to invade it unless prohibited by some specific constitutional provision." Because the Constitution by its specific terms provides no right of privacy as the Court described it, he could not find the anticontraceptive law unconstitutional. The law might be unwise or misguided, but, as Black saw it, a lack of wisdom did not make a law unconstitutional. The remedy for bad legislation was at the polls rather than in the courts.

Despite this criticism, the majority opinion remains a seminal statement of the right of privacy. The ruling launched the Court in a new and significant constitutional direction, but had limited impact when it was applied to the circumstances that generated the actual litigation. By its terms, the decision protected only the right of married persons to access contraceptives and receive counseling for their usage. Three years later, in Eisenstadt v. Baird (1968), the Court extended the right of privacy to unmarried persons. The guarantee since has been expanded to include a woman's liberty to choose an abortion, family freedom to live as an extended unit, the right to marry, and the right to refuse unwanted medical treatment. At the same time, the Court has determined that the right of privacy is not broad enough to include sexual orientation, parental rights for a father whose child was born from an extramarital affair, and a right to medically assisted suicide.

By the early 1970s, consistent with views expressed by Justice John Harlan, Jr., in *Griswold*, the right of privacy became grounded in the due process clause of the Fifth and Fourteenth Amendments. Perhaps in recognition of the artificiality of the penumbra concept, contemporary privacy decisions have abandoned reference to it. The debate over the judiciary as a source for developing rights not specifically enumerated by the Constitution, however, persists. Supporters of this role argue that the right of privacy is distinguishable from economic liberty because it is identified in a more objective way or is a more compelling interest. Detractors view the function, regardless of method or result, as a violation of democratic principles. The long history of this debate and the intensity of convictions on both sides suggest a controversy that is unlikely to be consensually resolved.

Bibliography

Louis D. Brandeis and Samuel D. Warren, "The Right to Privacy," 4 *Harvard Law Review* 193 (1890). A seminal work on privacy as a constitutionally protected interest.

David J. Garrow, *Liberty and Sexuality: The Right to Privacy and the Making of Roe v. Wade* (1994). Discusses the definition and development of the right of privacy in and after Griswold v. Connecticut.

Paul Kauper, "Penumbras, Peripheries, Emanations, Things Fundamental, and Things Forgotten: The Griswold Case," 64 *Michigan Law Review* 235 (1965). Discusses the concept of penumbras as used in *Griswold*.

Richard Posner, *Sex and Reason* (1992). Includes a critical perspective upon *Griswold* that questions its achievements and aims.

Roe v. Wade

The Supreme Court's identification of a right to privacy has been a source of relentless debate. Critics maintain that it enables the judiciary to tie the hands of the political process without having to rely upon constitutional specifics. Supporters contend that judicial development of fundamental rights is essential to ensure that individual freedom is not imperiled by legislative abuse or overreaching. Criticism of *Griswold v. Connecticut* (1965), although significant, may have been somewhat muted because the state law that prohibited distribution of contraceptives and birth-control counseling was perceived by many as obsolete. Controversy over the judiciary's role in developing fundamental rights was unleashed fully, however, when the Court determined that the right of privacy protected a woman's freedom to choose abortion as a way of terminating pregnancy.

By the early 1970s, most states outlawed abortion or allowed it on narrow grounds that typically included danger to the mother's life, pregnancy resulting from rape or incest, or the likelihood of birth defects. Regulation of abortion, although not common at the time of the Constitution's framing, had become pervasive by the middle of the nineteenth century. Restrictions on abortion originally paralleled increasing regulation of the medical profession. By the beginning of the twentieth century, most states strictly regulated abortion. As the decades unfolded, numerous states relaxed their laws in response to pressure for political reform. Because many states resisted such change, advocates of a woman's freedom to choose turned to the courts for a determination that restrictive abortion laws were unconstitutional.

Responding to these arguments in *Roe v. Wade*, the Court struck down a Texas law that prohibited abortion unless the pregnancy endangered the mother's life. The litigation commenced when Jane Roe, the pseudonym for a pregnant single woman, sued the District Attorney of Dallas County, Texas. The action sought a finding that the state's criminal abortions laws

Citation:	410 U.S. 113.
Issue:	Whether a state may prohibit or restrict the availability of abortion.
Year of Decision:	1973.
Outcome:	Laws barring abortion or allowing it only in extraordinary circumstances are at odds with the right of privacy, which secures a woman's freedom to obtain an abortion.
Author of Opinion:	Justice Harry Blackmun.
Vote:	7–2.

were unconstitutional and an injunction restraining the District Attorney, Henry Wade, from enforcing them. A federal district court concluded that the Texas laws were unconstitutional. In arguing to the United States Supreme Court, the state justified its laws on grounds that a fetus is a person whose interest in life is protected under the due process clause. Writing for the majority, Justice Harry Blackmun found that the unborn may be living beings under some theories of religion and morality but not under the Constitution. Although the Court acknowledged that the Constitution does not specify a right of privacy, it reaffirmed the validity of its earlier decision in *Griswold v. Connecticut* (1965), in which it had established this right. In *Roe v. Wade*, the Court believed that "[t]his right of privacy . . . is broad enough to encompass a woman's decision whether or not to terminate her pregnancy."

Freedom to obtain an abortion thus was established as a constitutionally protected right. This liberty, although fundamental, is not absolute. What had to be balanced, from the Court's perspective, was the woman's freedom to decide whether to terminate her pregnancy and the state's interest in the mother's well-being and in potential human life. To address these competing concerns, the Court established a trimester formula that established different priorities at different times. States were barred from regulating any interest but the mother's health during the first three months of pregnancy. Protection of a woman's freedom to choose during this period was the paramount concern, consistent with the fact that abortion during the first trimester of pregnancy is less risky than childbirth. During this period, states were limited to regulations clearly related to protection of the mother's health and safety, such as those requiring abortions to be performed in facilities and by professionals that are licensed. During the second trimester, a woman retained relatively unfettered freedom to elect an abortion as a means to terminate her pregnancy. Regulation at this point was found permissible to the extent it reasonably relates to protecting maternal health. Not until the onset of the third trimester, which the Court viewed as the point of fetal viability (the ability of the fetus to survive outside the womb), was the state's interest in prohibiting abortion perceived as compelling. Because the interest in life then outweighed the interest in choice, unless the woman's life was at stake, the state was free to prohibit abortion.

Perhaps anticipating arguments that it was creating rights from its own cloth rather than from actual constitutional fabric, the Court maintained that protecting a woman's freedom to choose under the Constitution was neither subjectively nor ideologically driven. It noted that judicial power to establish rights or liberties under the due process clause required a showing that they were indeed "fundamental" or "implicit in the concept of ordered liberty." The determination that the right of privacy includes the freedom to choose an abortion reflected the Court's sense that the interest is fundamental and of a constitutional nature. The stakes included a woman's physical, mental, and emotional well-being. Given the personal and intimate nature of the decision to terminate a pregnancy, the Court found that it was more aptly made by the individual than the state.

Detractors maintain that such standards as "fundamental" or "implicit in the concept of ordered liberty" do not protect against judicial invention of rights on the basis of whim. Critics such as Judge Robert Bork have characterized such limiting principles as "pretty vaporous stuff," hiding neither "an exercise in moral and political philosophy" nor the "assumption of illegitimate judicial power and a usurpation of the democratic authority of the American people."[1] Justice William Rehnquist in a dissenting opinion maintained that the majority opinion was an exercise in pure subjectivism. Noting that most states prohibited abortion, he considered it preposterous that a woman's freedom to obtain an abortion could be grounded in the nation's traditions and experience. Rehnquist believed that the Court should not strike down a law regulating abortion unless it determined that the measure had no rational relationship to a legitimate state objective. Such a standard, he maintained, best assured that the judiciary would not tamper with the political process merely because it disliked a particular policy or doubted its wisdom. Using reasoning similar to Rehnquist's, Justice Byron White dissented on grounds that the Constitution did not speak to abortion. Because abortion was not included as a constitutionally protected interest, White believed that resolution of the issue should be left to the people and their elected representatives.

The majority opinion has generated some of the most intense criticism ever directed toward a Supreme Court ruling. Critics typically echo the arguments of Justices Rehnquist and White in maintaining that the liberty is an invention of the judiciary rather than an actual constitutional right. Despite the heavy volume of criticism, the decision became the basis for striking down numerous state regulations that established roadblocks to a woman's freedom to choose. Laws that created unnecessary licensing procedures, imposed spousal consent requirements, or established waiting periods during the early months of pregnancy were examples of those that the Court routinely struck down through the late 1980s. Denial of public funding for abortions was found not to interfere with the right to choose. Regulation that required minors to obtain the approval of a parent or court prior to obtaining an abortion was also upheld.

Although the *Roe* decision may have been intended to resolve the debate over abortion, it instead fueled the controversy beyond its original boundaries. In the legislative context, the debate had focused exclusively on the merits and morality of abortion. Since *Roe*, the controversy has veered toward a focus on the function of the judiciary. Decisions since *Roe* not only have amplified the terms and conditions of the right of privacy, therefore, but have addressed the judiciary's role in defining and developing them. The aftermath of *Roe* thus has been characterized not only by un-folding terms and conditions of the right of privacy, but by an intensified debate over the Court's function.

Note

1. Robert H. Bork, *The Tempting of America* 118 (1990).

Bibliography

Robert H. Bork, *The Tempting of America* (1990). Includes a highly critical per-spective on the *Roe* decision and other rulings that establish a right of pri-vacy.

Archibald Cox, *The Role of the Supreme Court in American Government* (1976). Articulates a concern that the Court did not establish a legitimate principle in support of its decision.

Kenneth Karst, *Belonging to America* (1989). Offers a favorable characterization of the *Roe* decision.

Catharine MacKinnon, "Reflections on Sex Equality under Law," 100 *Yale Law Journal* 1281 (1991). Expresses the view that the *Roe* decision should have been based upon gender inequality.

Laurence H. Tribe, *Abortion: The Clash of Absolutes* (1990). Discusses the fervent political debate over abortion and constitutional positions that have been staked out.

Webster v. Reproductive Health Services

In *Roe v. Wade* (1973), the Supreme Court established that the Fourteenth Amendment protects a woman's freedom to obtain an abortion. Although the Court restricted state power to regulate abortion, it did not end debate over the right or its role in defining it. The aftermath of *Roe v. Wade* has been characterized by persistent challenges to its legitimacy. The decision generated an outpouring of critical commentary, even by those who favored liberalization or repeal of laws prohibiting abortion. As the constitutional scholar John Hart Ely put it, "The problem with *Roe* is not so much that it bungles the question it sets itself, but rather that it sets itself a question the Constitution has not made the Court's business."[1] From his perspective, "*Roe* is a very bad decision. . . . It is bad because it is bad constitutional law, or rather because it is *not* constitutional law and gives almost no sense of an obligation to try to be." Competing against such concern are other scholarly perspectives, including those of Professor Sylvia Law, who maintains that "[n]othing the Supreme Court has ever done has been more concretely important for women."[2]

Citation:	492 U.S. 490.
Issue:	Whether a state law that prohibited abortions in public hospitals and required fetal viability testing after twenty weeks violated a woman's freedom to obtain an abortion.
Year of Decision:	1989.
Outcome:	The enactment was upheld, and the *Roe* decision, although it was upheld, was narrowed.
Author of Opinion:	Chief Justice William Rehnquist.
Vote:	5–4.

Opinion polls that indicate that the public generally supports the availability of abortion on the terms set by the *Roe* decision have not appeased the ruling's detractors. They maintain that popular sentiment is an appropriate basis for assessing the quality of a legislature's performance, but it is entirely irrelevant in evaluating judicial review. Such criticism does not deny a public interest in the judicial process. Rather, it reflects a belief that quality should be measured on the basis of the judiciary's reasoning and fidelity to constitutional principle, rather than responsiveness to contemporary public preferences.

The *Roe* decision quickly became a political lightning rod. Even though restrictions on abortion invariably were struck down by federal courts, many states persisted in enacting them. The Democratic and Republican parties defined themselves politically in the era after *Roe* on the basis of their respective support for or opposition to the *Roe* ruling. Congressional critics of the decision unsuccessfully pushed for legislation to eliminate the judiciary's jurisdiction over abortion and for a constitutional amendment protecting the "right to life." In his 1980 presidential campaign, Ronald Reagan ran on an anti-*Roe* platform that included a pledge to appoint "strict constructionist" federal judges who would support "family values." The campaign promise was somewhat incongruous, as the Constitution speaks no more directly to family values than it does to privacy or abortion. The political implications of *Roe* perhaps were most effectively illustrated by the heavy outpouring of mail to the Supreme Court and widespread demonstrations by "prochoice" and "prolife" supporters. The level of protests and picketing outside the Court made it particularly evident that the judiciary itself had become a partisan focal point. This phenomenon was particularly distressful to Justice Antonin Scalia who observed, in *Webster v. Reproductive Health Services*, that the Court's constitutionalization of the abortion controversy "continuously distorts the public perception of the role of the Court. We can now look forward to at least another Term with carts full of mail from the public, and streets full of demonstrators, urging us—their unelected and life-tenured judges who have been awarded these extraordinary, undemocratic characteristics precisely in order that we might follow the law despite the popular will—to follow the popular will."

In *Webster*, the Court reviewed a Missouri law that prohibited abortion in state-funded hospitals and required fetal viability testing after twenty weeks. The statute was challenged by Reproductive Health Services and other providers of abortion counseling and services. Governor William Webster, who signed the law into effect in 1986, was named as a defendant. Although the Missouri statute was conceptualized and presented as a direct challenge to *Roe*, the Court upheld the law without overturning *Roe*. The timing of viability testing in particular contested the premise that viability, the ability of the fetus to survive outside the womb, commences with the third trimester of a pregnancy. The law required physicians to determine the possiblity of viability, therefore, relatively early in the second trimester of pregnancy. Making good on President Reagan's promise to challenge the *Roe* decision, the Department of Justice filed an *amicus curiae* (friend of the court) brief that asserted: "*Roe* rests on assumptions not firmly grounded in the Constitution; it adopts an unworkable framework tying permissible state regulation to particular periods of pregnancy; and it has allowed courts to usurp functions of legislative bodies in weighing competing social, ethical and scientific factors in determining how much state regulation is permissible." After sixteen years of striking down any state law that was viewed as imposing barriers to a woman's freedom to choose an abortion, the Court relented. Its course change, however, was not as dramatic as what the Reagan administration desired.

The Missouri law, in addition to prohibiting abortions in state-funded facilities and requiring viability testing after twenty weeks, contained a preamble that described the aims of the law in terms that appeared to attack *Roe* directly. The preamble included legislative findings to the effect that life begins at conception and unborn children have constitutionally protected interests in life and liberty. Noting that the preamble merely made "a value judgment favoring childbirth over abortion" and "impose[d] no substantive restrictions on abortions," the Court declined to rule on its constitutionality.

Because the Court previously had upheld laws that denied government funding of abortions, no significant new ground was broken by barring such procedures in public hospitals. The viability testing requirement imposed during the second trimester, however, presented the most significant challenge to *Roe*. The provision effectively extended the time during which states could prohibit abortion. Viability, which had been set at the beginning of the third trimester effectively was moved back to the fifth month of pregnancy if testing established the ability of the fetus to survive outside the womb. For practical purposes, the requirement presented a new risk and deterrent to physicians, so that abortions would be less likely to be performed after the fourth month. Writing for a plurality, Chief Justice William Rehnquist noted that the viability testing requirement properly responded to advances in medical technology. If technology supported viability earlier in the course of a pregnancy, states were allowed to establish their interest in protecting potential life sooner.

Although the Court was asked to overrule the *Roe* decision, the Rehnquist plurality stopped short of doing so. Because the *Roe* Court had struck down a law that banned all abortions except when a woman's life was endangered, and Missouri had identified viability as the point at which human life begins, the plurality concluded that the case was not an appropriate platform for reconsideration of a woman's freedom to obtain an abortion. Justice Sandra Day O'Connor, although she expressed discomfort with the *Roe* ruling, also concluded that the Missouri law did not present the right case for overruling it. She agreed that viability testing did not conflict with *Roe*'s identification of viability as the starting point for a state's interest in prohibiting abortion. From her perspective, states could enact any regulation aimed at protecting life when viability was possible.

In a strident dissent that urged the overturning of *Roe*, Justice Scalia asserted that the Court was ducking the key issue. As he saw it, the Court should have acknowledged that *Roe* was mistaken and overruled it. Given the choices that the case presented to the Court—"to reaffirm *Roe*, to overrule it explicitly, to overrule it *sub silentio* [that is, without actually saying so], or to avoid the question"—Scalia maintained that the Court's pursuit of the last alternative was "the least responsible." Although he concurred with the Court's judgment, he strongly disagreed with its method.

As the author of the Court's opinion in *Roe*, Justice Harry Blackmun was particularly distressed by the outcome in *Webster*. Blackmun maintained that the Court had destabilized *Roe* without being forthright about doing so. He acknowledged that viability testing might be supported by advances in medical technology since *Roe* had been decided. Because additional medical testing increased the cost of abortion, he also believed that the Missouri law imposed an undue burden upon a woman's freedom to choose. Responding to criticism that the *Roe* trimester framework was not specified by the Constitution itself, Blackmun noted that most tests and standards for determining the scope or nature of rights are judicially created. Although his observation on this point is correct and is attributable to the Constitution's general and sweeping nature, the argument bypassed the question of whether the Court should identify a right that is not enumerated in the text of the Constitution.

In closing, Blackmun warned that a woman's liberty to elect an abortion had become an endangered constitutional species. He expressed concern that unless there were compelling reasons for nullification, laws that promoted any permissible interest would be upheld even if they created an obstacle to obtaining an abortion. The modification of *Roe* led him to observe that "[f]or today, at least, the law of abortion stands undisturbed. For today, the women of this Nation still retain the liberty to control their destinies. But the signs are evident and very ominous, and a chill wind blows." What Blackmun perceived as dark skies eventually lightened. Despite modifications, the *Roe* framework has survived largely intact.

Notes

1. John Hart Ely, "The Wages of Crying Wolf: A Comment on Roe v. Wade," 82 *Yale Law Journal* 920, 947 (1973).
2. Sylvia A. Law, "Rethinking Sex and the Constitution," 132 *University of Pennsylvania Law Review* 955, 980 (1984).

Bibliography

Laurence H. Tribe, *Abortion: The Clash of Absolutes* (1990). Discusses the significance of the *Webster* decision in redefining *Roe v. Wade*.

Planned Parenthood of Southeastern Pennsylvania v. Casey

Two decades after the Supreme Court established a woman's freedom to obtain an abortion in *Roe v. Wade* (1973), prochoice advocates sensed impending doom for this liberty. This perception was heightened by the ominous tones of *Webster v. Reproductive Health Services* (1989), which expanded state power to regulate abortion. Three years after the *Webster* Court raised serious questions about the validity of *Roe*, the Court in *Planned Parenthood of Southeastern Pennsylvania v. Casey* reviewed a Pennsylvania law that imposed several restrictions upon abortion. The statute required physicians to provide information to patients about the physical and psychological risks of abortion. Following presentation of this information, the woman was reguired to wait twenty-four hours before an abortion could be performed. The law also required that in order to obtain an abortion, minors had to obtain the consent of a parent or judge, and a married woman had to notify her spouse. Physicians also were obligated to file with the state a report that documented compliance with the law for every abortion they performed. Except for the reporting requirement, each of the law's provisions was inapplicable in the event of a medical emergency. Planned Parenthood of Southeastern Pennsylvania, joined by other abortion clinics and by physicians providing abortion services, sued to have the law declared unconstitutional. Named as the lead defendant was Governor Robert P. Casey. Finding that the regulatory scheme violated a woman's constitu-

Citation:	505 U.S. 833.
Issue:	Whether a state law that imposed a waiting period, required parental consent for minors and spousal notification for married women, required physicians to inform patients of physical and psychological risks, and established reporting obligations upon physicians performing abortions invaded a woman's freedom to obtain an abortion.
Year of Decision:	1992.
Outcome:	Except for the spousal notification requirement, which imposes an undue burden upon a woman's liberty to choose, the law was constitutional.
Authors of Opinion:	Justices Sandra Day O'Connor, Anthony Kennedy, and David Souter.
Vote:	5–4.

tional freedom to terminate her pregnancy by means of an abortion, a trial court struck down the law. The court of appeals reversed the lower court's ruling, except that it found the spousal notification provision unconstitutional. The case was then presented to the Supreme Court as an opportunity to reaffirm or overturn *Roe*.

In an opinion jointly authored by Justices Sandra Day O'Connor, Anthony Kennedy, and David Souter, the Court restated the *Roe* decision's vitality but upheld all aspects of the challenged law except the spousal notification provision. The justices preceded their analysis of the law with a statement of what they understood to be the central principle of *Roe*. This core meaning is that a state cannot prohibit a woman from obtaining an abortion prior to viability of the fetus. Noting that medical technology had advanced viability since *Roe* had been decided, the Court nonetheless stressed that this moment still was the dividing line between the mother's interest in exercising her freedom and the state's interest in protecting potential life.

Although the justices upheld the "central" meaning of *Roe*, they observed that its "rigid trimester framework" too often had excluded legitimate regulatory interests. From their perspective, the focus should be on whether a regulation unduly burdened a woman's freedom to choose prior to viability. Measured against that standard, they concluded that the spousal notification requirement was unconstitutional. This condition transferred the power to choose from the woman to her spouse, even though she categorically was more affected both by the pregnancy and its regulation. The requirement was perceived as particularly burdensome to spouses of abusive husbands. These women might forgo abortion rather than risk harm to themselves or their children.

Because information concerning physical and psychological risk was viewed as a means of ensuring knowledgeable decision making, the justices found that the information requirement imposed no undue burden on a woman's freedom to choose. The twenty-four-hour waiting period posed greater uncertainty. Although the Court acknowledged that the requirement might increase the cost of abortion and be a source of delay, it was unwilling to conclude without more evidence that the provision was excessively burdensome. Because there was no demonstration that the waiting period unreasonably interfered with a woman's freedom to choose, the justices were satisfied that the waiting period aided informed decision making. Consistent with previous decisions that had upheld parental consent as a prerequisite to abortion for minors, provided they had the option to obtain court approval as an alternative, the justices found Pennsylvania's requirement unobjectionable. Because the state had correlated reporting requirements to the interest of medical research and maternal health, the justices concluded that they too were not unduly burdensome.

The *Casey* decision emerged against a backdrop of continuing political division over the abortion issue, and the Court was mindful of that reality. Responding to arguments that the *Roe* decision had injected the judiciary into the politics of abortion, O'Connor, Kennedy, and Souter maintained that institutional and national harm would result if the Court retreated in the face of political pressure. They relied on the principle of *stare decisis* (the rule that a court must adhere to a previous ruling unless it manifestly was in error) for the conclusion that *Roe*, or at least its central meaning, should be reaffirmed rather than overruled.

Not surprisingly, given the intensity of opinions on abortion, the reasoning of O'Connor, Kennedy, and Souter generated some sharp responses. Although Justice John Paul Stevens did not disagree with their general analytical framework, he maintained that they underestimated the severity of the burdens imposed by the Pennsylvania law. Particularly bothersome to Stevens were the requirement that physicians provide information on abortion's physical and psychological risks and the waiting period, which he viewed as impermissibly steering a woman from her preference to the state's. Justice Harry Blackmun, although pleased with the reaffirmation of the basic meaning of *Roe*, expressed concern that the standard for reviewing abortion regulations had been relaxed. He viewed the reporting requirement as an especially significant burden in that physicians who feared harassment might shy away from performing abortions. Blackmun also restated his preference for *Roe*'s trimester framework as a more rigorous protection of the freedom to choose.

Chief Justice William Rehnquist and Justice Antonin Scalia dissented. Asserting that *Roe* had been wrongly decided, and that the judiciary's reputation is enhanced rather than diminished when it acknowledges mistaken judgment, Rehnquist urged that the ruling should be overruled forthrightly. Referring back to his dissent in *Roe*, Rehnquist reiterated the point that the public's deep divisions on the abortion issue indicated a lack of necessary consensus for a woman's right to choose. As he viewed it, state regulation of abortion was permissible when any reasonable justification existed. Rehnquist would have upheld all provisions of the Pennsylvania law, including the spousal notification requirement because it protected the husband's interests, marital integrity, and potential life. Even if the wisdom of the policy might be debated, Rehnquist stressed that the Court's role was not to debate politics but to interpret a Fourteenth Amendment that does not set forth a comprehensive right of privacy.

Like Rehnquist, Justice Scalia urged repudiation of *Roe* and withdrawal of the judiciary from the abortion controversy. Because the Constitution does not enumerate a woman's freedom to choose abortion, and the nation's traditions do not foreclose prohibition of abortion, he argued that the people through their elected representatives should resolve the controversy. Scalia was particularly critical of the Court's reliance upon the doctrine of *stare decisis*. Although he conceded a strong interest in the law's certainty and predictability, he argued that such imperatives were second-ary when a case had been wrongly decided. The *Roe* decision was flawed, from his perspective, because it had bypassed the issue of whether a fetus is a human life and had not established a settled principle of law. Persistent criticism of and challenges to *Roe* indicated that uncertainty was a primary aspect of its legacy.

Although the decision stabilized judicial recognition of a woman's free-dom to obtain an abortion, albeit with less security than *Roe* provided, it did not preempt the underlying debate. The Court's ruling reaffirmed the "central meaning" of *Roe* in that viability remains the primary dividing line between maternal and state interests. Because the trimester framework was abandoned and replaced with a focus upon regulation that is "unduly burdensome," states were afforded more room to regulate. Justices Stevens and Blackmun viewed this softening of standards as a risk to a constitu-tionally protected freedom. Justice Scalia maintained that these criteria en-able a court to invalidate any abortion restriction that it disfavors as a matter of policy. For a Court that intervened in a particularly thorny and divisive debate, mixed sentiments about the decision may indicate that the ruling actually has defused some of the controversy over the judiciary's role. Because the decision reaffirmed the core liberty, but gave states more room to regulate abortion, the Court has returned much of the debate to the political process from whence it came.

Bibliography

Charles Fried, "Constitutional Doctrine," 107 *Harvard Law Review* 1140 (1994). Argues that *stare decisis* was used in *Casey* to shore up opinion that could not stand independently.

Cass Sunstein, *The Partial Constitution* (1994). Addresses the persistent question of how critics of the *Lochner* decision can support the right of privacy.

Bowers v. Hardwick

A basic premise of American constitutional law is that rights and liberties, no matter how profound, are not absolute. Inevitable questions about the right of privacy, like any other fundamental guarantee, are how far it extends and what interests may defeat it. From the early 1960s to the late 1970s, the right of privacy was expanded to include the rights to obtain contraceptives, terminate an unwanted pregnancy, marry, and live as an extended family. Indications that the right of privacy was reaching its limits became evident in the 1980s. A particularly forceful statement for curbing expansion of the right of privacy was articulated in *Bowers v. Hardwick*, in which the Court reviewed what it characterized as "the right of homosexuals to engage in acts of sodomy."

The case arose from the arrest of Michael Hardwick, who was charged with performing acts of homosexual oral sodomy in violation of

Citation:	478 U.S. 186.
Issue:	Whether a state law that forbids consensual homosexual sodomy violates the right of privacy.
Year of Decision:	1986.
Outcome:	The Constitution does not protect a right to engage in homosexual sodomy.
Author of Opinion:	Justice Byron White.
Vote:	5–4.

Georgia law. The actions for which he was prosecuted occurred in his bedroom. Although the charges were dropped without being brought to trial, Hardwick sued the Attorney General of Georgia, Michael J. Bowers, in an effort to have the state law declared unconstitutional. The Georgia law provided that "[a] person commits the offense of sodomy when he performs or submits to any sexual act involving the sex organs of one person and the mouth or anus of another." Hardwick challenged the law because it criminalized consensual sexual behavior and interfered with a constitutionally protected private association. Despite the law's application to both homosexual and heterosexual sodomy, the Court focused only upon the former aspect. Its decision is relevant not only to the constitutionality of sodomy laws but to regulation that discriminates on the basis of sexual orientation.

Justice Byron White, who wrote the majority opinion that upheld the Georgia law, defined the basic issue as "whether the Federal Constitution confers a fundamental right upon homosexuals to engage in sodomy and hence invalidates the laws of the many States that still make such conduct illegal and have done so for a very long time." Before the Court resolved this question, it set forth a narrow sense of the boundaries of the right of privacy. Noting that previous decisions had identified child rearing and education, family relationships, procreation, marriage, contraception, and abortion as dimensions of the right of privacy, the Court concluded that none of these rights "bears any resemblance to the claimed right of homosexuals to engage in acts of sodomy." As the Court saw it, no connection existed between family, marriage, and procreation and homosexuality. Nor did prior decisions support the proposition that sexual acts between consenting adults were constitutionally insulated from state regulation.

Even if precedent did not stand in its way, the Court indicated that it was "quite unwilling" to recognize "a fundamental right to engage in homosexual sodomy." To do so would breach those standards that the Court had established "to assure itself and the public that announcing rights not readily identifiable in the Constitution's text involves much more than the imposition of the Justices' own choice of values." Under these criteria, fundamental liberties are those that are "implicit in the concept of ordered liberty, such that neither liberty nor justice would exist if [they] were sacrificed," or that "are deeply rooted in this Nation's history and traditions." As the Court viewed it, a right to engage in acts of consensual homosexual sodomy failed both formulations. It noted that prohibition of such conduct has "ancient roots" and that sodomy was forbidden in all states at the time of the framing of the Constitution. Until the early 1960s, this prohibition still was a pervasive feature of American law. At the time of the Court's ruling, nearly half of the states still criminalized homosexual sodomy. The Court therefore rejected the argument that "such conduct is 'deeply rooted in this Nation's history and tradition' or 'implicit in the concept of ordered liberty.' "

The majority's hostility toward homosexual sodomy as a fundamental freedom also reflected a resistance against using the Court's power "to discover new fundamental rights embedded in the Due Process Clause." Reflecting the concerns of dissenters expressed in *Griswold v. Connecticut* (1965) and *Roe v. Wade* (1973), the Court observed that its legitimacy is most at risk when it develops constitutional law with "no cognizable roots in the language or design of the Constitution." Referring to the largely discredited legacy of *Lochner v. New York* (1905) and the damage it caused to the Court's reputation, Justice White stressed that the Court should shy away from expanding the reach of the due process clause, "particularly if it requires redefining the category of rights deemed to be fundamental. Otherwise, the Judiciary necessarily takes to itself further authority to govern the country without express constitutional authority."

In a concurring opinion, Chief Justice Warren Burger developed further the majority's point that "proscriptions against sodomy have very 'ancient roots.' " Burger stated that condemnation of homosexuality "is firmly rooted in Judeo-Christian moral and ethical standards," "was a capital crime under Roman law," was characterized under English law as "an offense of 'deeper malignity' than rape, a heinous act 'the very mention of which is a disgrace to human nature,' and a 'crime not fit to be named.' " Noting that Georgia had imported English common law and had enacted its sodomy statute in 1816, Burger rejected a right of homosexual sodomy that would "cast aside millennia of moral teaching."

The Court's opinion generated an impassioned dissenting opinion by Justice Harry Blackmun, who was joined by Justices William Brennan, Thurgood Marshall, and John Paul Stevens. From his perspective, the case was not about a fundamental right to engage in homosexual sodomy but "about 'the most comprehensive of rights and the right most valued by civilized men,' namely, 'the right to be let alone.' " Blackmun maintained that the Court not only had denied a right to engage in homosexual sodomy, but had refused "to recognize a fundamental interest all individuals have in controlling the nature of their intimate associations." Blackmun reduced the state's argument to the premise that sodomy has been condemned "for hundreds of years, if not thousands." In response, he maintained that neither the length of time a majority has held its convictions nor the depth of its passions can immunize a law from meaningful judicial scrutiny. Quoting from an opinion that had upheld a student's right not to salute the flag, West Virginia Board of Education v. Barnette (1943), he noted that "freedom to differ is not limited to things that do not matter much. That would be a mere shadow of freedom." Because the issue of homosexual sodomy "touches the heart of what makes individuals what they are," Blackmun believed that the Court should be particularly "sensitive to the rights of those whose choices upset the majority." He stressed, therefore, a need to analyze Hardwick's "claim in the light of the values that underlie the constitutional right to privacy." For that right to mean anything, it required Georgia to do more than assert "an abominable crime not fit to be named among Christians" as a basis for prosecuting persons "for making choices about the most intimate aspects of their lives."

The majority ruling represented a significant triumph for those who were concerned with the Court's role in defining and developing a right of privacy. Three years later, in Michael H. v. Gerald D. (1989), a four-justice plurality determined that fundamental rights must be defined specifically rather than generally. Such a focal point restricts significantly the judiciary's ability to establish a right as fundamental. Defined generally, the issue in Michael H. was whether a natural father could be denied visitation rights with his daughter. As the plurality framed the issue at a more specific level, however, the question was whether a state could deny visitation rights to the father of a child conceived in an extramarital affair. The nation's history and traditions may have supported the abstract concept of a parent-child relationship, but the plurality found no basis for acknowledging that the relationship between a parent and his or her child conceived in an extramarital affair was fundamental in a constitutional sense. To the contrary, it concluded that "[t]his is not the stuff of which fundamental rights . . . are made."

This narrowed frame of reference for the right of privacy postdated analysis of the Georgia sodomy law in Bowers v. Hardwick. It flows from the same sense, however, that a purported right must be referenced to specific circumstances rather than be viewed as a general concept. The law in Bowers v. Hardwick was measured against a specific "fundamental right to engage in homosexual sodomy" rather than the more general "right to be let alone." Exponents of judicial restraint cite the ruling as a model decision. Critics fault the Court for failing to understand that the right of privacy means little if it does not protect departures from societal norms.

Bibliography

Patrick Devlin, *The Enforcement of Morals* (1965). Sets forth philosophical underpinnings of the Court's decision in *Bowers v. Hardwick*.

H. L. A. Hart, *Law, Liberty, and Morality* (1963). Responds to and challenges Devlin's theory and arguments.

Donald E. Lively, *Foreshadows of the Law* (1992). Discusses the Court's evolution in defining, developing, and restricting the right of privacy.

Richard Posner, *Sex and Reason* (1992). Argues for decriminalizing sodomy.

Cruzan v. Director, Missouri Department of Health

The Supreme Court's decisions since the late 1970s have been cautious about developing the right of privacy. Determinations that this right included freedom to terminate a pregnancy (*Roe v. Wade* [1973]), marry (Zablocki v. Redhail [1977]), and live as an extended family (Moore v. City of East Cleveland [1978]) represented high points for the right of privacy. Since then, the Court largely has resisted arguments for opening new frontiers for the right of privacy. Instead, its decisions have reflected misgivings with a role in identifying and protecting rights and freedoms that are not enumerated in the Constitution.

Despite generally shying away from generation of fundamental rights, the Court has not abandoned the exercise altogether. The continuing vitality of the due process clause as a source of the right of privacy was evident in *Cruzan v. Director, Missouri Department of Public Health*. At issue was a parental request to discontinue medical treatment for a daughter whose death would result. The issue arose from an automobile accident that caused severe brain damage to the petitioner, Nancy Cruzan. Although it was likely that she never would regain consciousness, Cruzan was kept alive by artificial feeding and hydration. Recognizing the severity and implications of their daughter's injuries, her parents and co-guardians, Lester and Joyce Cruzan, sought a court order that would direct the hospital to remove her from life support. The state countered that such action could not be taken under Missouri law without clear and convincing evidence that Cruzan would have wanted this action. The Missouri Supreme Court agreed with the state and determined that the parents lacked authority for the decision.

In reviewing the state law and the lower court's ruling, the United States Supreme Court established first that "a competent person has a constitutionally protected liberty interest in refusing unwanted medical treatment." This

Citation:	497 U.S. 261.
Issue:	Whether parents whose daughter had no prospects for regaining consciousness had the right to withdraw her life-support systems.
Year of Decision:	1990.
Outcome:	The due process clause of the Fourteenth Amendment provides a right to refuse unwanted medical treatment, but, in this instance, it was outweighed by strong state regulatory interests.
Author of Opinion:	Chief Justice William Rehnquist.
Vote:	8–1.

determination was inferrable from earlier decisions that recognized an individual's liberty interest in refusing unwanted vaccines and drugs. Although the Court acknowledged a protected liberty interest under the due process clause, this finding did not resolve the case. Because Cruzan was incompetent, it did not follow that she had the same right to refuse lifesaving nutrition and hydration that a competent person would have. Rather, as the Court noted, "[a]n incompetent person is not able to make an informed and voluntary choice to exercise a hypothetical right to refuse treatment or any other right." For a right to be exercised under such circumstances, it "must be exercised for her, if at all, by some sort of surrogate."

Missouri law did not preclude a surrogate's power to terminate life support. However, it required compliance with procedures that were designed to ensure that the surrogate's action reflected the wishes expressed by the patient when competent. For this requirement to be satisfied, "the incompetent's wishes as to the withdrawal of treatment [must] be proved by clear and convincing evidence." The ultimate question for the Court, therefore, was whether the right to refuse unwanted medical treatment was outweighed by the state's regulatory concerns. In balancing these considerations, the Court found for the state. The Missouri law, from the Court's perspective, was based "on the state's interest in the protection and preservation of human life, and there can be no gainsaying this interest."

Acknowledging that a state need not "remain neutral in the face of an informed and voluntary decision by a physically able adult to starve to death," the Court observed that Missouri had even "more particular interests at stake" when a person is incompetent. Because "[t]he choice between life and death is a deeply personal decision of obvious and overwhelming finality," the Court determined that the state legitimately could safeguard the integrity of an individual's choice. It pointed out that incompetent patients are not always the beneficiaries of decision makers who love them or act in their best interest. Because abuse is possible, the Court found good reason for procedural safeguards. The Court emphasized that even when the decision is made by close family members, the state must ensure that the decision is truly the patient's. The Court conceded that family members may have strong feelings about a loved one's "hopeless, meaningless, and even degrading" condition. It further observed, however, that their concerns are "not entirely disinterested." Nor is there "automatic assurance" that the view of close family members will be the same as the patient's.

The Court also upheld the state's rule that, given the interests at stake, the standard for proving the patient's intent could be set at a higher level than in an ordinary civil dispute. This higher standard of proof also was justified on grounds that the party who was seeking to terminate life support should bear the risk of an erroneous decision. Although a decision to withdraw life support "is not susceptible to correction," a contrary ruling would maintain the status quo. A decision that erred on the side of life might be corrected or mitigated by advances in medical science, discovery of new evidence regarding the patient's intent, a change in the law, or the patient's eventual death.

Although Justice Antonin Scalia agreed with the majority's result, he authored a concurring opinion in which he expressed concern with usage of the due process clause. Scalia "would have preferred that we announce, clearly and promptly, that the federal courts have no business in this field; that American law has always accorded the State the power to prevent, by force if necessary, suicide" by any means. Reiterating the same criticisms that he had aimed at other decisions that established and developed the right of privacy, he contended "that the point at which life becomes 'worthless,' and the point at which the means necessary to preserve it become 'extraordinary' or 'inappropriate,' are neither set forth in the Constitution nor known to the nine Justices of this Court any better than they are known to nine people picked at random from the Kansas City telephone directory." From Scalia's perspective, because the Constitution did not address the issue, the Missouri citizenry through its elected representatives had sole authority to limit or facilitate any interest in refusing unwanted medical treatment. Noting that many "horribles" are not categorically prohibited by the Constitution, he observed that the "Court need not, and has no authority to, inject itself into every field of human activity where irrationality and oppression may theoretically occur; and if it tries to do so it will destroy itself."

In a dissenting opinion, Justice William Brennan noted that "no state interest could outweigh the rights of an individual in Nancy Cruzan's position." As he understood her condition, the state had "no legitimate general interest in someone's life completely abstracted from the interest of the person living that life." If the state had any regulatory interest, it was only in ensuring an accurate determination of her wishes. The real question, as Brennan saw it, was "whether the incompetent person would choose to live in a persistent vegetative state on life support or to avoid this medical treatment." Brennan rejected the notion that a patient's wishes must be established by clear and convincing evidence. He maintained that the state must leave the choice with the patient's family or the person most likely to have been chosen by the patient as proxy. He acknowledged the possibility that a surrogate might have improper motives, but he asserted that these concerns could be addressed by excluding any such person from the process.

Justice John Paul Stevens, in a separate dissent, did not dispute the "clear and convincing evidence" standard. Rather, he found Missouri's failure "to heed the interests of a dying individual with respect to matters so private [to be] ample evidence of the policy's illegitimacy." As Stevens viewed it, the conflict between life and liberty was an "artificial consequence of Missouri's effort, and this Court's willingness, to abstract Nancy Cruzan's life from Nancy Cruzan's person." Because the policy disconnected the existence of life from the person, Stevens maintained that the state's responsibility for protecting life was "desecrate[d]" rather than "honored."

The differing positions among the justices illuminate not only a thorny issue but a continuing challenge to the Court in determining whether to announce a right as fundamental. Chief Justice William Rehnquist, since *Roe v. Wade* (1973), has been a persistent critic of decisions that create and develop the right of privacy. He nonetheless authored the majority opinion in *Cruzan*. His hand in the decision suggests that even for ardent critics, the temptation to develop rights not specifically enumerated by the Constitution is difficult to resist.

Bibliography

Ronald Dworkin, *Life's Dominion* (1993). Explores the value of life in the context of abortion and medically distressed conditions.

Seth Kreimer, "Does Pro-Choice Mean Pro-Kevorkian? An Essay on Roe, Casey, and the Right to Die," 44 *American University Law Review* 803 (1995). Discusses the question of whether recognition of the freedom to obtain an abortion necessitates support for a right to die.

Glossary

Actual malice A standard that requires a public official or public figure who sues for defamation to demonstrate that an alleged falsehood was made with knowledge that it was untrue or with reckless disregard of the truth.

Affirmative action Governmental action that establishes a preference for a traditionally disadvantaged group, typically on the basis of race or gender, to compensate for past discrimination or to achieve diversification of an institution or program.

Alien The status of a person, for constitutional purposes, who is not a citizen of the United States.

***Amicus curiae* brief** A brief filed as a friend of the Court rather than by an actual party to the litigation. Such filings typically are made by individuals or entities with an interest in the outcome of the case.

Clear and present danger test A formula for determining whether speech that advocates illegal action may be regulated. The modern version of this standard focuses on whether speech is directed toward causing immediate harm, and whether such harm is likely.

Commerce clause A provision of Article 1, Section 8 [3], of the Constitution that vests Congress with the power to regulate commerce among the several states.

Commercial speech Expression, such as advertising, that invites an economic transaction.

Concurring opinion An opinion by one or more justices that agrees with the judgment of a court but offers separate reasons in support of that outcome.

De facto segregation A condition of segregation that is attributable to factors other than the law and is not constitutionally significant.

Defamation A false statement that injures a person's reputation either by slander (the spoken word) or libel (the published word).

De jure segregation A condition of segregation that intentionally was created by law and is illegal.

Dissenting opinion An opinion that disagrees with a court's judgment and typically its reasoning.

Dormant commerce clause A reference to Congress's power under Article I, Section 8[3] of the Constitution that, even if it is not used to enact a law, may preclude states from regulating in ways that burden interstate commerce or discriminate on the basis of a product's or service's place of origin.

Dual sovereignty A system dividing power between two governments, federal and state, in a single union.

Due process A guarantee secured by the Fifth and Fourteenth Amendments which, respectively, apply to federal and state governments. Due process originally was understood as an assurance that government, through the judicial process, could not deprive an individual of life, liberty, or property without fair procedures. Such fairness at a minimum would consist of notice and a hearing. Contrasting with procedural due process is the concept of substantive due process, which is a product of case law that has developed since the mid-nineteenth century. Substantive due process review is typified by the judiciary's identification of a fundamental right that it reads into the due process clause and uses as a basis for striking down legislation.

Equal protection clause A guarantee set forth in the Fourteenth Amendment against any state's denial of equal protection of the laws to any person in its jurisdiction. Equal protection emerged in the mid-twentieth century as the basis for eliminating official racial segregation.

Establishment clause A provision of the First Amendment which, as interpreted, prohibits government from promoting or favoring religion or a religious group.

Executive privilege The president's right to preserve the confidentiality of communications within the executive branch.

Ex post facto **law** A law that retroactively punishes or penalizes an individual. Article I, Sections 9 and 10, of the Constitution prohibit enactment of criminal laws that operate retroactively.

Fairness doctrine A requirement which, until abandoned in 1987, required broadcasters to cover and balance their reporting of controversial issues of public importance.

Fighting words Expression that by its very utterance inflicts injury or tends to incite an immediate breach of the peace.

In camera **review** A judicial proceeding, such as a review of documents claimed to be privileged, in private session.

Incorporation The process of applying provisions of the Bill of Rights to the states by including them within the meaning of the Due Process Clause of the Fourteenth Amendment.

Indecent expression Speech that offends because of its sexual content, but falls short of being obscene.

Injunction A court order that requires performance of a particular act or, more typically, prohibits a person from engaging in a specified activity. Violation of an injunction may result in a contempt citation.

Judicial review The power of courts to review legislation and determine its constitutionality.

Justiciability A self-imposed principle that limits the judiciary's power to hearing actual cases and controversies rather than, for instance, issues that are not truly adversarial, are premature, or are better left for the legislative branch to resolve.

Moot A determination that a case no longer presents a legal controversy because of subsequent events that have eliminated the dispute.

Natural law A theory of law that operates on the premise that basic rights and freedoms exist that are fundamental to human nature, even if they are not constitutionally enumerated, and the judiciary may refer to them as a basis for striking down legislation.

Necessary and proper clause A constitutional provision set forth in Article I, Section 8[18] which, as interpreted, enables Congress to employ any appropriate means to achieve a legitimate legislative end.

Obscenity Sexually explicit expression that fails to meet specific state standards of acceptability and thus is not protected by the First Amendment.

Overbroad A law that regulates so broadly that it prohibits constitutionally protected activity.

Penumbra A zone, extension, or radiation of an enumerated constitutional right or liberty that although not specified by the Bill of Rights, is found to be fundamental.

Per curiam An opinion authored by an entire court rather than under the name of a particular judge or justice. It typically is used when the law is settled and extensive reasoning is unnecessary.

Plurality opinion An opinion that attracts support from more than one justice but falls short of a majority.

Prima facie A case or proposition that, on its face, is accepted as true but may be disproved by further evidence.

Prior restraint Prohibition of speech or publication without official authorization.

Privilege A basis for confidentiality which protects individuals from having to testify or disclose information.

Privileges and immunities clause The privileges and immunities clause of Article IV, Section 2 [1], of the Constitution generally prohibits states from discriminating against citizens of other states. The privileges and immunities clause of the Fourteenth Amendment prohibits the states from impairing the privileges and immunities of federal citizenship.

Public figure A person who, because of pervasive fame or notoriety or having injected himself or herself into a public controversy in an attempt to influence the outcome, must prove actual malice to recover damages in a defamation action.

Public official A person who, because of his or her position in government, must prove actual malice to recover damages in a defamation action.

Rational basis A standard of judicial review which defers to legislative judgment and asks merely whether an enactment is supported by any state of facts known or which could be reasonably assumed.

Separation of powers The division of authority among the executive, legislative, and judicial branches as a safeguard against the risk of tyranny inherent in concentrated power.

Stare decisis A doctrine that requires courts to follow principles of law that have been established in preceding cases that are factually similar, unless the previous ruling manifestly was erroneous.

Strict scrutiny A standard of review which carefully reviews legislative means and ends by asking whether an enactment is justified by a compelling interest, the means necessarily achieve their ends, and any less constitutionally restrictive alternatives are available.

Subpoena duces tecum A judicial order that requires a person to produce documents or other materials. It must be complied with unless it is successfully resisted on grounds of privilege or some other legal basis.

Supremacy clause A constitutional provision set forth in Article VI[2] that requires preemption of state law that conflicts with federal law.

Symbolic speech Expression that communicates a point of view in a non-verbal way, typically through the use of symbols or by action.

Vagueness The state of a law that is not precise enough to provide adequate notice of the activity that is regulated or subject to prohibition.

Appendix A

Cases

Adamson v. California (Bill of Rights are incorporated through the Fourteenth Amendment on a selective basis)

Baldwin v. Fish and Game Commission of Montana (privileges and immunities of the citizens of each state, secured by Article IV, Section 2, are those fundamental rights "basic to the maintenance or well-being of the Union" or "bearing upon the vitality of the Nation as a single entity")

Bowers v. Hardwick (there is no fundamental right to engage in homosexual sodomy)

Brandenburg v. Ohio (speech advocating illegal action cannot be prohibited unless the expression aims to incite or produce imminent lawless action and is likely to produce such results)

Branzburg v. Hayes (First Amendment does not establish a privilege for news reporters seeking to protect the confidentiality of their sources from a grand jury)

Brown v. Board of Education (official segregation of public schools is unconstitutional)

Calder v. Bull (debates the terms and scope of judicial review)

Chaplinsky v. New Hampshire ("fighting words" are not protected by the First Amendment)

The Civil Rights Cases (Fourteenth Amendment applies only to state action)

Cohen v. California (expression cannot be punished merely because it is offensive)

Cooley v. Board of Wardens (barring a national interest in uniformity of the law, states may regulate activities affecting commerce)

Cooper v. Aaron (state could not nullify the constitutional requirement of school desegregation)

Craig v. Boren (official discrimination on the basis of gender violates the Equal Protection Clause unless justified by an important governmental objective which is achieved by methods substantially related to that goal)

Cruzan v. Director, Missouri Department of Health (person has a right to refuse unwanted medical treatment)

Dean Milk Co. v. Madison (city ban on milk not pasteurized within five miles of the municipality violated the Commerce Clause)

Dred Scott v. Sandford (persons of African descent could not be citizens of the United States, the federal government had no power to prohibit slavery in United States Territories, and the Fifth Amendment secured the right to own slaves)

Everson v. Board of Education (transportation reimbursement plan for parents of students, including those attending parochial schools, did not offend the Establishment Clause)

Federal Communications Commission v. Pacifica Foundation (indecent expression could be punished when broadcast by radio or television, even though such speech is protected under the First Amendment)

Furman v. Georgia (death penalty unconstitutional to the extent a system of capital punishment operates arbitrarily and randomly)

Gertz v. Robert Welch, Inc. (actual malice standard, applicable to public officials and public figures in defamation actions, does not extend to private persons)

Gibbons v. Ogden (Congress's power over interstate commerce is plenary and reaches to wherever commercial intercourse exists)

Gideon v. Wainwright (right to counsel applies in state criminal trials)

Globe Newspapers Co. v. Superior Court (First Amendment generally requires open trials)

Green v. County School Board (public school systems segregated by force of law must desegregate immediately)

Griswold v. Connecticut (right to privacy exists in penumbras of First, Third, Fourth, Fifth, Sixth, and Ninth Amendments)

Katz v. United States ("the Fourth Amendment protects people, not places")

Katzenbach v. Morgan (constitutionality of a congressional enactment enforcing the Fourteenth Amendment does not require proof of a Fourteenth Amendment violation)

Keyes v. School District No. 1 (*de jure* segregation violates the Equal Protection Clause, but *de facto* segregation does not)

Korematsu v. United States (race is a constitutionally suspect classification, but forced relocation and interment of Japanese-Americans during World War II upheld)

Lemon v. Kurtzman (Establishment Clause not violated so long as a statute has a secular purpose, neither advances nor inhibits religion, and does not foster an excessive government entanglement with religion)

Lochner v. New York (liberty of contract is secured by the Due Process Clause of the Fourteenth Amendment)

Loving v. Virginia (state's ban on interracial marriage violates the Equal Protection Clause)

Lynch v. Donnelly (municipally supported nativity scene did not violate the Establishment Clause)

Mapp v. Ohio (exclusionary rule bars the introduction of illegally seized evidence from state criminal proceedings)

Marbury v. Madison (judiciary has power to determine the Constitution's meaning, so its rulings bind the other branches of government)

McCulloch v. Maryland (state tax on the Bank of the United States impermissible pursuant to a broad reading of the Necessary and Proper Clause)

Miami Herald Publishing Co. v. Tornillo (state right to reply law violated the First Amendment)

Miller v. California (obscenity consists of expression that, taken as a whole, appeals to prurient interest in sex, portrays sexual conduct in a patently offensive way, and, taken as a whole, lacks serious literary, artistic, political, or scientific value)

Milliken v. Bradley (interdistrict desegregation plan impermissible unless segregation in one district intentionally caused by another)

Miranda v. Arizona (law enforcement officers must notify persons, prior to custodial interrogation, of their right to remain silent, right to have counsel present and paid for by the state, and consequences of waiving these rights)

NAACP v. Alabama (First Amendment implies the freedom of association)

Near v. Minnesota (First Amendment, barring exigent circumstances or unless the particular type of speech is constitutionally unprotected, prohibits systems of prior restraint)

New York Times Co. v. Sullivan (public official may not recover for defamation unless he or she establishes actual malice)

New York Times Co. v. United States (system of prior restraint has a strong presumption against its constitutionality and government has a heavy burden of justifying its operation)

Pacific Gas and Electric Co. v. State Energy Resources Conservation and Development Commission (federal interest in nuclear power safety did not preempt a state law establishing a moratorium on nuclear power plant development)

Planned Parenthood of South-Eastern Pennsylvania v. Casey (state may not impose undue burdens upon a woman's freedom to obtain an abortion)

Plessy v. Ferguson (separate but equal doctrine established as constitutional basis for official segregation)

Railway Express Agency v. New York (economic classifications do not warrant close attention under the Equal Protection Clause)

R.A.V. v. City of St. Paul (hate speech regulation violated First Amendment because it discriminated on the basis of content and viewpoint)

Red Lion Broadcasting Co. v. Federal Communications Commission (requiring broadcasters to provide balanced coverage of certain public issues does not violate the First Amendment)

Regents of the University of California v. Bakke (university admissions program may take race into account provided it is not the only factor used to achieve a diverse student body)

Reynolds v. Sims (state legislative districts must be apportioned on the basis of one person, one vote)

Richmond, City of, v. J. A. Croson Co. (municipality's requirement that contractors set aside percentage of public works opportunities for minority subcontractors violates Equal Protection Clause)

Roe v. Wade (Due Process Clause secures a woman's freedom to obtain an abortion)

Roth v. United States (obscene expression is not protected by the First Amendment)

San Antonio Independent School District v. Rodriguez (disparities in state funding of public education does not offend the Equal Protection Clause)

Schenck v. United States (advocacy of illegal action must be measured pursuant to clear and present danger test)

Shapiro v. Thompson (state's one-year waiting period for new residents to qualify for welfare benefits burdens the fundamental right of interstate movement)

Slaughter-House Cases (narrowly defines the privileges and immunities of federal citizenship)

Southern Pacific Co. v. Arizona (state's restriction on the length of trains unduly burdens interstate commerce and thus violates the Commerce Clause)

Strauder v. West Virginia (state's exclusion of African-Americans from juries violates the Fourteenth Amendment)

Swann v. Charlotte-Mecklenburg Board of Education (federal court has broad remedial power to enforce school desegregation including authority to redraw attendance zones and bus students)

Terry v. Ohio (officer may stop and frisk an individual based upon a reasonable suspicion that he or she is armed and dangerous)

Texas v. Johnson (state law prohibiting flag burning violates the First Amendment)

United States v. Carolene Products Co. (regulation of ordinary commercial transactions is presumed constitutional if supported by any rational basis)

United States v. Nixon (executive privilege claim outweighed by evidentiary needs of criminal justice system)

United States v. O'Brien (burning of draft card not protected by First Amendment)

Virginia State Board of Pharmacy v. Virginia Citizens Consumer Council, Inc. (commercial speech is protected by the First Amendment)

Washington v. Davis (violation of the Equal Protection Clause requires proof of discriminatory purpose)

Webster v. Reproductive Health Systems (state law prohibiting use of public facilities and employees for abortion and requiring fetal viability testing does not violate woman's freedom to obtain an abortion)

Wickard v. Filburn (federal quotas which prohibited small farmers from producing wheat for domestic consumption did not exceed Congress's power to regulate interstate commerce)

Wisconsin v. Yoder (state law requiring children to attend school through age 16 violated Free Exercise Clause)

Yakus v. United States (Congress allowed to delegate power to regulate consumer prices during World War II)

Youngstown Sheet and Tube Co. v. Sawyer (President's seizure of steel industry during Korean War violated separation of powers doctrine)

Zurcher v. Stanford Daily (Fourth Amendment does not confer immunity upon newsroom from search and seizure)

Appendix B

The Constitution of the United States

WE THE PEOPLE of the United States, in Order to form a more perfect Union, establish Justice, insure domestic Tranquility, provide for the common defence, promote the general Welfare, and secure the Blessings of Liberty to ourselves and our Posterity, do ordain and establish this CONSTITUTION for the United States of America

Article I

Section 1. All legislative Powers herein granted shall be vested in a Congress of the United States, which shall consist of a Senate and House of Representatives.

Section 2. [1] The House of Representatives shall be composed of Members chosen every second Year by the People of the several States, and the Electors in each State shall have the Qualifications requisite for Electors of the most numerous Branch of the State Legislature.

[2] No Person shall be a Representative who shall not have attained to the Age of twenty five Years, and been seven Years a Citizen of the United States, and who shall not, when elected, be an Inhabitant of that State in which he shall be chosen.

[3] Representatives and direct Taxes shall be apportioned among the several States which may be included within this Union, according to their respective Numbers, which shall be determined by adding to the whole Number of free Persons, including those bound to Service for a Term of Years, and excluding Indians not taxed, three fifths of all other Persons. The actual Enumeration shall be made within three Years after the first Meeting of the Congress of the United States, and within every subsequent Term of ten Years, in such Manner as they shall by Law direct. The Number of Representatives shall not exceed one for every thirty Thousand, but each State shall have at least one Representative; and until such enumeration

shall be made, the State of New Hampshire shall be entitled to chuse three, Massachusetts eight, Rhode Island and Providence Plantations one, Connecticut five, New York six, New Jersey four, Pennsylvania eight, Delaware one, Maryland six, Virginia ten, North Carolina five, South Carolina five, and Georgia three.

[4] When vacancies happen in the Representation from any State, the Executive Authority thereof shall issue Writs of Election to fill such Vacancies.

[5] The House of Representatives shall chuse their Speaker and other Officers; and shall have the sole Power of Impeachment.

Section 3. [1] This provision is superseded by Amendment XVII.

[2] Immediately after they shall be assembled in Consequence of the first Election, they shall be divided as equally as may be into three Classes. The Seats of the Senators of the first Class shall be vacated at the Expiration of the second Year, of the second Class at the Expiration of the fourth Year, and of the third Class at the Expiration of the sixth Year, so that one third may be chosen every second Year; and if Vacancies happen by Resignation, or otherwise, during the Recess of the Legislature of any State, the Executive thereof may make temporary Appointments until the next Meeting of the Legislature, which shall then fill such Vacancies.

[3] No Person shall be a Senator who shall not have attained to the Age of thirty Years, and been nine Years a Citizen of the United States, and who shall not, when elected, be an Inhabitant of that State for which he shall be chosen.

[4] The Vice President of the United States shall be President of the Senate, but shall have no Vote, unless they be equally divided.

[5] The Senate shall chuse their other Officers, and also a President pro tempore, in the Absence of the Vice President, or when he shall exercise the Office of President of the United States.

[6] The Senate shall have the sole Power to try all Impeachments. When sitting for that Purpose, they shall be on Oath or Affirmation. When the President of the United States is tried, the Chief Justice shall preside: And no Person shall be convicted without the Concurrence of two thirds of the Members present.

[7] Judgment in Cases of Impeachment shall not extend further than to removal from Office, and disqualification to hold and enjoy any Office of honor, Trust or Profit under the United States: but the Party convicted shall nevertheless be liable and subject to Indictment, Trial, Judgment and Punishment, according to Law.

Section 4. [1] The Times, Places and Manner of holding Elections for Senators and Representatives, shall be prescribed in each State by the Legislature thereof; but the Congress may at any time by Law make or alter such Regulations, except as to the Places of choosing Senators.

[2] The Congress shall assemble at least once in every Year, and such Meeting shall be on the first Monday in December, unless they shall by Law appoint a different Day.

Section 5. [1] Each house shall be the Judge of the Elections, Returns and Qualifications of its own Members, and a Majority of each shall constitute a Quorum to do Business; but a smaller Number may adjourn from day to day, and may be authorized to compel the Attendance of absent Members, in such Manner, and under such Penalties as each House may provide.

[2] Each House may determine the Rules of its Proceedings, punish its Members for disorderly Behaviour, and, with the Concurrence of two thirds, expel a Member.

[3] Each House shall keep a Journal of its Proceedings, and from time to time publish the same, excepting such Parts as may in their Judgment require Secrecy; and the Yeas and Nays of the Members of either House on any question shall, at the Desire of one fifth of those Present, be entered on the Journal.

[4] Neither House, during the Session of Congress, shall, without the Consent of the other, adjourn for more than three days, nor to any other Place than that in which the two Houses shall be sitting.

Section 6. [1] The Senators and Representatives shall receive a Compensation for their Services, to be ascertained by Law, and paid out of the Treasury of the United States. They shall in all Cases, except Treason, Felony and Breach of the Peace, be privileged from Arrest during their Attendance at the Session of their respective Houses, and in going to and returning from the same, and for any Speech or Debate in either House, they shall not be questioned in any other Place.

[2] No Senator or Representative shall, during the Time for which he was elected, be appointed to any civil Office under the Authority of the United States, which shall have been created, or the Emoluments whereof shall have been encreased during such time; and no Person holding any Office under the United States, shall be a Member of either House during his Continuance in Office.

Section 7. [1] All Bills for raising Revenue shall originate in the House of Representatives, but the Senate may propose or concur with Amendments as on other Bills.

[2] Every Bill which shall have passed the House of Representatives and the Senate, shall, before it become a Law, be presented to the President of the United States; If he approves he shall sign it, but if not he shall return it, with his Objections to that House in which it shall have originated, who shall enter the Objections at large on their Journal, and proceed to reconsider it. If after such Reconsideration two thirds of that House shall agree to pass the Bill, it shall be sent, together with the Objections, to the other House, by which it shall likewise be reconsidered, and if approved by two thirds of that House, it shall become a Law. But in all such Cases the Votes of both Houses shall be determined by Yeas and Nays, and the Names of the Persons voting for and against the Bill shall be entered on the Journal of each House respectively. If any Bill shall not be returned by the President within ten Days (Sundays excepted) after it shall have been presented to him, the Same shall be a Law, in like Manner as if he had signed it, unless the Congress by their Adjournment prevent its Return, in which Case it shall not be a Law.

[3] Every Order, Resolution, or Vote to which the Concurrence of the Senate and House of Representatives may be necessary (except on a question of Adjournment) shall be presented to the President of the United States; and before the Same shall take Effect, shall be approved by him, or being disapproved by him, shall be re-

passed by two thirds of the Senate and House of Representatives, according to the Rules and Limitations prescribed in the Case of a Bill.

Section 8. [1] The Congress shall have Power To lay and collect Taxes, Duties, Imposts and Excises, to pay the Debts and provide for the common Defence and general Welfare of the United States; but all Duties, Imposts and Excises shall be uniform throughout the United States;

[2] To borrow Money on the credit of the United States;

[3] To regulate Commerce with foreign Nations, and among the several States, and with the Indian Tribes;

[4] To establish an uniform Rule of Naturalization, and uniform Laws on the subject of Bankruptcies throughout the United States;

[5] To coin Money, regulate the Value thereof, and of foreign Coin, and fix the Standard of Weights and Measures;

[6] To provide for the Punishment of counterfeiting the Securities and current Coin of the United States;

[7] To establish Post-Offices and Post-Roads;

[8] To promote the Progress of Science and useful Arts, by securing for limited Times to Authors and Inventors the exclusive Right to their respective Writings and Discoveries;

[9] To constitute Tribunals inferior to the supreme Court;

[10] To define and punish Piracies and Felonies committed on the high Seas, and Offences against the Law of Nations;

[11] To declare War, grant Letters of Marque and Reprisal, and make Rules, concerning Captures on Land and Water;

[12] To raise and support Armies, but no Appropriation of Money to that Use shall be for a longer Term than two Years;

[13] To provide and maintain a Navy;

[14] To make Rules for the Government and Regulation of the land and naval Forces;

[15] To provide for calling forth the Militia to execute the Laws of the Union, suppress Insurrections and repel Invasions;

[16] To provide for organizing, arming, and disciplining the Militia, and for governing such Part of them as may be employed in the Service of the United States, reserving to the States respectively, the Appointment of the Officers, and the Authority of training the Militia according to the discipline prescribed by Congress;

[17] To exercise exclusive Legislation in all Cases whatsoever, over such District (not exceeding ten miles square) as may, by Cession of Particular States, and the Acceptance of Congress, become the Seat of the Government of the United States, and to exercise like Authority over all Places purchased by the Consent of the Legislature of the State in which the Same shall be, for the Erection of Forts, Magazines, Arsenals, dock-Yards, and other needful Buildings;—And

[18] To make all Laws which shall be necessary and proper for carrying into Execution the foregoing Powers, and all other Powers vested by this Constitution in the Government of the United States, or in any Department or Officer thereof.

Section 9. [1] The Migration or Importation of such Persons as any of the States now existing shall think proper to admit, shall not be prohibited by the Congress prior to the Year one thousand eight hundred and eight, but a Tax or duty may be imposed on such Importation, not exceeding ten dollars for each Person.

[2] The Privilege of the Writ of Habeas Corpus shall not be suspended, unless when in Cases of Rebellion or Invasion the public Safety may require it.

[3] No Bill of Attainder or ex post facto Law shall be passed.

[4] No Capitation, or other direct, Tax shall be laid, unless in Proportion to the Census or Enumeration herein before directed to be taken.

[5] No Tax or Duty shall be laid on Articles exported from any State.

[6] No Preference shall be given by any Regulation of Commerce or Revenue to the Ports of one State over those of another: nor shall Vessels bound to, or from, one State be obliged to enter, clear, or pay Duties in another.

[7] No Money shall be drawn from the Treasury, but in Consequence of Appropriations made by Law; and a regular Statement and Account of the Receipts and Expenditures of all public Money shall be published from time to time.

[8] No Title of Nobility shall be granted by the United States: And no Person holding any Office of Profit or Trust under them, shall, without the Consent of the Congress, accept of any present, Emolument, Office, or Title, of any kind whatever, from any King, Prince, or foreign State.

Section 10. [1] No State shall enter into any Treaty, Alliance, or Confederation; grant Letters of Marque and Reprisal; coin Money; emit Bills of Credit; make any Thing but gold and silver Coin a Tender in Payment of Debts; pass any Bill of Attainder, ex post facto Law, or Law impairing the obligation of Contracts, or grant any Title of Nobility.

[2] No State shall, without the Consent of the Congress, lay any Imposts or Duties on Imports or Exports, except what may be absolutely necessary for executing its inspection Laws: and the net Produce of all Duties and Imposts laid by any State on Imports or Exports, shall be for the Use of the Treasury of the United States; and all such Laws shall be subject to the Revision and Controul of the Congress.

[3] No State shall, without the Consent of Congress, lay any Duty of Tonnage, keep Troops, or Ships of War in time of Peace, enter into any Agreement or Compact with another State, or with a foreign Power, or engage in War, unless actually invaded, or in such imminent Danger as will not admit of delay.

Article II

Section 1. [1] The executive Power shall be vested in a President of the United States of America. He shall hold his Office during the Term of four Years, and together with the Vice President, chosen for the same Term, be elected, as follows:

[2] Each State shall appoint, in such Manner as the Legislature thereof may direct, a Number of Electors, equal to the whole Number of Senators and Respresentatives to which the State may be entitled in the Congress; but no Senator or Represen-

tative, or Person holding an Office of Trust or Profit under the United States, shall be appointed an Elector.

[3] This provision is superseded by Amendment XII.

[4] The Congress may determine the Time of chusing the Electors, and the Day on which they shall give their Votes; which Day shall be the same throughout the United States.

[5] No Person except a natural born Citizen, or a Citizen of the United States, at the time of the Adoption of this Constitution, shall be eligible to the Office of President; neither shall any Person be eligible to that Office who shall not have attained to the Age of thirty five Years, and been fourteen Years a Resident within the United States.

[6] In Case of the Removal of the President from Office, or of his Death, Resignation, or Inability to discharge the Powers and Duties of the said Office, the Same shall devolve on the Vice President, and the Congress may by Law provide for the Case of Removal, Death, Resignation or Inability, both of the President and Vice President, declaring what Officer shall then act as President, and such Officer shall act accordingly, until the Disability be removed, or a President shall be elected.

[7] The President shall, at stated Times, receive for his Services a Compensation, which shall neither be encreased nor diminished during the Period for which he shall have been elected, and he shall not receive within that Period any other Emolument from the United States, or any of them.

[8] Before he enter on the Execution of his Office, he shall take the following Oath or Affirmation: "I do solemnly swear (or affirm) that I will faithfully execute the Office of President of the United States, and will to the best of my Ability, preserve, protect and defend the Constitution of the United States."

Section 2. [1] The President shall be Commander in Chief of the Army and Navy of the United States, and of the Militia of the several States, when called into the actual Service of the United States; he may require the Opinion, in writing of the principal Officer in each of the executive Departments, upon any Subject relating to the Duties of their respective Offices, and he shall have Power to grant Reprieves and Pardons for Offenses against the United States, except in Cases of Impeachment.

[2] He shall have Power, by and with the Advice and Consent of the Senate, to make Treaties, provided two thirds of the Senators present concur; and he shall nominate, and by and with the Advice and Consent of the Senate, shall appoint Ambassadors, other public Ministers and Consuls, Judges of the supreme Court, and all other Officers of the United States, whose Appointments are not herein otherwise provided for, and which shall be established by Law: but the Congress may by Law vest the Appointment of such inferior Officers, as they think proper, in the President alone, in the Courts of Law, or in the Heads of Departments.

[3] The President shall have Power to fill up all Vacancies that may happen during the Recess of the Senate, by granting Commissions which shall expire at the End of their next Session.

Section 3. He shall from time to time give to the Congress Information of the

State of the Union, and recommend to their Consideration such Measures as he shall judge necessary and expedient; he may, on extraordinary Occasions, convene both Houses, or either of them, and in Case of Disagreement between them, with Respect to the Time of Adjournment, he may adjourn them to such Time as he shall think proper; he shall receive Ambassadors and other public Ministers; he shall take Care that the Laws be faithfully executed, and shall Commission all the Officers of the United States.

Section 4. The President, Vice President and all civil Officers of the United States, shall be removed from Office on Impeachment for, and Conviction of, Treason, Bribery, or other high Crimes and Misdemeanors.

Article III

Section 1. The judicial Power of the United States, shall be vested in one supreme Court, and in such inferior Courts as the Congress may from time to time ordain and establish. The Judges, both of the supreme and inferior Courts, shall hold their Offices during good Behaviour, and shall, at stated Times, receive for their Services, a Compensation, which shall not be diminished during their Continuance in Office.

Section 2. [1] The judicial Power shall extend to all Cases, in Law and Equity, arising under this Constitution, the Laws of the United States, and Treaties made, or which shall be made, under their Authority; to all Cases affecting Ambassadors, other public Ministers and Consuls; to all Cases of admiralty and maritime Jurisdiction; to Controversies to which the United States shall be a Party; to Controversies between two or more States; between a State and Citizens of another State; between Citizens of different States, between Citizens of the same State claiming Lands under Grants of different States, and between a State, or the Citizens thereof, and foreign States, Citizens or Subjects.

[2] In all Cases affecting Ambassadors, other public Ministers and Consuls, and those in which a State shall be Party, the supreme Court shall have original Jurisdiction. In all the other Cases before mentioned, the supreme Court shall have appellate Jurisdiction, both as to Law and Fact, with such Exceptions, and under such Regulations as the Congress shall make.

[3] The Trial of all Crimes, except in Cases of Impeachment, shall be by Jury; and such Trial shall be held in the State where the said Crimes shall have been committed; but when not committed within any State, the Trial shall be at such Place or Places as the Congress may by Law have directed.

Section 3. [1] Treason against the United States, shall consist only in levying War against them, or in adhering to their Enemies, giving them Aid and Comfort. No Person shall be convicted of Treason unless on the Testimony of two Witnesses to the same overt Act, or on Confession in open Court.

[2] The Congress shall have Power to declare the Punishment of Treason, but no Attainder of Treason shall work Corruption of Blood, or Forfeiture except during the Life of the Person attainted.

Article IV

Section 1. Full Faith and Credit shall be given in each State to the public Acts, Records, and judicial Proceedings of every other State. And the Congress may by general Laws prescribe the Manner in which such Acts, Records and Proceedings shall be proved, and the Effect thereof.

Section 2. [1] The Citizens of each State shall be entitled to all Privileges and Immunities of Citizens in the several States.

[2] A Person charged in any State with Treason, Felony, or other Crime, who shall flee from Justice, and be found in another State, shall on Demand of the executive Authority of the State from which he fled, be delivered up, to be removed to the State having Jurisdiction of the Crime.

[3] No Person held to Service or Labour in one State, under the Laws thereof, escaping into another, shall, in Consequence of any Law or Regulation therein, be discharged from such Service or Labour, but shall be delivered up on Claim of the Party to whom such Service or Labour may be due.

Section 3. [1] New States may be admitted by the Congress into this Union; but no new State shall be formed or erected within the Jurisdiction of any other State; nor any State be formed by the Junction of two or more States, or Parts of States, without the Consent of the Legislatures of the States concerned as well as of the Congress.

[2] The Congress shall have power to dispose of and make all needful Rules and Regulations respecting the Territory or other Property belonging to the United States; and nothing in this Constitution shall be so construed as to Prejudice any Claims of the United States, or of any particular State.

Section 4. The United States shall guarantee to every State in this Union a Republician Form of Government, and shall protect each of them against Invasion; and on Application of the Legislative, or of the Executive (when the Legislature cannot be convened) against domestic Violence.

Article V

The Congress, whenever two thirds of both Houses shall deem it necessary, shall propose Amendments to this Constitution, or, on the Application of the Legislatures of two thirds of the several States, shall call a Convention for proposing Amendments, which, in either Case, shall be valid to all Intents and Purposes, as Part of this Constitution, when ratified by the Legislatures of three fourths of the several States, or by Conventions in three fourths thereof, as the one or the other Mode of Ratification may be proposed by the Congress; Provided that no Amendment which may be made prior to the Year One thousand eight hundred and eight shall in any Manner affect the first and fourth Clauses in the Ninth Section of the first Article; and that no State, without its Consent, shall be deprived of its equal Suffrage in the Senate.

Article VI

[1] All Debts contracted and Engagements entered into, before the Adoption of this Constitution, shall be as valid against the United States under this Constitution, as under the Confederation.

[2] This Constitution, and the Laws of the United States which shall be made in Pursuance thereof; and all Treaties made, or which shall be made, under the Authority of the United States, shall be the supreme Law of the Land; and the Judges in every State shall be bound thereby, any Thing in the Constitution or Laws of any State to the Contrary notwithstanding.

[3] The Senators and Representatives before mentioned, and the Members of the several State Legislatures, and all executive and judicial Officers, both of the United States and of the several States, shall be bound by Oath or Affirmation, to support this Constitution; but no religious Test shall ever be required as a Qualification to any Office or public Trust under the United States.

Article VII

The Ratification of the Conventions of nine States, shall be sufficient for the Establishment of this Constitution between the States so ratifying the Same.

Articles in Addition to, and Amendment of, the Constitution of the United States of America, Proposed by Congress, and Ratified by the Legislatures of the Several States Pursuant to the Fifth Article of the Original Constitution.

Amendment I [1791]

Congress shall make no law respecting an establishment of religion, or prohibiting the free exercise thereof; or abridging the freedom of speech, or of the press; or the right of the people peaceably to assemble, and to petition the Government for a redress of grievances.

Amendment II [1791]

A well regulated Militia, being necessary to the security of a free State, the right of the people to keep and bear Arms, shall not be infringed.

Amendment III [1791]

No Soldier shall, in time of peace be quartered in any house, without the consent of the Owner, nor in time of war, but in a manner to be prescribed by law.

Amendment IV [1791]

The right of the people to be secure in their persons, houses, papers, and effects, against unreasonable searches and seizures, shall not be violated, and no Warrants shall issue, but upon probable cause, supported by Oath or affirmation, and particularly describing the place to be searched, and the persons or things to be seized.

Amendment V [1791]

No person shall be held to answer for a capital, or otherwise infamous crime, unless on a presentment or indictment of a Grand Jury, except in cases arising in the land or naval forces, or in the Militia, when in actual service in time of War or public danger; nor shall any person be subject for the same offence to be twice put in jeopardy of life or limb; nor shall be compelled in any criminal case to be a witness against himself, nor be deprived of life, liberty, or property, without due process of law; nor shall private property be taken for public use without just compensation.

Amendment VI [1791]

In all criminal prosecutions, the accused shall enjoy the right to a speedy and public trial, by an impartial jury of the State and district wherein the crime shall have been committed, which district shall have been previously ascertained by law, and to be informed of the nature and cause of the accusation; to be confronted with the witnesses against him; to have compulsory process for obtaining witnesses in his favor, and to have the assistance of counsel for his defence.

Amendment VII [1791]

In Suits at common law, where the value in controversy shall exceed twenty dollars, the right of trial by jury shall be preserved, and no fact tried by jury, shall be otherwise re-examined in any Court of the United States, than according to the rules of the common law.

Amendment VIII [1791]

Excessive bail shall not be required, nor excessive fines imposed, nor cruel and unusual punishments inflicted.

Amendment IX [1791]

The enumeration in the Constitution, of certain rights, shall not be construed to deny or disparage others retained by the people.

Amendment X [1791]

The powers not delegated to the United States by the Constitution, nor prohibited by it to the States, are reserved to the States respectively, or to the people.

Amendment XI [1798]

The Judicial power of the United States shall not be construed to extend to any suit in law or equity, commenced or prosecuted against one of the United States by Citizens of another State, or by Citizens or Subjects of any Foreign State.

Amendment XII [1804]

The Electors shall meet in their respective states and vote by ballot for President and Vice-President, one of whom, at least, shall not be an inhabitant of the same state with themselves; they shall name in their ballots the person voted for as President, and in distinct ballots the person voted for as Vice-President, and they shall make distinct lists of all persons voted for as President, and of all persons voted for as Vice-President, and of the number of votes for each, which lists they shall sign and certify, and transmit sealed to the seat of the government of the United States, directed to the President of the Senate;—The President of the Senate shall, in the presence of the Senate and House of Representatives, open all the certificates and the votes shall then be counted;—The person having the greatest number of votes for President, shall be the President, if such number be a majority of the whole number of Electors appointed; and if no person have such majority, then from the persons having the highest numbers not exceeding three on the list of those voted for as President, the House of Representatives shall choose immediately, by ballot, the President. But in choosing the President, the votes shall be taken by states, the representation from each state having one vote; a quorum for this purpose shall consist of a member or members from two-thirds of the states, and a majority of all the states shall be necessary to a choice. And if the House of Representatives shall not choose a President whenever the right of choice shall devolve upon them, before the fourth day of March next following, then the Vice-President shall act as President, as in the case of the death or other constitutional disability of the President.—The person having the greatest number of votes as Vice-President, shall be the Vice-President, if such number be a majority of the whole number of Electors appointed, and if no person have a majority, then from the two highest numbers on the list, the Senate shall choose the Vice-President; a quorum for the purpose shall consist of two-thirds of the whole number of Senators, and a majority of the whole number shall be necessary to a choice. But no person constitutionally ineligible to the office of President shall be eligible to that of Vice-President of the United States.

Amendment XIII [1865]

Section 1. Neither slavery nor involuntary servitude, except as a punishment for crime whereof the party shall have been duly convicted, shall exist within the United States, or any place subject to their jurisdiction.

Section 2. Congress shall have power to enforce this article by appropriate legislation.

Amendment XIV [1868]

Section 1. All persons born or naturalized in the United States, and subject to the jurisdiction thereof, are citizens of the United States and of the State wherein they reside. No State shall make or enforce any law which shall abridge the privileges or immunities of citizens of the United States; nor shall any State deprive any person of life, liberty, or property, without due process of law; nor deny to any person within its jurisdiction the equal protection of the laws.

Section 2. Representatives shall be apportioned among the several States according to their respective numbers, counting the whole number of persons in each State, excluding Indians not taxed. But when the right to vote at any election for the choice of electors for President and Vice President of the United States, Representatives in Congress, the Executive and Judicial officers of a State, or the members of the Legislature thereof, is denied to any of the male inhabitants of such State, being twenty-one years of age, and citizens of the United States, or in any way abridged, except for participation in rebellion, or other crime, the basis of representation therein shall be reduced in the proportion which the number of such male citizens shall bear to the whole number of male citizens twenty-one years of age in such State.

Section 3. No person shall be a Senator or Representative in Congress, or elector of President and Vice President, or hold any office, civil or military, under the United States, or under any State, who, having previously taken an oath, as a member of Congress, or as an officer of the United States, or as a member of any State legislature, or as an executive or judicial officer of any State, to support the Constitution of the United States, shall have engaged in insurrection or rebellion against the same, or given aid or comfort to the enemies thereof. But Congress may by a vote of two thirds of each House, remove such disability.

Section 4. The validity of the public debt of the United States, authorized by law, including debts incurred for payment of pensions and bounties for services in suppressing insurrection or rebellion, shall not be questioned. But neither the United States nor any State shall assume or pay any debt or obligation incurred in aid of insurrection or rebellion against the United States, or any claim for the loss or emancipation of any slave; but all such debts, obligations and claims shall be held illegal and void.

Section 5. The Congress shall have power to enforce, by appropriate legislation, the provisions of this article.

Amendment XV [1870]

Section 1. The right of citizens of the United States to vote shall not be denied or abridged by the United States or by any State on account of race, color, or previous condition of servitude.

Section 2. The Congress shall have power to enforce this article by appropriate legislation.

Amendment XVI [1913]

The Congress shall have power to lay and collect taxes on incomes, from whatever source derived, without apportionment among the several States, and without regard to any census or enumeration.

Amendment XVII [1913]

[1] The Senate of the United States shall be composed of two Senators from each State, elected by the people thereof, for six years; and each Senator shall have one vote. The electors in each State shall have the qualifications requisite for electors of the most numerous branch of the State legislatures.

[2] When vacancies happen in the representation of any State in the Senate, the executive authority of such State shall issue writs of election to fill such vacancies: *Provided*, that the legislature of any state may empower the executive thereof to make temporary appointments until the people fill the vacancies by election as the legislature may direct.

[3] This amendment shall not be so construed as to affect the election or term of any Senator chosen before it becomes valid as part of the Constitution.

Amendment XVIII [1919]

Prohibition of Liquor [Repealed by Amendment XXI]

Amendment XIX [1920]

[1] The right of citizens of the United States to vote shall not be denied or abridged by the United States or by any State on account of sex.

[2] Congress shall have power to enforce this article by appropriate legislation.

Amendment XX [1933]

Section 1. The terms of the President and Vice President shall end at noon on the 20th day of January, and the terms of Senators and Representatives at noon on the 3d day of January, of the years in which such terms would have ended if this article had not been ratified; and the terms of their successors shall then begin.

Section 2. The Congress shall assemble at least once in every year, and such meeting shall begin at noon on the 3d day of January, unless they shall by law appoint a different day.

Section 3. If, at the time fixed for the beginning of the term of the President, the President elect shall have died, the Vice President elect shall become President. If a President shall not have been chosen before the time fixed for the beginning of his term, or if the President elect shall have failed to qualify, then the Vice President elect shall act as President until a President shall have qualified; and the Congress may by law provide for the case wherein neither a President elect nor a Vice President elect shall have qualified, declaring who shall then act as President, or the manner in which one who is to act shall be selected, and such person shall act accordingly until a President or Vice President shall have qualified.

Section 4. The Congress may by law provide for the case of the death of any of the persons from whom the House of Representatives may choose a President whenever the right of choice may have devolved upon them; and for the case of the death of any of the persons from whom the Senate may choose a Vice President whenever the right of choice shall have devolved upon them.

Section 5. Sections 1 and 2 shall take effect on the 15th day of October following the ratification of this article.

Section 6. This article shall be inoperative unless it shall have been ratified as an amendment to the Constitution by the legislatures of three-fourths of the several States within seven years from the date of its submission.

Amendment XXI [1933]

Section 1. The eighteenth article of amendment to the Constitution of the United States is hereby repealed.

Section 2. The transportation or importation into any State, Territory, or possession of the United States for delivery or use therein of intoxicating liquors, in violation of the laws thereof, is hereby prohibited.

Section 3. This article shall be inoperative unless it shall have been ratified as an amendment to the Constitution by conventions in the several States, as provided in the Constitution, within seven years from the date of the submission hereof to the States by the Congress.

Amendment XXII [1951]

Section 1. No person shall be elected to the office of the President more than twice, and no person who has held the office of President, or acted as President, for more than two years of a term to which some other person was elected President shall be elected to the office of the President more than once. But this Article shall not apply to any person holding the office of President when this Article was proposed by the Congress, and shall not prevent any person who may be holding the office of President, or acting as President, during the term within which this Article becomes operative from holding the office of President or acting as President during the remainder of such term.

Section 2. This article shall be inoperative unless it shall have been ratified as an amendment to the Constitution by the legislatures of three-fourths of the several States within seven years from the date of its submission to the States by the Congress.

Amendment XXIII [1961]

Section 1. The District constituting the seat of Government of the United States shall appoint in such manner as the Congress may direct:

A number of electors of President and Vice President equal to the whole number of Senators and Representatives in Congress to which the District would be entitled if it were a State, but in no event more than the least populous State; they shall be in addition to those appointed by the States, but they shall be considered, for the purposes of the election of President and Vice President, to be electors appointed by a State; and they shall meet in the District and perform such duties as provided by the twelfth article of amendment.

Section 2. The Congress shall have power to enforce this article by appropriate legislation.

Amendment XXIV [1964]

Section 1. The right of citizens of the United States to vote in any primary or other election for President or Vice President, for electors for President or Vice President, or for Senator or Representative in Congress, shall not be denied or abridged by the United States or any State by reason of failure to pay any poll tax or other tax.

Section 2. The Congress shall have power to enforce this article by appropriate legislation.

Amendment XXV [1967]

Section 1. In case of the removal of the President from office or of his death or resignation, the Vice President shall become President.

Section 2. Whenever there is a vacancy in the office of the Vice President, the President shall nominate a Vice President who shall take office upon confirmation by a majority vote of both Houses of Congress.

Section 3. Whenever the President transmits to the President pro tempore of the Senate and the Speaker of the House of Representatives his written declaration that he is unable to discharge the powers and duties of his office, and until he transmits to them a written declaration to the contrary, such powers and duties shall be discharged by the Vice President as Acting President.

Section 4. Whenever the Vice President and a majority of either the principal officers of the executive departments or of such other body as Congress may by law provide, transmit to the President pro tempore of the Senate and the Speaker of the House of Representatives their written declaration that the President is unable to discharge the powers and duties of his office, the Vice President shall immediately assume the powers and duties of the office as Acting President.

Thereafter, when the President transmits to the President pro tempore of the Senate and the Speaker of the House of Representatives his written declaration that no inability exists, he shall resume the powers and duties of his office unless the Vice President and a majority of either the principal officers of the executive department or of such other body as Congress may by law provide, transmit within four days to the President pro tempore of the Senate and the Speaker of the House of Representatives their written declaration that the President is unable to discharge the powers and duties of his office. Thereupon Congress shall decide the issue, assembling within forty-eight hours for that purpose if not in session. If the Congress, within twenty-one days after receipt of the latter written declaration, or, if Congress is not in session, within twenty-one days after Congress is required to assemble, determines by two-thirds vote of both Houses that the President is unable to discharge the powers and duties of his office, the Vice President shall continue to discharge the same as Acting President; otherwise, the President shall resume the powers and duties of his office.

Amendment XXVI [1971]

Section 1. The right of citizens of the United States, who are eighteen years of age or older, to vote shall not be denied or abridged by the United States or by any State on account of age.

Section 2. The Congress shall have power to enforce this article by appropriate legislation.

Amendment XXVII [1992]

No law, varying the compensation for the services of the Senators and Representatives, shall take effect, until an election of Representatives shall have intervened.

Index

About the Author

DONALD E. LIVELY is Dean of the Florida Coastal School of Law. He is author of *Essential Principles of Communications Law* (Praeger, 1991), *Modern Communications Law* (Praeger, 1991), *The Constitution and Race* (1992), and *Foreshadows of the Law* (Praeger, 1992).